# Corporeal Politics
## Dancing East Asia

*Edited by*
*Katherine Mezur and Emily Wilcox*

University of Michigan Press
*Ann Arbor*

For questions or permissions, please contact um.press.perms@umich.edu

Published in the United States of America by
the University of Michigan Press
Manufactured in the United States of America
Printed on acid-free paper

First published September 2020

A CIP catalog record for this book is available from the British Library.

ISBN 978-0-472-07455-6 (hardcover : alk. paper)
ISBN 978-0-472-05455-8 (paper : alk. paper)
ISBN 978-0-472-12694-1 (ebook)

In Memory of Ting-Ting Chang

# Contents

Digital materials related to this title can be found on the Fulcrum platform via the following citable URL https://doi.org/10.3998/mpub.11521701

# Acknowledgments

Every book is an adventurous and unpredictable journey that relies on the support, expertise, and visionary belief of many people and their institutions. This one began with the Dance Studies Working Group at the University of California, Berkeley, the community that first brought us together and fostered early conversations that led to this project. UC Berkeley hosted our first exploratory conference, "Corporeal Nationalisms: Dance and the State in East Asia," co-organized with Laurence Coderre, on September 10–12, 2010. We received vital support from the Center for Korean Studies, the Center for Chinese Studies, the Center for Japanese Studies, the Department of Theatre, Dance, and Performance Studies, and the Townsend Center for the Humanities We are grateful to all invited participants for their stimulating contributions, which were formative in our early thinking about this project. They include Bruce Baird, Brandi Wilkins Catanese, Pheng Cheah, Xiaomei Chen, Tamano Hiroko, Naomi Inata, Andrew Jones, Hyang-Jin Jung, Laurel Kendall, Susan Klein, SanSan Kwan, Dohee Lee, Dongil Lee, Xiaozhen Liu, Khai-Thu Nguyen, Mariko Okada, Miryam Sas, Louisa Schein, Jacqueline Shea Murphy, Judy Van Zile, Elizabeth Wichmann-Walczak, Jia Wu, and Pacific Film Archive Film Collection Curator Mona Nagai. We especially thank Leonard Pronko (1927–2019) for his inspired workshop on Kabuki dance and gender roles. This diverse group of practitioner-scholars helped set the course of this collection. Thank you.

Several other venues also provided important early platforms for conversations about this project. One was the 2009 Danscross (now ArtsCross) international choreography research program jointly led by Christopher Bannerman at Middlesex University and Xu Rui at the Beijing Dance Academy. Another was the "Corporeal Nationalisms: Performance in Service of the State" roundtable at the 2014 Performance Studies international conference held at the Shanghai Theatre Academy. Copanelists were Ting-Ting Chang, Rachel Fensham, Sara Jansen, Daphne Lei, Tanja London, Geraldine Morris, Qing Qing, and Francis Tanglao-Aguas. Rachel Fensham particularly contributed to our corporeal politics trajectory with her suggestion for a focus on dance labor and how dance and dancers often "serve" the state or other institutions, which significantly influence dance forms, aesthetics, and individuals. Another was the "Migrant Choreographies" panel at the 2016 Association for Asian Studies Annual Conference, shared with Nan Ma, Okju Son, and Catherine Yeh. The discussions from this panel led to our focus on the pivotal connection of performers' innovations that resulted from their international exposure. In early discussions about the book project, we received helpful advice from Peter Boenisch, Rachel Fensham, Jenny McCall, Xiaobing Tang, and Mary Gallagher.

The establishment of our central theme and our contributors began with our second international conference, "Dancing East Asia: Critical Choreographies and Their Corporeal Politics," held at the University of Michigan, Ann Arbor, on April 7–8, 2017. This conference was made possible by generous financial and staff support from the University of Michigan Lieberthal-Rogel Center for Chinese Studies. Additional institutional support for this event also came from the International Institute and the Hatcher Graduate Library. Apart from the book contributors, several other individuals participated and generously contributed to the discussion. They include Rosemary Candelario, Amy Chavasse, Tarryn Chun, Clare Croft, Liangyu Fu, Beth Genné, Ellen Gerdes, Reginald Jackson, Sara Jansen, Angela Kane, Tsung-Hsin (Joda) Lee, Ruby MacDougall, Fangfei Miao, Se-Mi Oh, David Rolston, Debing Su, Xiaobing Tang, Hitomi Tonomura, Robin Wilson, Judy Van Zile, and others. The Society of Dance History Scholars adopted this event as their special theme conference for 2017, providing valuable guidance and increasing its visibility to a broader community of dance scholars.

We are so thrilled that this book is being published in the Studies in Dance History book series with the University of Michigan Press. We are extremely grateful to series editors Rebecca Rossen and Clare Croft, who supported our project and ushered it through the editorial board review. We are also very thankful to all members of both Studies in Dance History editorial boards, who reviewed our materials and provided generous comments and feedback on several early drafts of the book proposal and the full manuscript. At the University of Michigan Press, we were fortunate to enjoy the expert guidance of our book editor, LeAnn Fields, who is a leader in the field of theater and performance studies publications. Her careful honing of the book's focus drove our final, accumulative project into a forceful and clear publication. Christopher Dreyer, Anna Pohlod, Marcia LaBrenz, and members of the UM Press executive committee were exemplary in their help, communication, and expertise. We also benefited from and were inspired by the exacting and provoking critique of two anonymous reviewers.

The rich illustrations that appear in this book and the accompanying Fulcrum platform were made possible by the cooperation of photographers, choreographers, dancers, archivists, and librarians, many of whom are named individually in the image captions and notes to individual chapters. We are also grateful to the many unnamed individuals and organizations who helped us with photograph requests and provided access to other research materials. To pay for licensing fees, image production, and indexing, we are thankful for generous publication subventions from the University of Michigan Office of Research and the University of Michigan Lieberthal-Rogel Center for Chinese Studies.

We would like to thank each individual contributor to this volume, without whose tremendous dedication, brilliance, and insight this book would not have been possible.

Lastly, we would like to thank each other, our family and friends who support our work, and the artists who inspire us to write and dance. Thank you, to those who stand by, closely, to keep us going no matter what.

Every effort has been made to trace the copyright holders and obtain permission to reproduce the images and other audiovisual materials that accompany this book. Please do get in touch with any inquiries or any information relating to these materials or their rights holders.

# Note on Translation and East Asian Names

All translations from foreign languages are the individual essay contributors' own unless otherwise noted. When available, personal names, names of organizations, and titles of dance works are given in the original language, along with romanized transliteration and English translation, when relevant. Formats used for East Asian scripts and romanization systems are based on each individual author's discretion and at times differ between chapters. Sources in foreign languages are cited in the original language of publication, along with transliteration. Because of space limitations, supplementary English translations of foreign source titles are in most cases not provided.

The standard way of writing personal names in East Asian languages is to place the family name first. For example, in the name Mei Lanfang, the family name is Mei, and in the name Murayama Tomoyoshi, the family name is Murayama. In most cases, we follow this convention for East Asian names in this book. The exception is when citing scholarly work published in English, in which case the author's name is given following the English convention, with the family name placed last. This is also the format used for the names of the volume's contributors. So, for example, in the byline of Chapter 3, the author Nan Ma's family name is Ma, and in the byline of Chapter 4, the author Kazuko Kuniyoshi's family name is Kuniyoshi. All personal names in the Index are alphabetized by family name.

# Introduction

## Toward a Critical East Asian Dance Studies

*Emily Wilcox*

When wealthy people died in ancient China, their tombs were filled with objects representing things the deceased were thought to need in the afterlife. Statues of servants, horses and chariots, writing tools, vessels for storing food, musical instruments, and figurines of dancers are among the common items found in these heavenly entourages. Dance was something not to be without even in death.[1]

Throughout the centuries, dance has continued to be important to people across China and neighboring Japan and Korea—the region we today call East Asia.[2] Performed at royal banquets, diplomatic functions, and national pageants, dance has been imbued with the power of governance and the symbolic majesty of the realm, whether that of an emperor, a colonial regime, or a nation-state. Dance has also been woven into the mundane rhythms of social life, appearing in harvest celebrations, healing rituals, courtship, after-school and corporate leisure activities, and public parks. Dance is further ubiquitous in many forms of commercial entertainment, from tourism and art festivals to television and video games. Simply put, dance is an indispensable part of the cultural life of East Asia, whether past or present, elite or popular, public or private.

Despite its importance, dance in East Asia long eluded the academic attention of Anglophone scholars, for whom in the past it often fell into cracks between established disciplines. Scholars of East Asian studies, traditionally trained in the analysis of East Asian texts, often found dance difficult to engage with because its embodied expression seemed to defy text-based interpretative methods.[3] Meanwhile, scholars of dance studies, traditionally trained in Western ballet and modern dance, often lacked the kinesthetic, linguistic, and contextual knowledge to carry out primary research on East Asian source material.[4] Although anthropologists sometimes conducted research on non-Western dance, such research was rare and often did not address East Asia.[5] Moreover, while a vast and vibrant body of scholarship on East Asian dance has long been produced by scholars in East Asia, this research was rarely translated into English and thus remained largely inaccessible to Anglophone scholars who could not read Chinese, Korean, Japanese, or other languages in which this work was published.[6]

With the increased popularity of interdisciplinary methods and the rise of performance studies, along with other new fields, in the Anglophone academy at the end of the twentieth century, research in English on East Asian dance finally began to take off as a robust area of study in the 1990s.[7] During the last two decades, a burst of English-language academic monographs has appeared that examine, from a variety of perspectives, dance in diverse Chinese, Japanese, and Korean contexts.[8] Together with unpublished master's theses and doctoral dissertations, as well as published essays and article-length works, this marks the arrival of English-language East Asian dance studies as an established and rapidly growing multidisciplinary research field.

While East Asian dance studies is growing in the English-speaking academy, most books on dance in East Asia are framed around particular national or ethnolinguistic dance communities or dance forms, often treated in isolation from one another.[9] As the first book-length publication in English to take a regional approach to multiple forms of dance across East Asia, this volume seeks to expand the existing research by emphasizing transnational circulation, interconnections, and comparisons among different national communities and dance forms in the region. Bringing together sixteen essays by an interdisciplinary and international group of scholars based in East Asia and the United States, *Corporeal Politics: Dancing East Asia* builds on the new momentum in East Asian dance and performance research, while continuing to grow this field by taking up new themes and modeling new directions of inquiry. The concept of "corporeal politics" provides a unifying methodology for the case studies collected in this volume, which address a wide range of dance styles, time periods, and dance communities. Attending to issues such as gender, sexuality, class, race, religion, language, ethnic and national identity, imperialism, war, migration, revolution, activism, and technology, the essays in this volume each unpack the politics of bodily movement that emerge from particular bodies and choreographies located in specific places, times, and social settings.

There is no single, unifying definition of dance in East Asia. Thus, readers will encounter diverse kinds of performances examined as dance in this book. About two- thirds of the chapters in this volume focus on concert dance—choreographies of modern, folk, contemporary, classical, and other dance styles devised for the stage and conceived of as "art dance," distinct from theater, music, or popular performance (for examples, see Ma, Kuniyoshi, Son, Wilcox, Chen, Kim, Jiang, Chang, Mezur, and Lin). The remaining chapters examine dance in other contexts—as entertainment in private homes, in tourism and pageants, as movement sequences within operas and musicals, and in public protests (see Bossler, Yeh, Yuh, Okada, Rodman, and Yoon). The scope of dance forms and contexts discussed here is by no means exhaustive, and many important topics are not included. Overall, the volume aims to both reflect current directions in the field and introduce subjects and approaches not well represented in previous English-language scholarship. Each chapter poses some questions that are left unanswered, with the goal of initiating conversations and encouraging future research.

To frame the contents of the book, this introduction is organized into three parts. The first examines existing concepts of East Asia in area studies and considers how critical area studies methodologies can offer insights for East Asian dance studies. The second part looks at the recent critique of whiteness in dance studies and considers how anti-Orientalist approaches can inform scholarship on dance in East Asia. Finally, the third part introduces the concept of corporeal politics and explains how each section and chapter of the book addresses this theme through a different question or case study.

## DANCING EAST ASIA: A CRITICAL AREA STUDIES APPROACH

The term "East Asia" is a recent invention with multiple origins and a fraught past. In contemporary US area studies discourse, East Asia conventionally refers to the geographic region of northeast Asia, comprising the modern-day political entities of China (including Hong Kong, Macau, and Taiwan), Japan, and North and South Korea.[10] Within Asian studies, East Asia is often distinguished from two other major regions, namely, Southeast Asia (encompassing Indonesia, Vietnam, Thailand, Malaysia, Singapore, the Philippines, Cambodia, Laos, Myanmar, Brunei, and Timor-Leste) and South Asia (encompassing India, Pakistan, Bangladesh, Sri Lanka, Nepal, Bhutan, and sometimes Afghanistan).[11] While area studies scholars themselves often contest the usefulness and legitimacy of these regional categories, they nevertheless continue to have meaning as organizing structures for academic research and teaching. This contemporary US academic definition of East Asia forms the starting point for our conceptualization of this book and of the broader field of East Asian dance studies in the Anglophone context.

There are several historical premises for this definition of East Asia, each of which lends different political and cultural significance to the term today. In its oldest and most basic use, East Asia marks what was once understood as the sphere of Chinese cultural influence in Asia. If expanded to include Mongolia, Vietnam, and some other parts of Southeast Asia, the region designated today as East Asia roughly corresponds to places where, over a period of nearly two millennia, the Chinese writing system and cultural practices such as Confucianism were adopted by local governments and, to varying degrees, incorporated into average people's daily lives.[12] By around the fifth century CE, both Korea and Japan had adopted the Chinese writing system to record their local languages. Although Korea introduced the phonetic Hangul alphabet in the 1440s, Chinese characters (known in Korean as *Hanja*) were still regularly used in Korean texts through the mid-twentieth century. In today's Japan, Chinese characters (known in Japanese as *kanji*) remain integral to the Japanese writing system, along with two other phonetic Japanese scripts, *hiragana* and *katakana*. Some aspects of Confucian culture relating to family organization, the gender system, and ethical action continue to shape life in these places despite major social change. These historical connections link East Asia even during periods of regional conflict and disunity and despite the cultural distinctness of each locality within this broader region.

Another more recent historical premise for the contemporary concept of East Asia emerged at the end of the nineteenth century, when the region was facing intense threats from the violent expansion of Western empires. For a period of time, East Asian writers used the shared term "East Asia" 東亞 (*Dongya* in Chinese, *Tōa* in Japanese, and *Dong-a* in Korean) as a self-designation, as part of new political discourses of inter-Asian solidarity, later known as Pan-Asianism.[13] Initially, Pan-Asianism advocated Asian unity in opposition to Western European and US hegemony and racism. It represented "the agenda of a united Asia, an Asia with a common goal—the struggle against Western imperialism."[14] Eventually, however, Japan developed a Westernized military and began to establish its own empire in Asia, with Japanese intellectuals often using Pan-Asianism as a nationalistic justification to invade neighboring Asian states. After Japan's colonization of Taiwan in 1895 and then annexation of the Korean peninsula in 1910, the Japanese military conquered huge parts of mainland China, Hong Kong (then a British colony), and Southeast Asia (then predominantly under British, Dutch, French, and

US control). At the height of Japanese imperial expansion, in the early 1940s, Japan's leaders promoted the concept of the "Greater East Asia Co-Prosperity Sphere" as an idealized image of Asia under Japanese rule.[15] The discourse of Pan-Asianism and its related concept of "East Asia" thus acquired the dual meanings of resistance against Western imperialism and support for the Japanese Empire. In this way, the concept of East Asia also shifted from a Sino-centric order to a Japan-centric one.

The idea of East Asia gained yet a third set of meanings after the end of World War II, when area studies emerged as a recognized discipline in the US, one that was often interpolated to serve the military-intelligence work of US Cold War imperialism.[16] Although the US had long been involved in Asia as an imperial and colonial power (exemplified most clearly by the US colonization of the Philippines in 1898–1946, but also by US involvement in military ventures, missionary work, scientific and technical projects, and unequal trade agreements in Asia since the 1850s), direct intervention in East Asian political affairs increased dramatically following the US entry into World War II in 1941, following the Japanese strike on Pearl Harbor. It was during this war that the US government began recruiting large numbers of East Asian studies scholars into government jobs, a practice that continued through the US-led Allied Occupation of Japan in 1945–1952, the Chinese Civil War in 1946–1949, the Korean War in 1950–1953, and the Vietnam War in 1955–1975 (hence, the term "cold" in Cold War is largely a euphemism when it comes to East and Southeast Asia).[17] The US objective throughout this period was to expand its own influence and suppress left-wing revolutionary movements.[18] In this context, the field of East Asian studies often promoted the US Cold War political agenda, based on the ideology of anticommunism. East Asia itself was imagined as a battleground between so-called "free" territories (referring to US-allied areas such as Hong Kong, Japan, South Korea, and Taiwan, largely ruled by colonial regimes or right-wing military dictatorships) and so-called "unfree" territories (referring to areas initially allied with the Soviet Union, such as China and North Korea, which had socialist governments led by communist parties). By the late 1960s, as criticisms of the Vietnam War and other aspects of US Cold War foreign policy became increasingly widespread, many US-based East Asian studies scholars questioned their own field's complicity in these activities. This launched a new period of critical East Asian studies that continues in some ways today.[19]

Through its organization and chapter contents, this book builds on all three above meanings of "East Asia" and their related debates in the critical area studies scholarship as they apply to dance in and from the East Asia region. Part I, "Contested Genealogies," explores different ways historical Chinese cultural practices established foundations for dance in the East Asia region, looking at the traditions of female entertainers, operatic performance, and religious literary motifs as three examples. Part II, "Decolonizing Migration," looks at transnational circulations facilitated by imperialism, World War II, and post–Cold War neoliberal economic development, asking how East Asian dancers and choreographers embraced, rejected, and adapted performance forms and ideologies introduced from the West. Part III, "Militarization and Empire," examines how dance promoted the wartime propaganda of Japanese Pan-Asianism, as well as how militarization continued to shape bodily experience in Cold War–era Taiwan after fifty years of Japanese colonialism. Part IV, "Socialist Aesthetics," challenges the ideological legacy of US Cold War area studies, in which socialist art and culture created in the PRC and North Korea are often not taken seriously as artistic practices. Instead, it asks what communist revolutions and their aftermath contributed to dance culture in the region. Lastly, Part V, "Collective Technologies," looks at how dancers have collectively responded to periods of intense social change in contemporary East Asia, from the anti-US protests and feminist movement in 1960s Japan, to current pro- and anti-LGBTQ activism in South Korea and the boom of digital technology in Taiwan. In all five sections, the meanings of East Asia outlined above form an immediate context for each dance being explored.

The critical turn in area studies also forms the basis for many approaches and methodologies employed in this book. Following such work, for example, the essays in this volume attend closely to intersecting colonialisms and imperialisms as structuring forces in modern East Asian cultural history, including their relationships to the unequal power structures of global capitalism and the experiences of indigenous peoples and ethnic minorities within nation-states.[20] This book also affirms recent scholarship that defines an essential function of area studies as the decolonization of knowledge production, by countering the persistent overrepresentation and assumed universality of the US and Europe in the traditional disciplines—including dance.[21] Finally, this book follows the insights of critical area studies by reflecting on power structures that undergird knowledge production about East Asia, recognizing that these may include pressures from East Asian governments themselves. As critical area studies scholars have pointed out, the rapid growth of East Asian economies during the latter decades of the twentieth century, combined with US divestment from East Asian studies following the end of the Cold War, has prompted East Asian governments to sponsor US area studies scholarship through programs such as the Japan Foundation, the Korea Foundation, the Taiwan-based Chiang Ching Kuo Foundation, and, later, China's Confucius Institutes.[22] By pursuing a transnational research frame and reflecting on darker aspects of East Asian dance both past and present, this book challenges some of the outcomes of this new funding model, such as its tendency to promote nation-centered projects and discourage criticism of donor societies.

By invoking "East Asia" as a framing concept, this book embraces several methodological tenets that have long been foundational to area studies research and continue to be so today. These include (1) emphasis on deep historical and cultural contextualization, (2) use of original sources in East Asian languages, and (3) development of theoretical framings and historiographical timelines from within the logics of East Asian history, rather than treating US or European models as universal. While reinforcing these longstanding principles of area studies research, this book also builds on critical insights about how area studies can continue to grow and improve. To that end, this book disrupts nation-based models of "Chinese," "Japanese," or "Korean" culture, instead highlighting how these entities are constantly constructed, malleable, interconnected, and contested. Although the notion of "area" seems to imply a geographic region internally consistent and sealed off by fixed external boundaries, this is not the way East Asia is understood in critical area studies or in the methodology of this book. By contrast, as each chapter in this volume repeatedly asserts, dance and dancers in East Asia have always been internally diverse, moved across borders, and performed dances that are the products of transcultural processes.

The phrase "dancing East Asia" in the subtitle of this book encapsulates these many dimensions of a critical area studies approach to East Asian dance studies. East Asia here does not simply refer to a collection of political units that can be located on a map, nor does it refer to a fixed or homogenous cultural community defined by race, ethnicity, nationality, or language. Rather, "East Asia" points to a complex history of multidirectional exchanges, competing discourses and ideologies both internal and external to the region, and political struggles over East Asia—as a place, a transnational community, and a political idea. Dancing East Asia means looking head-on into these complexities and contradictions. It means locating where dance moves at the interstices of stable meanings to push forward this process of critical dialogue and self-reflection.

## DECENTERING WHITENESS:
## EAST ASIAN DANCE STUDIES AS ANTI-ORIENTALIST STRATEGY

Similar to critical area studies, critical dance studies emerged over the past several decades as a self-reflexive, politically engaged model of dance scholarship that attends to and seeks to challenge historical inequities and power structures shaping knowledge production in dance research. One theme that has been particularly important in critical dance studies is the critique of whiteness and its corresponding history of Western centrism in the discipline of dance studies. In accounts of dance in the US context, critical dance studies scholars have documented and challenged the tendency of dance critics and researchers to emphasize the contributions of white dancers and choreographers while discounting or ignoring those of artists of color.[23] These scholars have deconstructed the racial ideologies informing many persistent conceptual dichotomies in conventional US dance theory and historiography, such as those between "modern dance" and "ethnic dance," "contemporary" and "traditional," and "art" and "culture." By valuing the contributions of dancers classified as nonwhite, they have worked to identify and overcome racism in US dance practice, criticism, and research, while offering models for challenging racist narratives in the study of dance elsewhere in the world.

This book extends the critique of whiteness in US dance studies by foregrounding the voices and contributions of nonwhite artists in and from East Asia. The performers and choreographers discussed in this book include many influential figures in the modern history of East Asian dance—artists such as Mei Lanfang, Wu Xiaobang, Fujikage Shizue, Murayama Tomoyoshi, Park Yeong-in, Dai Ailian, Seo Jeongseon, Itō Michio, Lin Lee-chen, Choe Seung-hui, Chen Ailian, Yang Liping, Ashikawa Yoko, Furukawa Anzu, and Huang Yi. Many of these individuals have received little or no attention in previous English-language dance scholarship. Moreover, those who have are often studied from the perspective of how their work drew on or contributed to the activities of white artists based in the West, rather than contextualizing them in relation to other East Asian artists, artists of other nonwhite racial or ethnic backgrounds, or within the historical trajectories of dance in East Asia. By contrast, every essay in this volume prioritizes the ideas and voices of East Asian artists, by delving into their memoirs, essays, letters, interviews, and other textual traces that help us to better understand the intentions and concerns motivating their dance works in their own words. Thus, even when chapters in this book examine relationships between East Asian dancers and their white counterparts or audiences in the West, they do so from the perspective of the East Asian dancers. Additionally, the book not only prioritizes the contributions of East Asian artists but situates the significance of their work within historical narratives in which places, people, and issues of East Asia are at the center.

One important way that whiteness has been constructed historically is through the discourses of Orientalism, an ideology that posits radical difference between the East and the West, often as a justification for cultural, military, and economic interventions that advance the interests of people and groups associated with the West. The racist history of Orientalism in much English-language writing about Asian people and societies has meant that dancers from Asia have often been presented passively either as objects of representation or bearers of fixed ancient traditions, rather than actively as subjects who articulate their own ideas and create new artistic forms relevant to their contemporary lives. It has also meant that dance forms thought to have originated in the Western world and attributed to the innovations of white dancers are often treated as more modern, innovative, and meaningful than dances originating in Asia or attributed to Asian dancers. Such Orientalist narratives of Asian dance have furthered the imagined distinction between the East and the West, reinforcing the myth of absolute difference on which Orientalist discourses are based, by positing Asian dance forms as products of isolated national cultures separate from and irrelevant to global dance history.

An important development in critical dance studies has been the emergence of anti-Orientalist scholarship that explicitly challenges these views. Such work offers new ways of understanding dancers and dance practices in and from Asia, while also complicating received histories of Asian dancers' engagements with many so-called "Western" dance forms. Within this larger body of anti-Orientalist dance scholarship, work in South Asian dance studies has played an especially prominent role, producing important books that foreground the creative interventions of South Asian and South Asian diaspora artists working in a wide range of dance styles.[24] These projects do much to deconstruct the Orientalist notion that South Asian dance consists of static traditions perpetually rooted in the past and disconnected from the modern world (ideas often promoted by practitioners of these forms themselves). They also demonstrate the ways in which all dance practitioners— whether they work in the categories of classical, folk, modern, contemporary, or something else—are drawing on and responding to issues in their own lives and contemporary conditions. The divide between "traditional" and "contemporary" forms, as shown in this scholarship, is often more a matter of aesthetic choices, choreographic methods, and cultural discourses than it is about the temporality or creativity of such dances. Furthermore, they reveal that the imagined cultural purity or national origins associated with various dance forms (whether South Asian or Western) are also discursive constructions that mask historical and contemporary processes marked by hybridity and interaction. In sum, this anti-Orientalist scholarship has shown that no dance tradition has a monopoly on contemporaneity or creativity and that South Asian dance is as local and national as it is worldly and global.

*Corporeal Politics: Dancing East Asia* advances the project of de-Orientalizing Asian dance studies by similarly highlighting the inventiveness of East Asian dancers and choreographers and the contemporaneity, cultural hybridity, and worldliness of East Asian dance forms. Like South Asia, East Asia gave rise to a vast array of inherited, reconstructed, and newly created classical and folk dance forms during the twentieth century. Although they emerged in different historical conditions and followed different paths of development from their South Asian counterparts, many of these dance styles similarly remain central to the contemporary landscape of dance in East Asia and East Asian diaspora communities today. The contributors to this book provide varied approaches to the study of classical and folk dances in East Asia. However, what unites their accounts is a shared understanding that these forms are products of modern historical circumstances, not static traditions that have been handed down unchanged through time or that embody pure essences of local or national cultures. Bringing an anti-Orientalist approach to the study of these dance forms does not undermine their authenticity or cultural value, nor does it suggest that they are not grounded in longer traditions with deep meanings in their respective communities. In fact, as the essays in this volume show, many dances regarded in East Asia today as classical and folk forms do emerge out of sustained efforts by East Asian dancers and choreographers to learn from the past. By showing the contributions that individual artists have made toward developing and promoting these dance forms and by examining the historical conditions in which they have done so, anti-Orientalist approaches such as the ones demonstrated in this book add to, rather than take away from, the meaning and significance of these practices. They help to show how the concept of tradition itself is deeply entrenched in modern historical processes, meaning that the very act of claiming to embody tradition is part of a modern mindset and predicament. By showing differences, disagreements, and debates within the worlds of classical and folk dance in East Asia, the essays in this volume further challenge the common, though often misguided, view that a claim to represent tradition necessarily reinforces uniformity or suppresses artistic creativity.

One key way that East Asia differs from many other parts of Asia is that it was never fully colonized by a European government, as most of South Asia was by the British and different parts of Southeast Asia were by the British, Dutch, Spanish, French, and US. Nevertheless, this does not mean that East Asia lacked intensive cultural interaction with Europe or was immune from the cultural effects of Western imperialism. Cultural traffic between East Asia and Europe dates back centuries, first facilitated by land trade across the Silk Roads that traversed Central Asia from the start of the first millennium CE, and later through sea traffic that brought missionaries, merchants, and gunboats along with Western imperial expansion.[25] During the mid-nineteenth century, East Asia was forced to open its ports to European and US trade, and many coastal cities gained international settlements that operated under colonial or semicolonial conditions. During the early twentieth century, Tokyo emerged as a hub of Western culture within East Asia through its status as the local colonial metropole, and it was through this city that many dancers across East Asia gained exposure to Western concert dance forms such as ballet and early modern dance. The close contact and later political alliance between Japan and Germany made Berlin a common destination for East Asian dancers traveling abroad from the 1910s through the 1940s. This facilitated the emergence of an East Asian field of "New Dance" centered in Japan that arose in tandem with German expressionist dance or *Neue Tanz*.[26] During the Cold War, parts of East Asia that were aligned politically with the US, such as Japan, South Korea, and Taiwan, participated in intercultural exchange with dancers and other artists from North America and Western Europe.[27] Meanwhile, dancers and choreographers in North Korea and China participated in a different set of intercultural exchanges centered in the Soviet Union, Eastern Europe, and left-leaning countries in Asia, Africa, and Latin America.[28]

By addressing the many ways in which East Asian dancers and choreographers have traveled and worked abroad and engaged with dance communities beyond East Asia, this book challenges the Orientalist idea that East Asian dance exists in an exotic and distant vacuum separated from the rest of global dance history. Regardless of the dance styles and scenes in which they participated, the artists discussed in this book were all involved, to varying degrees, in processes and circulations that stretched beyond the geographic and cultural sphere of East Asia. When dance styles from outside the region circulated to East Asia, these dancers took them up and transformed them through their own visions. Moreover, when dancers from East Asia traveled abroad, their work too responded to their new environments. This movement across borders is an inherent part of the lives of dancers, dance works, and dance forms in East Asia, as it has so often been for dancers in other parts of the world. By showing that dance in East Asia has always been global, this book advances critical anti-Orientalist dance studies and identifies dance as a lens for the exploration of intercultural processes in East Asia past and present.

## CORPOREAL POLITICS: METHODOLOGY AND OVERVIEW OF CHAPTERS

A sustained attention to politics is one of the shared features of both critical area studies and critical dance studies. Thus, by proposing "corporeal politics" as an organizing theme, this book aims to bridge the insights of these two fields, while highlighting what critical East Asian dance studies can add to the existing discussions. The methodology of corporeal politics recognizes the central place of the artist's physical body in dance, in which the aesthetically structured body in motion serves as the primary medium for artistic expression and the production of meaning. This importance of the body in dance also means that aspects of an artist's identity that are physically marked on the body or inform the ways people move in the world—such as race, ethnicity, sex, gender, sexuality, class, nationality, and citizenship—are particularly highlighted in dance performance, and the political significance of dance is negotiated, felt, and performed first and foremost in bodily actions and experiences. A focus on corporeal politics pinpoints individual bodies located in specific historical contexts as the focus of our investigation. In this way, it discourages generalizations about national, ethnic, or cultural groups or dance forms, insisting that any analysis of East Asian dance must be located in concrete, historically specific bodies and sociopolitical situations. By offering politicized readings of dancing bodies in East Asia, this book locates dance within the broader structures of power and knowledge that critical area studies and critical dance studies scholars have expertly revealed, reflected upon, and challenged. Taking dance as an art that makes the politics of bodies visible, palpable, and transformable by displaying and manipulating them in ways uncommon in daily life, the methodology of corporeal politics models the investigation of these political interventions and the impacts of dance's bodily acts as one way to pursue critical East Asian dance studies.

Radical contextualization is at the heart of the methodology of corporeal politics. Therefore, each case study in this volume presents a slightly different articulation of this concept; no single, unified definition or model is held consistent across the book. It is important for this method that politics itself can mean different things in different contexts. Thus, in one essay, "politics" may refer to the nuances of interpersonal relations while in another it may refer to diplomatic negotiations between governments at war. Even definitions of the body can vary, ranging from the human dancer to the anthropomorphized robot. Rather than repeat a single view of corporeal politics in each case study, the chapters offer competing definitions that can be compared against one another. In this way, they produce not a normative, universal model but instead a spectrum of possibilities that reflects the many directions such analysis may take.

Part I, "Contested Genealogies," begins chronologically with the earliest case studies in the book, considering dance and performance in East Asia before and at the turn of the twentieth century. In chapter 1, "Sexuality, Status, and the Female Dancer: Legacies of Imperial China," historian Beverly Bossler traces the changing definitions and social contexts of dance in China from ancient times, paying special attention to gender, sexuality, and class as intersectional categories that shaped dancers' lives and social mobilities. Bossler shows that dance has often been closely connected to sexual allure in China and other parts of East Asia. She argues that this association made female dancers (and later boys and eunuchs who performed feminine roles) inherently transgressive figures capable of moving in unusual ways across social hierarchies.

In chapter 2, "Mei Lanfang and Modern Dance: Transcultural Innovation in Peking Opera, 1910s–1920s," literary scholar Catherine Yeh takes up the historical encounter between Chinese operatic theater and early Western modern dance in the opening decades of the twentieth century, through the lens of one of China's most famous actors—legendary Peking opera star and female impersonator Mei Lanfang. Analyzing Mei's cross-gender stage performances and the writings of his close artistic collaborator Qi Rushan, Yeh demonstrates that dance operated as a modernizing force in Chinese theater, while it also initiated the search for a new transcultural bodily aesthetic that would be capable of performing newly imagined ideas of Chinese cultural authenticity.

In chapter 3, "The Conflicted Monk: Choreographic Adaptations of *Si fan* (Longing for the Mundane) in Japan's and China's New Dance Movements," East Asian studies scholar Nan Ma looks at the transnational circulation of well-known story cycles—in this case *Si fan* 思凡, a story of a Buddhist monk's or nun's test of faith—as an enduring aspect of dance culture in East Asia. Ma compares two choreographies based on the *Si fan* story, one staged in 1921 by female Japanese dancer Fujikage Shizue and the other in 1942 by male Chinese dancer Wu Xiaobang. In her analysis of these two adaptations of the same tale, Ma considers how the dancers' gender and social status, as well as different local reactions to New Dance, influence their divergent choreographic renditions and the messages they relate about morality, desire, and modernity.

Part 2, "Decolonizing Migration," stretches the geographic boundaries of East Asia by considering people who traverse the region's borders as important creators and subjects of East Asian dance. In chapter 4, "Murayama Tomoyoshi and Dance of Modern Times: A Forerunner of the Japanese Avant-garde," and chapter 5, "Korean Dance Beyond Koreanness: Park Yeong-in in the German Modern Dance Scene," dance and performance scholars Kazuko Kuniyoshi and Okju Son both look at individuals who traveled from Japan to Germany during the early twentieth century and consider the impacts of these journeys on their dance careers. Murayama Tomoyoshi, who went to Berlin in 1922, is significant in that he was one of the only Japanese modern dancers of his time to be critical of influential German expressionist dancer Mary Wigman. As Kuniyoshi shows, Murayama chose not to adopt Wigman's style and instead developed his own dance theories. Park Yeong-in's case is different from Murayama's in that Park did not arrive in Germany until 1937, and before that he had already studied Western dance in Japan and staged new choreography inspired by Korean traditional performance, as was common for Korean colonial subjects in Japan at the time. As Son shows, Park was greeted in Germany as a professional dancer, and during his time abroad he acted as a performer and teacher of East Asian dance rather than a student of German dance.

In chapter 6, "Diasporic Moves: Sinophone Epistemology in the Choreography of Dai Ailian," and chapter 7, "Choreographing Neoliberal Marginalization: Dancing Migrant Bodies in the South Korean Musical *Bballae* (*Laundry*)," Chinese studies scholar Emily Wilcox and theater scholar Ji Hyon (Kayla) Yuh address the opposite direction of migration, not from the inside out but from the outside in. Examining the career of Trinidad-born Chinese diasporic dancer Dai Ailian, Wilcox shows how Dai's choreographic repertoires staged in Hong Kong and Chongqing during the 1940s enacted different place-based embodiments of Chinese identity. Wilcox argues that these embodiments, which were informed by Dai's intercultural upbringing as both a British colonial subject and a patriotic Overseas Chinese, performed what Shu-mei Shih calls the "multiply-angulated critique" of Sinophone epistemology. In her analysis of the 2005 original South Korean Broadway-style musical *Bballae* (*Laundry*), Yuh turns to a very different context of inward migration in East Asia, namely, racialized male Mongolian and Filipino labor immigrants and working-class women in contemporary urban South Korea. By reading movement together with song lyrics and dialogue, Yuh shows how *Bballae* depicts migrants as assimilable only when their range of expression is constrained and their ambitions align with neoliberal values.

Part 3, "Militarization and Empire," turns to dance and the Japanese Empire during and after World War II, looking at how performance can both serve and deconstruct militarized cultures. In chapter 8, "Masking Japanese Militarism as a Dream of Sino-Japanese Friendship: *Miyako Odori* Performances in the 1930s," performance scholar Mariko Okada delves into the popular Kyoto tradition of *Miyako Odori*, a public geisha dance that has been performed annually each spring since 1872. Okada shows how, in the late 1930s, *Miyako Odori* was turned into a tool for disseminating Japan's imperialist propaganda, with children portraying cheerful and idyllic images of Sino-Japanese friendship at a time when Japanese armies were waging a violent war in China.

In chapter 9, "Imagined Choreographies: Itō Michio's Philippines Pageant and the Transpacific Performance of Japanese Imperialism," performance scholar Tara Rodman looks at another example of dance in service of Japanese empire, but one with a very different genealogy. Analyzing an unrealized 1944 plan made by international modern dancer Itō Michio for a national festival pageant to be held in the Japanese-occupied Philippines, Rodman shows how Itō drew on his earlier experiences studying at the Jaques-Dalcroze Institute for Eurythmics in Hellerau, Germany, and staging mass performances in Washington, DC, and Los Angeles, California. Looked at together, Okada's and Rodman's chapters show how Western modern dance and Japanese traditional dance were equally susceptible to appropriation by Japan's war effort.

In chapter 10, "Exorcism and Reclamation: Lin Lee-chen's *Jiao* and the Corporeal History of the Taiwanese," dance scholar Ya-ping Chen discusses how, following fifty years of Japanese colonization in 1895–1945, the new KMT government on Taiwan imposed a period of martial law in 1949–1987 that continued, in new ways, the militarization of Taiwanese bodies and sensibilities. In this context, Chen reads Taiwanese contemporary dance choreographer Lin Lee-chen's 1995 work *Jiao* (Mirrors of Life) as an exorcism of the militarized body and a reclamation of sensuous and empathic life, which Lin achieves through her use of elements of indigenous and local culture and religious rites embedded in local Taiwan history.

Part 4, "Socialist Aesthetics," looks at the creation and transformation of socialist dance culture in postrevolutionary North Korea and the People's Republic of China. In chapter 11, "Choe Seung-hui Between Classical and Folk: Aesthetics of National Form and Socialist Content in North Korea," historian Suzy Kim excavates the post-1946 career of Choe Seung-hui (Choi Seung-hee), one of the most renowned figures in early twentieth-century East Asian dance. Challenging existing views of North Korean performance culture that emphasize its propaganda function, Kim explores the theoretical and artistic depth of Choe's dance writings, choreography, and pedagogy, showing her engagement with transnational socialist culture and her enduring legacy in Korean dance today.

In chapter 12, "The Dilemma of Chinese Classical Dance: Traditional or Contemporary?," and Chapter 13, "Negotiating Chinese Identity through a Double-Minority Voice and the Female Dancing Body: Yang Liping's *Spirit of the Peacock* and Beyond," dance scholars Dong Jiang and Ting-Ting Chang examine two of the most prevalent styles of dance performed in the PRC and Chinese diaspora communities worldwide today—Chinese classical dance and Chinese national folk dance—both of which were first canonized and promoted during the socialist era. Tracing the historical development of Chinese classical dance from the 1950s to the early twenty-first century, Jiang shows how constant debate within the field has encouraged continued new innovations and the emergence of multiple voices and competing styles of Chinese classical dance. At the same time, changes in Chinese classical dance serve as a barometer of the transformation of contemporary Chinese society. Chang analyzes the work of Yang Liping, the most influential ethnic minority dance performer and choreographer in the Chinese-speaking world today. Chang shows how, through her innovative renditions of Dai peacock dance, Yang molded a powerful personal and local brand, bringing economic opportunities to her home region of Yunnan and establishing herself as a feminist entrepreneur icon, while also continuing to insert female ethnic minority images into portrayals of Chinese culture domestically and globally.

Part 5, "Collective Technologies," examines dances that engage social issues through collective performance strategies in contemporary East Asia. In chapter 14, "Cracking History's Codes in Crocodile Time: The Sweat, Powder, and Glitter of Women Butoh Artists' Collective Choreography," performance scholar Katherine Mezur addresses the work of Ashikawa Yoko and Furukawa

Anzu, two Japanese women artists who were central to the domestic and transnational evolution of butoh from the 1970s to the 2000s. Taking a feminist revisionist view of butoh history, Mezur shows how official histories have minoritized these major women performer-choreographers by placing them within the genealogies of male figures such as Hijikata Tatsumi. Attending to their work in Japan and abroad, Mezur shows how these women artists' innovations grew out of historically specific experiences of gender, class, and labor.

In chapter 15, "Fans, Sashes, and Jesus: Evangelical Activism and Anti-LGBTQ Performance in South Korea," performance scholar Soo Ryon Yoon analyzes the use of dance in anti-LGBTQ activism by right-wing Christian Protestant groups in South Korea. Yoon shows that conservative nationalism plays an important role in anti-LGBTQ evangelical activism and shows how Christianity and nationalism have been linked through choreographed performances in South Korea since the early twentieth century. Yoon argues that the seeming spectacularity of dance in contemporary evangelical activism conceals the visibility of a larger community of "respectable" groups who also push forward homophobic nationalist ideologies. She also considers how queer activists and their allies reappropriate national dance styles and imbue them with new meanings.

In chapter 16, "Choreographing Digital Performance in Twenty-First-Century Taiwan: *Huang Yi & KUKA*," dance scholar Yatin Lin concludes the book by investigating new dances by Taiwan-based choreographer Huang Yi that reflect on relationships between humans and digital technology. First, Lin traces the development of digital performance as a new creative industry in Taiwan that links choreographers such as Huang to transnational communities of digital artists, programmers, and dancers. The focus of the chapter is Huang's 2012–2015 work *Huang Yi & KUKA*, a dance featuring collaborative performances between human dancers and KUKA, an anthropomorphic industrial robot. The work poses existential questions about agency, mortality, and human-machine bonds. Lin argues that by exploring such questions through new technology, Huang has established himself within a new generation of "culturepreneurs" in the dance field of contemporary Taiwan and East Asia more broadly.

Each chapter includes illustrations of the dances discussed. Additionally, readers are encouraged to visit the Open Access *Corporeal Politics* Fulcrum multimedia platform at https://doi.org/10.3998/mpub.11521701. A list of relevant materials on Fulcrum, including videos, additional images, and links to external sources, can be found at the end of each chapter.

## *Notes*

1. Angela Falco Howard, Li Song, Wu Hung, and Yang Hong, *Chinese Sculpture* (New Haven, CT: Yale University Press, 2006), 17–200.

2. For more on definitions of "East Asia," see below.

3. For some exceptions, see A. C. Scott, *Literature and the Arts in Twentieth-Century China* (Garden City, NY: Doubleday, 1963); Lee Hye-gu, *An Introduction to Korean Music and Dance* (Seoul: Seoul Royal Asiatic Society, Korea Branch, 1977); Frank Hoff, *Song, Dance, and Storytelling: Aspects of the Performing Arts in Japan* (Ithaca, NY: China-Japan Program, Cornell University, 1978).

4. For some exceptions, see Carl Wolz, *Bugaku: Japanese Court Dance, with the Notation of Basic Movements and of Nasori* (Providence, RI: Asian Music Publications, 1971); Judy Van Zile, ed., *Dance in Africa, Asia, and the Pacific: Selected Readings* (New York: MSS Information Corporation, 1976); Adrienne L. Kaeppler, Judy Van Zile, and Carl Wolz, eds., *Asian and Pacific Dance: Selected Papers from the 1974 CORD-SEM Conference* (New York: Committee on Research in Dance, 1977).

5. See, for example, Anya Peterson Royce, *The Anthropology of Dance* (Bloomington: Indiana University Press, 1977).

6. For some exceptions, see Masakatsu Gunji, trans. Don Kenny, with an introduction by James R. Brandon, *Buyo: the Classical Dance* (New York: Walker/Weatherhill, 1970); Masataro Togi, trans. Don Kenny, with an introduction by William P. Malm, *Gagaku: Court Music and Dance* (New York: Walker/Weatherhill, 1971).

7. On the development of performance studies in the United States, see Shannon Jackson, *Professing Performance: Theatre in the Academy from Philology to Performativity* (New York: Cambridge University Press, 2004).

8. See, for example, Jennifer Robertson, *Takarazuka: Sexual Politics and Popular Culture in Modern Japan* (Berkeley: University of California Press, 1998); Sondra Fraleigh, *Dancing Into Darkness: Butoh, Zen, and Japan* (Pittsburgh: University of Pittsburgh Press, 1999); Judy Van Zile, *Perspectives on Korean Dance* (Middletown, CT: Wesleyan University Press, 2001); Katherine Mezur, *Beautiful Boys/Outlaw Bodies: Devising Kabuki Female-Likeness* (New York: Palgrave Macmillan, 2005); Nathan Hesselink, *P'ungmul: South Korean Drumming and Dance* (Chicago: University of Chicago Press, 2006); Tomie Hahn, *Sensational Knowledge: Embodying Culture Through Japanese Dance* (Middletown, CT: Wesleyan University Press, 2007); Andrew Field, *Shanghai's Dancing World: Cabaret Culture and Urban Politics, 1919–1954* (Hong Kong: Hong Kong Chinese University Press, 2010); Sondra Fraleigh, *Butoh: Metamorphic Dance and Global Alchemy* (Urbana: University of Illinois Press, 2010); Bruce Baird, *Hijikata Tatsumi and Butoh: Dancing in a Pool of Gray Grits* (New York: Palgrave Macmillan, 2012); SanSan Kwan, *Kinesthetic Cities: Dance in Chinese Urban Spaces* (Oxford: Oxford University Press, 2013); Yatin Lin, *Sino-Corporealities: Contemporary Choreographies from Taipei, Hong Kong, and New York* (Taipei: Taipei National University of the Arts, 2015); Eun-Joo Lee and Yong-Shin Kim, *Salpuri-Chum, A Korean Dance for Expelling Evil Spir-*

*its: A Psychoanalytic Interpretation of Its Artistic Characteristics* (Lanham, MD: Hamilton Books, 2017); Emily Wilcox, *Revolutionary Bodies: Chinese Dance and the Socialist Legacy* (Oakland: University of California Press, 2019).

9. Apart from the monographs listed above, see also Ruth Solomon and John Solomon, eds., *East Meets West in Dance: Voices in a Cross-Cultural Dialogue* (Chur, Switzerland: Harwood Academic, 1997); Wang Yunyu and Stephanie Burridge, eds., *Identity and Diversity: Celebrating Dance in Taiwan* (New Delhi: Routledge, 2012); Shih-Ming Li Chang and Lynn Frederiksen, *Chinese Dance: In the Vast Land and Beyond* (Middletown, CT: Wesleyan University Press, 2016); Bruce Baird and Rosemary Candelario, eds., *The Routledge Companion to Butoh Performance* (London: Routledge, 2018).

10. Both the US and China recognize Taiwan officially as part of China. However, Taiwan has its own political system and a dance history distinct from that of the Chinese mainland. Hong Kong was a British colony until 1997, and Macau was a territory of Portugal until 1999. Both are now Special Administrative Regions of the PRC. For a general introduction to politics, society, and culture in contemporary East Asia, see Anne Prescott, *East Asia in the World: An Introduction* (New York: Routledge, 2015).

11. The Middle East and Central Asia are also considered part of Asia, but they are typically not included in "Asian studies." The US-based Association for Asian Studies, for example, excludes most of these two regions from its academic purview.

12. For a historical overview of these relationships and their different trajectories in each place, see Charles Holcombe, *A History of East Asia: From the Origins of Civilization to the Twenty-First Century* (Cambridge: Cambridge University Press, 2017).

13. Although Pan-Asianism was not limited to East Asia, Japan and China were important centers for this discourse, and concepts of East Asian unity and cooperation were one important component of this broader phenomenon. See Sven Saaler and Christopher Szpilman, eds., *Pan-Asianism: A Documentary History* (Lanham, MD: Rowman & Littlefield, 2011); Torsten Weber, *Embracing "Asia" in China and Japan: Asianism Discourse and the Contest for Hegemony, 1912–1933* (Palgrave Macmillan, 2018).

14. Saaler and Szpilman, *Pan-Asianism*, 5.

15. Jeremy Yellen, *The Greater East Asia Co-Prosperity Sphere: When Total Empire Met Total War* (Ithaca, NY: Cornell University Press, 2019).

16. Numerous studies have established the historical connections between area studies and US foreign policy during the postwar period, particularly regarding the Cold War. For a short overview, see Hossein Khosrowjah, "A Brief History of Area Studies and International Studies," *Arab Studies Quarterly* 33, no. 3/4 (2011): 131–42.

17. Two key history textbooks for East Asian studies produced during this period, *East Asia: The Great Tradition* (1960) and *East Asia: The Modern Transformation* (1965), were authored by Harvard professors who worked for the US State Department during World War II and subsequently helped facilitate East Asian studies' service to US Cold War interests.

18. For a historical account, see Xiaobing Li, *The Cold War in East Asia* (London: Routledge, 2018).

19. Fabio Lanza, *The End of Concern: Maoist China, Activism, and Asian Studies* (Durham, NC: Duke University Press, 2017).

20. See, for example, Tani E. Barlow, ed., *Formations of Colonial Modernity in East Asia* (Durham, NC: Duke University Press, 1997); Bruce Cumings, *Parallax Visions: Making Sense of American–East Asian Relations* (Durham, NC: Duke University Press, 2002); Kuan-Hsing Chen, *Asia as Method: Toward Deimperialization* (Durham, NC: Duke University Press, 2010); Shu-mei Shih, Chien-hsin Tsai, and Brian Bernards, eds., *Sinophone Studies: A Critical Reader* (New York: Columbia University Press, 2013).

21. David Szanton, ed. *The Politics of Knowledge: Area Studies and the Disciplines* (Berkeley: University of California Press, 2004).

22. Masao Miyoshi and H. D. Harootunian, eds., *Learning Places: The Afterlives of Area Studies* (Durham, NC: Duke University Press, 2002).

23. For a small sampling of influential monographs in this broad field, see, for example, Brenda Dixon Gottschild, *Digging the Africanist Presence in American Performance: Dance and Other Contexts* (Westport, CN: Greenwoord Press, 1996); Ananya Chatterjea, *Butting Out: Reading Resistive Choreographies Through Works by Jawole Willa Jo Zollar and Chandralekha* (Middletown, CT: Wesleyan University Press, 2004); Susan Manning, *Modern Dance, Negro Dance: Race in Motion* (Minneapolis: University of Minnesota Press, 2004); Jacqueline Shea Murphy, *The People Have Never Stopped Dancing: Native American Modern Dance Histories* (Minneapolis: University of Minnesota Press, 2007); Yutian Wong, *Choreographing Asian America* (Middletown, CT: Wesleyan University Press, 2010);  Adria Imada, *Aloha America: Hula Circuits through the U.S. Empire* (Durham, NC: Duke University Press, 2012); Priya Srinivasan, *Sweating Saris: Indian Dance as Transnational Labor* (Philadelphia: Temple University Press, 2012); Rebecca Rossen, *Dancing Jewish: Jewish Identity in American Modern and Postmodern Dance* (Oxford: Oxford University Press, 2014); Anthea Kraut, *Choreographing Copyright: Race, Gender, and Intellectual Property Rights in American Dance* (New York: Oxford University Press, 2016).

24. See, for example, Chatterjea, *Butting Out*; Avanthi Meduri, ed., *Rukmini Devi Arundale, 1904–1986: A Visionary Architect of Indian Culture and the Performing Arts* (Delhi: Motilal Banarsidass Publishers, 2005); Janet O'Shea, *At Home in the World: Bharata Natyam on the Global Stage* (Middletown, CT: Wesleyan University Press, 2007); Pallabi Chakravorty, *Bells of Change: Kathak Dance, Women and Modernity in India* (Calcutta, London, and New York: Seagull, 2008); Susan A. Reed, *Dance and the Nation: Performance, Ritual, and Politics in Sri Lanka* (Madison: University of Wisconsin Press, 2010); Davesh Soneji, ed., *Bharatnatyam: A Reader* (New Delhi: Oxford University Press, 2010); Prarthana Purkayastha, *Indian Modern Dance, Feminism and Transnationalism* (Houndsmills, UK: Palgrave Macmillan, 2014); Royona Mitra, *Akram Khan: Dancing New Interculturalism* (Houndsmills, UK: Palgrave Macmillan, 2015).

25. See Bossler, Yeh, and Yoon, this volume.

26. For English-language studies of Tokyo's role as a hub of Western dance culture in East Asia during this period, see Kazuko Yamazaki, "Nihon Buyo: Classical Dance

of Modern Japan" (PhD diss., Indiana University, 2001); Toshiharu Omuka, "Dancing and Performing: Japanese Artists in the Early 1920s at the Dawn of Modern Dance," *Experiment* 10 (2004):157–70; Yukihiko Yoshida, "National Dance Under the Rising Sun, Mainly from National Dance, Buyō Geijutsu and the Activities of Takaya Eguchi," *International Journal of Eastern Sports and Physical Education* 7, no. 1 (October 2009): 88–103; Ya-ping Chen, "Colonial Modernity and Female Dancing Bodies in Early Taiwanese Modern Dance," in *Identity and Diversity: Celebrating Dance in Taiwan,* eds. Wang Yunyu and Stephanie Burridge (New Delhi: Routledge, 2012); Faye Yuan Kleeman, "Dancers of the Empire," in *In Transit: the Formation of the Colonial East Asian Cultural Sphere* (Honolulu: University of Hawai'i Press, 2014), 186–210; Nan Ma, "Transmediating Kinesthesia: Wu Xiaobang and Modern Dance in China, 1929–1939," *Modern Chinese Literature and Culture* 28, no. 1 (2016): 129–73. See also Ma, Kuniyoshi, and Son, this volume.

27. On dance exchange in US-allied East Asia during the Cold War, see Ruth Solomon and John Solomon, eds., *East Meets West in Dance: Voices in a Cross-Cultural Dialogue* (Chur, Switzerland: Harwood Academic, 1997); Ya-ping Chen, "Dance History and Cultural Politics: A Study of Contemporary Dance in Taiwan, 1930s–1997" (PhD diss., New York University, 2003). See also Yuh, Mezur, and Yoon, this volume.

28. On North Korea and China's intercultural dance exchange during the Cold War, see Emily Wilcox, "Performing Bandung: China's Dance Diplomacy with India, Indonesia, and Burma, 1953–1962," *Inter-Asia Cultural Studies* 18, no. 4: 518–39; Emily Wilcox, "The Postcolonial Blind Spot: Chinese Dance in the Era of Third World-ism, 1949–1965," *positions: asia critique* 26, no. 4 (2018): 781–815; Emily Wilcox, "Crossing Over: Choi Seunghee's Pan-Asianism in Revolutionary Time," 무용역사기록학 (*The Journal of Society for Dance Documentation and History*) 51 (December): 65–97. See also Kim and Jiang, this volume.

# PART 1

# Contested Genealogies

# CHAPTER 1

# Sexuality, Status, and the Female Dancer

## Legacies of Imperial China

*Beverly Bossler*

This chapter explores the social conditions of dance and dancers in imperial China, a period of two millennia stretching from the third century BCE through 1911. Developments in the first half of this era established general social and performance structures that prevailed through later centuries in China and influenced Korea and Japan as well. A salient figure within these structures was the female dancer, who, like other female entertainers, had a special place in the East Asian social world.[1] Surviving textual as well as archeological sources show that the female dancer in imperial China was mobile across social statuses, social spaces, and social roles. The opportunities and constraints that dancers faced, like the dances they performed, changed over time. Chinese dance practices were subject to cultural influences from outside China and to changing political conditions and shifting social structures within China: there was no static, unchanging "traditional" Chinese dance. For all this mobility, however, some salient aspects of dancers' social position—especially Confucian-influenced attitudes about the relationship of female performance, sexuality, and status—remained in place throughout the later imperial period and into the twentieth century. Moreover, those attitudes, along with specific performance practices, were exported into Korea and Japan. In this sense, Chinese dance was "transnational" long before "nations" in the modern sense existed. As a result, the legacies of imperial Chinese practices and attitudes still influence the social conditions and meanings of dance and dancers in East Asia today.

## EARLY UNDERSTANDINGS OF "DANCE" IN CHINA

To trace the origins of the mobile female dancer in China, it is useful to have some understanding of early attitudes toward dance in China. The modern

Chinese word for dance is composed of two characters, *wu* (舞) and *dao* (蹈). Early uses of the term *wu* associate it with movement of the upper body, while *dao* originally implied stamping the feet. We see this in a statement by the early Confucian philosopher Mencius (c. 372–289 BCE), who said that in the state of joy brought on by the practice of benevolence, unconsciously "one's feet begin to step and one's hands to dance" (*bu zhi zu zhi dao zhi, shou zhi wu zhi* 不知足之蹈之、手之舞之).[2] Mencius's claim also reflects another very important early Chinese view, which had significant implications for ideas about dance: that human beings are intimately connected to the larger workings of the cosmos. In fact, Confucian thought asserted that the role of human beings in the world is to facilitate or extend the development of the cosmos through proper (moral) action. Benevolent action puts one in accord with the cosmos and thus brings joy; dance is the spontaneous human physical expression of that joy.

But if "dance" was understood as the spontaneous expression of being in tune with the cosmos, from there it was a small step to the notion that, conversely, the practice of dance could help one become more in tune with the cosmos. Early Chinese ritual texts accordingly included dance among the activities young men were to practice to cultivate their bodies and grow into proper gentlemen.[3] Moreover, dance was not only a mechanism for individual moral and physical self-cultivation: it was also one of the ways that human beings could address broader cosmic dislocations, such as droughts, floods, and earthquakes. Many early texts describe dance as a central aspect of ritual ceremonies designed to ward off natural calamities, and the altars at which prayers for rain were offered were called *wu yu* (舞雩), literally "dance rain-sacrifice."[4] The prayers at such alters were often offered up by female shamans, whose dances were meant to please the gods.[5] Dance was likewise integral to ceremonies designed to exorcise evil influences or to ensure bountiful harvests.[6] In short, dance (and music with it) was understood to have cosmic significance.

As China became an organized empire under the Qin (221–206 BCE) and Han (206 BCE–220 CE) dynasties, dance remained central in court ritual sacrifices. In accord with the admonition that "Ritual restrains the people's hearts, and music accords with the people's voices," Chinese rulers understood ritual and music to be critical to proper governance.[7] They organized elaborate court ceremonies involving musicians, singers, and dancers. Mirroring earlier practice, court rituals often had exorcistic or propitiatory functions, although they could also serve as displays of dynastic grandeur, inspiring awe and obedience in the population. Either way, the association of dance and court ritual continued to be salient in China through most of the imperial period. It also came to influence understandings of dance in Korea and Japan, and we see obvious vestiges of this idea in the later Japanese performance arts of Noh and butoh.

Still, the role of dance in early China was not limited to quasireligious or moral functions: dance was also widely appreciated simply as a form of entertainment. Arguably, of course, rituals themselves were a form of entertainment, but we know from both archeological and textual sources that dance was also enjoyed in more informal settings such as banquets. In some cases, the banquet participants themselves danced,[8] but banquets at which dancers and musicians performed for a seated audience of guests were probably more common. In archeological artifacts, the audiences most often appear to be male; the dancers are sometimes female and sometimes male and are engaged in a wide variety of movements and styles. Extra-long sleeves (extending well beyond the length of the arms) were a common feature in the costumes for both male and female dancers, with those of women tending to be longer than those of men. In fact, female dancers gesturing with long, swooping sleeves—a stylistic element that remains emblematic of Chinese dance even today—already figure prominently in Han images and may have once had talismanic significance.[9] Such long-sleeved female figures are often depicted in static positions, with dramatically arched or twisted torsos. In contrast, male figures tend to brandish weapons or appear in acrobatic poses, such as flips and summersaults, in scenes vaguely suggestive of martial arts competitions. A variety of musicians playing drums, flutes, and stringed instruments often accompany the dancers, and textual sources show that dancers could also be accompanied by singers or could accompany their own movements with song. This points to yet another important aspect of pre-twentieth-century Chinese notions of dance, which is that dance was seldom a stand-alone art. Chinese "dancers" in the imperial period—and in imperial Japan and Korea—as often as not were also singers, acrobats, musicians, and in later imperial China, actors.[10]

Whatever the nature of her performance, however, the potential cosmic significance of music and dance early on gave rise to concerns about the figure of the female performer. Confucian philosophers worried about the moral implications of musical entertainments, and in particular they recognized—and roundly condemned—the erotic undercurrent inherent in male enjoyment of female performance. They warned that at best such entertainments would distract men from their duties and at worst could lead to failure of the state. The Confucians' attitudes reveal the very early association of female dancers with sexual allure, and their opprobrium led to distinctly contradictory attitudes toward dance and music in the Chinese tradition.[11] On the one hand, music and dance were celebrated as critical elements in the ritual performances necessary to the proper functioning of the universe; on the other, music and dance as entertainment—especially when it involved women—was seen as threatening to morality. This ambivalent moral attitude toward performance (and especially female performers) was to last well into the twentieth century.[12] It helped to define the female performer as an inherently transgressive figure.

## THE MOBILE PERFORMER: GENDER AND CLASS

In imperial China the professional practice of music or dance, like that of other arts, was not regarded as an elite activity. (In China throughout the imperial period, elite status was mostly reserved to those who served in government.) Han dynasty texts generally refer to performers as *chang* (倡, an obvious cognate of the word *chang* 唱, to sing). Not much is known about how people became *chang* in early China, but in surviving sources the great majority appear as dependents or slaves of the imperial palace or in the houses of the nobility.[13] As dependents of the government or of private households, both male and female performers were regarded as *jian* 賤 or "dishonorable": that is, they were legally and socially of lower status than free, tax-paying commoners, who were designated as *liang* 良 or "respectable." Intermarriage of *jian* and *liang* individuals was prohibited, and punishments for crimes were harsher when the perpetrator was of *jian* status.

Although *jian* status affected males and females alike, the position of female performers was doubly complicated by the broader gender norms of the society. Among the most important of these norms was the ideal of separation of the sexes. Early Chinese ritual texts posited the separation of the sexes as central to a properly ordered society: men and women who were not spouses or blood relatives were not to interact with one another. Women were nominally confined to the "inner" realm of the household and ideally did not appear in public spaces, which were the domain of men. How strictly these norms were observed undoubtedly varied over time and space and by social position, but for most of imperial China, upper-class women were indeed customarily kept "cloistered," out of sight of outside males. Even farmers' wives were supposed to focus on "inner" work like cloth-making and sewing rather than outside labor, and the idea that "respectable" women did not casually interact with outside males came to be widely accepted at all levels of society.

The impact of these norms on dance is evident in surviving artifacts as well as textual sources, which depict dance as largely a single-sex activity. Men and women might dance singly or with others of their own sex, but men and women rarely danced as partners. Even Chinese folk dances—at least those known to contemporary scholars—tended to be single-sex affairs. These norms also meant that the female entertainer, whose profession was to be viewed by "outside" males, necessarily occupied different spaces than either ordinary "respectable" commoner women or the cloistered women of well-to-do families. Although female entertainers could and did become wives, concubines, and mothers, their accessibility to the gaze of strange males tainted them with the stain of moral laxity, reinforcing their already-low social status.

Ironically, however, in spite of attitudes about their social inferiority, their exposure to the gaze (and desires) of upper-class males sometimes enabled female entertainers to enjoy spectacular social mobility. Among the most famous examples in early times was Zhao Feiyan 趙飛燕, a palace slave who so captivated the emperor with her dancing that he eventually promoted her to be his empress, overriding those who objected to her lowly background.[14] Zhao was just one of several performers who ended up as consorts of emperors. To be sure, imperial favorites everywhere, male as well as female, used their ability to earn the favor of powerful men to improve their social positions. But in China, such opportunities were greater for women than men, and not only at court. This was because the institution of concubinage provided a woman who had earned favor through sexual allure with the possibility to become a socially legitimate consort of the master and mother of his children. Because female performance in China was at times closely connected to the institution of concubinage, the legal relationship between these two social practices requires further explanation.

For most of the imperial period, Chinese law stipulated that a man could have only one legal wife: she was married with special ritual ceremonies, and she was the legal mother of all of her husband's children, including those born to concubines. A concubine was a lesser consort, at least theoretically expected to serve the wife as well as the husband, and legally prohibited from ever becoming her master's wife. A concubine could also be sold off at any point. Also by law, a concubine was required to be a person of "respectable" (*liang*) status: she was not a slave or dependent. That meant that, at least theoretically, performers were not legally eligible to become concubines, for as we have seen they were by definition "dishonorable" (*jian*). The law, however, provided a convenient loophole that allowed a master to first free a dependent into "respectable" status and then take her as a concubine; moreover, as long as the father acknowledged them, a concubine's children were legitimate. A slave or dependent who became a favored concubine could thus not only enjoy a place in the household well beyond her own original status, she could see her descendants become members of the upper class. This was true of any slave, not just performers—but female entertainers, and perhaps especially dancers, were in an unusually good position to attract the master's attention. Still, the relationship between entertainers, dependency, and concubinage changed significantly over the centuries, in turn transforming the roles of female dancers in the society of imperial China.

### HISTORICAL SHIFTS: THE RISE OF DANCE AS ENTERTAINMENT

For several centuries after the fall of the Han dynasty in 220, "China" as a unified political entity did not exist: rather, the territory we understand today as China was ruled by many independent, often competing, states. The changing political situation had several important effects on dance and dancers. Shortly after the Han fell, invaders from the north and west, beyond the Chinese cultural sphere, took over much of the northern territory that had once belonged to the Han. They intermarried with indigenous Chinese, and new cultural values from outside China became amalgamated into "Chinese" culture. Probably the most obvious were those associated with Buddhism, which had been introduced into China during the Han but became popular and widespread during this "Period of Disunity" (220–581 CE). New Buddhist aesthetics strongly influenced indigenous art forms, and popular dance forms brought by Central Asian tribes who now ruled much of the north spread throughout the north and into southern regions as well. Chinese Buddhist art from this period shows scenes of paradise featuring buxom dancers in diaphanous, even transparent garb, and textual sources comment on new musical instruments and styles from India and Central Asia.[15]

The period after the fall of the Han dynasty also saw important changes in the social settings of entertainment. During the several centuries of political disunity that followed the Han, either some entertainers became free of dependency or perhaps erstwhile free people took up performance, for we see references to *chang* who were publicly available for hire. By no later than the sixth century, *chang* were typically associated with places where travelers spent the night, as well as with licentiousness.[16] In other words, in this period, if not before, *chang* performers became linked with the sale of entertainment that included sexual as well as other sorts of pleasures. Meanwhile, wealthy and powerful families continued to keep troupes of entertainers as dependents in their households, but now these entertainers were called *ji* (伎 or 妓), which in this context we might translate as "artiste," because the term originally referred to skill. The distinction between *chang* and *ji* was important, for *ji* in this period did not sell their services or perform publicly—they entertained only for the master and his guests. Still, *ji* entertainers were certainly sexually available to their masters, and female performance of both the *chang* and *ji* varieties continued to be associated with sexual allure, whether in public brothels or the mansions of the wealthy.

The *chang* of the Period of Disunity are largely anonymous figures, alluded to but rarely described. The presence of *ji* performers in the households of the rich and famous is more frequently noted, but even they appear mostly in anonymous groups, as symbols of the wealth, luxury, and titillation of their owners. One performer who does stand out as an individual in this period was the talented flautist Green Pearl (*Lüzhu* 綠珠). Her master, a man of great wealth, doted on her, and ultimately lost his life for refusing to turn her over to a powerful warlord who wanted her.[17] Their story was celebrated in later centuries as a moving love tragedy, and the name "Green Pearl" became synonymous with a beautiful and talented serving woman. Significantly, by the tenth century Green Pearl was imagined as a dancer, suggesting that dance was becoming an increasingly important element in the image of a beloved entertainer.[18]

The basic structures of entertainment that prevailed during the Period of Disunity continued well into the Tang dynasty (618–907), which brought lasting political integration back to China. The Tang founders were northerners whose families had long intermarried with the tribal aristocrats who had dominated northern China over the preceding centuries. Though they certainly viewed themselves as "Chinese," the Tang emperors nonetheless exhibited a number of traits inherited from their non-Chinese ancestors. In addition, they were highly cosmopolitan in their attitude to outside cultural influences. Foreign fashions were popular among court women, and foreign music and dance styles were enthusiastically embraced. Names of Tang dances that have come down to us include "Foreign Spinning" (*hu xuan* 胡旋) and "Foreign Prancing" (*hu teng* 胡騰), and Tang dance images show the continued influence of Buddhist iconography, also an originally foreign import.[19]

Even more important, the Tang dynasty served as a cultural model across

East Asia. By the seventh and eighth centuries, if not before, Chinese governing institutions, religion, and even the written Chinese language were being adopted and adapted by ruling elites in the Korean peninsula and the Japanese islands. Court music and dance were among the cultural forms transmitted, and in both Korea and Japan indigenized forms of "Tang music" (Korean: Dangak; Japanese: Tōgaku) continued to be performed into the twentieth century.[20]

In China, the middle and later Tang began to see important changes in the institutional structures of performance at court and the role of performers in society.[21] Already in the early Tang, a new court institution had been created to train performers and develop entertainments for the emperor and his ladies within the palace. Called the "Inner Court Entertainment Bureau" (*nei jiao fang* 內教坊), this institution was distinct from the "Court of Imperial Sacrifices," which was in charge of the ritual performances of the outer court that had existed since the Qin and Han periods. In other words, the Tang was the first Chinese dynasty in which the court had an office explicitly charged with providing performances for entertainment, rather than ritual.

Not much is known about how this early Entertainment Bureau functioned. However, in 714, shortly after he came to the throne, the emperor Xuanzong felt compelled not only to re-establish the Inner Court Entertainment Bureau, but also to establish two additional Entertainment Bureaus outside the imperial palace: a "Left Entertainment Bureau" for dancers and a "Right Entertainment Bureau" for singers.[22] Moreover, unlike the palace performers, who essentially became part of the imperial harem, the female denizens of the Right and Left Entertainment Bureaus were not cloistered as palace women. That is, although they performed for the emperor and his ministers, some of them were married to male performers within the bureaus.

Initially, the Entertainment Bureau performers do not seem to have been available for hire by those outside the court: their performances were reserved for the imperial family and their guests. Accordingly, for most of the early Tang, officials and others who wanted to enjoy song and dance entertainments generally followed the custom of earlier eras and kept *ji* entertainers as dependents (slaves) in their own households. But late in Xuanzong's reign, and especially after the cataclysmic An Lushan rebellion (755–763) nearly brought down the Tang dynasty, this state of affairs changed dramatically.

As the central Tang state became weaker, private commerce expanded, and trade cities began to develop. The Court Entertainment Bureau was reduced in size, and erstwhile Entertainment Bureau performers found a place for themselves in the growing pleasure quarters of Chang'an, Luoyang, and other urban areas, as well as at the courts of regionally powerful military commissioners. In other words, the boundary between entertainers at the court and those in the city was breaking down. We also begin to hear about *guan ji* (官妓), or "government entertainers," who, like the Entertainment Bureau performers, were essentially government dependents. But where the Entertainment Bureau performers were registered to the court or palace, "government entertainers" were registered to *local* government offices. Their job was to perform at the banquets held by and for local officials. Other social changes also affected the context of performance culture in the late Tang: the civil service examinations became increasingly prestigious, and romance—often with female entertainers—became an important literary theme.[23] Tang men began to write poetry to and about the entertainers they saw perform in the homes of their acquaintances. In a drunken poem composed for "the entertainers Li and Ma," the famous Tang poet Bai Juyi compared the "voluptuous movements of their dancing skirts" to fire and "their singing eyebrows, set in sadness" to smoke. In response to a request from another official's "little entertainer" (*xiao ji* 小妓), Bai wrote a poem describing how the girl's "fragrant sweat" had penetrated her "singing scarf," while her "dancing skirts" were decorated with wild pomegranate blossoms.[24] In short, by the late ninth century, musical entertainments (including dance) had begun to transition from being largely a privilege of high political status to being more widely available, both at home and in public settings such as government offices and urban teahouses.[25] Meanwhile, the connection between dance and sexual allure remained.

## BLURRING BOUNDARIES: ENTERTAINERS IN PUBLIC AND CONCUBINES WHO DANCED

These trends continued even after the Tang dynasty officially fell in 907, brought down by several decades of rebellion and violence. During the so-called Five Dynasties period (907–960) that followed the Tang, the economy continued to expand. In 960, the Song dynasty (960–1279) succeeded in reunifying most of historical China. Under the Song, the aristocratic ethos that had dominated the Tang dynasty was replaced by a new emphasis on meritocracy, epitomized in the expansion and opening of the civil service examination system. The elite class grew dramatically, and entertainments of all types became accessible to a wider public than ever before.

The early Song emperors re-established the Court Entertainment Bureau, and, as in the late Tang, the Entertainment Bureau performers were able to leave the palace and interact with the public. On some festival occasions, the court even sponsored public performances by Entertainment Bureau performers.[26] Bureau performers were far from the only professional performers out in public, however. The Song continued the Tang tradition of maintaining government entertainers at its local government offices, and commercial entertainments unconnected to government offices flourished as well. The capital city had numerous pleasure districts that encompassed dozens of theaters, the largest of which could hold "several thousand" onlookers.[27] In addition, over the course of the dynasty itinerant performing troupes (*san yue* 散樂) proliferated in the countryside. Now even villagers in the countryside could see professional performances.

The long tradition of keeping entertainers at home underwent changes as well. Significantly, whereas household entertainers in the Tang and earlier had been essentially chattel slaves, private slavery disappeared in the Song.[28] Instead, entertainers—like other servants—were typically brought into a household on term contracts, in a system closer to indentured servitude. Many if not most entertainers in the Song originated in "respectable" commoner families: sometimes a crisis in family circumstances, such as the death or disgrace of a father, meant that even girls of elite family background ended up as entertainers. When their contracts were up, however, they were once again free, and their status reverted from "dishonorable" to "respectable" persons. This greater fluidity of social status meant that the social gap that had once separated a "dishonorable" slave entertainer and a concubine of "respectable" commoner status largely disappeared. The two statuses blurred, and increasingly "concubines" were expected also to possess entertainment skills such as singing, dancing, or playing an instrument. Song anecdotal sources are full of amusing tales describing parties at which the host's entertainer concubines performed, often inspiring poetry by the guests. The official Guo Xiangzheng described such an outing on a lake[29]:

> Together the dancing courtesans sing a boating song
> As if it were the place where [the famed beauty] Xi Shi washed gauze.
> Luminous wrists flutter like ribbons of white lotus
> Graceful like a playful dragon, then suddenly recoiling.

Similarly, the scholar Li Zhi, in a slightly risqué move, penned a poem directly on the sash of his host's dancing serving maid[30]:

Twisting and cutting, the fragrant gauze drifts on the ground
The seductive red and lovely green trace elegant patterns
Before the flowers I wish to make layers and layers of knots,
Binding up the springtime aura and not letting it leave

By the end of the Song dynasty, then, the performing arts could be found in a variety of disparate locations throughout the society: at banquets of court and government offices, in commercial teahouses and brothels, and in elite homes. Equally important for our discussion here is that this general framework of performance culture also influenced Korea and Japan. In Korea, under the Goryo (Koryo) dynasty (918–1392), "government entertainers" on the Tang-Song model—and called, as they were in Chinese, *kwangi* (*guan ji*) 官妓—served the governing class. As in China, such women were often skilled and educated but were considered to be of "dishonorable" status (the same Chinese character, 賤, was used to describe them).[31] Dance in Japan in this period was likewise associated with dishonorable status and the sex trade.[32] Yet despite this stigma and in spite of the quite different social systems of China, Korea, and Japan, in all three countries elite men continued to pursue liaisons with female entertainers.[33]

## DANCE IN THE LATE IMPERIAL PERIOD

After the Song dynasty, performance in China increasingly took the form of the musical dramas that we today broadly call "Chinese opera." In Chinese opera, as in Western musical theater, the performer employed a combination of stylized movement (sometimes including acrobatics), acting, and singing, in the service of a narrative plot.

Forms and styles of Chinese opera developed significantly across the later imperial period, and many regions had their own particular styles. But in general, Chinese opera focused more on singing skill than on dance, with song used to express the emotions of the characters. Despite the emphasis on song, however, movement remained important. In some cases, as the repertoire became standardized, specific movements were choreographed to accompany each aria.[34] So, although there seem to have been no groups of performers who trained exclusively in dance, all performers were in some senses "dancing" whenever they were on stage.

Moreover, some operas incorporated extended dance sequences as part of the opera's story. For example, the opera *Washing Silk* (*Huan sha ji* 浣紗記) revolves around the heroine, Xi Shi, who is sent to seduce an enemy king to help undermine his rule. One scene highlights the dance that Xi Shi performs for the king in hopes of attracting his favor.[35] Because many operas took a full day or longer to perform in their entirety, often only certain famous scenes would be performed. The popularity of Xi Shi's dance scene suggests that it may well have been performed as a dance-only sequence.

Unfortunately, we know very little about what dance looked like in the Ming (1368–1644) and Qing (1644–1911) dynasties. We have only occasional descriptions, such as that by the late Ming scholar Zhang Dai (1597–1679), who described a performance of Xi Shi's dance:

> The song and dance of Xi Shi [had] five dancers dancing together, with long sleeves and flowing sashes, "coiling their bodies into rings, at once brushing the ground, then twisting elegantly," delicate as autumn herbs. The [dancers playing] female officials and inner attendants raised their fans to make a sky; more than twenty [dancers held] golden lotus candelabras, round silk fans, and palace lanterns, flashing and glittering. Loveliness upon loveliness: the audience was dumbstruck.[36]

Unfortunately, part of Zhang Dai's description here is a quotation from a classic text dating from 139 BCE, so it tells us little about what the dancers he saw actually looked like.[37] Similarly, illustrations of dance from the Ming and Qing tend to show a single performer or two, often female, with flowing sleeves, bending and twisting in a manner reminiscent of the earliest Chinese dance images.[38] How the actual content of specific dances changed over time is therefore unclear.

## PERFORMERS IN MING-QING SOCIETY

In most respects, the social position of performers in the later imperial period remained similar to what it had been during the Song. As in earlier eras, during the Ming and Qing dynasties some performers came from families of "dishonorable" hereditary musicians; others, originally of "good commoner" status, received training in music and dance after being sold into brothels. Still others were sold into wealthy households to be trained as performers in household drama troupes. But over the course of the Ming and Qing, the public presence of female performers came increasingly to be viewed as a

Fig. 1.1. Two dancers performing in front of a group of several men. From Tang Xianzu 湯顯祖 (1550–1616), *Mu dan ting huan hun ji: Yu ming tang yuan ben 8 juan* 牡丹亭還魂記: 玉茗堂原本 8 卷 (Shanghai: Sao ye shan fang, [18??]), j. xia.51b. Courtesy Hathi Trust).

threat to social order. This in turn led to the most significant change in stage practices of the late imperial period: the gradual replacement of female performers on the public stage by adolescent boys playing female roles.

The first sign of changing attitudes came in the 1430s, when the Ming government abolished the institution of government courtesans and prohibited officials from frequenting courtesan houses.[39] It seems to have been at about this time that adolescent boys began to play female roles in operas.[40] Even so, women continued to perform throughout the Ming dynasty. Moreover, perhaps ironically, male performers in female roles turned out to be as much associated with sexual allure and erotic excitement as female performers had been, and by the late Ming young male actors were often kept as performers and paramours by well-to-do literati males.[41]

The Qing dynasty was founded in 1644 by a foreign invading force from northeast of China. The new Manchu rulers quickly set out to reform what they saw as corrupt and decadent practices of the late Ming, including those associated with theater. Almost immediately, they barred women from performing at court, replacing them with eunuchs.[42] Over the course of the next hundred years, the Qing government issued a series of ever-stricter edicts designed to keep women off the stage and even out of public theater audiences. Although the edicts initially applied to public performances in the capital, in 1774 the government issued a ban on keeping any type of female performer in one's home, "in the capital and outside." An 1811 edict demanded that all female performers should be "expelled and returned to the registers [of commoners]."[43] Chinese theater thus became a largely male domain.

Still, is not clear that, outside of the capital, the Qing government ever totally succeeded in keeping women off the stage, and by the 1860s new forces were limiting their ability to do so. As foreign powers came to dominate cities such as Shanghai, all-female troupes of Chinese opera performers re-emerged and gained popularity.[44] The influx of Westerners also meant that, over the late nineteenth century, Chinese elites were absorbing new ideas about dance and theater from abroad. By 1900, even the daughter of a Manchu nobleman could be found studying with Isadora Duncan in Paris.[45]

## CONCLUSION: THE ENDURING ENTERTAINER

We have seen that, with the rise of Chinese opera after the thirteenth century, dance as a stand-alone art was somewhat eclipsed in China. Still, the tradition of salon performances continued throughout most of the late imperial era. In such performances, a lone dancer, perhaps accompanied by a musician or two, entertained a small audience in a salon setting. The sparse written records of such performances suggest that the dances performed often bore the same names as those created in the Tang and Song.[46] More broadly, throughout East Asia, the tradition of female entertainers serving wine, providing clever banter, and performing dance and music for the entertainment of men prevailed into the early twentieth century. Although the extent of Chinese influence and the precise process of transmission remain obscure, in all of these countries, performance was long associated with the sex trade; music and dance were important aspects of the courtesan's arts, and private

Fig. 1.2. Nine cloud dream (gu'unmong), approx. 1800–1900, Detail. Korea; Joseon
dynasty (1392–1910). Ink and colors on paper. Photo © Asian Art Museum of San
Francisco. Acquisition made possible in part by the Korean Art and Culture
Committee, 1997.21. This detail of a salon dancer accompanied by female musicians
aptly illustrates the circulation of ideas and images throughout East Asia. The screen
depicts scenes from the famous 17th century Korean novel *Nine Cloud Dream*, which
is itself set in Tang dynasty China and centers on the conflict between Buddhist and
Confucian values.

salon performances by women (or boys dressed as women) for small groups of men remained central to how "dance" was understood. As a result, across East Asia, the emergence of "dance" as a respectable and "modern" art form required a liberation from—or more accurately, an erasure of—the mobile entertainer and her problematic past.

## ADDITIONAL RESOURCES

Full resolution color versions of Figure 1.1 at https://doi.org/10.3998/mpub.11521701.cmp.1 and Figure 1.2 at https://doi.org/10.3998/mpub.11521701.cmp.2

Figure 1.3: Two dancers entertain three men enjoying tea and snacks. From Pu Songling 蒲松齡, *Liao zhai zhi yi xin ping* 聊齋誌異新評 (with commentaries by Wang Shizhen and Dan Minglun). Shanghai : Zhong xin shu ju, Minguo 7 [1918]. (Courtesy Hathi Trust). Available at https://doi.org/10.3998/mpub.11521701.cmp.33

Link 1.1: Han Dynasty dancer on Metropolitan Museum of Art Website. Available at https://doi.org/10.3998/mpub.11521701.cmp.34

## *Notes*

I would like to express my gratitude to the editors for their hard work and patience in shepherding this volume through publication. Research on this article was facilitated by a Faculty Research Grant from University of California, Davis.

1. I adopt the term "East Asia" here for convenience. The term originated in nineteenth-century imperialism and obscures many important differences among the countries and cultures of the region, but it also acknowledges the considerable and long-standing historical interactions among them.

2. *Mengzi* [Mencius] Li Lou 1, 7.27, trans. James Legge (London: Clarendon, 1985), Chinese Text Project, https://ctext.org

3. *Li ji* 禮記 [The Book of Ritual], trans. James Legge (1885), "Nei ze" [Inner Principles] 79, Chinese Text Project, http://ctext.org

4. See *Lun yu* [The Analects of Confucius], trans. James Legge (1861), Xian Jin, 26; Yan Yuan, 21, Chinese Text Project, http://ctext.org

5. Sun Jingchen 孙景琛, *Zhongguo wudao tong shi—xian Qin* 中国舞蹈通史——先秦 [History of Chinese dance, pre–Qin dynasty] (Shanghai: Shanghai yinyue chubanshe, 2010), 64–65.

6. Peng Song 彭松, *Zhongguo wudao tong shi—Qin-Han* 中国舞蹈通史——秦汉卷 (Shanghai: Shanghai yin yue chu ban she, 2010), 131–57.

7. Peng Song, *Qin-Han*, 112–13; Erica Brindley, *Music, Cosmology, and the Politics of Harmony in Early China*, SUNY Series in Chinese Philosophy and Culture (Albany: State University of New York Press, 2012).

8. Peng Song, *Qin-Han*, 110–11.

9. Susan Erickson, "'Twirling Their Long Sleeves, They Dance Again and Again': Jade Plaque Sleeve Dancers of the Western Han Dynasty," *Ars Orientalis* 24 (1994): 39–63.

10. Xing Fan, "Dance in Traditional Asian Theatre—China," in *Routledge Handbook of Asian Theatre*, ed. Siyuan Liu (London: Routledge, 2016), 101–5.

11. Joseph S. C. Lam, "The Presence and Absence of Female Musicians and Music in China," in *Women and Confucian Cultures in Premodern China, Korea, and Japan*, ed. Jahyun Kim Haboush and Dorothy Ko (Berkeley: University of California Press, 2003), *passim*.

12. Ritual performers, at least those at court, were men. Since performances involving female performers generally fell into the category of entertainment, I use the terms "female performers" and "female entertainers" interchangeably.

13. Peng Song, *Qin and Han*, 87–89; Anne Behnke Kinney, *Chinese Views of Childhood* (Honolulu: University of Hawai'i Press, 1995), 129.

14. Ban Gu 班固, *Han shu* 漢書 (Beijing: Zhonghua shu ju, 1962), 93.3730.

15. Peng Song 彭松, *Zhongguo wudao tong shi—Wei, Jin, Nan bei chao juan* 中国舞蹈通史——魏晉南北朝卷 (Shanghai: Shanghai yin yue chu ban she, 2010), 15 (illustration); 107 ff.

16. Beverly Bossler, "The Vocabularies of Pleasure: Entertainers in the Tang Dynasty," *Harvard Journal of Asiatic Studies* 72, no. 1 (2012), 75–76.

17. Liu Yiqing [Liu I-ch'ing] 劉義慶, Liu Jun [Liu Chün] 劉峻, trans. Richard B. Mather, *A New Account of Tales of the World* [Shi shuo xin yu], (Minneapolis: University of Minnesota Press, 1976), 489–90.

18. Liu Xu 劉昫, *Jiu Tang Shu* 舊唐書 (Beijing: Zhonghua shu ju, 1975), 29.1063.

19. Wang Kefen 王克芬, *Zhongguo wudao tong shi, Sui, Tang, Wu dai juan* 中国舞蹈通史,隋,唐,五代卷 (Shanghai: Shanghai yin yue chu ban she, 2010), 4–20.

20. Terauchi, Naoko, "Ancient and Early Medieval Performing Arts" in *The History of Japanese Theatre*, ed. Jonah Salz (Cambridge: Cambridge University Press, 2016), 4–9.

21. Bossler, "Vocabularies," 76–79.

22. Cui Lingqin 催令欽, *Jiao fang ji jian ding* 教坊記箋訂, ed. Ren Bantang 任半塘 (Shanghai: Zhonghua shu ju, 1962), 13–14.

23. Stephen Owen, *The End of the Chinese "Middle Ages": Essays in Mid-Tang Literary Culture* (Stanford, CA: Stanford University Press, 1996), 130–48.

24. Bai Juyi 白居易, "Zui hou ti Li Ma er ji" 醉後題李馬二姬 and "Lu shi yu xiao ji qi shi zuo shang liu zeng," 盧侍御小妓乞詩座上留贈 in *Bai shi Changqing ji* 白氏長慶集, SKQS, vol. 1080 (Taipei: Taiwan shang wu yin shu guan, 1983), 15.27–27b.

25. Bossler, "Vocabularies," 83–99.

26. Beverly Bossler, "Gender and Entertainment at the Song Court," in *Servants of the Dynasty*, ed. Anne Walthall (Berkeley: University of California Press, 2008), 265–66.

27. Wilt L. Idema and Stephen H. West, *Chinese Theater 1100–1450, A Source Book*, Münchener Ostasiatische Studien 27 (Wiesbaden: Franz Steiner Verlag GMBH, 1982), 14–16.

28. Takahashi Yoshirō 高橋芳郎, *Sō-Sei mibunhō no kenkyū* 宋清身分法の研究 (Hokkaido: Hokkaido University Publishing Group, 2001), 11–12, 157–67.

29. Guo Xiangzheng 郭祥正, *Qing shan ji* 青山集, SKQS, vol. 1116 (Taipei: Taiwan shang wu yin shu guan, 1983), 8.9b.

30. Li Zhi 李廌, *Jinan Ji* 濟南集, SKQS, vol. 1115 (Taipei: Taiwan shang wu yin shu guan, 1983), 4.39.

31. Lee Insuk, "Convention and Innovation: The Lives and Cultural Legacy of the Kisaeng in Colonial Korea (1910–1945)," *Seoul Journal of Korean Studies* 23, no. 1 (2010), 74–75. See also the important dissertation by Hyun Suk Park, "*The Government Courtesan: Status, Gender, and Performance in Late Choson Korea*" (University of Chicago, 2015).

32. Katharine Mezur, *Beautiful Boys/Outlaw Bodies: Devising Kabuki Female-Likeness* (New York: Palgrave Macmillan), 205, 52.

33. Terauchi, "Performing Arts," 13; Park, "Courtesan," 1–2.

34. Wang Kefen 王克芬, *Zhongguo wudao tong shi, Ming-Qing juan* 中国舞蹈通史明清卷 (Shanghai: Shanghai yin yue chu ban she, 2010), 31–36.

35. Wang Kefen, *Ming-Qing*, 9.

36. Zhang Dai 張岱, *Tao an meng yi* 陶庵夢憶, as cited in Wang Kefen, *Ming-Qing*, 9.

37. *Huainanzi* 淮南子, Xiu wu xun 修務訓, Chinese Text Project, https://ctext.org. The phrase in quotation marks comes directly from the *Huainanzi*'s description of dancers in the Han dynasty. The reference to "autumn herbs" is also an allusion to the *Huainanzi*, which includes the line, "bodies like autumn herbs in the breeze." Wang Kefen, in quoting Zhang Dai, does not seem to recognize that Zhang is using language from centuries earlier.

38. See, for example, Wang Kefen, *Ming-Qing*, 31, 40, and 41.

39. The abolition is known only from later references to it. See Zhang Tingyu 張廷玉 et al., *Ming shi* (Beijing: Zhonghua shu ju, 1991), 151.4185; Shen Defu 沈德符 (1578–1642), *Wanli ye huo bian* 萬曆野獲編, bu yi 3, "Jin ge ji" 禁歌妓, Wikisource. https://zh.wikisource.org/wiki/%E8%90%AC%E6%9B%86%E9%87%8E%E7%8D%B2%E7%B7%A8/%E8%A3%9C%E9%81%BA%E4%B8%89#%E7%A6%81%E6%AD%8C%E5%A6%93; Zhou Hui 周暉 (1546–?), *Jinling suo shi* 金陵瑣事, j. 2, Wikisource. https://zh.wikisource.org/wiki/%E9%87%91%E9%99%B5%E7%91%A3%E4%BA%8B

40. Wang Anqi 王安祈, *Xing bie, zheng zhi, yu Jing ju biao yan wen hua* 性別, 政治與京劇表演文化 (Taipei: Guo li Taiwan da xue chu ban zhong xin, 2011), 3. Grant Shen cites an anecdote indicating the existence of male actors playing female roles in the

reign of Yingzong (1457–1464), but the anecdote suggests this was unusual at the time. See Grant Guangren Shen, "Theatre Performance during the Ming Dynasty" (PhD diss., University of Hawaii at Manoa, 1994), 49.

41. See Sophie Volpp, "The Literary Circulation of Actors in Seventeenth-Century China," *Journal of Asian Studies* 61, no. 3 (August 2002): 949–84.

42. Ye Xiaoqing, "Imperial Institutions and Drama in the Qing Court," *European Journal of East Asian Studies* 2, no. 2 (2003), 332; Wang Anqi, *Xing bie*, 4.

43. Ding Shumei 丁淑梅, "Qing dai jin hui shen gui ju, qu ju, yu di fang yan ju" 清代禁毀神鬼劇、凶戲與地方演劇, *Si fang wen zhang* 四方文章, August 9, 2018. https://www.4way.tw/a/16312018.html. Authors give varying dates for the important edicts banning female players in the Qing: it seems likely that the edicts were issued more than once.

44. Wang Anqi, *Xing bie*, 30–31.

45. Ma, Nan, "Dancing Into Modernity: Kinesthesia, Narrative, and Revolutions in Modern China, 1900–1978" (PhD diss., University of Wisconsin at Madison, 2015), 29–87.

46. Wang Kefen, *Ming-Qing*, 156.

# CHAPTER 2

# Mei Lanfang and Modern Dance

## Transcultural Innovation in Peking Opera, 1910s–1920s

*Catherine Yeh*

The first years of the Republic of China (est. 1912), with their promise of a break with the imperial past and the coming of a "new culture," created a high-temperature environment auspicious for radically new ideas and practices in all domains, including the stage. Qi Rushan 齊如山 (1877–1962), the playwright and mentor of the then young male *dan* 旦 actor of female roles, Mei Lanfang 梅蘭芳 (1894–1961), believed in the power of aesthetic appeal to shape a new citizenry for modern China. Qi's aim was to elevate the aesthetics of Peking opera so that new social values, which he labeled "civilized" (*wenming* 文明), could be transmitted through beauty to the audience by touching their feelings and moving their hearts. Qi, like Cai Yuanpei 蔡元培 (1868–1940), the educator with similar ideas, drew on foreign travel experience—in this case exposure to the art of dance—to form the core of a new and modern aesthetic language of emotions.[1] Cai's insertion of the concept of dance (*wu* 舞) into aesthetic education in China as a representation of the modern, and Qi's insertion of dance itself into Mei Lanfang's Peking opera performance, mark a recrafting and realignment of all features of this art form, guided by a new outlook on the world. Dance, thus, came to Peking opera with a modernizing mission: through the new aesthetic form of dance, Peking opera would bring new social values to the hearts and minds of its audiences.

Scholars of Mei Lanfang have used the concept of "dancification" to describe the reforms he (in collaboration with Qi) enacted in Peking opera. However, these studies have tended to regard Mei's innovations as an instance of the internal development of Chinese theater, rather than considering the importance of dance in Mei's aesthetic experiments.[2] A number of questions have not been asked: Why dance? What was dance for Mei and his contemporaries? What motives drove Mei's particular configuration of Peking opera dance? What were the choreographic principles along which this dance was developed? Here, my goal is to answer these questions, while also considering how singling out dance as a modernizing force influenced the overall aesthetics of Peking opera. The transcultural encounter with modern dance had an unforeseen outcome for Chinese theater and performing arts. While embracing the concept of dance, this encounter stimulated Mei and Qi and motivated them to create their own brand of Chinese dance that was to represent both Chinese modernity and cultural identity.

In 1911, the literary historian Georgy Lukács played with the thought that "in literature what is truly social is form. . . . Form is social reality, it participates vivaciously in the life of the spirit. It therefore does not operate only as a factor acting upon life and molding experiences, but also as a factor which is in its turn molded by life."[3] I suggest that the same might hold true for the stage in early twentieth-century China. Thus, I will probe the "social" inscribed into the aesthetics of Mei Lanfang's revolutionized Peking opera dance.

THE CONCEPTUAL FRAME:
AESTHETICS OF DANCE IN SOCIAL REFORM

In the early twentieth century, modern dance became a highly visible part of a new aesthetics on the European stage. An integral part of what Schiller called "aesthetic education," dance was needed to supplement a purely utilitarian and rational education to form a truly civilized human being. As a result, dance came to be seen in Europe as an indispensable marker of a civilized nation.[4]

The most influential proponent of aesthetic education (*meiyu* 美育), including the importance of dance in China, was educational reformer Cai Yuanpei. In 1912, Cai was studying philosophy, psychology, and art history at Leipzig University in Germany, when the Chinese Republic's first president, Sun Yat-sen, called on him to become his minister of education.[5] Aesthetic education, Cai argued, had to be part of China's modern transformation, replacing outdated religious education. Cai also proposed that if art and beauty were in the everyday life of society, the human spirit and emotions would mobilize toward a higher realm of enlightenment. Aesthetic education is above the three principles guiding political education, namely, militarism, utilitarianism, and moral education. Cai's belief, that every "civilized" nation must emphasize dance on stage and in education, became the reality.

Cai believed that dance as the oldest art form acted as one of the most powerful stimuli of human emotions because it continued to include song, poetry, sculpture, painting, and music while these other forms became independent of each other. In the West, dance already had become part of the conversation about aesthetic education, and China had no time to lose.[6] Cai's first educational decree included making dance part of a new aesthetic education that was to form the counterpart to science education. The new Republican government introduced dance in all schools.[7]

The idea of the centrality of aestheticism in the cultural modernization of China fell on fertile ground. By the mid-1910s, Qi Rushan and Mei Lanfang began advocating for what was later called the aestheticization (*meishuhua* 美術化) of Peking opera and the transformation of stage acting by dance (*xiqu wudaohua* 戲曲舞蹈化).[8] They saw dance as characterized by "civilized" cultural refinement, as a globally recognized modern aesthetic, and they became convinced that it should become the artistic engine of Peking opera reform. The task was urgent. As Chinese society was changing and audiences developed new preferences, the relevance of Peking opera and with it the fate of the *dan* actor as a man playing women roles in this changing world was at stake. The "aestheticization" and modernization in the new operas they created had dance at its heart but extended beyond the libretti, the acting style, and the music to stage design, lighting, costume, and even theater architecture. When they started, however, aesthetic dance was still considered a complete novelty on the Peking opera stage.

In 1915, the first beginnings were made with a new set of movements for Mei's rendition of Chang'e, a beautiful young woman from the traditional fairy tale *Chang'e Escapes to the Moon* (*Chang'e ben yue* 嫦娥奔月). By 1917, when Mei Lanfang performed his famous *Goddess Spreads Flowers* (*Tiannü sanhua* 天女散花), with two full acts entirely dominated by the sash dance, the artistic focus had altogether shifted to dance. Taking their cue from Mei Lanfang's huge success with this piece, other *dan* actors joined in with new dance operas of their own.

## PEKING OPERA MODERNITY: TRANSCULTURAL SOURCES

This project began when I was studying the new operas performed by *dan* actors during the 1910s and the 1920s and noticed that historical photographs showed most of them in unfamiliar dance poses in unusual costumes. I had never seen these poses or costumes on stage in Beijing during the early 1960s when I grew up. They had disappeared.

These costumes and dance poses suggest a transcultural context specific

Fig. 2.1. Mei Lanfang in the role of Yang Guifei in the new opera *The Unofficial Biography of Taizhen* [*Yang Guifei*]" [Taizhen waizhuan 太真外傳], created circa 1925. Mei's flowing garments and bare arms are completely foreign to Peking opera. Source: Liang She-Ch'ien, ed., *Mei Lanfang: Foremost Actor of China* (Shanghai: Commercial Press, 1929), 6.

to the period in which they emerged. Mei Lanfang's 1917 new signature piece *The Goddess Spreads Flowers*, with its stunning sash dance and five-color light-streams tracking the dancer on a semidark stage, can be ascribed to his choreographer and libretto writer Qi Rushan. Qi's pivotal role became clear—he can be considered Peking opera's earliest modern-period playwright, historian, choreographer, director, and theorist.[9] According to Qi, the changes were inspired by his experiences in Europe between 1908 and 1913, during which he saw stage performances in France, Germany, Austria, Belgium, and England. Like other Chinese drama reformers of that time, Qi felt that Chinese opera was uncivilized, primitive, and in urgent need of a new aesthetic system. He set out to develop this new system through a series of new dance-driven operas.[10]

A reconstruction of Qi's European experience offers insight to this new development. During the time of Qi's visits in Paris, the American modern dance pioneer Loïe Fuller (1862–1928), at the time "the most famous dancer in the world," performed her sash dances.[11] She had first established her fame with *Serpentine Dance* (1891) and *Fire Dance* (1895), both considered emblematic of Art Nouveau in their attempt to get away from the ballet tradition and link artistic innovation in dance with technical invention in lighting and stage design. Mei's sash dance and the lighting effects in *The Goddess Spreads Flowers* clearly echo Fuller's performances,[12] which were not only well-known and appreciated across Europe[13] but had been seen in Hong Kong, Shanghai, and Tianjin via the Lumière Brothers' films.[14]

Mei Lanfang also interacted directly with dance innovators from the United States and Japan, who became an important source of inspiration in his dance-driven Peking opera experiments.[15] A contemporary review of Mei's *Goddess* identified these sources of inspiration, pronouncing it a combination of ancient Chinese ritual, Japanese quick *odori* dance, and Western dance.[16]

For Qi Rushan and Mei Lanfang, the attraction of the idea of dance as performed in Europe, the United States, and Japan was that it represented a new language of the "civilized" vitality of modernity that could be incorporated into Peking opera.[17] For them, the martial art forms that already existed in Peking opera were not dance, because these movements represented the old social and aesthetic order that they were trying to overcome. In contrast to many other Chinese drama reformers of the time, Qi and Mei's experimentation with dance-driven dramas realized new social values within the genre of Peking opera. This set them apart from the completely Western-oriented young radicals from the May Fourth new culture movement who wanted to do away with Peking opera altogether.

CREATIVE ENERGIES RELEASED:
DISCOVERING THE WORLD AT HOME

While *Goddess* was a huge success that also earned Mei Lanfang a Japan tour,[18] it triggered questions characteristic of transcultural interactions, such as whether *Goddess* with its dance, music, light, and stage was truly Chinese theater.[19] Both critics and audiences sensed the "foreignness" of the piece. This was not due to its being a Buddhist story from the *Vimalakīrti nirdeśa*, because this sutra was widely known, there was a widespread interest in Buddhism at the time, and the theme of the goddess spreading flowers from this *sutra* was often used in Chinese painting. What made the piece look "foreign" was the unacknowledged aesthetic inspiration, particularly that of Fuller.

There were rather sharp exchanges in the press, with some critics defending the piece as representing "world dance" (*shijie de wu* 世界的舞).[20] The central issue was the cultural identity of the dance form. This was crucial, since it implied that modernization threatened one's own cultural identity. Faced with this dilemma, Qi Rushan began to formulate the idea that Chinese theater had included dance in ancient times but that it had long since vanished from the stage. [21] The task of modernizing Chinese drama, to have it represent China as a "civilized" nation, was to revive this long-lost Chinese tradition.

Thus, while transcultural interaction remained a vital factor in this revitalization of the genre,[22] the new Peking opera now set out to become the new national Chinese theater, which would be both truly international and truly Chinese and be able to conquer the world stage with the recast best of Chinese culture. To successfully link the new forms with old traditions meant to reinvent forgotten dance forms based on surviving heritage records and artistic imagination. Much like the US and European modern dance movements with their borrowings from classical, oriental, and "primitive" dance forms, Qi Rushan and Mei Lanfang returned to China's "classical" Han and Wei (second to sixth centuries) and high Tang (eighth and ninth centuries) periods to seek inspiration.[23] The new works that resulted were later classified as "dance drama" (*wudaoju* 舞蹈劇) or "song-and-dance drama in historical costumes" (*guzhuang gewuju* 古裝歌舞劇).[24]

The effort to transform the foreign cultural resource of modern dance into something authentically "Chinese" released vast creative energies. After their beginnings with *Goddess*, Qi and Mei inserted newly created traditional elements, while continuing to put "equal emphasis on singing and dancing" (*ge wu bing zhong* 歌舞并重) and going by the rule "no sound that is not song, no movement that is not dance" (*wu sheng bu wu, wu dong bu wu* 无声不歌,无动不舞) in their new works.[25] As a result, their new dance dramas no longer had a foreign look. While the new works were as unfamiliar to audiences as the presence of dance in Peking opera, they put an end to the discussion about their authentic Chineseness. One way Qi and Mei achieved this result was by introducing visibly "Chinese" objects as markers—most of them associated with literati culture—into the works: the revised *Chang'e Escapes to the Moon* features sleeves, a fan, and a flower sickle (*hualian* 花鐮); *Ma Gu Offers Birthday Gifts* (*Ma Gu xian shou* 麻姑獻壽) uses the tray (*pan* 盤), the flower basket (*hualan* 花籃), and the flower sickle; in *Lady Shangyuan* (*Shangyuan furen* 上元夫人), the cloud-broom (*yunzhou* 雲帚); in *The Drunken Beauty Guifei* (Guifei zuijiu 貴妃醉酒), the wine-cup; in *Daiyu Buries the Fallen Blossoms* (*Daiyu zang hua* 黛玉葬花), the flower-sickle (*huachu* 花鋤); in *The Goddess of the*

*River Luo* (*Luo shen* 洛神), the flowers; in *Hongxian Steals the Seal of Power* (Hongxian dao he 紅綾盜盒), the whisk (*fuchen* 拂塵); in *Hegemon King Bids Farewell to His Concubine* (*Bawang bieji* 霸王別姬), the sword; in *Beauty in the Fisherman's Net* (*Lian jin feng* 廉錦楓), the double sword; in *The Patriotic Beauty* (*Xi Shi* 西施), the sword; and in *The Life of Yang Guifei* (*Taizhen wai zhuan* 太真外傳), the feather fan and the cloud-broom. These dance-driven works make up the majority of Mei Lanfang's new operas of the 1910s and '20s.

With their now distinctly Chinese cultural markers, these dance pieces come into Peking opera with a double agenda: their dances link up with modern world theater aesthetics as reflecting the aspirations of the new Republic to develop a new social order in a modernized state, and they enhance the appeal of the new form with markers signifying authentic Chineseness while maintaining the dialogue with "world dance."

## THE SWORD DANCE: A TRANSCULTURAL PRODUCT RECAST INTO CHINESE LITERATI CULTURE

An examination of the use of the sword in these works helps to deepen our understanding of the particular dynamics of Qi's and Mei's creative process. If "what is truly social is form," such a new form needs to interact with the "social" in local culture. Qi and Mei used many different sources to recreate their brand of Chinese dance drama included written and pictorial records of music and dance in historical documents and literature, dance manuals, fresco paintings, stone carvings, woodblock illustrations, poetry, and Buddhist temple sculptures. Most of these in fact reflected earlier stages of transcultural interaction, primarily between China and Central Asia.[26]

For men of letters such as Qi Rushan, true Chineseness was to be found only in traditional literati culture. In other words, the various dance elements had to satisfy the criterion of being "refined" (*ya* 雅), which Qi and Mei recast in their modernizing agenda as beauty (*mei* 美) and aestheticism. Mei's new sword dance scene in *Hegemon King Bids Farewell to His Concubine* (hereafter *Farewell*), first presented in 1921, is a case in point. With its own style and narrative language based on different cultural traditions, this work illustrates the dynamics of transcultural exchanges in the localization of dance form.

Highly developed martial dance has appeared in Chinese records since the early Western Zhou period, when it formed an important part of state ritual (eleventh century BCE).[27] Between the fifth century BCE and the second century CE, sword dance as a form of entertainment became independent of the martial dance of state ritual to become a popular dance form during the Tang dynasty (618–907).[28] The sword dance of this era appears in a poem composed by Du Fu in 767 about a female dance virtuoso Gong Sun:

> Once there was a fair lady by the name of Gongsun,
> She used to cause a great sensation all over when she danced with
>     swords.
> Crowds would gather and build up, surprised and astonished they would
>     be,
> Even heaven and earth would come together for her performance in
>     accord.
> Her dancing shone like the flare when Hou Yi shot down the nine suns,
> And her moves were as swift as the heavenly gods on the fly in dragon
>     chariots,
> She used to commence a dance with the power of thunderbolts topping
>     all fury,
> And end like still rivers and seas where a clear reflection of the moon
>     would come to port.[29]

This is an example of a sword-dance performance exhibiting virtuosity in swordsmanship as an aesthetic dance form for public entertainment independent from martial arts performed at banquets and in state ritual.[30] From surviving records, we know that Chinese culture had absorbed many dance forms from Central Asia since the Han dynasty and especially during the "foreign" Northern Qi, Northern Wei, and Zhou (200–600 CE) dynasties and throughout the Tang (see Bossler, this volume). Historical sources link the popular Tang sword dance with other Central Asian dances.[31] If swords were included, ritual martial dance was a collective dance performed by many dancers, even hundreds. Contemporary records characterize its style as deliberate and slow in motion. We may assume that the Central Asian dances helped transform the previously existing Chinese ritual sword dance into a single-dancer performance without either ritual functions or sword fighting. Since the Tang, sword dances seem to have been performed mainly by female professionals.[32]

The sources of Mei Lanfang's sword dance for *Farewell* came in part from this cultural tradition.[33] To create it, he took lessons from a martial-arts teacher and incorporated sword-dance movements from two other Peking opera pieces.[34] The resulting dance style, however, seems rather different from the dynamic, fast-paced, and high-spirited dance of the Tang period.

Fig. 2.2. Mei Lanfang in *Hegemon King Bids Farewell to His Concubine* (*Bawang bieji* 霸王別姬), created circa 1922. Photo courtesy Kyushu University library.

The reason might be loss of knowledge—the sword dance disappeared as a form of dance after the Tang, resurfacing on stage only over 400 years later.[35]

The style of Mei's actual sword dances with their strong psychological implications, however, suggests other sources as well. As Mei commented later, Qi often offered a perspective on the sword dance that differed from what Mei had learned.[36] It appears that Qi Rushan incorporated yet another tradition, that of the literati sword dance, which also dates to the Tang. Literati were expected to carry a sword, and as studies on swordsmanship have pointed out, the sword acted as a soul mate. Dancing with the sword in this context was a way to express deeply felt emotions.[37] This differed from the popular sword dance, in which the sword functioned only as a dance prop and not an expression of individual sentiments.[38] As literati culture developed during the Song period, the literati sword dance expressed patriotic feeling and cultural identity.[39] Associated with Daoism and Buddhism, it signaled freedom from fear of death.[40] It also took on the significance of uprightness, valor, and patriotism. These literati refinements came to be reflected in Mei's civilized, personalized, and emotional sword dance. Elegant, psychological, and expressive of the female character's emotions and passions, this new dance was performed by a single *dan* actor. Mei's new Peking opera sword dance combined the literati sword dance of psychological performance with the motion and speed of the Central Asian sword dance.

American modern dancer Ted Shawn wrote the following after seeing Mei perform the sword dance in *Farewell* in 1925:

In this dance the first movement was done with an enormous circular cape and consisted largely of postures with the cape and soft graceful movements of the hands. After the cape was removed two swords came out of the sheath, trick swords in that they appeared to be one sword at first glance, but at a certain movement in the dance suddenly became two. As the dance grew livelier the footwork became evident for the first time. The actual steps were simple and limited in variety, not exceeding a few rapid turns executed with both feet on the ground and once or twice a movement that was similar to an inhibited *Jeté tour*. Toward the end of the dance the use of the two swords became very intricate and as the swords were polished silver he achieved an effect of a network of flashing light surrounding his entire body. The power and charm, however, seem to reside mainly in his own personality, for later, when we saw other young actors attempt the same style, we realized even more the vitalizing power which Mei Lan-Fang possesses.[41]

In 1955, a motion picture was made of *Farewell* featuring Mei Lanfang, then aged sixty-one. The sword dance piece starts with Mei's character Lady Yu trying with her dance and lyrics to comfort the King, who had been lured into an ambush and is now surrounded by enemy troops. The steps are measured, and each dance sequence ends with an aesthetically arresting pose. After this introductory dance with its singing, Mei continued the core section without singing, just dancing accompanied by music. The dance steps become increasingly structured by musical phrasing with poses conveying determination. The speed quickens, the double swords flash, and movements suggest an attack mode and express a spirit of defiance, courage, and moral resolve. Finally, the King cries out with a sense of rejuvenation and a will to fight for victory. The meaning is more tragic, however. Lady Yu turns away from the King to wipe a tear; she foresees that all is lost and is no longer able to suppress her grief. She expressed her hope that the King has the will to escape with his men without her. He, she, and the audience all know her fate: she must now take her own life.[42]

In the dance sequence at the heart of this scene, Mei's sword represents the fighting spirit, the moral conviction, and the loving heart of Lady Yu, who is preparing for self-sacrifice. She expresses these emotions entirely through dancing with the sword. The irony of her sword dance surely was not lost on the audience. Instead of the martial man or the man of letters expressing his fighting will, spirit of self-sacrifice, and devotion to the moral cause of his country and his lord, the dancing character who expresses all these lofty sentiments, together with love and inner conflicts, is a woman. The corporeal politics here is truly intriguing. Before the rise of the *dan* in Mei's generation, the traditional focus of Peking opera performance was the senior male (*laosheng* 老生) character. Through innovations such as Mei's, however, female *personae* (impersonated by male *dan* actors) took the lead. This reversal of roles might explain the popularity of the piece. During the turbulent early years of the Republican period with different warlords ruthlessly vying for power, it was much easier for the audience to identify with the figure of Lady Yu; she is without political power, but she alone stays true to normative moral values.

## CONCLUSIONS

The core of this sequence, with its dance accompanied by music but not singing, marks the realization of modern aesthetic understanding in Peking opera: the form of dance takes over the function of lyrics. Dance becomes the vehicle to evoke the hidden psychological and emotional state of the character. Thus, as Zou Yuanjiang has suggested, Mei and Qi pushed Chinese theater performance from a nonidentification with the characters (abstract aesthetics) toward twentieth-century realism.[43] The term "realism" might not be appropriate, however. What Qi and Mei envisioned as modern and civilized was very much a vision of art that reflected life, and they did so with what might better be called psychological acting. May Fourth youth regarded traditional theater as a lifeless form without value for the demands of new society. Thus dances were choreographed with dance movements and gestures that responded to the criticism of the May Fourth youth.[44]

This new dance and music combination also changed how audiences behaved in the theater. Where once there had been loud music and audience chatter, audiences of the dance-driven opera audiences became quiet.[45] Full of emotion and character interpretation, the new dance aesthetics directly engaged the audience and fostered identification with the main protagonist.

Dance entered Peking opera as an aesthetic form that embodied the spirit of what reformers like Qi, Cai, and Mei all envisioned as a civilized modernity. Through multilayered transcultural interaction, dance became the emblem of cultural renewal on China's stage, and its artistic form signaled that Peking opera was joining the world.

The resulting form, however, also had to satisfy longings for cultural authenticity. This longing for the cultural authenticity of a transculturally shared concept and practice presented the main challenge to Peking opera reform, and it released the creative energies to recreate this shared form from rediscovered or reimagined local material. In the process, an imagined Chinese past of modern dance was created. This is apparent in Qi and Mei's new sword dances. In these, they reimagined a Chinese sword dance that would be visibly authentic and at the same time fit the new agenda of presenting on stage characters who had refined and civilized emotions, which they expressed through psychological acting. They drew on both living popular traditions preserved in martial arts and on the visual and textual heritage.

The creative energy used to evoke Chinese authenticity in this mostly silent international exchange produced dance pieces that displayed the very spirit that was characteristic of the transcultural models. In this sense, Peking Opera modernity shares the trajectory of modern dance in the US and Europe, tapping into the creative offerings of foreign cultures and the past, but taking its own path by introducing emblems of classical Chinese authenticity.

ADDITIONAL RESOURCES

Full resolution versions of Figure 2.1 at https://doi.org/10.3998/
mpub.11521701.cmp.3 and Figure 2.2 at https://doi.org/10.3998/
mpub.11521701.cmp.4

Figure 2.3: Mei Lanfang demonstrates the dance steps in *Hegemon King Bids
Farewell to His Concubine*. Source: Bai mei tu 百美圖, no. 1 (1938), 7. Available
at https://doi.org/10.3998/mpub.11521701.cmp.35

Video Clip 2.1: Final dance scene in the film *Hegemon King Bids Farewell
to His Concubine* performed by Mei Lanfang. Source: Film, Beijing film
studio 北京電影製片廠, 1956. Video accessible at https://doi.org/10.3998/
mpub.11521701.cmp.36

## Notes

1. Qi Rushan 齊如山, "Shuo xi" 說戲 [On drama, 1913], in Qi Rushan, Qi Rushan
wenji 齊如山文集, ed. Liang Yan 梁燕 (Shijiazhuang: Hebei jiaoyu chubanshe and
Beijing: Kaiming hubanshe, 2010), vol. 1, 3–15.

2. Chen Weizhao 陳維昭, "'Mei Qi hebi' yu Zhongguo xiqu de jiyihua qingxiang"
'梅齊合璧'與中國戲劇的技藝化傾向 [Mei Lanfang and Qi Rushan's collaboration
and the move toward technical skills and artistry in Chinese theater], *Shantou daxue
xuebao* 汕頭大學學報 17, no. 3 (2001): 19–27; Wang Anqi 王安祈, "Jingju Meipai yishu
zhong Mei Lanfang zhuti yishi zhi tixian" 京劇梅派藝術中梅蘭芳主體意識之體現
[The reflection of Mei Lanfang's subjective consciousness within Peking opera Mei
style], in *Ming Qing wenxue yu sixiang zhong zhuti yishi yu shehui* 明清文學與思想中
主體意識與社會 [Society and subjectivity in Ming and Qing thought and literature],
ed. Wang Ailing 王愛玲 (Taipei: Zhongyang yanjiuyuan wenzhesuo, 2004), 705–62;
Liang Yan 梁燕, *Qi Rushan juxue yanjiu* 齊如山劇學研究 [A study on Qi Rushan's theater research] (Bejing: Xueyuan chubanshe, 2008), 33–42.

3. György Lukács, *Il drama moderno*, trans. Luisa Coeta (Milan: Sugar Co., 1967),
8; qtd. in Franco Moretti, *Signs Taken for Wonders: Essays in the Sociology of Literary
Forms* (London: Verso, 1983), 10.

4. Friedrich Schiller, "Über die ästhetische Erziehung des Menschen in einer Reyhe
von Briefen," *Die Horen*, 1, 2, and 6 (Stück, 1895).

5. Although Cai resigned and returned to Europe when Yuan Shikai took over the
presidency in the same year, he remained an influential public voice as president of
Peking University beginning in 1916.

6. Cai Yuanpei, "Yi meiyu dai zongjiao shuo" 以美育代宗教說 [On aesthetic education replacing religion] in *Cai Yuanpei meiyu lunji*, ed. Gao Pingshu 高平叔, (1917), 90.

7. Dance entered the Chinese social and political reform vocabulary as early as in the 1880s. Influenced by the missionary girls schools and modeled on the reformed Japanese educational system, dance was introduced through physical education, one of the educational reforms in newly established modern schools at the time. See Zhou Xueting 周雪婷, *Minguo shiqi xuexiao jiaoy yanjiu* 民國時期學校舞蹈教育研究 [A study on dance education in schools during the Republican period] (Shanghai shifan daxue, unpublished MA thesis, 2013), 6–7.

8. Mei Lanfang, *Wutai shenghuo sishinian* 舞台生活四十年 [Forty years on stage] (Beijing: Zhongguo xiju chubanshe, 1987), 513–14; Qi Rushan, *Guoju gailun* 國劇概論 [Introduction to Chinese theater, 1953], in Qi Rushan, *Qi Rushan quanji*, vol. 3, 1335.

9. Liang Yan 梁燕, "Qi Rushan xijuxue yanjiu de guoji shiye" 齊如山戲劇學研究的國際視野 [The international perspective of Qi Rushan's theater study], *Yishu Xuejie* 藝術學屆 2 (2010): 264–76.

10. Qi Rushan, *Qi Rushan huiyilu* 齊如山回憶錄 [Qi Rushan memoirs] (Beijing: Zhongguo xiju chubanshe, 1998), 72–73, 81–82, 101.

11. Richard Nelson Current and Marcia Ewing Current, *Loie Fuller: Goddess of Light* (Lebanon NH: Northeastern University Press, 1997), 1.

12. At the center of this new opera were new dance arrangements that were integrated with singing. Other new elements included the insertion of Kunqu musical elements into the *beihuang* musical rhythms characteristic of Peking opera; a new type of costume for the goddess designed to suggest otherworldliness; a new makeup including hairdo that was based on historical murals, sculptures, and paintings; masks for the Buddha's disciples; a cloud-patterned stage backdrop suggesting a celestial environment; and a "cloud stage" 雲台 made up of sixteen large tables at the back of the stage with cloud-shaped coverings on which the "spreading flowers" dance was performed. Lighting was another breakthrough: five-color light-streams tracked the dancer's moves across the semidark stage, evoking, as one member of the audience recalled later, a dream with the most exquisite dancing beauty gliding by. The silk used for the colored sash was light Indian silk gauze, and the petals were changed from silk to paper because they flowed better. See Mei Lanfang, *Wutai shenghuo sishinian*, 412–13, 515–19, 526–27, 530.

13. Jacques Rancière, *Aisthesis: Scenes from the Aesthetic Regime of Art*, trans. Zakir Paul (London: Verso, 2013), 93–109.

14. Loïe Fuller's "Serpentine Dance" film was first shown in Shanghai (Tian Hua Tea Garden), Peking, Tianjin, and Hong Kong to foreign and Chinese audiences in 1898. See Law Kar, Frank Brenn, and Sam Ho, *Hong Kong Cinema: A Cross-Cultural View* (Lanham, MD: Scarecrow Press, 2004), 12–18.

15. Catherine Yeh, "Mei Lanfang, the Denishawn Dancers, and World Theater," in *A New Literary History of Modern China*, ed. David Wang (Cambridge, MA: Harvard University Press, 2017), 311–19; Ted Shawn, *Gods Who Dance* (New York: E. P. Dutton & Co. 1929), 50.

16. Chunliu jiuzhu 春柳舊主 (Zhang, Taohen 張濤痕), "Tiannü sanhua" 天女散花

[The goddess spreads flowers], in *Mei Lanfang* 梅蘭芳 [Mei Lanfang], ed. Mei she 梅
社 (Shanghai: private printing, 1918), 75–76. It is likely that the author referred to the
type of dance recorded in an 1894 film by William K. L. Dickson, https://en.wikipedia.
org/wiki/File:Japanese_Traditional_Dance.oggtheora.ogv, accessed April 3, 2017. The
"Mikado Dance" here, performed by the Sarashe sisters, was part of the hugely popular Gilbert and Sullivan comic opera *The Mikado*.

17. Although not mentioned here, the Japanese influence was equally important.
See Catherine Yeh, "Experimenting with Dance Drama: Peking Opera Modernity, Kabuki Theater Reform and the Denishawn's Tour of the Far East," *Journal of Global Theatre History* 1, no. 2 (2016): 28–37.

18. Catherine Yeh, "Politics, Art and Eroticism: The Female Impersonator as the National Cultural Symbol of Republican China," in *Performing the "Nation": Gender Politics in Literature, Theatre and the Visual Arts of China and Japan, 1880–1940*, eds. Doris
Croissant, Catherine Yeh, and Joshua S. Mostow (Leiden: Brill, 2008), 215–32.

19. Chunliu jiuzhu (Zhang, Taohen), "Tiannü sanhua," 76.

20. Liaozi 膠子 (Zhang Liaozi 張膠子, Qinggong 卿公, Houzai 厚載, "Mou mingshi
lai jian lun 'Tiannüsanhua'" 某名士來柬論 '天女散花' [A general man of letters sent
his comments on *The Goddess Spreads Flowers* (to our newspaper)], *Gongyanbao* 公言
報 (Dec. 22, 1917): 7.

21. Qi Rushan, *Qi Rushan huiyi lu*, 114; Qi Rushan, *Guowu mantan* 國舞漫談 [On national dance], in Qi Rushan, *Qi Rushan quanji* 齊如山全集 [The complete works of Qi
Rushan] (Taipei: Qi Rushan yizhu bianying weiyuanhui, 1977), vol. 5, 2964.

22. Ouyang Zhesheng 歐陽哲生, *Fu Sinian yisheng zhiye yanjiu* 傅斯年一生志業研
究 [A study of Fu Sinian's life ambition] (Taipei: Xiuwei zixun keji gufen youxian gong-
si, 2014), 199–200.

23. Chen Weizhao, "Qi Rushan de xiju shijian yu Han,Wei suwu" 齊如山的戲曲實踐
與漢魏俗舞 [Qi Rushan's opera practice and folk dance of the Han and Wei dynasties],
*Zhejiang daxue xuebao* 浙江大學學報 42, no. 3 (2012): 150.

24. Qi Rushan, *Qi Rushan huiyilu*, 113.

25. This theory had already dominated the aesthetics of Chinese theater outlined in
Qi Rushan, *Zhongguoju zhi zuzhi* 中國劇之組織 [The constituents of Chinese theater,
1928], but the actual formula first occurs in his 1962 *Guoju de yuanze* 國劇的原則 [The
principles of Chinese theater], in Qi Rushan, *Qi Rushan quanji*, vol. 3, 1466.

26. Qi Rushan, *Guowu mantan*, vol. 5, 2961; Ted Shawn, *Gods Who Dance* (New York:
E. P. Dutton & Co. 1929), 50.

27. Wang Kefen 王克芬, *Wan wu yiyi: Zhongguo wudao tushi* 萬舞翼翼: 中國舞蹈圖
史 [A pictorial history of Chinese dance] (Beijing: Beijing Zhonghua shuju, 2012), 35–
36.

28. Yang Ming 楊名, "Tangdai jianwu ji jianwu shi kao lun" 唐代劍舞及劍舞詩考論
[On sword dance and poetry about sword dance in the Tang period], *Yinyue yu biaoyan* 音樂與表演 2 (2016): 127–31.

29. Betty Tseng, translation of Du Fu's poem "Guan Gongsun daniang dizi wu ji-

anqi xing" 觀公孫大娘弟子舞劍器行, in *English Translation of Chinese Poetry*, https://28utscprojects.wordpress.com/2011/01/18/064/, accessed April 3, 2017.

30. Tian Muhe 田沐禾 and Zhu Jiaying 朱家英, "Xian Tang jianwu yuanliu kaolun" 先唐劍舞源流考論 [Research on sword dance before the Tang dynasty], *Tiyu janjiu* 体育研究 37, no. 1 (2016): 81.

31. Yang Ming, "Tangdai jianwu ji jianwu shi kao lun," 128.

32. "Liu Xuegang 劉學剛, "Zhongguo gudai jianwu biaoyan fengge de fazhan liubian" 中國古代劍舞表演風格的發展流變 [The development and transformation of ancient Chinese sword dance performance style], *Yihai* 藝海 6 (2016): 97.

33. Liu Xuegang, "Zhongguo jianwu de fazhan liubian" 中國劍舞的發展流變 [On the development and transformation of Chinese sword dance], *Yihai* 藝海 10 (2013): 125.

34. Mei Lanfang, *Wutai shenghuo sishinian*, 670.

35. Liu Xuegang, "San lun jianshu yu jianwu de guanlianxing" 三論劍術與劍舞的關聯性 [Three points on the relatedness between fencing and sword dance], *Yishu yanjiu* 藝術研究 4 (2015): 60; Yang Ming, "Tangdai jianwu ji jianwu shi kao lun," 128.

36. Mei Lanfang, *Wutai shenghuo sishinian*, 670.

37. Yan Yufeng 閆玉鋒, "Tangdai jianwu wenhua tanjiu" 唐代劍舞文化探究 [Study on Tang dynasty sword dance culture], *Mang Zhong* 芒种 17 (2012): 197.

38. Cui Ping 崔兵, "Lun Zhongguo chuantong jianshu de wenhua jiazhi" 論中國傳統劍術的文化價值 [On the cultural value of China's traditional sword art], *Hebei tiyu xueyuan xuebao* 河北體育學院學報 20, no. 3 (2006): 81.

39. Liu Xuegang, "Zhongguo gudai jianwu biaoyan fengge de fazhan liubian," 97.

40. Luo Liqun 羅立群, "Gudai xiaoshuo dui 'jianshu' de biaoxian jiqi yiyun" 古代小說對'劍術'的表現以及意蘊 [Depiction and significance of sword art in premodern Chinese fiction], *Nankai xuebao* 南開學報 6 (2006): 117–18.

41. Ted Shawn, *Gods Who Dance*, 54.

42. Mei Lanfang performing the sword dance in the film *Hegemon King Bids Farewell to His Concubine* (Beijing: Beijing Dianying zhibianchang, 1955). See https://www.youtube.com/watch?v=63iYpn2v2HM, time: 39:00–42:12.

43. Zou Yuanjiang 鄒元江, "Mei Lanfang de 'biaoqing' yu 'Jingju jingshen'" 梅蘭芳的'表情'與'京劇精神' [On Mei Lanfang's "expressive acting" and the "spirit of Peking opera"], *Xiju yanjiu* 戲劇研究 2, no. 7 (2008): 145–68.

44. See Ted Shawn's interview with Mei Lanfang, in Ted Shawn, *Gods Who Dance*, 50.

45. Chunliu jiuzhu (Zhang, Taohen), "Tiannü sanhua," 76.

# CHAPTER 3

# The Conflicted Monk

## Choreographic Adaptations of *Si fan* (Longing for the Mundane) in Japan's and China's New Dance Movements

*Nan Ma*

> In days long ago, there was a monk named Mulian. On one end [of his carrying pole] he balanced his mother, on the other the sutras. If he carried the pole so that the sutras were in front, then he turned his back on his mother; if he carried it so that his mother was in front, then he turned his back on the sutras. [And so] he had no choice but to carry the pole across both shoulders, parting the trees on both sides. On his left shoulder it caused his skin to rip open and on the right it chafed so that blood streamed down his body....
>
> —*Xiao nigu* 小尼姑 (The little nun), 1571 AD[1]

Quoted above are the opening lines of *The little nun*, an early predecessor of the Kun Opera (or *Kunqu* 昆曲) work *Si fan* 思凡 (Longing for the mundane) of late sixteenth-century Ming China.[2] The quotation is an allusion to the allegory of Mulian 目连, a virtuous monk who sacrifices his flesh and blood to balance two conflicting faiths—Confucianism (or familial obligations, represented by the mother in the text above) and Buddhism (or the renunciation of secular life, represented by the sutras). In this image of the monk balancing his carrying pole awkwardly and painfully sideways, in an effort to avoid preferring either the mother or the sutras, the dilemma of the mind is externalized, "choreographed" into a self-mutilating, un/balancing act of the body.[3]

About 370 years after *The little nun*, this figure of the conflicted monk reentered the stage spotlight in China. It appeared in a "new dance" adaptation of *Si fan* composed in 1942 by Wu Xiaobang 吳曉邦 (1906–1995), the widely regarded "father of China's new dance," who launched China's "new dance movement" (*xin wuyong yundong* 新舞踊運動) during the mid-1930s. In Wu's solo *Si fan*, instead of balancing Confucianism vis-à-vis Buddhism, however, the monk struggles internally between a different pair of conflicting forces—

now, he is balancing religious faith (*shen* 神) against worldly desire (*yu* 欲). Confined within the temple walls, the monk's inner peace in Wu's dance is disturbed by the voices and laughter of young men and women passing by on the street outside the monastery. While pretending to stay calm by chanting Buddhist scriptures, the monk is deeply attracted to the secular life he hears outside the walls. In his dance, Wu choreographs the monk's psychological struggle through subtle and contrasting movements of body parts. Ankles, torso, hands, neck, and head simultaneously respond to two competing centers of gravity: the sounds outside the walls symbolizing secular desires and the Buddhist altar representing religious faith.

Wu regarded *Si fan* as a representative work of his new dance, a genre derived partly from the German school of modern dance Wu learned via his Japanese colleague Eguchi Takaya 江口隆哉 (1900–1977) in 1936 Tokyo.[4] According to Wu, *Si fan* reconfirmed his "unshakable confidence in modern dance."[5] Matching this modernist form of dancing is Wu's modern interpretation of the *Si fan* theme. For Wu, the *Si fan* story centers on "the sharp conflict between faith and desire, which had been widely employed by many great artists since the European Renaissance."[6] That is, Wu justifies the modern significance of the *Si fan* theme by comparing it to European arts since the Renaissance, the supposed origin of Western modernity.[7]

In most scholarship today, the narrative about Wu composing *Si fan* and its significance seems to conform to a typical account of the rise of modernist arts in East Asia: the art form (e.g., modern dance) diffuses from its European origin to Japan and then to China, and the "modern" quality of the local adaptations (e.g., Wu's new dance) must be evaluated against the European authority. However, what this narrative cannot fully explain in the case of Wu's *Si fan* is the surprisingly "conservative" and even "backward" ending Wu gives to his work. In contrast to the so-called "liberating" and "progressive" ideology of modern dance and the exhilarating and rebellious ending of the original *Si fan* story (in which secular longings triumph over religious asceticism), religion unexpectedly emerges as the final winner in Wu's version. After an exhausting struggle, Wu's monk smothers his desires and returns to chanting scriptures at the end of the dance; the balance is upset, tilting toward the repressive religion.

Rather than judging this ending as conservative or backward, which may be the initial impression it suggests without further context, it may be more productive to instead see Wu's unexpected ending as symptomatic of the ambiguity and polysemy inherent in perceptions and conceptions of "modernity" in the East Asian dance worlds. What constituted the "new" or

Fig. 3.1. Wu Xiaobang
performing *Si fan*,
1942, Qujiang,
Guangdong Province,
China. Source: Yu
Ping 余平 and Feng
Shuangbai 冯双白,
eds. 2006. *Bai nian Wu
Xiaobang* 百年吴晓
邦 (A hundred years
of Wu Xiaobang),
Beijing: Wenhua yishu
chubanshe 文化艺术
出版社, p. 19.

the "modern," the "old" or "tradition," the "national" and the "foreign," the
"progressive" and the "backward" turned out to be quite blurry, and it varied greatly for individual dancer-choreographers in different places, times,
and historical contexts. The dance fields revolving around these definitional
issues became a murky yet generative ground where various historical agents,
ideas, and art forms contacted, conflicted, negotiated, or collaborated with
each other.

Despite their ambiguities, these processes of modernization in East
Asian dance spheres had their distinctive mechanisms. This essay uses the
imagery of the impossible corporeal balance—embodied by the image of the
carrying pole on the bloody shoulders of the conflicted monk Mulian—as
both a unifying theme and an analytical concept. That is, the "modernity"

(or "modernities") reflected in different new dance versions of *Si fan* in early twentieth-century China and Japan can be seen as a dynamic un/balance. This dynamic un/balance of modernity is characterized by the ever-shifting trade-offs and ups and downs of competing discourses, praxes, and cultural and political forces across space and time, which are measured up against each other along the "carrying pole" of dance. In other words, the conflicted monk becomes a metaphor for the choreographer who uses dance to maneuver amid competing forces of modernity in East Asia.

This un/balancing process of choreographic modernities was not a passive response jump-started by the arrival of Western modern dance in East Asia, as is often assumed. Rather, it had followed its own dynamics for centuries before modern dance appeared on the scene. During my years of researching Wu Xiaobang, I have been especially fascinated by his modern-dance-influenced "new dance" *Si fan*. I came to realize that the theme has a long and rich history of adaptation in both textual and performance forms that can be traced back to the mid-sixteenth-century drama *The little nun*. Moreover, I found that this theme traveled beyond China's borders and inspired an important Japanese work of "new dance" in the early twentieth century. Thus, *Si fan*'s transhistorical and transnational adaptations offer an opportunity to reflect on the intrinsic tensions and ambiguities of modernity in the East Asian new dance movements.

Adaptation as a choreographic strategy is both practically and theoretically significant for understanding the Chinese and Japanese new dance movements. Practically, in much of the early-twentieth-century East Asian dance world, it was a common practice to choreograph dance works by adapting existing literary or theatrical narratives, and this allowed dancer-choreographers to create and stabilize meaning in dance.[8] Theoretically, each adaptation of a familiar theme may be seen as a strategic reweighing process in which the dancer-choreographer decides what should be added to or removed from the previous un/balance(s), on which side, with how much weight, and for what purposes. Thus, adaptation is the dancer-choreographers' continuous negotiation between contemporary urgencies and the textual and/or performance history of the work in its changing historical contexts. The remainder of this essay traces the ever-un/balancing adaptation process of *Si fan,* first within the late imperial and early twentieth-century male-centered Chinese theatrical and operatic tradition, then in a 1921 choreography by Fujikage Shizue, a female Japanese choreographer and former geisha, during Japan's new dance movement, and finally in Wu's 1942 Chinese version. Through this chronological comparative study of trans-genre and cross-gender adaptation, this essay shows that definitions of the "new," the "modern," and the "national," often weighed against "foreign" influences and local theatric "traditions," were a shared theme in both Japan's and China's new dance movements. Yet, it also demonstrates their contrasting manifestations in the works of different artists due to the divergent, yet intertwined, cultural and political environments of the two countries.

## SI FAN IN THE CHINESE THEATRICAL TRADITION

The plot of *Si fan* remained stable across centuries in the Chinese theatrical tradition. It tells a story about a young girl named Zhao Sekong 趙色空 (meaning "physicality/desire is emptiness"), who was forced by her parents to become a Buddhist nun when she was a child, as a sacrifice for the parents' redemption. Her life in a convent secluded in the mountain goes by peacefully until she turns sixteen. Thereafter, her mood and emotion change, as she desires mundane life and sexual pleasure, which conflicts with her religious education. The conflict is resolved as Zhao finally runs out of the temple and down the mountain to pursue her mundane happiness. The performance takes the form of a soliloquy, often featuring a long uninterrupted dance solo by the heroine (typically performed by a male actor who specializes in female roles), accompanied by her *nianbai* 念白 (the spoken part of the drama).[9]

Despite the relative stability of its plot, *Si fan* went through a series of transformations across the centuries, enacting constant recalibrations in relation to ever-shifting cultural and ideological forces.[10] For example, the initial integration of *Si fan*, an originally independent operatic work, into the larger story cycle of Mulian during the sixteenth and early seventeenth centuries served as a "sensual and vulgar" counterweight to the Buddhist-Confucian moralist narrative ascendant in that era. However, ironically, due to its popularity, *Si fan* largely remained as a stand-alone drama, outliving the longer Mulian plays of which it was once a part. To further counterbalance the "sensual and vulgar" through their many adaptations of *Si fan*, the Ming playwrights then strove to strike a new balance—one between *qing* 情 (pure sentiment, love), a highly coded elitist concept closely related to "authenticity," and *qi* 奇 (the strange), which generates entertainment value.[11] Thus, the *Si fan* play became the fulcrum for negotiating pairs of polarities that further counterbalanced each other: Buddhism and Confucianism on the one end, and *qing* and *qi* on the other.

This balance was by no means a static one. By the early 1910s, the highly refined Kun opera form had reached its nadir, while the more vernacular Peking opera was gaining popularity. However, around this time, *Si fan*, one of the few Kun operas that still retained some degree of fame, attracted the attention of Mei Lanfang 梅蘭芳 (1894–1961), the preeminent master practitioner-reformer of the Peking opera. Mei and his associates subsequently revived the play in the mid-1910s.[12]

Chasing the demands of China's mass-mediated cultural market of the 1910s, Peking opera increasingly appealed to female sensuality and visuality, which explains Mei's rise to fame as the top *dan* 旦 (female role) actor during this period, replacing the previous centrality of *sheng* 生 (male-role) actors in Peking opera.[13] As Catherine Yeh (in this volume) points out, a major problem facing Peking opera during this period was its lack of well-organized and visually pleasing dance movements. According to Yeh, this motivated Mei and his associates to "dancify" Peking opera by learning from early Western modern dance. The dance-rich Kun opera was another source for Mei's "dancification" endeavor in Peking opera, however. In Mei's words, "when [we] mention 'the integration of song and dance, and the dual emphasis on singing and gesturing,' the Kun opera fully deserves this [praise]."[14] By studying the Kun opera *Si fan*, Mei thus enriched his choreographic vocabulary and dance skills for Peking opera performance.

By the 1910s, the theme of rebellion highlighted in the plot of *Si fan* had also gained new meanings in China. It became subsumed into the rising discourse of antifeudalism that would prevail in the brewing New Culture (May Fourth) movement of the mid-1910s and early 1920s. This mass modernizing and Westernizing enlightenment campaign marks the beginning of China's "modern era" in official historical periodization.[15] As Mei puts it, "ideologically, it [*Si fan*] has the positive quality of resistance [to feudalist oppressions]."[16] That is, a new layer of dynamic dis/equilibrium was added to the many meanings of *Si fan*, one between a mass-mediated culture of feminine sensuality and visuality on the one end and mass-enlightening ideals of (gendered) individual freedom and self-liberation on the other.

This new interpretation of the "old drama" *Si fan* as a vessel of "modern" desires and ideals needs to be understood in relation to its Western counterpart, a point best expressed in an essay by Hu Shi 胡適 (1891–1962), one of Mei's contemporaries.[17] As a prominent leader in the New Culture movement, Hu was a major opponent of China's "old drama," represented by Mei's performances, which he and others regarded as "feudal." In his essay, Hu employs an evolutionary perspective to frame traditional Chinese theater (including *Si fan*) as a form with "every historical survival" that is primitive compared to

Western theater. However, Hu points out a curious similarity between *Si fan* and an early modernist poem: he writes that *Si fan* "is a soliloquy throughout and reads like one of Robert Browning's dramatic poems portraying the psychology of a Medieval artist in a cell of his monastery."[18]

Here, Hu seems to refer to Browning's (1812–1889) poem "Fra Lippo Lippi," which is a dramatic monologue of Brother Lippo Lippi, a famous medieval Florentine monk-painter. The poem opens with the monk being caught seeking pleasure in the red-light district by the police, defending himself in the street against the accusation.[19] The story does resemble that of *Si fan*: the orphan Lippo is forced by hunger to become a Catholic monk at a church. As he grows up, his reflection on human desires and the essence of art leads him into confrontation with his religious faith. One night, seduced by the laughter of young girls passing by the church, Lippo climbs out the window and follows the girls into the street, which leads to the opening scene of the poem.

Fu Sinian 傅斯年 (1896–1950), another leader in the New Culture movement, made a similar comparison in 1918. He writes, "when I tried to find a work from the old drama that is compatible with the new ideology, [I] cannot find any, except the Kun opera *Si fan*: [it] reads like an essay on religious revolution. . . . Therefore, as far as the ideology of this opera is concerned, it is very radical."[20] By weighing the centuries-old script of *Si fan* against the Reformation and a recognized work of early English poetic modernism in both form and content, Fu and Hu, despite their generally critical attitude toward traditional Chinese theater with *Si fan* being a representative, contributed to unearthing the modernity of this so-called old drama.

## *SI FAN* IN JAPAN'S NEW DANCE MOVEMENT

In Japanese dance historiography, modernism in Japanese dance began with Japan's new dance movement (*shin buyō undō* 新舞踊運動), predecessor to and inspiration for China's movement of the same name.[21] Japan's new dance movement started with the publication in November 1904 of *Shin gakugekiron* 新楽劇論 (On the new musical drama) by Tsubōuchi Shōyō 坪内逍遙 (1859–1935). Calling for reforming the traditional Japanese *buyōgeki* 舞踊劇 (dance drama), the manifesto had a lasting impact on Japan's new dance movement.[22] Motivated by Japan's victories in the Russo-Japanese War (1904–1905), Tsubōuchi hoped that a "new national dance drama" could demonstrate to the world powers "the ideal taste of the Japanese civilization."[23] In this "epoch-making" statement, Tsubōuchi maintains that Japan's new dance should be developed by condensing and amplifying the "essences" of traditional Japanese theatrical forms, such that it would be comparable to but distinct from Western dances.[24] In the context of this highly nationalist background of Japan's new dance movement, it is remarkable that the 1921 adaptation of the Chinese drama *Si fan* (*Shi han* in Japanese) by Fujikage Shizue 藤蔭靜枝 (1880–1966) has been widely considered a milestone and a "much-awaited" work in the movement.[25]

Brought up to be a geisha, the beautiful and talented Fujikage received systematic training in traditional Japanese performing arts, especially Kabuki 歌舞伎. Moreover, she was a lover of literature and was known as the "literary geisha."[26] These qualities enabled her to build a broad social network with many influential Japanese male intellectuals, writers, artists, and critics, who later turned out to be crucial to her success (for more on the history of female entertainers and their relationships to male patrons in East Asia, see Bossler, this volume).[27] Only after her short marriage to the famous writer Kafū Nagai 永井荷風 (1879–1959) ended in 1915 did Fujikage, then in her late thirties, embark on the arduous journey of transforming herself from a geisha-entertainer to one of the few early independent female artistic dancers in Japan.[28]

Fujikage regarded *Shi han* as a breakthrough both in theme and form in her dance career, as it contrasted with her former works, which were characterized mostly by a pessimistic, tepid style.[29] Fujikage based her choreography for *Shi han* on paintings, a story outline, and props from Mei Lanfang's *Si fan*, which she obtained from the Japanese geologist and theater-lover Fukuchi Nobuyo 福地信世 (1887–1934, a friend of Mei), who had sketched, painted, recorded, and brought them with him back to Japan from China. Fujikage's *Shi han* quickly became a success after its premiere in Tokyo in 1921.[30] *Shi han* followed the original story line, and "at every key juncture of the choreography, the postures [of Mei in *Si fan*] in Mr. Fukuchi's paintings were borrowed"; even the horsetail whisk used as a prop by Fujikage was the same one used by Mei in his *Si fan* (Mei gave it to Fukuchi as a gift). Yet Fujikage strove to prevent her choreography from "being trapped in the style of traditional Chinese theater."[31] Fujikage's associates (many of whom were trained in Western arts) also redesigned the music, costume and makeup, and stage setup in experimental ways. In this way, Fujikage's *Shi han* became distinct from its Chinese counterpart.[32]

In Fujikage's *Shi han,* the stage is divided into two sections. The front is a courtyard, and in the back towers the main hall of the convent, with red pillars on both sides. Further to the sides are red fences, beyond which stand peach and cherry trees in full blossom, contrasting against the monotonous life within. As Fukuchi sings the line "My body that retreats into the gate of Buddha," the young nun (Fujikage) emerges from the shadows of pillars on the left side, dressed in a white floral kimono under black Kasaya decorated with Tang style embroidery, with her head covered by a dark-amber-colored Buddhist hood. Stepping across the stage to the right, the nun removes the hood to let her long dark hair cascade down over her shoulders, and then takes off the black Kasaya to reveal her true self as a beautiful girl in a secular kimono; these actions go against the line of the accompanying song, foreshadowing the nun's final escape from the "gate of Buddha."[33] Adding to the intercultural aspects of this dance, the choreography of this opening scene was inspired by the Korean "monk dance" described by the painter Tanaka Ryo 田中良, who also designed the stage background.[34]

In *Shi han*, Fujikage appropriated the modernity that came to be associated with *Si fan*'s rebellion theme, here understood as individual freedom and self-actualization, to make a gesture of "breaking away" from the formal and thematic constraints of traditional Japanese dance, which she felt had limited her possibilities of innovation.[35] The borrowed Chinese and Korean dance motifs further allowed her to bring something new, yet different from Western dances, into the Japanese choreography.[36] Thanks to the shared cultural legacies among China, Japan, and Korea, these innovations did not run directly against the nationalist imperatives of Japan's new dance movement, though *Shi han* did incite some criticisms for "grafting the postures of Chinese performance onto a Japanese dance."[37]

The image of the rebellious nun may be interpreted as Fujikage's declaration of her identity as an independent female artist, freeing herself from the constraints of various gendered social roles—a geisha, wife, and apprentice in the Kabuki world dominated by men.[38] As a former geisha in her late thirties, Fujikage's odyssey to become an independent artistic dancer was indeed challenging.[39] She faced several major obstacles. First, while the new dance needed to acquire an identity relatively independent of traditional Japanese theatrical forms, especially Kabuki, the male masters of these forms were so well established that they often resisted reform. Second, on the female side, geishas, who were master dancers, tended to be hostile toward independent artistic dancers due to fierce competition in the profession, which is reflected in the famous 1917 novel *Udekurabe* 腕くらべ (translated as *Rivalry: A Geisha's Tale*) by Kafū, Fujikage's ex-husband.[40]

To overcome these obstacles, Fujikage adopted a two-pronged strategy. On the one hand, she collaborated with male intellectuals, writers, and artists in her dance productions to elevate her dance to the status of a serious art, thus distinguishing her works from the competing geisha "entertainment." On the other hand, she highlighted her gender identity as an independent woman, as represented by the image of the rebellious nun in *Shi han*, to maintain some autonomy and freedom in the male-dominated discourses and praxes of the Japanese dance world. Fujikage's *Shi han* registers a distinct un/balance of power relations in Japan's new dance movement—a fraught negotiation between the traditional and the new, the national and the foreign, the gendered social roles and self-liberation, the female dancer and the male patrons, intellectuals, and critics.

## *SI FAN* IN CHINA'S NEW DANCE MOVEMENT

In contrast to its Japanese counterpart, the historical background in which China's new dance movement unfolded in the mid-1930s was characterized by a deep sense of national crises: the loss of Manchuria to Japan (1931) and the Japanese total invasion (1937) culminated a series of humiliating defeats in China's century-long struggles against foreign colonial powers. Despite the persisting tensions between the two countries, Japan, as the major cultural mediator between the West and East Asia, was a popular destination for Chinese students to study abroad. Like many of his contemporaries and predecessors in the New Culture movement, Wu Xiaobang went to Japan to learn modern arts. However, Wu was the only one who seriously studied dance and chose dance as his lifelong career.

From 1929 to 1936, Wu studied modern dance in Tokyo, first with Takada Seiko 高田原世子 (1895–1977) and then briefly with Eguchi Takaya. Unlike Fujikage and other dancer-choreographers of the new dance movement, who were experts in traditional Japanese theater forms and devoted to reforming the dance components in them, Takada and Eguchi belonged to another lineage of modern Japanese dancers, who were trained in European ballet at the Imperial Theatre Training School Opera Section and later studied various schools of Western modern dance (see Kuniyoshi, this volume). In the mid-1930s, Wu brought modern dance back to China and almost single-handedly launched China's new dance movement on its foundation. Thus, although Wu borrowed the term "new dance movement" from Japanese, the dance form the term signified in China was closer to Western, especially German, modern dance, rather than dances derived from traditional theater forms.[41]

Within these contexts, Wu adopted the typical ideology of the New Culture movement for his new dance, emulating the various associated "new" movements in literature and arts in China. These movements typically regarded Western(ized) arts as "superior" to so-called "backward" local forms. Therefore, unlike its Japanese counterpart, which was conceived as the essentialist "refinement" and reformation of traditional theatrical forms, China's new dance movement had to justify its "newness" by antagonizing itself against so-called "traditional" theater forms such as Kun and Peking operas, at the same time stressing its "authoritative" Western modernist origins. These ideals are reflected in the choreographic and narrative decisions Wu made in his 1942 adaptation of *Si fan*, which was different from and even opposite to the other versions.[42]

In Wu's *Si fan*, the stage set features a red wall topped by glazed tiles separating the monastery interior from the outside world, a spatial symbolization of the character's internal conflict. Beyond the wall one can see the top of a willow with crooked branches and a distant mountain peak, which transform the stage into a secluded space. Accompanied by a Chinese-styled lyrical violin solo (composed according to the principles of Western classical music), the dance begins with Wu as a barefooted young Buddhist monk, sitting cross-legged on a cattail hassock. The monk, in gray-and-black Kasaya with a string of prayer beads hanging around his neck, is chanting scriptures piously with his eyes closed. The monk's palms are put together in a praying gesture, which becomes a persisting motif throughout the whole dance. This rigid gesture—which greatly restrains the freedom of movement of the arms, hands, fingers, and the upper torso—symbolizes the constant self-discipline of religious spirituality. It contrasts with the tender, rich, and subtle movements of the arms, hands, and fingers in Mei's *Si fan* and Fujikage's *Shi han*.

As time goes by, more and more tourists, supposedly young men and women, pass by the monastery. Their voices disturb the internal tranquility of the monk. He gradually loses his composure and leans his head slightly and slowly to each side, listening attentively to the sounds of the mundane world. The monk cannot help but stand up and, attracted to the voices outside, walk slowly toward the red wall while still praying toward the Buddhist altar. The subsequent dance movements then unfold in the push and pull between these two opposite directions, making visual the character's internal struggle. At first, the wavering of faith is expressed by small movements of body parts, such as a quivering motion of a raised ankle. As the outsiders get closer and their voices louder, the internal conflict of the monk intensifies, represented by larger movements such as stretching his body and raising his head to peek beyond the wall. The brewing tension culminates in a sweeping

Fig. 3.2. Wu Xiaobang performing *Si fan*, 1942, Qujiang, Guangdong Province, China. Source: Yu Ping 余平 and Feng Shuangbai 冯双白, eds. 2006. *Bai nian Wu Xiaobang* 百年吴晓邦 (A hundred years of Wu Xiaobang), Beijing: Wenhua yishu chubanshe 文化艺术出版社, p. 19.

action of "scratching his head with his right hand." This breaks the motif of the "two palms put together," suggesting the monk's frustration and failure to conceal his inner struggle. After the climax, as the tourists wander away and their voices fall to distant whispers, the monk gradually gathers his mind, puts his two palms back together, and resumes chanting scriptures against the ringing of the temple bell to express his repentance.[43] Both Mei's *Si fan* and Fujikage's *Shi han*, though visually rich in symbolic and expressive dance movements, anchor their meanings on the *nianbai* and the lyrics of arias (or the lyrics of accompanying songs in *Shi han*). Wu's version, without any assistance from language, instead centers on the monk's conflicting bodily reactions to the acoustic stimuli inside and outside the temple walls.

Two other major differences distinguish Wu's *Si fan* from Mei's and Fujikage's. First, Wu changed the character of the teenage nun to a young monk. In the Chinese context, this was especially important because it also abandoned the tradition of cross-gender performance used in Mei's version.[44] Following the ideology of the New Culture movement, Wu criticized cross-gender performance in China's "old drama" as a form of "backward feudalistic oppression" of the body that was contradictory to the modern-dance principle of "natural" body movement.[45] Although men dominated theatrical performance, in 1940s China dance was still widely deemed a profession for women, and being a male dancer was highly scandalous. Wu himself was often sneered at and criticized.[46] In this context, Wu attempted to dance as a "man" to "masculinize" his new dance.[47] This attitude is reflected too in Wu's choreography: after hearing the voices of young women outside the temple, the monk walks several steps forward in an awkwardly feminine gait, mocking the gender-crossing performance in traditional theater.[48]

The second difference is the seemingly conservative ending of Wu's version. To understand this paradoxical choice, one needs to consider the status of dance in relation to Chinese theater in the early twentieth century. By the 1930s, Peking opera had largely succeeded in striking a balance between *ya* 雅 (refined) and *su* 俗 (popular/vulgar), as manifested in its status being elevated to the "national drama."[49] However, dance was still struggling at the *su* and sensual end of this dis/equilibrium. In early twentieth-century China, dance was almost entirely identified as a low art, or even anti-art, that relied on sensuality to serve the purpose of entertainment. It was seen as devoid of intellectual content and often associated with debauchery.[50] As Wu remarked in 1941 (one year before he choreographed *Si fan*), dance had been "the commodity in the hands of merchants selling laughter, the martial arts of peddling kung fu performers, or interludes for [the performance of] magicians on stage," where the phrase "selling laughter" connotes prostitution in Chinese.[51] Therefore, Wu's new ending may be interpreted as his attempt to portray the triumph of "masculine" intellectualism over "feminine" sensuality, implying Wu's fear of his new dance being associated with sensual desires.

However, this "victory" of faith and rationality over the mundane and bodily incurs a heavy cost. According to the dance script, after his agonizing conflict, though still chanting scriptures, the monk's mind "cannot return to the realm of Buddha anymore."[52] Just as in the allegory of Mulian, where the impossibility of balance is evidenced by self-mutilation, the trauma of the repenting monk seems to suggest Wu's concern that the unity of the mind and the body, spirituality and corporeality—which modern dance had been striving to achieve—was ultimately a utopia in the age of mass popular culture, in which the dancing body was irreversibly objectified and commodified.

CONCLUSION

The centuries-long adaptation process of *Si fan* traced in this essay began with the corporeal un/balance between Confucianism and Buddhism in the Sinicized Indic allegory of Mulian, on which was added another dis/equilibrium between *qing* and *qi* in the Ming-dynasty Kun opera *Si fan*. In the mid-1910s, Mei Lanfang's "dancified" version added a new calibration between the mass-mediated feminine sensuality-visuality and the antifeudalist discourse of China's New Culture movement that called for the creation of a new, or Westernized, Chinese culture as a means of nation-building. Developed during a period when Japan was expanding its hegemonic influences in northern China, Mei's *Si fan* inspired Fujikage Shizue's 1921 Japanese dance version *Shi han*. Fujikage's adaptation of the Chinese drama paradoxically became a milestone in Japan's new dance movement that was initially intended to distill the national cultural "essences" of traditional Japanese theater forms into modernized dance works. In Fujikage's version, more un/balances accrued to the *Si fan* theme between national and foreign dance forms, and between the precarious status of the female dancer and male dominance in Japan's dance world during the liberal Taishō period (1912–1926). Finally, in 1942, at the height of the Second Sino-Japanese War and the Pacific War, Wu Xiaobang choreographed a modern-dance version of *Si fan*. Wu distinguished his adaptation from both Mei's and Fujikage's versions by highlighting two more points of calibration, one between cross-gender performance in Chinese theater and the "natural" body movement of modern dance, and the other between rationality-intellectuality and sensual desires.

Using this layering of negotiated relationships, the essay demonstrates how the same *Si fan* theme was seen variously as new and old, refreshing and decadent, progressive and backward, liberating and oppressive in the eyes of Japanese and Chinese dancer-choreographers and intellectual-critics in the two countries' new dance movements. Their specific choreographic and narrative decisions depended on which way they intended to tilt their "carrying pole" of dance, which was in turn shaped by the positions of the artists and their arts in their respective cultural and political environments. Though different, the Chinese and Japanese versions of *Si fan* were also intertwined through transnational cultural exchanges, colonial and anticolonial struggles, and world wars. By incorporating competing concepts into one spatiotemporal framework, measured against one another, the un/balances of modernity revealed in *Si fan*'s choreographic history make explicit the often-implicit power structures underlying binary logics of exclusion and inclusion.[53] In so doing, this history challenges the boundaries between Western modernism and its East Asian "adaptations," between "traditional" and "new," and between "national" and "foreign."

### ADDITIONAL RESOURCES

Full resolution versions of Figure 3.1 at https://doi.org/10.3998/ mpub.11521701.cmp.5 and Figure 3.2 at https://doi.org/10.3998/ mpub.11521701.cmp.6

Link 3.1: Japanese Wikipedia page for Fujikage Shizue, including photograph of her performing *Si fan (Shi han)*. Available at https://doi.org/10.3998/ mpub.11521701.cmp.37

### *Notes*

1. Translated by Andrea S Goldman, "The Nun Who Wouldn't Be: Representations of Female Desire in Two Performance Genres of 'Si Fan,'" *Late Imperial China* 22, no. 1 (2001): 71–138, 85.

2. Kun opera originated in southeast China in the late 1300s and enjoyed its greatest popularity from the mid-sixteenth to late eighteenth centuries. While the performance of Kun opera centers on singing with a refined and subtle vocal style, it is an integrative art that organically incorporates rich, smooth, and elegant dance movements. For a detailed performance history of the Kun opera, see Lu O-t'ing 陸萼庭, *Kun ju yanchu shigao* 昆劇演出史稿 (Taiwan: Guojia chubanshe, 2002).

3. The carrying pole is a common device in China used to transport heavy loads by foot. It consists of a pole balanced over the shoulder with buckets or packages hanging on each end. Usually, the pole is held in line with the road. In the image above, the monk carries the pole sideways, hence the description "parting the trees on both sides."

4. For a detailed account of Wu's experiences of learning dance (especially the German school of modern dance) in Japan and transforming it into China's new dance,

see Nan Ma, "Transmediating Kinesthesia: Wu Xiaobang and Modern Dance in China, 1929–1939," *Modern Chinese Literature and Culture* 28, no. 1 (2016): 129–73.

5. Wu Xiaobang 吳曉邦, *Wu Xiaobang wudao wenji (di yi juan)* 吳曉邦舞蹈文集 (第一卷), ed. Feng Shuangbai 馮雙白 and Yu Ping 余平 (Beijing: Zhongguo wenlian chubanshe, 2007), 56.

6. Wu, *Wu Xiaobang wudao wenji (di wu juan)*, vol. 5, 74.

7. On the significance of Wu's *Si fan* in modern Chinese dance history, see Nan Ma, "Dancing into Modernity: Kinesthesia, Narrative, and Revolutions in Modern China, 1900–1978" (PhD dissertation, University of Wisconsin–Madison, 2015), 142–201.

8. Ma, "Transmediating Kinesthesia"; Nishikata Setsuko 西形節子, *Kindai nihon buyōshi* 近代日本舞踊史 (Tōkyō: Engeki Shuppansha, 2006).

9. Mei Lanfang 梅蘭芳, *Wutai shenghuo sishi nian* 舞臺生活四十年 (Beijing: Zhongguo xiju chubanshe, 1987), 336–54.

10. Goldman, "The Nun Who Wouldn't Be," 80–94.

11. Ibid., 74; Wai-yee Li, *Enchantment and Disenchantment: Love and Illusion in Chinese Literature* (Princeton: Princeton University Press, 1993), 47–88.

12. Mei Lanfang 梅蘭芳, *Mei Lanfang tan yi lu* 梅蘭芳談藝錄 (Changsha: Hunan daxue chubanshe, 2010), 124.

13. Joshua Goldstein, *Drama kings: Players and publics in the re-creation of Peking opera, 1870–1937* (Berkeley: University of California Press, 2007), 118–28.

14. Mei, *Mei Lanfang tan yi lu*, 123–24.

15. Frustrated by a series of less-than-effective attempts to modernize China through top-down social, economic, and political reforms since the mid-nineteenth century, many elite Chinese intellectuals in the mid-1910s came to agree that a major obstacle to China's modernization and self-strengthening was the "feudalist ideology" (mainly Confucianism) deeply rooted in the minds of the masses. Therefore, they proposed to establish and disseminate a "new culture" (mainly Western or Westernized cultures) to replace or reform the "old feudalist culture." For a conventional account, see Jonathan Spence, *The Search for Modern China*, 3rd ed. (New York: Norton, 2013), 279–95.

16. Mei, *Mei Lanfang tan yi lu*, 123.

17. Hu Shi 胡適, "Mei Lanfang and the Chinese Drama," in *The Pacific Coast tour of Mei Lan-fang, under the management of the Pacific Chinese Dramatic Club, San Francisco, Cal*, ed. Ernest K. Moy (publisher unidentified, around 1930), 1.

18. Ibid. Cited in Mei Shaowu 梅紹武, *Wo de fuqin Mei Lanfang* 我的父親梅蘭芳 (Beijing: Zhonghua Shuju, 2006), 216–18.

19. Robert Browning, "Fra Lippo Lippi," in *Men and Women* (Boston: Ticknor and Fields, 1856), 25–38.

20. Fu Sinian 傅斯年, "Xiju gailiang ge mian guan" 戲劇改良各面觀, *Xin qingnian* 新青年 4 (1918): 14–15. Cited in Mei, *Wo de fuqin Mei Lanfang*, 218–19.

21. The two movements have the same written name but are pronounced differently.

22. Tsubōuchi Shōyō 坪內逍遙, *Shin gakugekiron* 新楽劇論 (Tōkyō: Waseda Daigaku Shuppanbu, 1904); Chao Chi-Fang 趙綺芳, "Quanqiu xiandaixing, guojiazhuyi yu 'xinwuyong:' yi 1945 nian yiqian riben xiandaiwu de fazhan wei li zhi fenxi" 全球現代性, 國家主義與"新舞踊": 以 1945 年以前日本現代舞的發展為例之分析, *Yishu pinglun* 藝術評論 (Taipei: Taipei National University of Arts) 18 (2008): 27–55, 42; Kuniyoshi Kazuko 國吉和子, *Yumeo no ishō kioku no tsubo: buyō to modanizumu* 夢の衣裳・記憶の壺：舞踊とモダニズム (Tōkyō : Shinshokan, 2002).

23. Nishikata, *Kindai nihon buyōshi*, 11.

24. Ibid., 11–12.

25. Fujikagekai 藤蔭會, ed., *Fujikage Shizue* 藤蔭静枝 (Tōkyō: Fujikagekai, 1934), in Tsubōuchi Memorial Theater Museum of Waseda University 早稻田大學演劇博物館, Tōkyō, Japan; Chao, "Quanqiu xiandaixing, guojiazhuyi yu 'xinwuyong,'" 42.

26. Nishikata, *Kindai nihon buyōshi*, 68; Akira Shioura, *Kafū to Shizue: Meiji Taigyaku Jiken no inga* 荷風と静枝：明治大逆事件の陰画 (Tōkyō : Yōyōsha, 2007), 48.

27. Nishikata, *Kindai nihon buyōshi*, 77.

28. Ibid., 69–74.

29. Ibid., 108.

30. Ibid., 108–9; Kuniyoshi, *Yumeo no ishō kioku no tsubo*, 119. Although *Si fan* was in the repertoire of Mei's 1919 sensational Japanese tour, it seemingly received less attention from Mei's troupe, because Mei himself never performed it during the tour. Thus, compared with other highly promoted Peking opera works, the Kun opera *Si fan* had a limited impact in Japan's literary and artistic circles during this tour. Ōshima Tomonao 大島友明, *Hinbaiki* 品梅記 (Kyōto: Ibundō Shoten, 1919).

31. Nishikata, *Kindai nihon buyōshi*, 109.

32. Ibid., 107–11.

33. Ibid., 109. Available information about the exact choreography of Fujikage's *Shi han* is scarce, to the author's knowledge.

34. Ibid., 110.

35. Ibid., 108, 111.

36. Fujikage did choreograph many dances with clear influences from Western modern dance later in her career. Kuniyoshi, *Yumeo no ishō kioku no tsubo*, 113–29; Fujikagekai, *Fujikage Shizue*.

37. In 1922, the year after *Shi han*'s premiere, Tsubōuchi reiterated his nationalist vision for Japan's new dance, which again emphasized the importance of pure "Japaneseness" against foreign, especially Western, dances. However, (Japanified) traditional Chinese literary themes were not uncommon among the choreographies in Japan's new dance movement. Nishikata, *Kindai nihon buyōshi*, 119–20.

38. For the patriarchal and condescending attitude of a typical Japanese male intellectual, Kafū Nagai (Fujikage's ex-husband), toward his beloved geisha-turned-wife, see Kafū Nagai 永井荷風, *Yongjing hefeng sanwen xuan* 永井荷風散文選, trans. Chen Dewen 陳德文 (Tianjin: Bai hua wen yi chubanshe, 1997), 205–24.

39. Uri Miyama 牛山充, "Namanama hatten no gei-jutsu" 生生發展の藝術, in *Fujikage Shizue*, ed. Fujikagekai; Eiji Wada 和田英作, untitled article in *Fujikage Shizue*.

40. Fujikage could also exploit new opportunities. Nishikata, *Kindai nihon buyōshi*, 124–25; Kafū Nagai 永井荷風, *Rivalry: A Geisha's Tale*, trans. Stephen Snyder (New York: Columbia University Press, 2007).

41. On Wu's contributions to China's new dance movement in the 1930s and 1940s, see Ma, "Transmediating Kinesthesia."

42. Considering Wu's experience of studying dance in Japan, he might have known about the Japanese *Shi han*. Perhaps because Wu intended to position his *Si fan* as a work of Chinese origin, he never confirmed any connection to Fijikage's adaptation.

43. Wu, *Wu Xiaobang wudao wenji (di yi juan)*, vol. 1, 59; vol. 5, 71–74.

44. Fujikage did cross-gender performance too. In the mid-1930s, Fujikage choreographed the work *Saba daishi* 鯖大師 (Master Mackerel), in which she danced the role of the famous Japanese monk *Kūkai* 空海, who went to Tang China to study Buddhism in the early ninth century and brought what he learned back to Japan. Fujikagekai, *Fujikage Shizue*.

45. Wu, *Wu Xiaobang wudao wenji (di san juan)*, vol. 3, 46, 121–22.

46. Wu, *Wu Xiaobang wudao wenji (di si juan)*, vol. 4, 164.

47. In the Kun opera repertoire, there is a sequel to *Si fan*, named *Seng ni hui* 僧尼會 (The rendezvous between the monk and the nun). After running away from the convent, the nun Zhao Sekong meets a young monk who has likewise abandoned his religious faith, and the two become lovers. Wu's *Si fan* may thus be seen as related to the story of the monk in *Seng ni hui* as well. However, the story of *Si fan* is much more popular than *Seng ni hui*. Goldman, "The Nun Who Wouldn't Be," 72–73.

48. Wu, *Wu Xiaobang wudao wenji (di wu juan)*, vol. 5, 71.

49. Goldstein, *Drama Kings*, 118–28.

50. Wu, *Wu Xiaobang wudao wenji (di san juan)*, vol. 3, 124.

51. Wu Xiaobang 吳曉邦, "Zai kangzhan zhong shengzhang qilai de wuyong yishu" 在抗戰中生長起來的舞踊藝術, *Zhong Su wenhua* 中蘇文化 9, no. 1 (1941): 96–98, 96.

52. Wu, *Wu Xiaobang wudao wenji (di wu juan)*, vol. 5, 72.

53. Susan Stanford Friedman, *Planetary Modernisms: Provocations on Modernity across Time* (New York: Columbia University Press, 2015), 37–43.

## PART 2

## Decolonizing Migration

# CHAPTER 4

# Murayama Tomoyoshi and Dance of Modern Times

## A Forerunner of the Japanese Avant-garde

*Kazuko Kuniyoshi* 國吉和子,
*translated from Japanese by Yuda Kenji* 湯田賢司

Murayama Tomoyoshi 村山知義 (1901–1977) is well known as a theater direc-tor and fine artist, but he has rarely been spoken of as a dancer in writings on modern Japanese dance history. Only recently have a few articles and books touched on his very brief dancing career.[1] Murayama danced in public and private from June 1923 until he founded the avant-garde fine-art group Mavo (マヴォ) in 1925. Only a handful of photographs tell us what his dance might have been like. He had a significant role as the first dancer in Japan in the modern age to create a movement expression based on body awareness—perception of the body. On the other hand, conventional modern Japanese dance history writing has only focused on the assimilation and development of new techniques from Western dance. As a researcher of butoh, I am inter-ested in this missing link in the history of body awareness in the Japanese avant-garde.

The Imperial Theatre Training School Opera Section (帝国劇場付属養成所) was established in Hibiya, Tokyo, during the Taishō Era (1912–1926). It is generally believed that modern Japanese dance started when this school offered Western dance, that is, classical ballet lessons, for the first time. At that point, Japan was gaining international attention because although it was a small country, it successively won the First Sino-Japanese War (1894–1895) and the Russo-Japanese War (1904–1905). Foreign dignitaries started to fre-quently visit Japan, and Japanese officials felt a growing need to modernize Japanese culture and society, as well as to demonstrate Japanese military power. From the end of the Tokugawa Era (1603–1868) through the Meiji Era (1868–1912), Japan sent a number of diplomatic missions to Western coun-tries to witness the progress of modern nations and societies and to learn how Westerners built and structured their nations. Japanese leaders were interested in the role of theater arts in a modern society, especially in France, England, and Germany.[2]

At that time, Japanese theaters consisted of relatively small playhouses for Kabuki (歌舞伎), Noh (能), and Kyōgen (狂言); there were no other venues available in Japan for large public performances. Construction of modern Western theaters was becoming a pressing matter, together with a government initiative called the Theatrical Play Improvement Movement. Planning for the development of modern Western theater started under the auspices of top politicians and government officials, but leaders of the business world were the actual driving force. Japan's government was financially strained after the Russo-Japanese War, and private resources achieved the plan more quickly. As a result, the palatial Imperial Theatre Company was established with private capital instead of government funding. Music, new opera, new Kabuki, dance, and other performances were held at this theater.

When the Imperial Theatre opened, its main program was Western opera, and an Opera School was established. It is interesting that many leading figures of Japanese Western dance were graduates of the Imperial Theatre Opera School's inaugural class and the succeeding class. Many scholars believe that most of the pioneers of Western dance in Japan generally were alumni from this school, including Ishii Baku 石井漠 (1886–1962), Takada Masao 高田雅夫 (1895–1929), Hara Seiko 原せい子 (Takada Seiko 高田せい子 1895–1977), Itō Michio 伊藤道郎 (1893–1961), Sawa Morino 沢モリノ (1890–1933), and Komori Toshi 小森敏 (1887–1951), among others. In fact, however, historians of modern Japanese dance never looked outside of Imperial Theatre pedigrees—the Imperial Theatre was that powerful a symbol of cutting-edge culture in the Japanese capital. I would like to include another person in this history: Murayama Tomoyoshi, a complete outsider to the Imperial Theatre, and an indispensable dancer in the formative years of Japanese dance in modern times.

Dancers from the Imperial Theatre Opera School would build a foundation for Japanese dance in the modern age. The Imperial Theatre did not impose any strict control over the development of the Japanese dance world, nor did it provide ample support for any dancers. For instance, Ishii Baku rebelled against the Imperial Theatre's policy and explored his own dance style. The individual efforts of dancers themselves laid out and expanded the groundwork of Japanese Western dance. They were pioneers who studied and introduced modern Western dance to Japan, but they cannot be called avant-garde. In the beginning of the twentieth century, modernization in Japan meant Westernization. Murayama did not have any disciples or a connection to the Japanese dance world, but his interdisciplinary and social-movement approaches as an artist were true to the spirit of the avant-garde.

The history of Japanese avant-garde art is said to have begun with the introduction of the Futurist Manifesto from Italy in 1909.[3] The Japanese avant-garde art movement actually started in the early 1920s. It was created by a group of artists who advocated a new artistic concept of free expression emancipated from conventional aesthetics or value systems. These artists were engaged in multiple disciplines at the same time; for example, one might be both a fine artist and a poet. In Japan, as in Italy, the avant-garde was embraced as a product of Western modernism. Avant-garde artists chose to criticize existing conventional aesthetics or value systems; they freely traversed multiple methods for expression and engaged in a social movement to explore them. This type of approach was common in European avant-garde art movements in the twentieth century, including Futurism, Constructivism, and Dadaism. Likewise, Murayama formed an artistic group, called Mavo, and after his short stint as a dancer, he shifted his focus to fine art and theater. Mavo performances in the 1920s were eccentric productions enacted by painters and sculptors, not by dancers. Ishii Baku was a pioneer of modern Japanese dance who dedicated his life to completing his own dancing. Murayama was different. He was the first Japanese artist who questioned the characteristics of somatic expression and the common threads between dance and other genres of art. This essay focuses on what Murayama Tomoyoshi tried to achieve in his short dance career and why his dance activity was so brief, from the perspective of Japanese avant-garde art.

## BERLIN IN 1922

Murayama Tomoyoshi visited Berlin in 1922, and he absorbed an astonishing variety of cutting-edge fine art and performing arts in less than one year.[4] His encounter with dance was especially electrifying. Murayama originally wanted to major in philosophy and intended to study early Christianity at the University of Berlin. He went to Germany by himself to fulfill his very personal interest, but he gave up on the entrance examination and devoted himself to various arts. He was especially infatuated with dance and called himself a dancer after coming back to Japan. Berlin at that time must have been spellbinding. I can imagine the young Murayama wandering the streets, excited and full of energy. In Berlin in the 1920s where he studied, Dadaism was past its heyday, but in around 1922 the Romanisches Café and West Berlin were full of bohemians and Russian émigrés, both famous and unknown.

From a dance-history perspective, in German culture at the beginning of the twentieth century a very Expressionist form of dance was emerging as a successor to classical ballet. This new dance was called *Neue Tanz* (new dance) or *Freier Tanz* (free dance) and was gaining attention as leading toward a liberated body expression and not conforming to the techniques of ballet. Music theorist Émile Jaques-Dalcroze (1865–1950) invented eurhythmics theory, which later developed into a dance theory that formed the foundation for German Expressionist dance. Rudolf von Laban (1879–1958) promoted eurhythmics as a new dance theory with great success. Pioneering modern Japanese composer Yamada Kōsaku 山田耕筰 (1886–1965) studied eurhythmics as a new music theory in Berlin as early as the 1910s and subsequently introduced it to Japan. Ishii Baku was a friend of Yamada, and it is highly likely that Ishii was aware of German eurhythmics theory. The forerunner of German Expressionist dance was Mary Wigman (1886–1973), who made her debut in 1914 under the auspices of Laban. I assume that Murayama saw Wigman's solo performances as well as the choreography of her dance company in Berlin.

## IMPRESSIONS OF WIGMAN'S DANCE

Murayama wrote, "There were hardly any dance performances that I didn't attend in 1922 Berlin."[5] He seemed to see every one of them. His notes were full of legendary dancers at work: Anna Pavlova (1881–1931), Michael Fokine (1880–1942), and Vaslav Nijinsky (1889–1950) of Ballets Russes; prima ballerina Carina Ari (1897–1970), who was based in Berlin at the time; Sent M'Ahesa (1883–1970) and Ruth St. Denis (1879–1968) of Oriental dance fame; Gret Palucca (1902–1993), the Wiesenthal sisters (Grete, 1885–1970, and Elza, 1887–1967); Alexander Sakharoff (1886–1963); Clotilde Sakharoff (1892–1974); among other *Neue Tanz* dancers.

Murayama described the shock of witnessing Mary Wigman's dance:

I've never seen such a serious dance before. Her skeletal face and serpentine body were brimming with ghastly power from fingertips to toes. She was at times nearly naked, with her discerning eyes closed to refuse the notion of interpretation, throwing her limbs to the floor and crawling. Always with astonishing solemnity and an exquisitely refined taste.[6]

Descriptions of Wigman's dance convey her frightening concentration as she worked to convert volatile feelings and the unstably changing human soul into definitive forms of movement. It's difficult to know which dance piece Murayama saw, but it may have been her signature solo piece *Witch Dance*, premiered in 1914, or a similar work. Murayama keenly recognized the characteristics of Wigman's highly Expressionist dance style. At the same time, he criticized Wigman's dance. The following passage, his parting words to Wigman, so to speak, is quoted from Murayama's dance theory, which he published immediately after his return to Japan. His shocking encounter with Wigman's dance is expressed in meandering poetic prose; he seemed to be repulsed by her dance, which powerfully combined beauty and ugliness:

> Of course I was terribly moved by it, but I didn't want to see it again—
> because I already saw them all,
> because she presented through and through,
> because too much perfection betrayed her ignoble taste,
> because her wrists turned in unworldly daintiness.[7]

Awash in strong emotions, Murayama immediately had an insight into the limitation of Wigman's notion of dance principle and necessitarianism. Individual experience and forms were the most important elements in Expressionist dance. Wigman believed that by presenting these forms, dancers were able to break through the confinement of individual experiences and gain empathy from a wider audience.

The principle of Wigman's Expressionist dance was that the pursuit of forms transcended individuals and sublimated universal expressions. Expressionist dance tried to attain perfect forms, to match the underlying emotions with expressed forms. Murayama thought that as their pursuit approached immaculate perfection, the intent to be Expressionistic revealed dancers' internal limitations. Murayama commented on Wigman's dance with irony: "It looked like a pitiful, lovely, and brave worm doing the most expert dance allowable for worms."[8]

Later, Ishii Baku, Eguchi Takaya 江口隆哉, and other leading figures of modern Japanese dance studied German Expressionist dance, especially by their favorite dancer, Wigman, and introduced it in Japan. It is obvious that Murayama had a completely opposite perspective. Murayama didn't try to learn the techniques of Western dance of that time as an advanced style of expression; instead, he attempted to grasp it as an equal and from a contemporary perspective. It seems he was criticizing the subjectivism of the artist at the center of Expressionism, which had a tendency toward fatalistic, pre-destinate, or universal themes. He also commented that many Expressionist dancers didn't reach for such themes, and only resorted to "cheap, obtrusive, and out-front histrionics" to pour out their personal distress.[9] At this point, Murayama hadn't ascribed such significance to dance.

## THE IMPEKOVEN SENSATION

Half a year after arriving in Berlin, in the autumn of 1922, Murayama became infatuated with the dance of Niddy Impekoven.[10] Murayama was in tears when a "little girl, with an ashen, swan-like body" quietly hopped three steps facing the audience to the strains of Beethoven's *Moonlight Sonata*.[11] This unusual excitement cannot be attributed only to the extreme stress of living abroad. He wrote,

> What great care for the sound, what great love for human emotions, what humble kindness that permeates to the atmosphere itself—she must have been raised by a modest and admirable mother. Or perchance—No, she is a sorceress. A tremendous witch.[12]

In addition to the wonder of simultaneously finding both innocent and demonic qualities in a small body, her "angular cheekbones, sunken eyes, too modest lips as if her teeth had fallen out, pale translucent skin, [and] dishev-eled blond hair" could not be simply considered lovely.[13] Her "otherworldly" bizarre appearance is reminiscent of the notion of decadence.

The Tanz Archive in Germany owns the actual footage of Niddy Impek-oven's dance piece *Life of a Flower*.[14] Let me provide the synopsis: on a dimly lit stage, a young girl in a simple one-piece dress desperately raises her arm to the sky as if she is pleading for a ray of light—it is a moment when a flower blooms in a faint light. The flower quietly opens and enjoys life for a while, but withers in the cold the next moment. In time it lays itself down on the ground, as if to return to the soil, and dies. This short dance piece depicts the modest life of a flower in approximately three minutes. Impekoven's delicate hand movements and the dramatic look of her eyes are striking. In another small piece called *Doll*, she dances as a puppet with clumsy movements. Wearing a striped coverall and a three-cornered hat like a Pierrot, her movements look painfully fragile, as if she is a brittle creature at the mercy of fate. Murayama wrote, "I fell headlong into Impekoven, and her dance drove me crazy night and day. I was beginning to wonder would there be any Art comparable to dance?"[15] His whole being was devastated by Impekoven's dance. Murayama commented that this encounter was only surpassed by his enlightenment when he read about Marxism.

## ESSENCE OF DANCE: THE DISCOVERY OF GESTICULATION

Captivated by Impekoven, Murayama started to reexamine dance as bodily expression. As soon as he returned to Japan, he published an idiosyncratic dance theory, "On the Essence of Dance." He summarized the following two points regarding the nature of dance in his study:

1. Dance must present the supreme wisdom of incompleteness.
2. Dance must present boundless love for music and spectators' emotions.
      The synthesis of the two is the biggest requirement; the heart of the dancer—the creator of dance—must be filled with the Ideal, i.e., a true existence.[16]

He reconsiders what a dance must be by questioning the awareness of the dancer, instead of utilizing existing dance theories.

The first essence says that a dance must be "incomplete." Then what is the complete dance? It is a dance as composite art, typically represented by classical ballet. Classical ballet inherits strict forms and style derived from the cultivated etiquette and attitudes of aristocrats and royalty. Murayama called ballet "engineered completeness," and he openly criticized it, saying "The same old theme is endlessly repeated with ridiculously superficial skills, cheap emotions, malicious music, and conspiring lights. As the time progresses, one cannot be always fooled by such things."[17]

Another example of "completeness" can be seen in the earlier quoted passage on Wigman's dance, "because too much completeness betrayed her ignoble taste." *Neue Tanz* defied classical ballet, but their effort to be faithful to their own new methodology led to a self-contained dance. Murayama criticized this closed system. Its "completeness" became an end unto itself. That's why Murayama could not be sympathetic toward *Neue Tanz*.

Instead of such "complete" dance, Murayama proposed the dance "as a whole life" as an example of "incomplete" dance. He stated, "Dance must present the supreme wisdom of incompleteness." This revelation was brought about by Impekoven's dance. Let me quote his detailed description of her movements:

> The technique of turning right with raised right shoulder and bringing her face up with a sudden grin from ear to ear, the technique of giving the impression that her upper right arm is partly sclerosed, and the technique of ascending to heaven at the moment when people were about to shout out "There's no hope!" in despair, all of these felt completely and terribly sacred to me.[18]

Murayama repeatedly called Impekoven's extremely natural movement expressions "techniques." The first two "techniques" of grinning and the upper arm are not "dancy" movements, but rather gesticulations. It is difficult to pinpoint the movements of the third "technique to ascend to heaven." This can be interpreted as something related to the music in the second essence, but the flow of dance here is an unexpected sudden movement. Verbal description of her movements becomes somewhat peculiar, because as professional as she was, Impekoven's dance was supposed to be composed of these innocent gesticulations. Innocent gesticulations are not limited by existing dances; they are newly born and immature, but their honesty and freedom easily transcend what dance is. Murayama dared to call these movements "techniques" as exemplary of "the supreme wisdom of incompleteness," that is, his essence of dance.

After coming back to Japan, Murayama commented on *Twelve Dances* (*Juuni no dansu* 十二のダンス), to be premiered in the autumn of 1923. He explained that he himself was going to put the "incompleteness led by wisdom" into practice.

> Throughout all these twelve dances, my left shoulder joint will be wobbly, leaving my left arm longer and hanging a little bit lower than the right arm, so my left and right arms would be very unevenly swinging—this would be the theme for this dance. Usually hand movements should change at the chord change of the music, but I could pretend not to notice it and keep the same motion.[19]

*Twelve Dances* was cancelled because of the Great Kantō Earthquake in September 1923, but it is very interesting that Murayama was planning to use unbalanced arm positions as a theme for the new dance piece. A wobbly left shoulder joint, lowered left arm, and uneven swinging would create a very peculiar movement for audiences accustomed to classical ballet or other

Fig. 4.1. Murayama Tomoyoshi dancing at Jiyū Gakuen in 1923. Source: *Murayama Tomoyoshi: Get All of Me Seething* exhibition catalogue, 2012. Photo no. III-134, p. 117.

existing dances' aesthetics of symmetry. There is something strange about this gesticulation. Also, hand movements usually change at a chord change in the music, but he said, "I could pretend not to notice it and keep the same motion." He was trying to avoid a conventional "dance" by intentionally continuing the movement.

Impekoven's innocent gesticulation and the peculiar gesticulation Murayama planned for *Twelve Dances* were human movements, but both were difficult to fit into the framework of dance. In spite of this, Murayama sensed future possibilities in such gesticulations, but he also warned that such engineering could "quickly degenerate into a crummy job" unless it was led with "extremely sensible guidance."[20]

## CONSCIOUS CONSTRUCTIVISM AND DANCE

The second essence of dance that Murayama proposed was "Dance must present boundless love for music and spectators' emotions." What did he mean by this? His explanation was insufficient and difficult to comprehend. At least for a dance accompanied by music, the ideal is when a dancer's existence becomes rhythm itself or melody itself, instead of audiences watching a dancer's bodily motions. Sensory perception of the body should be led by a transcending Ideal, a true existence. According to Murayama, such mystery of creation was unconsciously embodied in the dance of Impekoven.

Murayama was an avid fan of Impekoven, but he also wrote a scathing criticism at the end of "On the Essence of Dance." He flatly rejected a dance piece in which Impekoven interpreted four temperaments, saying it was "nothing but an obtrusive peddling of cheap emotions," just like what many other Expressionist dancers produced. A genius dancer like Impekoven cannot continue the unconscious innocent dance forever. That's why he concluded his study by stating that "Even a dazzling genius, if one is a true genius, must fall into my arms of Conscious Constructivism (*Ishiki-teki Kōsei shugi* 意識的構成主義) in the end."

Conscious Constructivism is a new concept of fine art proposed by Murayama based on his study in Germany. He explained that it was his inventive way of presenting fresh and powerful visual materials, rather than a direct influence of Russian Constructivists.[21] Visual objects in nature could be combined with abstract colors or shapes on canvases, but these were not simple abstraction because "No matter how abstract, these things are inevitably accompanied with a variety of suggestions."[22] Murayama proposed

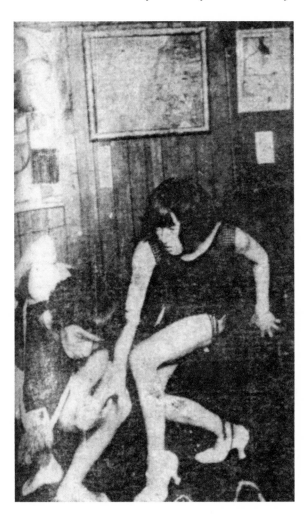

Fig. 4.2. Murayama
Tomoyoshi and Okada
Tatsuo dancing at
Chieruteru no kai
in 1924. Source:
*Murayama Tomoyoshi:
Get All of Me Seething*
exhibition catalogue,
2012. Photo no. III-137,
p. 119.

that "Artists should use this suggestion effect to make the content of painting richer and more complex," and he expanded this thought further: "In the
mixture of abstract colors and shapes, some materials can be introduced to
suggest concrete objects."[23] He developed a method to collage various materials with paint on canvases. Other than paints and canvases, these collages
were composed of cutouts of photographs and printed paper, metal springs,
pieces of wood, women's hair, slippers, and other elements. The interesting
point is that the suggestive effect of these materials attracts thoughts of other
materials to the minds of viewers, making the work richer and more com-

plex. Likewise, I assume, the human body can be attracted to these materials. For instance, it is possible to trace people's movements by looking at an object; an object can entice people to move, and some objects or fragments that are profoundly connected with somebody's life are left with their footprints. I would like to propose that Murayama used "gesticulations" to extract such vestigia of human bodies embedded in objects. These gesticulations are inherently antisocial. Let me put it this way: Murayama aspired to a supreme dance, but he proposed a factor—gesticulation—to destroy the dance itself from within. This contradictory relationship between the dance and gesticulation was, in other words, an expression beyond the framework of dance "as a whole life." This foreshadows Murayama's complete shift to theatrical plays at a later point.

*Gekijō no Sanka* (劇場の三科 *The Third Section in the Theater*) was premiered at Tsukiji Little Theatre (築地小劇場) in 1925. Artists advocating Futurism, Expressionism, Constructivism, Cubism, and Dadaism participated in this performance. It was a forerunner of the Neo Dadaism Organizers art movement in 1960s Japan. According to Yoshida Kenkichi 吉田謙吉 (1897–1982), who acted the role of newspaper deliveryman along with Yanase Masamu 柳瀬正夢 (1900–1945), Murayama gave them the direction, "Walk across downstage with clumsy movements."[24] And at the ending Murayama "danced two legitimate dance pieces, then danced an improvisation without music wearing only underwear and a bold hairpiece, accompanied by several other naked Mavoists."[25] This "legitimate dance" seems like dance accompanied by music and refers to the dance Murayama was practicing alone at Jiyū Gakuen (自由学園) Auditorium in Toshima, Tokyo. At that time, he was also involved with the Mavoist movement. Ishii Baku saw *Gekijō no Sanka* and his comment, "This is a very original dance, but it needs a little bit more physical training to improve it," probably referred to this "legitimate dance" (*chantoshita odori*).[26] Murayama Kazuko, Murayama's wife and a poet, wrote a poem called "Minuet in G" in which she described Murayama's dance as "beautiful on stage" accompanied by Beethoven's piece with the same title.[27] Murayama himself quoted her poetry and wrote, "This is proof that my dance belonged to a different dimension from my Mavoist compositions."[28] Senda Koreya 千田是也 (1904–1994) wrote an article on Murayama's dance, stating, "I was fairly impressed by Tom's dance. At least it was more beautiful than Baku Ishii. It was straightforward and refreshing compared to the very snobbish dance à la Sakharoff by Iwamura Kazuo 岩村和雄 (1902–1932)."[29] This too must have been Murayama's "legitimate dance."

Murayama must have separated improvisational bodily expressions as a Mavoist from dance accompanied by the music of Beethoven or Hummel. He seemed to be practicing completely different body expressions in parallel. While engaged in the Mavoist art movement, he was also practicing such "legitimate dance" (*chantosita odori*) alone at Jiyū Gakuen Auditorium with a Victor portable phonograph.

> It didn't use any conventional techniques like ballet, but it wasn't a novelty-seeking or grotesque movement; and it was certainly not a movement to symbolize sexual behaviors; it was something in the style of Impekoven. Guided by music, I tried to fuse the music with body movement; I only had four or five repertoires, but I honed them over and over, night after night.[30]

People who felt Murayama's dance was "beautiful" watched this free-style "legitimate dance" accompanied by music. The dance Murayama performed at Hongō Buddhist Hall (本郷仏教会館) in the spring of 1925 and the two pieces at the end of *Gekijō no Sanka* the same year must have been this kind of dance. His comment "in the style of Impekoven" must refer to the musicality of her dance. He was practicing four or five repertoires of "legitimate dance" for a couple of years, but then moved away from dancing to focus on designing stage sets and directing theater plays.

According to his second essence of dance, "Dance must present boundless love for music and spectators' emotions." And if the realization of this essence was the "legitimate dance," it might contradict his own invention, Conscious Constructivism. His "legitimate dance" sublimated presentable movements from the feelings inspired by music; it was a pure dance. Contrary to this, he proposed Conscious Constructivism because only gesticulations based on sensory perception of the body can make expressions richer and more complex. As he leaned toward Conscious Constructivism, Murayama's dance must have been directed away from "legitimate dance."

The dancer Murayama Tomoyoshi didn't even leave a trace at the beginning of Japanese dance in modern times, mainly because he actually danced for a very limited time, didn't take disciples, and didn't form an organization to hand down his dance to posterity. It should be pointed out that he was able to deepen his own dance philosophy because he did not have any connections with the dance world. Although he admitted it must always change, Murayama stated Conscious Constructivism's interpretation of the notion of beauty as follows:

Ultimately it is always vibrating at any moment, from extreme opposite to another extreme opposite.

That's why if an Artist wants to get closer to the truth, they must always consciously deny their tendency to fixate, and vibrate toward the opposite tendency.[31]

The two elements that Murayama identified as "the essence of dance" contradicted each other; this could have contributed to the brevity of his active period as a dancer. His endeavor to achieve more clarity in expression by constantly going back and forth between conflicting elements was quite modernistic. This internal conflict also forced Murayama to perceive the body as a sensory existence that cannot be fully aggregated into the domain of expression called dance. He pursued dance as a history of body awareness rather than a history of dance techniques in modern times. In this respect, Murayama was a noteworthy dancer who differed substantially from other representatives of modern Japanese dance history.

CONCLUSION

This essay examines Murayama Tomoyoshi and dance in relation to the emerging German dancer Niddy Impekoven in the 1920s. Murayama received two paradoxical revelations from Impekoven: the discovery of gesticulation and pursuit of a pure dance. After his return from Germany, Murayama called himself a dancer, and although it was only for a brief couple of years, he actively performed on and off stage. Murayama created a highly improvisational performance with other members of the Mavoist movement. This might be linked with the origin of performance art as gesticulations of living artists that was spread all over Europe by Italian Futurists in the beginning of the twentieth century. At the same time, Murayama was also developing dance pieces accompanied by music; this coincided with abstract dance that rose to prominence alongside Expressionist dance in the world dance history of modern times. Likewise, Murayama advocated a stage constructed with materials for expression based on the Ideal, instead of dance that expressed the internal nature of individuals.

Murayama came back to Japan in 1923. At that time, Ishii Baku and the other leading figures of modern Japanese dance in later years were away in Europe or the United States. A foundation for the acceptance of new Western dances had not been established yet in Japan. It was understandable that Murayama was critical of the gradual popularization of modern Japanese dance, which leaned on Expressionism, and never took part in it. It was a fact that the contradiction between two elements he pointed out as the essence of dance and Conscious Constructivism alienated him from dancing. In the latter half of the 1920s, Murayama turned toward left-wing theater and concentrated on his work as a stage set designer and director.

Impekoven's dance taught Murayama two elements of the nature of dance. He embraced the aspect of pure dance and the gesticulation that presented incomplete bodily existence. Murayama realized that these elements contradicted each other, and their offsetting nature led him away from dance. Dance expression has both spiritual and extremely corporeal natures at the same time. In the 1920s Murayama was already aware of this radical issue: dance as a sublimation of the Ideal, a true existence, and dance as ultimate bodily expression. Modern Japanese dance history has always been discussed as a part of the history of the importation of Western culture to Japan and has only highlighted the Imperial Theatre. By introducing Murayama Tomoyoshi as a dancer, this accepted view should be reassessed as a history of body awareness.

ADDITIONAL RESOURCES

Full resolution versions of Figure 4.1 at https://doi.org/10.3998/ mpub.11521701.cmp.7 and Figure 4.2 at https://doi.org/10.3998/ mpub.11521701.cmp.8

Link 4.1: Encyclopedia entry "Murayama, Tomoyoshi (1901–1977)" by Diane Wei Lewis in *Routledge Enclyclopedia of Modernism.* Available at https://doi. org/10.3998/mpub.11521701.cmp.38

## Notes

1. Kuriyama, Jun 栗山淳, "*Niddy Impekoven o meguru oboegaki 1, 2, 3,*" ニディ・イ ンペコーフェンをめぐる覚え書き1, 2, 3 [Notes on Niddy Impekoven 1,2,3], in *Taishō Engeki Kenkyū* 大正演劇研究, vols. 28, 29, 30 (Tokyo: Taisho Engeki Kenkyu-kai, 1990), vol. 28, 6–9; vol. 29, 8–11; vol. 30, 25–27. Kanbe, Keiko 神戸圭子, "*Impekoven o tazunete: part 1, 2, 3*" インペコーフェンを訪ねて上・中・下 [Visiting Impekoven 1, 2, 3], in *Taishō Engeki Kenkyū* 大正演劇研究 , vols. 28, 29, 30 (Tokyo: Taishō Engeki Kenkyū-kai, 1990), vol. 28, 5; vol. 29, 6–7; vol. 30, 21–24. "Niddy Impekoven o tazunete jou, chu, ge," *Suisei Tsushin* 水声通信, vol. 3 (January 2006). See also Gennifer Weis-

enfeld, *Mavo: Japanese Artists and the Avant-Garde 1905–1931* (Berkeley: University of California Press, 2002).

2. These diplomatic missions reported back to Japan that theaters had much significance as a place for social interactions, and that it was standard practice in Western countries to invite diplomatic state visitors to the theater.

3. Mori Rintarō 森林太郎 / Mori Ōgai 森鴎外 (1862–1922) translated the Futurist Manifesto into Japanese only three months after it was published by Filippo Tommaso Marinetti. Also, in 1911, poet and sculptor Takamura Kotarō 高村光太郎 published his art theory in "Midori iro no taiyō" 緑色の太陽 [*Green Sun*], *Subaru* スバル. (Tokyo) (April 1910), 170.

4. The voyage to Europe usually took approximately two months at that time. According to Senda Koreya (Tomu to Odori, 81). Murayama arrived in Berlin in February 1922. His departure must have been in December 1921. Murayama came back to Japan at the end of January 1923, so he probably left Berlin around November 1922. He stayed in Germany for ten months or so.

5. Murayama, Tomoyoshi 村山知義, " Engekiteki jijoden" 演劇的自叙伝 2    [*Theatrical Autobiography 2*], Tōhō Shuppannsha 東邦出版社 (Tokyo) (1970): 86.

6. Ibid., 87.

7. Murayama, Tomoyoshi 村山知義, "Dansu no honshitsu ni tsuite" ダンスの本質について [ On the Essence of Dance], *Chuou Bijutsu* 中央美術 (Tokyo) (July 1923): 169.

8. Ibid., 169.

9. Ibid., 176.

10. Details about Niddy Impekoven can be found in Senda Koreya 千田是也, "Tomu to odori" トムと踊り[*Tom and Dance*], *Teatoro* テアトロ (Tokyo) (June 1977): 80–86.

11. Ibid.,170–71.

12. Ibid., 172.

13. Ibid., 171.

14. 16 mm film transferred to videotape by Tanz Archive.

15. Murayama (1923): 173.

16. Ibid., 164. Throughout this essay, Murayama's use of the word *Ideal* refers to Plato's Theory of Ideas. According to this theory, the true existence is Idea. What a human being perceives and the world that a human being feels and touches are only a Nemesis, similitude of Idea.

17. Ibid., 165.

18. Ibid., 172.

19. Ibid., 177.

20. Ibid., 177.

21. Murayama, "Engekiteki jijoden."

22. Ibid., 147

23. Ibid.,147.

24. Yoshida, Kenkichi 吉田謙吉, "Gekijō no Sanka" 劇場の三科 [The Third Section in the Theater], *Hon no Techō* 本の手帖 (Tokyo) (May 1963): 146.

25. Murayama, "Engekiteki jijoden," 293.

26. Ibid., 293.

27. Ibid., 186.

28. Ibid., 286.

29. Senda Koreya, "Tomu to odori," 80.

30. Murayama 1970, "Engekiteki jijoden," 280.

31. Murayama, Tomoyoshi 村山知義, "Watashi no avant garde jidai" 私のアバンギャルド時代 [My Avant-garde Days], *Hon no Techou* 本の手帖 (Tokyo) (May 1963): 14.

# CHAPTER 5

# Korean Dance Beyond Koreanness

## Park Yeong-in in the German Modern Dance Scene

*Okju Son* 손옥주

> Westerners in general laugh at the Japanese when the Japanese play the piano, sing opera, and perform ballet. [ ... ] However, we have felt hostility against such views by Westerners. We are just as good as they are. [ ... ] We have believed we can achieve better results than Westerners in culture and the arts by learning theirs like we already have in science and sports. [ ... ] But, can we actually overcome them by learning their arts? Is it really possible?[1]

In his essay quoted above, the Korean-Japanese modern dancer Park Yeong-in (박영인, 朴永仁, also known by his Japanese name, Kuni Masami 邦正美, 1908–2007)[2] reveals a stereotypical way of thinking about the Japanese (with whom he identifies) and Westerners that was widespread in East Asia during the modern era. He sees the possibility of "successful" Westernization in a modernized Japan, yet he also anticipates the impossibility of "complete" or "perfect" Westernization by the Japanese, or rather Asians in general. As a symbolic figure from East Asia who moved between Korea, Japan, and Germany in the early and mid-twentieth century, Park embodied the intercultural and political conflicts of this turbulent era. Interestingly, however, Park's stereotypical imaginings, which were closely related to the modern idea of the nation-state, dissolved in his dancing body. Park's dancing body became a cultural melting pot through his studies of different movement languages, such as ballet, Western modern dance, Japanese dance, and Korean dance. This enabled him to create hybrid, multilayered dance characters and, finally, to perform modernized Korean dances on European stages.

The hybridity and complexity of Park's dances reflect two distinct features of modernity in Korean dance. First, "Korean dance" was established as a concept in contrast to "Western dance" during the modern era. Second, representative Korean dances were ironically born through an "inversion of perspective" of Korean modern dancers, who began their careers practicing Western modern dance but then changed their choreographic style from

Western modern dance to Korean dance.[3] This means that many dances introduced as "traditional Korean dance" on the modern global stage were not transmitted from generation to generation, but instead were largely initiated by Korean modern dancers known as *Sinmuyongga* 新舞踊家 (literally, "artists of New Dance"), of whom Park is one example. The work of these *Sinmuyongga* is closely related to the development of dance in Japan. This is because *Sinmuyongga* began their dance careers learning Western dance genres such as classical ballet, rhythmic gymnastics, and expressive dance in Japan during the period when Korea was under Japanese colonial occupation (1910–1945). In the early and mid-1930s, many *Sinmuyongga* were studying in Japan (as were dancers from elsewhere in the Japanese empire) when they began to create new works on traditional Korean themes. These works, though initially known as *Sinmuyong* (新舞踊, New Dance), came to be understood by many as traditional Korean dance.

In this chapter, I pose the following questions: What did "Dancing Korean" actually mean to Korean *Sinmuyongga* such as Park, especially when they left Japan in the late 1930s and began to tour outside East Asia? Why did they sometimes strive to erase their educational background in Western dance and instead display their dancing bodies in a framework of "premodern, authentic" Korean images? The complex trajectories of the life and dance of Park Yeong-in can offer one starting point to answer these questions. By concentrating on his experiences in Japan in the mid-1930s and his career in Germany from 1937 to 1945, I explore how Park negotiated complex political and cultural positions and expressed hybridity in the movement language that characterized his Korean-themed *Sinmuyong* dance pieces performed in Europe.

## INFLUENCE OF THE GERMAN *AUSDRUCKSTANZ* ON KOREAN *SINMUYONG*

Early Western modern dance artists, especially practitioners of German *Ausdruckstanz*, exerted a crucial influence on Korean *Sinmuyongga* such as Park in Japan before they left Asia. This is because many of the *Sinmuyongga's* Japanese teachers were renowned Japanese modern dancers who had either seen Western modern dance performances in the West while they were on tour or actually trained with European teachers.[4] Some of these Korean dancers also developed their own approaches on the basis of Western dance practices, combining Émile Jaques-Dalcroze's rhythmic training, Mary Wigman's use of percussion instruments, and even classical ballet movements to create new experiments.[5]

The *Ausdruckstanz* (sometimes translated as "expressionist dance") was a social movement in the European dance community that emerged during World War I, with the goal of liberating art from a dehumanized sociocultural environment and returning its focus to human nature.[6] The creators of this new form of dance conceptualized it as an alternative to conventional European dance forms such as classical ballet and as being "concerned with dance as a philosophical, metaphysical or even spiritual statement."[7] However, we should not overlook that such a paradigm shift in dance was brought about by the advent of a modern dance education system, which many Asian dancers experienced directly or indirectly at the same time as their European counterparts. Western modern dancers, including the dancers of the *Ausdruckstanz*, actively established their own training methods, opened private dance schools, and organized workshops for both professional and amateur dancers. As a result, dance movements became more than technical feats performed by professionals and expanded into everyday physical training for everyone.

In this context, there are two important advocates of *Ausdruckstanz*, Émile Jaques-Dalcroze (1865–1950) and Mary Wigman (1886–1973), whose different perspectives on the essence of dance are important for contextualizing Park's work, because their theories and practical training methods were crucial for the development of *Sinmuyong* in Korea. Émile Jaques-Dalcroze, the Swiss music educator and a forerunner of *Ausdruckstanz*, argued that "the rhythmicity comes from an embodiment of music," and that this kind of embodiment is oriented toward the "regulation of natural rhythm of the body."[8] Based on this theoretical foundation, Jaques-Dalcroze created a unique teaching method that involved the accompaniment of a musical instrument such as the piano. In a typical class at Jaques-Dalcroze's school in Hellerau, students in dance leotards would improvise their steps and hand movements, accompanied by music of constantly varying tempo, duration, and dynamics. As a group, their dancing would create a mysterious, almost ritualistic atmosphere.[9] Contrary to Jaques-Dalcroze, who put more emphasis on the embodiment of rhythm and experiencing music through movement, the German dancer Mary Wigman was concerned with expressing one's inner feelings through movement without the accompaniment of carefully constructed rhythms. Hence, spontaneous physical movements form the core of her artistic statement: "Body and physical movement are one in dance!"[10] The beat from a percussion instrument played a decisive role in Wigman's dance to stimulate the body's natural rhythms, whereas for Jaques-Dalcroze the diversity of musical tempo in eurhythmics controlled those rhythms.[11] Both of these training concepts were deep and fundamental principles that worked together or in tension in the dancers of *Ausdruckstanz*.

For Korean *Sinmuyongga*, in contrast to the advocates of European *Ausdruckstanz*, dancing as a medium for expressing one's inner feelings did not mean emancipation from conventional dance, since they had no specific dance genre that they passionately wished to overcome or from which they sought to free themselves. Instead, Korean *Sinmuyongga* perceived the theories and practices of Western modern dancers as symbols of modernization, enlightenment, and development. Like many artists and intellectuals across East Asia during the early twentieth century, the Korean *Sinmuyongga* saw the physical distance between the East and West as corresponding to a temporal distance between the premodern and modern eras. By internalizing the modern "temporal" spirit of dance, they believed that the East and West would ultimately become one. For instance, Park Yeong-in wrote in an undated essay,

> As far as body technique is concerned, West and East have been going their own ways for many centuries. The New Dance Movement initiated in the Central European countries, however, has changed this disparate phenomenon and extinguished the line between East and West once and for all. The New Dance—*Der Ausdruckstanz*—advocated the expression of feeling through total body movement. [ ... ] At once, East and West, past and present, rediscovered one another, and so the course was set for future innovation and delight.[12]

This essay suggests that Park struggled to become proficient in the New Dance with the aim of approaching the same level as Western dancers in (e)motional expressivity. Accordingly, he strove to learn Western modern dance without considering what that endeavor actually meant in the Korean or Japanese context. Such voluntary efforts to learn Western modern dance were mainly made by Korean *Sinmuyongga* within the context of a modern education system in Japan that encouraged the study of Western ideas in many fields. The *Sinmuyongga* therefore came to view and study indigenous (Korean) dance culture through a modern lens that led them to alienate themselves from their own dance heritage.

## A REVERSAL OF WHAT IT MEANS TO DANCE:
## FROM CREATING THE NEW TO DISCOVERING THE OLD

To understand modern Korean dance history, we must first understand that its chronology may appear to be reversed. A reverse chronology of dance in this context entails the question of why Korean *Sinmuyong*, which literally means "New Dance" in Korean, is today paradoxically associated with stylized, reformed, or even "pseudo" Korean dance.[13] This is because in the 1930s, *Sinmuyongga* such as Park Yeong-in, Choe Seung-hui 최승희/崔承喜 (aka Choi Seung-hee, 1911–1969), and Cho Taek-won 조택원/趙澤元 (1907–1976) radically switched their dance styles from modern Western to Korean, a style that in many cases they had never learned before. One significant impetus for these dancers' interest in the indigenous dance of Korea was, paradoxically, the 1936 Anti-Comintern Pact between Japan and Germany, which enabled Japanese and Korean dancers to have more advanced cultural exchanges with European dancers.[14] Following the Pact, many Korean *Sinmuyongga* had opportunities from the mid-1930s to tour Germany and other Western countries or to study in Europe with financial support from the Japanese government. One result of such exchanges was that many *Sinmuyongga* tried to locate themselves as "the Korean" or rather "the Asian" in the European dance scene, rather than position themselves as "modernists." Many chose to Koreanize or Asianize their dances during their time abroad, even though they were regarded as pioneers of New Dance in their home country (although most began this process of Koreanization or Asianization before they left Japan). I will suggest some explanations for why they did not articulate their own modernized artistic presence on the European stage by examining the trajectory of Park Yeong-in's dance career before and after he left Tokyo for Berlin, using newspaper articles, magazine stories, and dance programs of the time.[15]

Park Yeong-in was born in a liberal Korean family in 1908 in Ulsan, Korea, two years before the Japanese annexation of Korea. After attending primary and middle schools in Japan-colonized Korea, he moved to Japan for higher education and to experience culture. Park entered the Matsue High School in Japan and then went on to study aesthetics in the renowned Tokyo Imperial University.[16] While at university, for around six months Park studied dance at the private dance school of Ishii Baku 石井漠 (1886–1962), who is considered the father of Japanese modern dance. Additionally, Park got in touch with several Western dancers, who also taught him the basics of ballet and Western modern dance.[17] Those experiences motivated him to organize his first dance recital at the Japan Youth Hall in Tokyo on January 18, 1933. At that time, Park's dance program consisted mainly of abstract and expressive dance pieces, some of which, including *The Genesis* (創世記) and *The fin de siècle* (世紀末), were thought to reveal the intellect of the choreographer.[18] Afterward, Park met Gertrud Bodenwieser (1890–1959) from Austria, a pioneer of *Ausdruckstanz*, when she visited Park's dance recital during her tour in Japan in 1934.[19] This encounter marked a turning point in Park's dance career and provided momentum for his decision to move to Europe. In fact, Park had been keenly interested in German philosophy and music since his studies in aesthetics, so much so that he confessed in his autobiography, *Berurin Sensō* (Berlin War), that he went to Berlin because he "dreamed of this city."[20] Park's statement unveils his adoration for Berlin, which functioned as a central metropolis for European culture at the time.

Park finally departed for Europe in September 1936 and arrived at Berlin in late February of 1937.[21] Shortly after, on March 7, Park got an opportunity to give the Berlin audience his first dance recital. While working as a professional dancer, Park continued learning dance under Mary Wigman and others at the *Deutsche Meisterwerkstätte für Tanz* (the German Master Workshops for Dance) in Berlin. According to a Korean newspaper, Japanese dancers "have received enthusiastic response from the audience" since the Anti-Comintern Pact between Japan and Germany, and among them Park was working hard "for the dance scene of the Korean peninsula."[22] Another Korean newspaper reported that Park's most popular dances in Berlin were *Seungmu* (Monk Dance) and *Nongbuui Chum* (Farmer's Dance),"[23] both of which were associated with traditional Korean dances. These reports indicate that Park presumably preferred to perform, not Western modern dance inspired by his *Ausdruckstanz* training, but rather "Asian" dances associated with traditional Korean forms on the German stage. The *Maeil Sinbo* article included a letter that Park wrote to his friend:

> I arrived in Berlin in late February, and I was already able to give a dance performance on March 7 at the National Theatre (Editor's note: On this day, Mr. Park performed the Korean Farmer's Dance). No one could've imagined that an Asian dancer would perform at the National Theatre, and I was moved to tears because it was a great honor for me. [ ... ] My dance is the so-called "New Dance" based on Western dance. But many favorable comments from the audience here prove how much they are interested in my dance. Apart from going on stage, I am also teaching classes at dance schools, and newcomers from the German artistic scene are learning my dance with great passion [ ... ].[24]

In this letter, Park pointed out a noticeable difference between his choreographic intention and the reaction of the German audience. While he himself regarded his dances as a kind of "new dance" that emphasized its Western philosophical and artistic roots, a German journalist nevertheless introduced Park to the German audience as a paragon of "ancient Japanese dance culture and mime art."[25] On the one hand, Park's dancing body represented a specific understanding of antiquity that corresponded to the stereotypes the German audience had of Asian art. On the other hand, Park recognized the antiquity or tradition of Asian dance as a creative source for his own choreography. In this sense, Park demonstrated on stage the intertwined relationship between tradition and modernity by creatively and intentionally "Asianizing" his dance program. To do this, he built on the *Sinmuyong* repertoire already being developed by Korean *Sinmuyongga* (including himself) in Japan.

Apart from giving stage performances, Park taught "Asian dance" at the *Deutsche Meisterwerkstätte für Tanz* beginning in late 1938 and worked as a correspondent for *Dōmei Tsūshin* (Domei News), which published propaganda for the Japanese Empire aimed at foreign countries, until the end of World War II.[26] After the war, Park returned to Japan after a short stay in Korea and was naturalized as a Japanese citizen instead of returning to Korea. In 1961, he immigrated to the United States. Park regularly traveled back and forth between the US and Japan until his death in Tokyo in April 2007.[27]

### SHOWCASING ETHNICITY ON THE MODERN GERMAN STAGE

When creating his Asian-themed *Sinmuyong* works, Park found his artistic impulse in existing Korean dances, which he used as the subject matter for his choreography, creating expressive dance pieces with the results of his research. There seem to be three stages to Park's choreographic choices during this period: first the impulse from tradition, then the exploration of that subject matter, and finally a filtering through his physical knowledge of expressive dance training. Each of these stages needs to be carefully examined in the context of his "Asian" position in 1937 Berlin.

Park's dance program for a recital on June 3, 1937, in the *Kuppelsaal* makes possible a more concrete approach to Park Yeong-in's work on the Berlin stage. As the recital was held about four months after his arrival in Berlin, the program especially reflects his initial early work in the city. The printed program not only tells us the title of each dance performed, but also the intent of some of his choreography. According to the program, he presented eight pieces under the main title, *Japanische Tänze* (Japanese Dances), in the following order: *Erinnerung an ein altes Schloß* (Memory of an Old Castle), *Yamabushi* (*Bergpriester*, or Mountain Priest), *Tsurugi-no-mai* (*Dolchtanz*, or Sword Dance), *Haya-bikyaku* (*Bote*, or Messenger), *Tsukushi-mai* (*Tsukushi* Dance, a folk dance), *Shi-ki* (*Die vier Jahreszeiten*, or the Four Seasons), *Tanz eines koreanischen Bräutigams* (Dance of a Korean Bridegroom), and *Träumereien eines Anglers* (Woolgathering of a Fisherman). As these titles indicate, most of them borrowed their subject matter from Japanese fairy tales, literature, music, and costume. The printed program shows that Park wore a "Fujiwara era [tenth- to eleventh-century]–style costume" and played "an old [Japanese] folksong" as background music for the first piece, *Erinnerung an ein altes Schloß*. In addition, he integrated elements of a Japanese folk dance that appeared in "the thirteenth century in the Kyushu region" of southern Japan into his *Tsukushi-mai*. For his performance of *Shi-ki*, he danced wearing a "half mask" that was modeled after the ones excavated at "the Imperial Treasury of Nara in the seventh and eighth centuries."[28]

In some of these pieces Park chose Korean culture as a central theme. He also mentions clearly on the program that some of his choreography was inspired by Korean art and culture. For example, he describes the *Tsurugi-no-mai* as a "sword dance" that has been performed "in Japan and Korea since the Tempyō period (around 800)."[29] Due to the lack of footage or still images of this piece, however, it is impossible to describe its composition and characteristics in detail or to draw an in-depth comparison with other extant sword dances from Korea. Nevertheless, we can suppose that Park's solo sword dance, which his printed program describes in relation to the Japanese *Komagaku* 高麗樂 (a section from the Japanese court performance *Gagaku* that is based in ancient Korean music), would probably not have been exactly the same as the Korean *Geommu* 劍舞 (sword dance). This is because the Korean *Geommu* is known to have appeared in about 660 CE during the Silla period (57 BCE–935 CE) as a public mask dance to console the spirit of deceased warriors, before being performed actively in the royal court from the Sunjo period (1800–1834).[30] According to historical records, Korean *Geommu* was typically a group dance, not a solo, and the number of group performers varied depending on the situation or context of each dance performance.[31] This suggests that, like the other works on the program, the *Tsurugi-no-mai* was an original choreography of Park's making, not an inherited court or folk dance.

Another noteworthy example referring to Korea is the *Tanz eines koreanischen Bräutigams*. Even though no extra explanation was added to this dance on the program, we can find more clues in a picture published by the German Nazi propaganda magazine *Freude und Arbeit* (Joy and Work) in 1937. One page of this magazine features seven photographs of Park, including those capturing his dance poses, backstage preparation, and rehearsal with a German pianist.[32] This page also contains a short introduction about the dancer for the benefit of readers. In the third photograph, entitled *Mikonshano Odori/Koreanischer Hochzeitstanz* (Korean Wedding Dance), Park appears in a traditional Korean male costume and a small straw hat.[33] The photograph shows Park in front of the theater stairs striking a pose: he is standing and stretching out his right arm, with his wrist and fingers looking slightly relaxed because they are drooping down. This particular pose has elements of both Western dance (the arm held out rigidly straight) and Korean dance (the wrist and fingers relaxed and pointing downward). These elements, combined with Park's ethnic costume, give his performance a hybrid character to observers today.[34] The scene depicted in the photograph very closely resembles a widely performed Korean *Sinmuyong* choreography called *Choripdong* (초립동), or the dance of a straw-hatted child, which expresses the joy of a young bridegroom after his marriage. Both male and female Korean *Sinmuyongga* liked to perform the dynamic, diversified movements of such bridegrooms in *Hanbok*, or traditional Korean attire. Likewise, Park would have also choreographed his own version of *Choripdong*. It is possible that the extreme cheerful and rhythmical movements of *Choripdong* led *Sinmuyongga* such as Park to discover a core of modern expressive dance in this kind of movement vocabulary.

Such visual hybridity is also seen in *Nembutsu/Koreanischer Priestertanz* (Korean Monk Dance). This dance is not listed on Park Yeong-in's dance program cited above, but it is captured in the fourth of the seven photographs printed by *Freude und Arbeit*. Therefore, we can guess that Park would have either actually performed it at his Berlin recital or at least tried to introduce this important *Sinmuyong* piece to the German audience by demonstrating a pose for the magazine's photo shoot.[35] What is most remarkable about the *Nembutsu* photograph is the costume, which clearly represents the Korean *Seungmu* 僧舞, or monk dance. *Seungmu* was created in the early twentieth century by various *Sinmuyongga*, who "elaborated" on an old Buddhist dance named *Beobgomu* 法鼓舞 (Buddhist Drum Dance) and "created an adaptation of it for performance in a concert setting."[36] The newly created dance was typically performed as a solo and "begins with a lengthy, slow introduction" that involves "the manipulation of extremely long sleeves."[37] The piece gradually builds to the climactic scene of drum playing. A tremendous con-

Fig. 5.1. Masami Kuni (Park Yeong-in) in *Mikonshano Odori*, n.d. Photographer unknown. Courtesy Deutsches Tanzarchiv Köln.

trast between the sweeping movements of long sleeves and the powerful, rhythmic beat of the drum portrayed the diversity of human life. To maximize such aesthetic effects, *Seungmu* uses a special costume comprising three parts: *Jangsam* 장삼 (a white or black robe with long sleeves), *Gasa* 가사 (a red band draped across the chest from shoulder to waist), and *Gokkal* 고깔 (a white peaked hat). In the *Nembutsu* photograph, Park is wearing a typical *Seungmu* costume and putting his hands together in front of his chest as if in prayer. The symmetry of his hands and arms in the center of the photograph gives the impression of a systematic movement, reflecting artistic trends of the early twentieth century such as Constructivism. Park stares intensely into the air in a standing position, creating the impression not only of a well-constructed dance movement, but of a spiritual aura befitting the portrayal of a monk.[38]

The above examples all show that Park appropriated his knowledge of

Fig. 5.2. Masami
Kuni (Park Yeong-in)
in *Nembutsu*, n.d.
Photographer
unknown. Courtesy
Deutsches Tanzarchiv
Köln.

a type of alienated and neutralized Korean and Japanese culture to choreograph a new kind of dance that connected him to his European audiences.
Park's enhanced ability to communicate with the Western audience eventually converged with his aesthetic experiments to "Koreanize" his dance
style. Moreover, within the wartime context, this aestheticization of Korean
dance, which was interpreted at the time as a local culture of the Japanese
empire, also contributed to promoting Japanese art as a way to counteract
the threat of Japanese military activity in the 1930s and 40s. This is because
while Park Yeong-in resided in Berlin in the 1930s and 1940s, in addition to
performing and teaching, he was highly admired as a Japanese dance scholar
who provided a wealth of information about Japanese dance culture to locals
by publishing articles in German. Park's German-language dance writings
strengthened existing stereotypical images about traditional Japanese dance

in Europe, which contrasted sharply with the violent and barbaric image of modern Japanese imperial power. [39]

## THE PROBLEM OF MULTILAYERED IN-BETWEENNESS
## IN PARK'S DANCE

> What the dancer needs most is to have his own superior *weltanschauung*. Only dance based on that is real dance.[40]

Park's interest in East Asian material did not begin after his arrival in Germany. Rather, in the beginning of 1936, before his departure to Europe, Park had already spoken of his aspirations to research Korean dance.[41] His concern from the outset, however, was not to reenact Korean dance, but to try to infuse his distinctive weltanschauung, or worldview, into it. Accordingly, he strove to craft a unique dance that would not eliminate the nuances of old Korean dance but would propose a "contemporary tradition" by Koreanizing Park's own expressive dance movements. Like other *Sinmuyongga*, Park regarded his artistic experiments on Korean dance as a means to modernize dance. His understanding of ethnicity or indigenousness in the framework of modern discourse enabled him to invent an ambiguous and multidimensional tradition by choreographing dance pieces that spoke to multiple audiences.

If we consider the process of representing Korean tradition revealed in Park's dance during the turbulent Japanese colonial era, we can recognize a link between the mechanism of modernizing tradition triggered by Korea's colonial experience and Park's internalization of the philosophy, artistic statements, choreographic direction, and dance-training techniques of the *Ausdruckstanz* pioneers. For Korean *Sinmuyongga* such as Park, choreographing dance required understanding it, which they did using the criteria for "reading" dance as laid down by the modern education system. Yet, the *Sinmuyongga* did not deeply reflect on these criteria as specific tools for a representation of their own "in-betweenness"—"between Asia and Europe, between dance tradition and dance modernity, and between dance theory and dance practice."[42] Thus, their self-represented expression was bound to a preexisting framework for interpreting the meaning behind their dance movements. Precisely because they were created within this externally derived framework, however, Park's Korean dance also became readable internationally.

ADDITIONAL RESOURCES

Digital versions (with institutional watermark) of Figure 5.1 at https://doi.org/10.3998/mpub.11521701.cmp.9 and Figure 5.2 at https://doi.org/10.3998/mpub.11521701.cmp.10

Link 5.1: Homepage of the *Kuni Institute of Creative Dance* (in Japanese). Available at https://doi.org/10.3998/mpub.11521701.cmp.39

Link 5.2: TV Program: Finding Your Roots—Fred Armisen on his grandfather Park Yeong-in. Available at https://doi.org/10.3998/mpub.11521701.cmp.40

Link 5.3: News Report (USA Today)—Fred Armisen. Available at https://doi.org/10.3998/mpub.11521701.cmp.41

Link 5.4: Review of the Book *Masami Kuni* (Tokyo: Ronsosha, 1998) (in Japanese. Available at https://doi.org/10.3998/mpub.11521701.cmp.42

Link 5.5: Web Magazine Article about Park Yeong-in, part 1 (in Korean). Available at https://doi.org/10.3998/mpub.11521701.cmp.43

Link 5.6: Web Magazine Article about Park Yeong-in, part 2 (in Korean). Available at https://doi.org/10.3998/mpub.11521701.cmp.44

*Notes*

1. Park Yeong-in 朴永仁, "Naui Hoeui" 나의 懷疑, qtd. in Cho Taek-won 趙澤元, "Joseon Muyongui Sae Jillo" 朝鮮舞踊의 새進路, *Donga Ilbo* 東亞日報, Evening Edition, November 23, 1938, 5. Another Korean *Sinmuyongga*, Cho Taek-won, quoted Park's essay entitled *Naui Hoeui* to support his opinion that Western dancers cannot surpass Korean dancers in Korean traditional dance. However, as Park's full essay was not included in Cho's article, it is unfortunately only partially available.

2. In this essay, I deliberately use Park's Korean name rather than his Japanese name, Kuni Masami, which was officially used at the time. This essay aims to trace Park's ambivalent self-(re)presentation as a modern Japanese dancer from colonized Korea. Therefore, recalling his original Korean name is the first step toward accessing the multidimensionality of Park's life and dance.

3. In his book *Origins of Modern Japanese Literature*, Karatani Kōjin (柄谷 行人), a Japanese radical philosopher of the "modern" in Japanese literature, politics, society, and aesthetics, understands "inversion" not as "a matter of vision," but as something

that "transforms our mode of perception" and as "a semiotic configuration" that "does not take place either inside of us or outside of us." Karatani Kōjin, *Origins of Modern Japanese Literature*, trans. Brett de Bary, (Durham, NC: Duke University Press, 1998 [1993]), 27. If this notion is applied to the modernity of Korean dance, such inversion can be understood as a nexus that connects an external, politico-cultural framework (of the colonizer) to an internal, spontaneous assimilation (of the colonized), so that it takes place neither inside nor outside of Korean *Sinmuyongga*, but in between.

4. Cultural exchanges, including those in dance, between Japan and European countries were frequent during the modern period. For instance, many pioneers of Japanese modern dance, such as Ishii Baku, Itō Michio, Eguchi Takaya, Miya Misako, Takada Masao, and Takada Seiko went to Germany beginning in the early 1920s to study or perform. See Son Okju, "*Zwischen Vertrautheit und Fremdheit: Modernismus im Tanz und die Entwicklung des koreanischen Sinmuyong*" (PhD diss., Freie Universität Berlin, 2014), 52.

5. For example, Choe Seung-hui incorporated ballet such as basic barre exercises and arabesque into her dance training and even into her own choreography to re-form Korean dance. During exercises, Choe's students kept time by doing basic movements such as standing jumps and forward rolls while she beat the drum. See Mun Ae-ryeong 문애령, *Hanguk Hyeondae Muyongsaui Inmuldeul* 한국 현대 무용사의 인물들 (Seoul: Noonbit, 2001), 86. In the case of Cho Taek-won, he evidently constructed his training method based on the rhythmic exercises of Jaques-Dalcroze and thus stressed the role of musical accompaniment for his rehearsals. Cho's dance training is featured in a Korean film entitled *Mimong* (Sweet Dream, 1936). According to this film, five to six female students receive rhythmic training by moving in a circle to Cho's piano accompaniment. This is very similar to Jaques-Dalcroze's rhythmic training in Hellerau in the early twentieth century. Such movement training aimed to strike a constant balance between quantity (calculation of tempo) and quality (improvisation of movement). See *Mimong* 미몽, DVD, directed by Yang Ju-nam 양주남 (Seoul: Korean Film Archive, 2008).

6. German dance scholar Gabriele Brandstetter identifies two stages in the development of *Ausdruckstanz*. The first phase was World War I; the next phase was in the 1920s, during which it was called *Deutscher Ausdruckstanz* and progressed in conjunction with Expressionism and New Objectivity. See Gabriele Brandstetter, *Tanz-Lektüren* (Frankfurt am Main: Fischer, 1995), 33–34.

7. Claudia Jeschke and Gabi Vettermann, "Between Institutions and Aesthetics: Choreographing Germanness?" in *Europe Dancing: Perspectives on Theatre Dance and Cultural Identity*, ed. Andrée Grau and Stephanie Jordan (London: Routledge, 2000), 55.

8. Émile Jaques-Dalcroze, *Rhythmus, Musik und Erziehung*, trans. Julius Schwabe (Basel: Benno Schwabe & Co, 1921), 166, 171.

9. Czechoslovak writer Camill Hoffmann reported on his visit to Dalcroze's school *Bildungsanstalt für Musik und Rhythmus* (Educational Institution for Music and Rhythm) in Hellerau in the 1910s and precisely described how classes were run. See

Hedwig Müller, *Mary Wigman: Leben und Werk der großen Tänzerin* (Weinheim: Quadriga, 1986), 29–30.

10. Mary Wigman, *Deutsche Tanzkunst* (Dresden: Carl Reißner, 1935), 25.

11. "In her understanding, creative movement was no longer dominated by rhythm (as it had been for Jaques-Dalcroze), nor by expressive space (as it had been for Laban), but emanated from individual creative genius; in other words, from innermost feelings and from the mind." Jeschke and Vettermann, "Between Institutions and Aesthetics: Choreographing Germanness?," 58.

12. Kuni Masami, "Kuni Dance Newsletter," publication date unknown, archived in: Masami Kuni Collection at Deutsches Tanzarchiv Köln, Bestand: Masami Kuni nr.: 366, 2.2. Zeitungsartikel von und über Masami Kuni 1937–1985, undatiert.

13. Such semantic reversal of *Sinmuyong* is interestingly not shown in Japanese dance history, even though this terminology was originally brought to Korea in the 1920s as a direct translation of Japanese *Shinbuyō*.

14. Another reason for *Sinmuyonggas'* radical change to Korean dance was the encouragement of their Japanese dance teachers. Ishii Baku suggested, for example, that Choe Seung-hui's dance should incorporate both "uniqueness" and "Korean mind." This example indicates the strong external influences on the creation of hybrid *Sinmuyong* pieces, which exposed cultural trends of the time such as modernism and orientalism in dance. See Son, "*Zwischen Vertrautheit und Fremdheit*," 171–72.

15. Compared to other *Sinmuyongga* who promoted themselves as dancers from the Korean peninsula, Park defined himself as a Japanese in Europe, even though he was originally a Korean-Japanese and was received as a Korean dancer in his homeland, thereby enhancing the national prestige of colonized Korea in Europe. This dislocation between his stance as a Japanese and his border-crossing cultural experiences discloses a symptom of modernization in East Asia. That is, Park's self-designation as Japanese reflects his belief that Japan is the only Asian country that successfully assimilated Western civilization. This self-identification further leads to his assimilation into "the German" that he always admired as a role model of modernization in general. On the basis of this view, Park even applied to the Nazi propaganda bureau to give performances for German soldiers at the front during the World War II. See "Nyuseu Depateu—Bando Muyongga Dokjeonseon Wimun" 뉴스데파트—半島舞踊家 獨戰線慰問, *Maeil Sinbo* 每日申報, Morning Edition, October 25, 1939, 3.

16. The biography of Park Yeong-in refers to *Kyeongsang Ilbo* 경상일보 articles written by the Korean journalist Seo Dae-hyeon. These articles were published online on May 15, 16, 18, and 21, 2006.

17. Oh Byeong-nyeon 吳炳年, "Ijijeokeuro Mireul Guseonghaneun Sinheungmuyongga Park Yeong In ssi" 理智的으로 美를 構成하는 新興舞踊家 朴永仁 氏, *Donga Ilbo* 東亞日報, Morning Edition, September 10, 1937, 6.

18. Baek Hae-nam 白海南, "Donggyeong Muyonggyeui Jeonmang" 東京舞踊界의 展望, *Samcheonri* 三千里, vol. 6, nr. 7, 1934, 173.

19. "Dongyangmuyongeul gyosuhareo Park Yeong In guni Dogu Otaerigug Gwonwijaui Chobingeul Badeo Muyong Joseone tto Nangbo" 東洋舞踊을 教授하려 朴永仁

君이 渡歐 오태리국 권위자의 초빙을 바더 舞踊朝鮮에 또 朗報, *Maeil Sinbo* 每日申報, Morning Edition, September 20, 1936, 7. For the unique dance style of Bodenwieser, see Gunhild Oberzaucher-Schüller, "A Driving Force towards the New. Bodenwieser—Exponent of Ausdruckstanz," in *Gertrud Bodenwieser and Vienna's Contribution to Ausdruckstanz*, ed. Bettina Vernon-Warren and Charles Warren (Amsterdam: Harwood Academic Publishers, 1999), 19–28.

20. Kuni Masami 邦正美, *Berurin Sensō* ベルリン戦争 (Tōkyō: Asahi Shinbunsha, 1993), 21.

21. It has not yet been clearly proved whether Park first arrived in Berlin or in Vienna. A Korean newspaper, *Maeil Sinbo*, reported on September 20, 1936, that Bodenwieser became fascinated with Park's Asian art and invited him to teach Asian dance at her dance school as well as to work with her dance company in Vienna. However, his autobiography *Berurin Sensō* mentions that he boarded a ship to Germany after receiving a scholarship from the Japanese Ministry of Education to study abroad in September 1936. See "Dongyangmuyongeul gyosuhareo Park Yeong In guni Dogu Otaerigug Gwonwijaui Chobingeul Badeo Muyong Joseone tto Nangbo," 7; Kuni, "Berurin Sensō, " 20; Son Okju 손옥주, "Jagiminjokjijeok Eungsi: Park Yeong Inui Jakpume Natanan Joseonmuyongui Jaebalgyeon" 자기민족지적 응시: 박영인의 작품에 나타난 조선무용의 재발견, *Inmunyeonggu* 인문연구, no. 81 (2017): 293–94.

22. "Baengnimseo Hwaryakjungin Bandochurui Muyongga Park Yeong In gunui Geunhwang" 伯林서 活躍中인 半島出의 舞踊家 朴永仁 君의 近況, *Maeil Sinbo* 每日申報, Evening Edition, May 20, 1937, 8.

23. "Park Yeong In ssi Muyong Baengnimseo Daehopyeong" 朴永仁氏舞踊 伯林서 大好評, *Donga Ilbo* 東亞日報, Morning Edition, June 8, 1937, 8.

24. "Baengnimseo Hwaryakjungin Bandochurui Muyongga Park Yeong In gunui Geunhwang," 8.

25. "Masami Kuni," *BZ am Mittag*, June 2, 1937, archived in: Masami Kuni Collection at Deutsches Tanzarchiv Köln, II. Beruf und Werk Bestand: Masami Kuni, Nr.: 366 2.2. Zeitungsartikel von und über Masami Kuni 1937–1985, undatiert.

26. Katrin Endres, "Der Tänzer Kuni Masami (1908–2007)—Die Berliner Jahre (1936–1945)" (Magister thesis, Ruprecht-Karls-Universität Heidelberg, 2012, 73; "Ilseonbodojeonsaro Baengnimseo Hamnakjeonkkaji Hwaryak" 一線報道戰士로 伯林서 陷落前까지 活躍, *Maeil Sinbo* 每日申報, Morning Edition, May 30, 1945, 2. Park's role was actually not limited to a spreader of Asian dance and a correspondent for a Japanese propaganda news agency in Europe. Furthermore, it turns out that he was a Japanese espionage agent who collected intelligence about Nazi Germany for Japan. Park's ambivalent position as a pro-Nazi artist on the one hand and as a spy on Nazi Germany on the other hand reflects a double meaning of modernization in East Asia. See Frank Hoffmann, *Berlin Koreans and Pictured Koreans* (Vienna: Praesens, 2015), 111–27 on Park's espionage during the war.

27. Son Okju, "Between Self-Appropriation and Self-Discovery: Park Yeong-in in German Dance Modernity," published in 2014 in the official proceedings of the 7th World Congress of Korean Studies, https://congress.aks.ac.kr:52525/korean/files/2_1413536315.pdf, 7–9; Endres, "Der Tänzer Kuni Masami," 8.

28. "Japanische Tänze," *Programm des Tanzabends Masami Kunis am 3. Juni 1937 um 20.15Uhr im Kuppelsaal (Reichsportfeld, Haus des Deutschen Sports)*, 1937, archived in: Masami Kuni Collection at Deutsches Tanzarchiv Köln, Bestand: Masami Kuni Nr.: 366, 2.1. Programm-Material 1937–1961.

29. Ibid.

30. Kim Cheon-heung 김천흥, "Geommu 劍舞," in *Simso Gim Cheon Heung Seonsaengnimui Urichum Iyagi* 심소 김천흥 선생님의 우리춤 이야기, ed. Ha roo-mi, Choi Sook-hee, and Choi Hae-ree (Seoul: Minsokwon, 2005), 448–51.

31. For more on the history of Korean "*Jinju Geommu*" (Jinju Sword Dance), see Judy Van Zile, *Perspectives on Korean Dance* (Middletown, CT: Wesleyan University Press, 2001), 129.

32. "Ein junger japanischer Tänzer: Masami Kuni," *Freude und Arbeit*, Jg. 2, Heft. 6, 1937, 66.

33. Image from the Masami Kuni Collection, Bestand Nr. 366, 2.2. Zeitungsartikel von und über Masami Kuni 1937–1985, Deutsches Tanzarchiv Köln.

34. Son, "Jagiminjokjijeok Eungsi: Park Yeong Inui Jakpume Natanan Joseonmuyongui Jaebalgyeon," 299–301.

35. Image from the Masami Kuni Collection, Bestand Nr. 366, 2.2. Zeitungsartikel von und über Masami Kuni 1937–1985, Deutsches Tanzarchiv Köln.

36. Van Zile, *Perspectives on Korean Dance*, 17.

37. Ibid.

38. The choreography list in Choe Seung-hui's US tour programs, for example, also shows *Sword Dance* (or *Dagger Dance*) and *Young Korean Bridegroom* (or *Child Bridegroom*). See Van Zile, *Perspectives on Korean Dance*, 259–62. While these titles are very similar to Park's, the two choreographers differed substantially in movement composition and artistic strategy. Choe's *Sword Dance* "attempted to restore the dance," which was "originally created to portray the manly appearance and heroic spirit of ancient warriors" (Van Zile, *Perspectives on Korean Dance*, 261), whereas Park introduced his *Sword Dance* to the German audience "as a ceremonial dance called *Komagaku*" held in "the Japanese imperial palace" ("Japanische Tänze").

39. See "Vom japanischen Tanz," *Programm des Tanzabends Masami Kunis am 28. März 1943 um 11½ Uhr bei der Volksbühne*, 1943, 3, Archived in: Masami Kuni Collection at Deutsches Tanzarchiv Köln, Bestand: Masami Kuni Nr.: 366, 2.1. Programm-Material 1937–1961.

40. Park Yeong-in 朴永仁, "Segyegwan, Ingyeogeun Muyongui Pilsunjogeon" 世界觀, 人格은 舞踊의 必順條件, *Donga Ilbo* 東亞日報, Morning Edition, April 12, 1936, 7.

41. "I Haee Gidaedoeneun Sininui Hwaryak. Muyongga Park Yeong In ssi" 이 해에 期待되는 新人의 活躍. 舞踊家 朴永仁 氏, *Donga Ilbo* 東亞日報, Evening Edition, January 1, vol.7, 1936, 3.

42. Son, "Between Self-Appropriation and Self-Discovery," 1.

# CHAPTER 6

# Diasporic Moves

## Sinophone Epistemology in the Choreography of Dai Ailian

*Emily Wilcox*

Dai Ailian 戴爱蓮 (also spelled Ai-lien Tai, 1916–2006) was one of twentieth-century East Asia's most influential dance leaders. During the 1940s, she launched the effort to create "Chinese Dance" (*Zhongguo wu* 中國舞), a genre of contemporary concert dance that enjoys widespread popularity today in China and around the world.[1] Dai also promoted ballet, Asian dance, and Labonotation in China. After the establishment of the People's Republic of China (PRC) in 1949, Dai served as the founding head of several important PRC dance institutions, including the Chinese Dancers' Association, the Central Song and Dance Ensemble Dance Group, the Beijing Dance School, and the National Ballet of China. In 1981–1985 she served as vice president of UNESCO's International Dance Council.[2] On her death, China's media pronounced Dai the "Mother of Chinese dance" (*Zhongguo wudao zhi mu* 中國舞蹈之母).[3]

Despite her profound influence on China's dance world, Dai's relationship with China was complicated. Born and raised in Trinidad, she was a third- or fourth-generation diasporic Chinese (third on her father's side and fourth on her mother's side). Born Eileen Isaac, Dai spoke English as her native language and, like most young Chinese Trinidadians of her generation, was highly assimilated into British colonial culture.[4] Dai's grandfather on her father's side and great-grandparents on her mother's side were Cantonese- and Hakka-speaking immigrants from southern China who arrived in Trinidad during the nineteenth century. Dai never learned to speak either of their native tongues, although she did eventually learn Mandarin as an adult. Around the age of fourteen, Dai left Trinidad and moved with her mother and two sisters to London, where she launched her professional dance career by studying ballet and German modern dance. Nine years later, World War II broke out in Europe, and Dai left for Hong Kong, which like Trinidad was a British colony. From there, Dai moved on to China, settling in Chongqing in 1941, in the midst of the Second Sino-Japanese War. In China, Dai was often referred to as a "*Guiqiao*" 歸僑 (short for *guiguo Huaqiao* 歸國華僑), or "returned Overseas Chinese."[5] She was among hundreds of thousands of diasporic Chinese who "returned" to China from Southeast Asia, the Western Hemisphere, and other places during the mid-twentieth century.[6] Although Dai resided in China for the remainder of her life, she occupied an unusual position there. Like other returned ethnic migrants, Dai was "marked [ ... ] as a kind of permanent 'outsider' whose peculiarity or 'special features' (*tedian* 特點) were defined by their connection to foreign worlds."[7]

When speaking publicly about her own life, Dai often downplayed her intercultural upbringing and embraced an unqualified Chinese identity. For example, when she was asked in a 1983 television interview why she chose to emigrate to China, she replied, "Well, I know that I am Chinese. I mean, it's very strong to know that you're Chinese. And there's a big country there. It is your motherland."[8] That Dai saw herself as unequivocally Chinese, despite having grown up outside China, is consistent with a state ideology of diasporic Chineseness promoted in China since the late nineteenth century. Although emigration out of China dates back hundreds of years, it was long officially banned in China, and people of Chinese descent living abroad were often criminalized, viewed as "wanderers, fugitives, traitors and conspirators."[9] Then, in the late 1870s, China's leaders started to regard Chinese emigrants as an asset to China's modernization, and the Qing government began actively cultivating their support, starting in places such as Singapore (then a British colony with a large Chinese diasporic population). In 1893, the Qing formally repealed its ban on emigration and decreed that henceforth all Chinese "honest merchants and common people, no matter how long they have been abroad, along with their wives and children, shall be issued passports [ ... ] to allow them to return to China."[10] The term Overseas Chinese (*Huaqiao* 華僑), which emerged at this time, meant "Chinese sojourner." It assumed that Chinese migrants and their descendants living abroad still saw China as their home; moreover, it expected that they would remain loyal to China and one day eventually return.[11]

This essay builds on recent scholarship that problematizes this notion of Overseas Chinese identity, asking how such questions might change our understanding of the life and work of Dai Ailian. It draws on the work of Shu-mei Shih, a leading figure in this critical wave of scholarship, who has proposed the concept of the "Sinophone" as a new approach to what have traditionally been called Overseas Chinese communities or the Chinese diaspora. For Shih, the Sinophone concept shifts focus away from China-centric theorizations in which China remains the imagined homeland and destination for return. It proposes an emphasis on place-based cultures, as well as an acknowledgment of the idea that many people of Chinese descent do not embrace a Chinese identity. It also considers that many ethnic minorities in China have complex relationships to Chineseness.[12]

Not all of Shih's theorizations of the Sinophone are relevant or applicable to Dai. The fact that Dai did not speak or read any Chinese language before she moved to China means that she was technically not "Sinophone" by Shih's definition, according to which "Sinophone culture [ . . . ] is defined not by ethnicity [ . . . ] but by language."[13] Moreover, as cited above, Dai readily embraced the identities of "Chinese diaspora" and "Overseas Chinese." As a dancer Dai created cultural expressions that are difficult to analyze by the traditional approaches of Sinophone studies, which has tended to focus on written and spoken language.[14] Nevertheless, some aspects of Sinophone studies are useful for examining Dai's case, particularly the notion of "the Sinophone . . . as an epistemology."[15] As discussed further below, this concept highlights the potential of diasporic or Sinophone subjects to engage in "multiply-angulated critique," producing work that is highly local and yet transcends singular identities or affiliations. Such an approach, I argue, can enrich our understanding of Dai's work and the power of her choreography.

In this essay, I examine just two of the many locations in which Dai worked during her life: Hong Kong, a city on the southern coast of China that was a British colony from 1842 to 1997, and Chongqing, an inland city in the southwest that was China's provisional capital in 1937–1946, during the Second Sino-Japanese War. Specifically, I look at one major performance Dai gave in each locale: her September 1940 recital in Hong Kong, just six months after she arrived in Asia, and her March 1946 performance in Chongqing, after she had been residing in remote areas of China for nearly five years. By focusing on these two events, I show that Dai's choreography embodied a localized and evolving, rather than universal and static, approach to representing Chinese identity, performing a Sinophone epistemology enabled by her diasporic experiences.

## DAI AILIAN IN HONG KONG: DANCING PATRIOTISM IN THE COLONY

When Dai landed in Hong Kong in March of 1940, the local Chinese and English-language presses responded to her arrival in different ways, indicating divergent local audiences for whom she would soon perform. *Ta Kung*

*Pao*, a Chinese-language newspaper, highlighted her patriotism by noting her participation in benefit concerts for the China Campaign Committee, a UK-based group that advocated for support for China in the war against Japan.[16] To emphasize her Chinese cultural roots, the article featured a photograph of Dai performing *The Concubine Beauty Dances Before the Emperor*, a solo dance in which she portrayed the famed Tang dynasty consort Yang Guifei. In the photo, Dai is dressed in an embroidered gown with long drooping sleeves, resembling paintings of Tang court ladies. Her upper body is slightly arched, head tilted to one side and eyes cast down demurely, and her fingers point upward, delicately arrayed like flower petals, similar to postures from Chinese opera.[17] The *South China Morning Post*, an English-language newspaper, wrote instead about the artists Dai had worked with while she was living in England and the venues where she performed, such as the Embassy and Mask Theatres, the Ernest and Lotte Berk Group, the Dance Centre, and the Ballets Jooss at Dartington Hall. In an indication of Dai's cross-cultural appeal, the article quoted a review of Dai's dance from *The New Statesman and Nation*, which stated, "To see her was to participate, for a moment, in the exaltation of good art of whatever country and century."[18]

Details about Dai's Hong Kong performance schedule also appeared in local newspapers, again with different information to appeal to different readers. After a June benefit concert for the Guiyang Red Cross had to be cancelled, Dai finally appeared at a private event in September, which *Ta Kung Pao* used as publicity for an upcoming public recital.[19] An advertisement for the recital in *South China Morning Post* indicated joint British and Chinese support for the event, while clearly labeling Dai as "Chinese":

> Under the patronage of His Excellency the Acting Governor, Lt. General E. F. Norton, who has kindly consented to be present, a Dance Recital will be held in the Rose Room of the Peninsula Hotel on Friday evening, October 18th, at 9:30 PM. The performance is to be sponsored by the China Defence League, of which Madame Sun Yat-sen is Chairman; and the proceeds will be in aid of Chinese War Orphans. Star performer of the evening will be the well-known Chinese dancer, Miss Ai-Lien Tai.[20]

The *Da Kung Bao* advertisements for this event had a slightly different emphasis. One, for example, introduced the history of ballet to prepare audiences for Dai's presentation of excerpts from *Les Sylphides*.[21] Another offered a biographical essay that again lauded Dai's patriotism toward China. It read, "Ten years of difficult study made her achieve artistic success, with great acclaim abroad. However, she sincerely misses her motherland and hopes to use her art to serve it [. . . .] [S]he is an artist with a conscience."[22]

A detailed program from the recital, which appears in *Ta Kung Pao*, offers a valuable historical document of Dai's first public performance in Asia. It reflects both the Europeanized culture of British colonial Hong Kong at the time and a sense of the complex national and cultural affiliations of Dai's local audiences:

> Opening: British national anthem; national anthem of the Republic of China; 1. Chamber music: movements from Bach's suite in D Major, arranged by J. R. M. Smith; 2. Dance: Prelude and Waltz from *Les Sylphides* 嬋娟舞, to music by Chopin, danced by Dai Ailian; 3. Solo songs: "Elegie" (Massenet), "Palisir d'Amour" (Martini), "La Calunnia" (Rossini) and "Song of the Volga Boatmen" (Russian folk song, arranged by Koenemann), sung by Y. K. Sze, bass; 4. Flute solo: "Variations on Ancient Dances" (Telemann), played by Walter Yeh; 5. Dance: *La Glaneuse* 拾穗女, to music by Debussy, danced by Dai Ailian; Intermission; 6. Chamber music: "A Sonata a Quartre" (Telemann), played by Walter Yeh (flute), Chao Pu-wei (first viola), Ho On-tung (second viola), and J. R. M. Smith (piano); 7. Dance: *The Concubine Beauty Dances Before the Emperor* 楊貴妃唐宮舞, to "Rainbow Skirt and Feathered Dress" 霓裳羽衣 (Tang composition) on Western wind, and *Willow* 垂楊舞, to "Wandering in the Garden" 遊園 (Kunqu tune) on flute, both danced by Dai Ailian; 8. Chamber music: "Handel in the Strand" (Grainger's Clog Dance), arranged by J. R. M. Smith; 9. Dance: *Alarm!* 警醒, to drum solo, and *Guerilla March* 前進, to music by Prokofiev, both danced by Dai Ailian; Closing: British national anthem.[23]

The *South China Morning Post* reported on the reception of Dai's dances as follows:

> The most outstanding of the dances were two modern expressive numbers interpreting different moods of China's struggle against Japan. The first 'Ching Hsing' (Alarm!), in which the artist dramatized a night alarm to the self-accompaniment of a small drum was a most realistic portrayal, with the percussion adding to the general effect of the dance. 'Guerilla March' proved even more popular with the audience. Wearing a striking costume symbolic of the Chinese flag, Miss Ai-Lien Tai gave a most spirited performance in which gestures of defiance and victory were predominant. 'La Glaneuse,' a lyrical dance on the Biblical theme of Ruth the Gleaner to music of Debussy

was in contrast in a quieter mood. The handicap of a small stage detracted from her classical numbers, two dances from *Les Sylphides*. Two dances from old opera were beautifully rendered.[24]

Although there are no known film recordings of these dances, published photographs and drawings offer ideas of what they looked like. A photograph of Dai in *La Glaneuse* shows her in a white blouse and a nun-like head-covering squarely facing the audience with both hands solemnly crossed over her chest.[25] A drawing of *Alarm!* depicts Dai dancing barefoot in rolled-up pants and a button-down-collared shirt with rolled-up sleeves, a swath of fabric tied around her head and a large drum under her left arm.[26] She balances on a turned-out left foot with her right knee lifted to the side, the sole of her right foot pressed against her left inner thigh. Tilting her head to the left with her gaze forward, she beats the drum with her right hand.

Only one photograph from this concert appeared in the Hong Kong newspapers. It depicted Dai standing outdoors, seemingly on the edge of a cliff overlooking the ocean, in a pose from *Guerilla March*.[27] Dai stands in a costume matching the description in her oral history: "the top a blue sky with white sun and the bottom red; on the right wrist is attached a square piece [of fabric] lined up with the bottom, to look like a flag."[28] The costume only covers Dai's torso and one arm, exposing her bare legs and feet in a style reminiscent of 1930s German modern dance, which Dai had studied in England. Dai stands in a lunge with her feet spread wide, chest and face turned upward, and arms drawing a long diagonal from front to back. Her palms face upward and fingers curl in as if grasping invisible balls. With her muscular legs firmly planted, her arms rotating dynamically upward from the shoulder sockets, and her gaze looking up toward the sky, she presents a powerful, statuesque image that exudes patriotism and hope, embodying Chinese nationalism in a time of war, invoked through movement qualities drawn from European modern dance.

*The South China Morning Post* declared Dai's Hong Kong recital "an outstanding success, both as a concert and as a benefit performance."[29] Dai and the other artists reportedly donated their performances for free, so the only expenses were for constructing the stage and printing programs. With an audience of 500, the event raised HK$4,255.55, of which HK$3,685.35 went to the China Defence League War Orphans' Fund. According to the report, "So much interest was taken in the recital that numerous requests have reached the Committee for a repeat performance in a theatre in Hongkong, and at the present time this is under consideration."[30]

Fig. 6.1. Dai Ailian in Hong Kong performing a dance pose from her solo dance
*Guerilla March. South China Morning Post*, October 16, 1940. Photographer unknown.
Used with permission of South China Morning Post.

A repeat performance did occur on January 22, 1941, this time with the addition of Christian hymns by the Chinese Choral Society and *East River* 東江, a new war-themed modern dance by Dai. Also organized by the China Defence League, proceeds went to the International Peace Hospital in North China and the Kunming Huidian Hospital in Yunnan.[31] Once again, *Guerilla March,* which Dai performed to the third movement of Russian composer Sergey Prokofiev's modernist piano composition "The Love for Three Oranges," was an audience favorite. According to the *South China Morning Post*, "Most popular of her numbers was the stirring 'Guerrilla March,' [ . . . ] in which she so strikingly captured the spirit of China's resistance to the Japanese. The effect of the dance was heightened by her costume[. . . .] She was forced to give this dance twice."[32] Dai's reputation as a powerful and patriotic dancer now solidified, she soon left Hong Kong for Chongqing, where she developed a new repertoire for new audiences.

## DAI AILIAN IN CHONGQING:
## PERFORMING ETHNICITY ON THE FRONTIER

For Dai, life in Chongqing was very different from life in Hong Kong. Because Dai spoke no Chinese, she relied for interpretation on her husband (the Chinese painter Ye Qianyu 葉淺予, whom Dai met and married during her stay in Hong Kong), an arrangement that proved frustrating for them both.[33] Spaces equipped for dance were rare and often in poor condition, and the ongoing war meant that air raids and bombings were frequent, making everyday life unpredictable and dangerous.[34] Dai also experienced health problems, including a serious illness for which she had to return to Hong Kong for surgery in the fall of 1941. Dai's convalescence coincided with the Japanese invasion of Hong Kong, leading to a perilous escape that nearly cost her life.[35]

Despite the harsh conditions, Dai took every opportunity to study and perform in each place she visited. In April of 1941, while she and Ye were passing through Guilin, Dai joined a local benefit concert held to raise funds for an airplane donation in honor of the women's movement. Dai performed alongside a group of female actors who specialized in Gui opera (*Guiju* 桂劇), the local Han dialect theater of that area.[36] This led Dai to study the movements in a comic scene from Gui opera, in which one actor plays the roles of two characters—a woman holding a fan and handkerchief and a man carrying the woman on his back. She later developed this into one of her most iconic solo choreographies, *The Mute Carries the Cripple* 啞子背瘋.[37]

*The Mute Carries the Cripple* was just one of a series of new dances Dai created over the next several years based on similar encounters with other local communities in Chongqing and surrounding areas of southwest China. *Nostalgia* (*Sixiang qu* 思鄉曲), a solo inspired by Dai's meeting with composer Ma Sicong 馬思聰 in Chongqing in 1941, portrayed the homesickness of a wandering woman refugee, a common sight in the wartime capital during these years.[38] Many dances Dai created during this period had ethnic minority themes, reflecting the region's demographics. One of these, *Yao Drum* (*Yaoren zhi gu* 瑤人之鼓), was inspired by Dai's visit to a Yao mountain community in Guizhou in around 1941 or 1942.[39] Danced with drumsticks around a large floor drum, it was loosely based on dances she had observed, recreated for the concert stage.[40] Another minority-themed work, *Dance of Youth* (*Qingchun wu qu* 青春舞曲/*Qingchun zhi wu* 青春之舞), was inspired by a Uyghur dance Dai learned in 1943 from a friend in Chongqing who had recently visited Xinjiang.[41] In 1945, Dai traveled to Kangding, in what is now central Sichuan, where she stayed with a Tibetan trader from Batang (Ba'an) and learned several Tibetan dances. *Ba'an Xianzi* (巴安弦子) was a new choreography Dai created based on these studies.[42] Similar to many Tibetan-themed dances presented in China today, it was performed in a long skirt and striped apron and featured bending and straightening of the torso, lowered stamping actions with flat-bottomed boots, and curving arm actions tossing elongated sleeves.

In 1946, Dai put on a major concert in Chongqing presenting this and other new choreography she had created during the five years since she had arrived in China. Known as the *Frontier Music and Dance Plenary* (*Bianjiang yinyue wudao dahui* 邊疆音樂舞蹈大會), it opened on March 6 at the Chongqing Youth Hall. The term "frontier" (*bianjiang* 邊疆) in the show's title referred to places in the northern and western parts of China, such as Xinjiang, Tibet, Yunnan, Inner Mongolia, and Guangxi, which have large non-Han communities.[43] Reflecting this theme, the program was dominated by dances associated with or thought to represent these regions and ethnic groups:

1. *Yao Drum* (trio version); 2. *Jiarong Drinking Party* 嘉戎酒會, group dance adapted from Tibetan *guozhuang* song and dance; 3. *Duan Gong Exorcises Ghosts* 端公驅鬼, duet adapted from Qiang exorcism rituals; 4. *The Mute Carries the Cripple*; 5. *Luoluo Love Song* 倮倮情歌, group dance based on court dance of the aristocratic Black Yi; 6. *Auspicious Dance* 吉祥舞, excerpt from Tibetan opera; 7. *Amitābha Dance* 彌陀舞, Buddhist-themed group dance; 8. *Ba'an xianzi* (group version); 9. *Tap Dance* 踢踏舞, Llasa-style Tibetan dance in which the dancers' feet produce sound by hitting the floor; 10. *Goddess*

Fig 6.2. Dai Ailian performing her Tibetan dance *Ba'an xianzi*, which she premiered in Chongqing in 1946. *Yiwen huabao* 艺文画报 2, no. 5, 1947, p. 6. Reproduction provided by the Chinese Periodical Full-text Database (1911–1949), Quan Guo Bao Kan Suo Yin (CNBKSY), Shanghai Library.

*Yi Zhu* 意珠天女, excerpt from Tibetan opera; 11. *Spring Outing* 春游, dance adapted from Tibetan dance, similar in style to *Ba'an xianzi*; 12. *Kanba'erhan* 坎巴爾韓, duet inspired by Uyghur dance, set to a folk song of the same name; 13. *Xinjiang Folk Song* 新疆民歌, a solo by a female singer; 14. *Dance of Youth* (group version).[44]

Eight of these dances were new choreographies Dai had created since leaving Hong Kong: *Yao Drum, The Mute Carries the Cripple, Luoluo Love Song, Amitābha Dance, Ba'an Xianzi, Spring Outing, Kanba'erhan,* and *Dance of Youth*.[45] She performed in all of these except *Ba'an xianzi*, which was danced by a group of Tibetan students, and possibly *Spring Outing*.[46] Dai also performed in *Jiarong Drinking Party*, a work choreographed by Peng Song 彭松 (1916–2016), Dai's close colleague and student. The remaining items on the program were presented by visiting performers from Tibet and members of Chongqing's Tibetan and Xinjiang community organizations, making it a collaborative production by artists of diverse ethnic backgrounds.

The participation of Han and ethnic minority artists in the same performance was a new trend in China during this period, in which this event was particularly large and influential.[47] Reflecting on its significance, one critic wrote, "In the wake of victory against Japan, as we are aiming for the peaceful unification of the country, the meaning of this type of event to the good terms between nationalities through artistic and cultural exchange is very great. It's really unprecedented."[48] Dai presented a lecture at the beginning of the performance that linked her new dances to local discussions about the future of the performing arts in China.[49] This launched a nationwide arts discussion, showing that Dai's ideas tapped into major concerns animating the country at this time.[50]

Like Dai's debut in Hong Kong, the Chongqing *Plenary* too was a resounding success. According to one report, the opening night alone attracted an audience of about 2,000, including many cultural luminaries and political leaders, marking the start of "a new epoch for the future of China's new dance."[51] During the next few months, a "frontier dance" (*bianjiang wu* 边疆舞) movement spread across China, leading to a series of other performances and tours. In August, Dai performed in Shanghai, at the time China's cultural capital, and received rave reviews.[52] Then, after a year in the United States in 1946–1947, Dai returned to Shanghai and eventually moved to Beijing, where by 1949 she emerged as leader of the dance field in the newly established PRC.

SINOPHONE EPISTEMOLOGY:
EMBODYING MULTIPLY-ANGULATED CRITIQUE

In one of her early formulations of Sinophone studies, Shu-mei Shih writes, "[T]he Sinophone stands as an open category that views China and Chineseness at an oblique angle in light of place-specific experiences."[53] This aptly describes Dai's dance performances in Hong Kong and Chongqing, both of which embodied China and Chineseness but did so in contrasting ways that reflected place-based concerns situated at "oblique angles" to China's traditional cultural centers. Even though about 90 percent of the Hong Kong population was of Chinese ethnicity, many of whom were recent immigrants, the city's status as a British colony set it apart from China proper. Similarly, although Chongqing served as the temporary wartime capital, it was an inland city in a "frontier" region long imagined to be on the nation's cultural periphery.

In both these locations, Dai leveraged distinctive local conditions to develop her own interpretation of China and Chineseness that also drew on her experiences as a diasporic subject. In Hong Kong, she used her unusual dual identity as a London-trained dancer and a patriotic Overseas Chinese to bridge Chinese- and English-speaking communities. In choreographies such as *Guerilla March,* she used her German modern dance training to construct an image of Chinese patriotism that aroused nationalist sentiment, while still affirming the colonial preference for European art forms. In Chongqing, Dai's diasporic background posed a challenge because of her inability to speak the local language. However, by learning from local artists and conducting her own field research, she developed a new approach to dance that quickly gained followers across China. Moreover, through the cross-ethnic collaboration of the *Plenary* performance, Dai responded to a local need for national unity following the devastating Second Sino-Japanese war.

Beyond offering new perspectives on China, Dai responded to other aspects of her intercultural experiences through these choreographies, and this is an important part of what makes the concept of a "Sinophone epistemology" useful for analyzing her work during this period. The key to Sinophone epistemology, as Shih explains, is the notion of "multiply-angulated critique," which acknowledges multiple cultural affiliations while maintaining a critical distance from them. Outlining this idea, Shih writes,

> Transcending national borders, Sinophone communities can maintain a critical position toward both the country of origin and the country of settlement.

[ . . . ] A Chinese American can be critical of China and the United States at the same time. [ . . . ] The Sinophone as a concept, then, allows for the emergence of a critical position that does not succumb to nationalist and imperialist pressures and allows for a multiply-mediated and multiply-angulated critique. In this way, Sinophone can be considered a method. Starting from being a historical and empirical category of communities, cultures, and languages, the Sinophone can also be rearticulated as an epistemology.[54]

Such "multiply-angulated critique" is evident in Dai Ailian's life choices and her choreography. Dai's decision to leave England and move to China at the peak of her dance career can be seen as a critique of British colonial values, in which London was supposed to be the world's cultural center and thus the ideal destination for aspiring artists. Thus, Dai's "return" to China can also be read as a rejection of British cultural superiority and a reversal of the racist notion that the colonies, by virtue of their distance from Europe, lacked sophisticated artistic life. Additionally, when Dai performed for benefit concerts in Hong Kong in 1940 and 1941, Dai introduced vivid embodiments of Chinese nationalism into programs that otherwise consisted largely of European classics. Her dances presented potent political symbols such as the Chinese national flag and moving images of Chinese resistance at a time when many colonized subjects across Asia were rebelling against their colonial overlords. Although these choreographies were designed to stir up Chinese patriotic sentiment directed against the Japanese, they could also carry a potential added effect as expressions of anticolonial Chinese nationalism directed against Hong Kong's British rulers. From this perspective, the British national anthem at the beginning and end of this performance hardly diffused the infectious potential of Dai's explosive bodily energy in her patriotic dances.

Dai's "multiply-angulated critique" also targeted the ballet and modern dance culture that she experienced in 1930s London. When Dai was living in London, she, like many other artists of color, experienced racism in daily life and in her career. In her memoir, she reflected that because people of Asian descent were few, "People were always 'paying attention' to me, and I always found it very uncomfortable."[55] London's dance publications sometimes wrote about Dai in racist terms, and the roles she received were often typecast and portrayed negative images of Chinese people.[56] By performing ballet and German modern dance in her Hong Kong concerts, Dai asserted the right of non-European bodies to perform European dance forms on stage, something she was often denied in London. Moreover, by devising her own dances that experimented with Chinese aesthetic elements and portrayed Chinese people, Dai wrested the creative agency to represent Asia away from the white choreographers she had often danced for in London.

One example of the latter case are Dai's works adapted from Tibetan dance in Chongqing, such as *Ba'an xianzi*. In 1937–1938, while Dai was working in London, she had played the role of a Tibetan girl in the Tibetan-themed stage production *Djroazanmo*, choreographed by German modern dancer Ernest Berk.[57] The Chinese newspapers reported approvingly on this performance when Dai arrived in Hong Kong.[58] However, it also displayed elements of Orientalism, common in European modern dance during this era, including having most of the Tibetan characters performed by European dancers. Because Dai was not of Tibetan ethnicity, performing the Tibetan dances was also an act of cross-ethnic representation for Dai herself. However, when viewed in relation to the *Djroazanmo* production in London, Dai's approach in Chongqing gave more agency to Tibetan communities. For example, Dai studied with Tibetan dancers to prepare the work, and she worked and performed alongside Tibetan artists in a collaborative performance process. In the final production, Dai's choreographies on Tibetan themes were presented alongside performances of Tibetan dance by Tibetan artists, and the entire production advocated multiethnic nation-building and respect for non-Han cultural traditions.[59]

Some of Dai's Chinese-themed dances, even when they had little or no basis in local performance culture, also embodied potential for multiply-angulated critique insofar as they could be interpreted differently by Chinese and British audiences. Dai's dances *The Concubine Beauty Dances Before the Emperor* and *Willow* were given little attention by the critic of the English-language *South China Morning Post*, who described them simply as "two dances from old opera."[60] However, like her modern-dance works, these dances were also Dai's creations and contained cultural messages about the wartime situation and Chinese patriotism. *Willow*, for example, created by Dai in London in 1936, took the weeping willow tree as a symbol for China's suffering during the Japanese military invasions.[61] *The Concubine Beauty Dances Before the Emperor*, also created in 1936 in London, depicted Yang Guifei, a woman famous for being blamed for a rebellion and killed during war. "Multiply-angulated critique" could thus be achieved in the double meanings of such cultural symbols that spoke distinct messages to different audiences.

## CONCLUSION: DAI AILIAN'S DIASPORIC MOVES

Dai's many contributions to the development of modern Chinese dance came not in spite, but rather because, of her identity as a diasporic artist. Without her experiences growing up abroad, she never would have received the dance training and professional opportunities she did. These experiences allowed her to master diverse dance knowledge and skills and to develop critical perspectives and learn to adapt to a wide range of cultural environments and audiences. Among her many talents, Dai excelled at learning from those around her and knowing the right kind of dance to create at a particular place and time. This versatility as a human being who could move between different cultural worlds was also reflected in her dancing body. Thus, Dai performed "diasporic moves" both in her everyday migrations and in her staged choreographies.

While Dai harnessed the power of her diasporic experience to contribute to the creation of new approaches to dance in China, she also laid a foundation for new Sinophone epistemologies in dance by helping to influence dance developments among other Sinophone communities. As Ya-ping Chen has documented, several students Dai taught in Chongqing later emigrated to Taiwan at the end of the Chinese Civil War. There, these dancers helped establish *minzu wudao* 民族舞蹈, a place-based version of Chinese Dance in Taiwan, which took a different direction from Chinese Dance on the mainland.[62] Some of Dai's students and contemporaries also took her Chongqing repertoires to Sinophone communities in Hong Kong and Southeast Asia in the late 1940s, where they helped initiate new dance movements in Hong Kong, Singapore, Malaysia, and Thailand.[63] In the succeeding decades, the dance styles Dai helped foster in China also circulated back to Chinese heritage communities in North America.[64]

Dai's story challenges a bounded geographic definition of East Asia that excludes overseas diaspora communities. At the same time, Dai's story calls into question notions of biological determinism that assume people in the diaspora remain culturally linked to East Asia. Dai's innovative and multivalent choreographies benefited from the fact that, for her, Chineseness was not inherited or innate, but had to be actively sought out, researched, and reimagined.

ADDITIONAL RESOURCES

Full resolution versions of Figure 6.1 at https://doi.org/10.3998/mpub.
mpub.11521701.cmp.11 and Figure 6.2 at https://doi.org/10.3998/
mpub.11521701.cmp.12

Link 6.1: Dai Ailian Foundation (see Gallery for additional photographs of
Dai Ailian). Available at https://doi.org/10.3998/mpub.11521701.cmp.45

Link 6.2: *Dance On* Interview with Dai Ailian, 1983 (institutional login
required). Available at https://doi.org/10.3998/mpub.11521701.cmp.46

Link 6.3: Video of Dai Ailian performing *The Mute Carries the Cripple*, 1947.
Available at https://doi.org/10.3998/mpub.11521701.cmp.47

Link 6.4: Video of Dai Ailian performing *Yao Drum*, 1947. Available at https://
doi.org/10.3998/mpub.11521701.cmp.48

## Notes

I am grateful for comments on earlier drafts of this essay from Elizabeth Chan, participants in the *Dancing East Asia* conference, and two anonymous reviewers.

1. On the history of Chinese Dance and Dai's leading role in it, see Emily Wilcox,
*Revolutionary Bodies: Chinese Dance and the Socialist Legacy* (Oakland: University of
California Press, 2019). See also Jiang and Chang, this volume.

2. For Dai's Chinese memoir, see Dai Ailian 戴爱莲, transcribed and edited by Luo
Bin 羅斌 and Wu Jingshu 吳靜姝, *Dai Ailian: wo de yishu yu shenghuo* 戴爱莲: 我的藝
術与生活 (Beijing: Renmin yinyue chubanshe, 2003). For her English biography, see
Richard Glasstone, *The Story of Dai Ailian: Icon of Chinese Folk Dance Pioneer of Chinese Ballet* (Hampshire, UK: Dance Books, 2007).

3. Wang Guobin 王國賓, "Zai Dai Ailian xiansheng zhuisihui shang de jianghua"
在戴爱莲先生追思會上的講話, *Beijing Wudoa xueyuan xuebao* 北京舞蹈學院學報,
March 30, 2006: 3–4.

4. Walton Look Lai, "The Chinese of Trinidad and Tobago: Mobility, Modernity, and
Assimilation During and After Colonialism," in *Chinese Transnational Networks*, ed.
Tan Chee-Beng (New York: Routledge, 2007), 191–210.

5. Wang Kefen 王克芬 and Long Yinpei 隆蔭培, *Zhongguo jinxiandai dangdai wudao
fazhanshi* 中國近現代當代舞蹈發展史 (Beijing: Renmin yinyue chubanshe, 1999), 72.

6. Between 1949 and 1960, an estimated 600,000 *Guiqiao* immigrated to the PRC.
Technically, because Dai moved to China prior to 1949, her official status would have

been "domestic overseas Chinese," which also included people born in China with family members abroad. There were around ten million people in this category in 1960. Glen Peterson, *Overseas Chinese in the People's Republic of China* (London: Routledge, 2012), 2–3.

7. Peterson, *Overseas Chinese*, 3. On ethnic return migrants worldwide, see Takeyuki Tsuda, ed., *Diasporic Homecomings: Ethnic Return Migration in Comparative Perspective* (Stanford, CA: Stanford University Press, 2009).

8. "Dai, Ailian," produced by Billie Mahoney and directed by William Hohauser, in *Dance On* (Kansas City, MO: Dance On Video, 1983), 22:25–23:05.

9. Peterson, *Overseas Chinese*, 15. See also Philip Kuhn, *Chinese Among Others: Emigration in Modern Times* (Lanham, MD: Rowman and Littlefield Publishers, 2008).

10. Cited in Kuhn, *Chinese Among Others*, 241.

11. Kuhn, *Chinese Among Others,* 243; Peterson, *Overseas Chinese*, 15. This was further reinforced in 1909 by the Qing Nationality Law that declared "law of the bloodline" (*jus sanguinis*), in which the children of Chinese nationals born abroad were considered Chinese nationals. This law was reaffirmed in 1928 by the Republic of China, extending the legal basis of "Overseas Chinese" identity into the modern era. Kuhn, *Chinese Among Others,* 266.

12. Shu-mei Shih, "The Concept of the Sinophone," *PMLA* 126, no. 3 (May 2011): 709–18; Shu-mei Shih, "Introduction: What Is Sinophone Studies?" and "Against Diaspora: The Sinophone as Places of Cultural Production," in *Sinophone Studies: A Critical Reader*, eds. Shu-mei Shih , Chien-hsin Tsai, and Brian Bernards (New York: Columbia University Press, 2013), 1–42.

13. Shu-mei Shih, "Introduction," 7.

14. See, for example, Shih, Tsai, and Bernards, *Sinophone Studies*; Audrey Yue, and Olivia Khoo, eds., *Sinophone Cinemas* (Houndsmills, UK: Palgrave Macmillan, 2014).

15. Shu-mei Shih, "Against Diaspora," 39.

16. "Dai Ailian nüshi zhi wuzi" 戴爱蓮女士之舞姿, *Da Kung Bao* 大公報, March 31, 1940.

17. For a reproduction of this photograph, see Glasstone, *The Story of Dai Ailian*, 9.

18. "Miss Tai Ai-lien: Famous Dancer in the Colony," *South China Morning Post,* April 1, 1940.

19. "Ben Gang jianxun" 本港簡訊, *Da Kung Bao* 大公報, June 26, 1940; "Si Guiyi duchang hui" 斯桂義獨唱會, *Da Kung Bao* 大公報, September 15, 1940.

20. "Dance Recital for War Orphans," *South China Morning Post*, September 21, 1940.

21. Ma Lai 馬萊, "Ballet Music," *Da Kung Bao* 大公報, October 13, 1940.

22. Zhi An 之安, "Ji yi wei you liangxin de yishujia" 記一位有良心的藝術家, *Da Kung Bao* 大公報, October 13, 1940. All translations from Chinese are mine.

23. "Baowei Zhongguo tongmeng yinyue wudao hui" 保衛中國同盟音樂舞蹈會, *Da Kung Bao* 大公報, October 15, 1940.

24. "Miss Ai-lien Tai: Assists War Orphans in Hongkong Debut Interpretive Dancing," *South China Morning Post,* October 19, 1940

25. Dai, *Dai Ailian*, 86.

26. Glasstone, *The Story of Dai Ailian*, 37.

27. "The Spirit of China," *South China Morning Post*, October 16, 1940.

28. Dai, *Wo de yishu*, 72.

29. "Aid for War Orphans," *South China Morning Post*, October 26, 1940.

30. Ibid.

31. "Huidian yiyuan ben Gang mujuan weiyuanhui jiang jüxing yuewuchoukuan" 惠滇醫院本港募捐委員會將舉行樂舞籌款, *Da Kung Bao* 大公報, January 4, 1941; "Baowei Zhongguo tongmeng jüxing yuewu dahui" 保衛中國同盟舉行樂舞大會, *Da Kung Bao* 大公報, January 20, 1941; "Benefit Performance to be Given on Wednesday," *South China Morning Post*, January 20, 1941; "Yinyue wudao dahui" 音樂舞蹈大會, *Da Kung Bao* 大公報, January 22, 1941; H.W.C.M., "Chinese Artistes: Fine Entertainment At King's Theatre to Aid Defense League," *South China Morning Post*, January 23, 1941.

32. H.W.C.M., "Chinese Artistes."

33. Dai, *Dai Ailian*, 111–112. Many articles about Dai published in the Chinese press during this period noted her inability to speak Chinese and her ongoing struggle to learn the language. See, for example, Mozi 墨子, "Ye Qianyu furen: Dai Ailian" 葉淺予夫人: 戴爱蓮舉辦蒙疆舞蹈會, 重慶市長, *Haijing* 海晶 no. 5 (1946): 1; Ren Feng 刃鋒, "Dai Ailian he ta de wudao" 戴爱蓮和她的舞蹈, *Minjian* 民間 5 (1946): 10; "Bianjiang wudao hui dayou xuetou: Ye Qianyu Dai Ailian fuchangfusui" 邊疆舞蹈會大有噱頭: 葉淺予戴爱蓮夫唱婦隨, *Kuaihuolin* 快活林 8 (1946): 3; "Bu hui jiang Zhongguo hua de nü wudao mingshou, Dai Ailian de Yangjingbang" 不會講中國話的女舞蹈名手,戴爱蓮的洋涇浜, *Shanghai tan* 上海灘 11 (1946): 10.

34. A 1941 article describes Dai having to perform on a dance space with floorboards so loose they "started dancing along with [her]." Xu Chi 徐遲, "Ma Sicong, qiren ji qi yinyue" 馬思聰, 其人及其音樂, *Da Kung Bao* 大公報, September 29, 1941. During their first summer in Chongqing, Dai and her husband witnessed a ten-day bombing of the city, which Ye documented in a series of drawings and watercolors. "China's Ordeal," *South China Morning Post*, October 7, 1941.

35. Dai, *Dai Ailian*, 90–100.

36. Qian Fei 茜菲, "Chunguang li de Guilin funü" 春光里的桂林婦女, *Da Kung Bao* 大公報, April 21, 1941.

37. For video, see https://doi.org/10.1525/luminos.58.1

38. Dai Ailian, *Dai Ailian*, 103; Danke Li, *Echoes of Chongqing: Women in Wartime China* (Urbana: University of Illinois Press, 2010).

39. Dai Ailian, *Dai Ailian*, 134.

40. For video, see https://doi.org/10.1525/luminos.58.2

41. Dai Ailian, *Dai Ailian*, 134.

42. Dai Ailian, *Dai Ailian*, 135.

43. On the history of this term, see Pamela Kyle Crossley, Helen Siu, and Donald Sutton, eds., *Empire at the Margins: Culture, Ethnicity, and Frontier in Early Modern Chi-

*na* (Berkeley: University of California Press, 2006); James Leibold, *Reconfiguring Chinese Nationalism: How the Qing Frontier and Its Indigenes Became Chinese* (New York: Palgrave Macmillan, 2007). On the construction of Han identity, see Thomas Mullaney et al., *Critical Han Studies: The History, Representation, and Identity of China's Majority* (Berkeley: University of California Press, 2012).

44. Chen Zhiliang 陳志良, "Lüetan minjian yuewu: 'Bianjiang yinyue wudao dahui' guanhou gan" 略談民間樂舞: '邊疆音樂舞蹈大會'觀後感, *Keguan* 客觀18 (1946): 10.

45. Dai, *Dai Ailian*, 131.

46. Chen Zhiliang, "Lüetan minjian yuewu."

47. Wilcox, *Revolutionary Bodies*, 34–43.

48. Chen Zhiliang, "Lüetan minjian yuewu."

49. See, for example, "Dai Ailian lingdao biaoyan bianjiang wudao" 戴爱莲領導表演邊疆舞蹈, *Zhongyang ribao* 中央日報, April 10, 1946; Dai Ailian 戴爱蓮, "Zhongguo wudao di yi bu" 中國舞蹈第一步, *Qingming* 清明 (Shanghai), 1946, no. 2: 9–12.

50. See, for example, Yu Wenzhou 宇文宙, "Dai Ailian de wudao" 戴爱蓮的舞蹈, *Xiao Shanghairen* 小上海人, 1946 1(1): 10–12.

51. Jing Pu 鏡溥 "Wudao kui bianqing, lianqing ru liehuo" 舞蹈窺遍情,戀情如烈火, *Xiang-Hai huabao* 香海畫報 1946(2): 1–2.

52. See, for example, "Dai Ailian biaoqing shenke bianjiangwu xiaokou changkai" 戴爱蓮表情深刻邊疆舞笑口常開, *Shenbao* 申報 August 27, 1946; Shang Guanyao 上官瑤 "Shanghai de bayue feng: kan Dai Ailian da tiao bianjiang wu" 上海的八月風-看戴爱蓮大跳邊疆舞!, *Hai chao zhoukan* 海潮週刊 20 (1946): 8; "Haofang reqing Dai Ailian de wudao tian" 豪放熱情戴爱蓮的舞蹈天, *Piao* 飄 1946(5): 2.

53. Shu-mei Shih, *Visuality and Identity: Sinophone Articulations Across the Pacific* (Berkeley: University of California Press, 2007), 34.

54. Shih, "Against Diaspora," 38–39.

55. Dai, *Dai Ailian*, 76.

56. Wilcox, *Revolutionary Bodies*, 18–19.

57. "Arts Theater: A Tibetan Fairy Tale," *The Times* (London), October 13, 1937, 2; "From Tibet to Troy," *The Sunday Times*, August 7, 1938, 15.

58. Zhi An, "Ji yi wei you liangxin de yishujia."

59. For more on the politics of representation in Chinese ethnic minority dance, see Emily Wilcox, "Beyond Internal Orientalism: Dance and Nationality Discourse in the Early People's Republic of China, 1949–1954," *Journal of Asian Studies* 75, no. 2 (May 2016): 363–86.

60. "Miss Ai-lien Tai."

61. Dai, *Dai Ailian*, 72–73.

62. Ya-Ping Chen, "Dancing Chinese Nationalism and Anticommunism: The *Minzu Wudao* Movement in 1950s Taiwan," in *Dance, Human Rights, and Social Justice: Dignity in Motion, eds.* Naomi M. Jackson and Toni Shapiro-Phim (Lanham, MD: Scarecrow Press, 2008), 34–50.

63. "Dance in Wartime China: Liang Lun's Choreographic Migrations of the 1940s," 무용역사기록학 (*Journal of Society for Dance Documentation and History*) 52 (March): 45–75.

64. See, for example, Sau-ling Wong, "Dancing in the Diaspora: Cultural Long-Distance Nationalism and the Staging of Chineseness by San Francisco's Chinese Folk Dance Association," *Journal of Transnational American Studies* 2, no. 1 (2010): electronic.

# CHAPTER 7

# Choreographing Neoliberal Marginalization

## Dancing Migrant Bodies in the South Korean Musical *Bballae* (*Laundry*)

*Ji Hyon (Kayla) Yuh*

In March 2017, a local newspaper based in Seoul, South Korea (hereafter, Korea), featured an article addressing the persistent racism that continues to plague Korean society, despite the growing number of foreigners residing in Seoul. Based on a survey and interviews, the writer revealed the implicit bias that Koreans have, mostly toward Chinese and Southeast Asian migrant workers; it ranged from assumptions that they are dirty to a sense of fear that they are potential terrorists.[1] At around the same time, Mamamoo, a female K-pop band that sings retro pop, faced significant criticism from English-speaking fans for their blackface performance in a music video intended to "show their respect" for Bruno Mars and his song "Uptown Funk."[2] In fact, such conventions of blackface have persisted in South Korea since the mid-twentieth century, in K-pop as well as comedic skits and theater; its perpetrators have little knowledge of the troubling history of American blackface minstrelsy.[3]

These examples of casual racism and lack of critical awareness, if not willful dismissal, of race relations and histories of racialized representations are not limited to Korea. Examples from neighboring Japan and China in the music industry as well as in TV commercials reveal a similar lack of critical engagement with issues of race and racial relationships; these countries and their collective experiences and exposure to issues of race differ greatly from those of other nations. I believe that the aforementioned Korean examples reflect how race is understood and consumed in contemporary neoliberal South Korea. In what follows, I examine *Bballae* 빨래 (*Laundry*), a popular and well-known Korean musical that broke ground by having an ethnically non-Korean character as the male lead for the first time in the history of contemporary musical theater.[4] By providing an analysis of the production and the historical and sociocultural contexts of musical theater and racial identities in Korea, I argue that the dramatic and physical representation of non-Korean characters on the musical stage through music, book, and choreography reveals how Koreans understand race and racialized others within the current neoliberal, multicultural political economy in South Korea.

Musical theater, among other forms of popular culture, provides a particularly interesting site for investigating Korea's relationship to ideas of race and racialized identities. This is due to the musical's sociopolitical and cultural position as a genre with a quintessentially US American heritage, which lent itself to the Americanization of Korea and thereby became a tool for individual and state advancement in a realm of global competition.[5] Examining the role of race and racialization in *Bballae*, especially in terms of the physical and bodily movements, reveals the web of desires of neoliberal multicultural subjects and the state, especially in relation to people of non-Korean ethnicity, many of whom are migrant workers living in Korea.

## A BRIEF HISTORY OF KOREAN MUSICALS

While indigenous forms of Korean theater that used music to tell stories predated the arrival of Broadway-style musicals in the second half of the twentieth century, it was during the 1960s that this quintessentially American genre was first produced in South Korea with the government's support, in part as cultural competition with North Korea. However, the current popularity of Korean musical theater is a direct result of a series of economic and cultural events that occurred during the early 2000s, a period when Korea had just emerged from the national bailout program following the Asian financial crisis that started in 1997. During the financial crisis, the Korean government struck down a number of trade barriers to solicit the IMF's bailout package. To avoid a debt moratorium, massive restructuring plans were imposed on big corporations under the IMF's austerity measures, which meant widespread worker layoffs. Such measures together increased the value of liquid assets, because such investments guaranteed a quick turnaround. Workers became increasingly expendable, and neoliberal ideals were ushered in with the South Korean government's blessing as a means to revive the nation's economy. This changing economic climate coincided with the unprecedented success of a local, Korean-language production of *The Phantom of the Opera*, which opened in December 2001 and ran for approximately seven consecutive months to largely sold-out houses. The success of *The Phantom* drew corporate investors' attention. It provided an influx of capital to the market and inspired more producers, creators, and policymakers to enter the musical theater industry.[6]

## *BBALLAE* BREAKS GROUND IN 2005

Following the success of *The Phantom*, South Korea's musical theater industry grew rapidly, and the number of productions of both licensed and original musicals increased.[7] Reflecting these changes and interests, more universities started musical theater programs that provided classes for aspiring actors and writers. *Bballae* resulted from one such initiative; the writers Chu Minju 추민주 and Min Chanhong 민찬홍 created the musical as their thesis project at Korean National University of the Arts (한국 종합 예술 대학교, KNUA) in 2003. Conceived by Chu, *Bballae* tells the story of Nayoung, a young woman in her twenties who moves to Seoul (South Korea's capital city) from Kangwon province, a less-developed region on the northeastern coast of South Korea. The musical begins as Nayoung moves into a small room in a house in the so-called *daldongne* 달동네, or moon-towns. This romantic term is employed for low-income neighborhoods, which are typically located at higher elevations and therefore closer to the moon. The reality of many *daldongne* is that they are located in the least accessible parts of Seoul and are thus less developed and less expensive, attracting a lower-income demographic.

In the story, Nayoung moved to Seoul five years earlier to pursue her dream of becoming a writer. However, the material reality of life as a perpetual part-time worker moved her further from her dream, forcing her to move six times during her five years in Seoul. At her new home in the *daldongne*, she meets new neighbors. *Jooin Halmoenee* is an older landlady who makes her living by collecting rents from her two tenants and by collecting refuse such as paper and rags. Jooin Halmoenee has a daughter who is never shown but is said to be developmentally challenged and severely paralyzed. The daughter exists only as a sound effect consisting of a monstrous scream; she is a dramaturgical tool that serves Jooin Halmoenee's story. Another tenant in the house is a character named *Heejung umma* (Heejung's Mother), who works at a small clothing shop in Seoul's night market. Her boyfriend, Mr. Ku, is a regular visitor and a constant cause of the landlady's grievances against Heejung umma, since Mr. Ku does not pay the bill for the water he uses when he visits. Another important character is Solongos, a twenty-something illegal migrant worker from Mongolia who lives in an adjacent building and works at a factory. An additional key character, Michael, is an illegal migrant worker from the Philippines and Solongos's friend. While Michael primarily offers comic relief throughout the story, he is also a dramaturgical device to show the plight of illegal laborers in Korea as he suffers unjust treatment from his employer. Taken together, this is a group of economically marginalized characters marked by their ethnic, class, and bodily differences. They represent those displaced from their respective homes who end up finding a new family in the *daldongne*.

Since *Bballae* opened in 2005, the production has been revived almost annually and has had more than twenty different casts since its premiere.[8] One of *Bballae's* many appeals is that Nayoung's struggles as a precarious part-time female worker under a misogynistic and egotistical male manager resonate with female audiences in their twenties and thirties, the main demographic of avid musical-theater-goers in South Korea. Another initial appeal of the story was that Solongos, who becomes Nayoung's love interest, is an illegal migrant worker from Mongolia. *Bballae* received significant attention because its premiere and history coincided with a period during which the Korean government was trying to raise awareness of the value of a multicultural society.[9] In other words, some of *Bballae's* sociocultural appeal came from its ability to capitalize on the government's multiculturalism initiatives, thanks to the presence of an ethnically non-Korean, racialized male protagonist. Subsequently, casting this particular role became important and competitive. Many current South Korean musical theater "stars" were discovered via their performances as Solongos, which further popularized this character.

However, precisely what Korean audiences saw in Solongos's performance remains an open question. Chu, *Bballae's* writer and director, stated in an interview that she chose to create a character from Mongolia because in the Korean imagination the Mongolian landscape is characterized by open, green pastures, a clear contrast to the cramped rooms in Solongos's impoverished urban neighborhood in Seoul. Further, Chu stated that she made Solongos Mongolian because Mongolians are viewed as phenotypically similar to Koreans.[10] This then begs the questions—what marked the character of Solongos as Mongolian, if not his looks? How was Solongos's non-Koreanness embodied? And, more importantly, how did Solongos's non-Koreanness function in *Bballae*? To answer these questions, it is helpful to first examine how Koreans typically understand race and racialized others within domestic contexts.

## RACE AND CLASS IN KOREA

*Injong* (인종), a Korean word used for the English term "race," is a transliteration of a Chinese (and Japanese) word, 人種, which literally means "human type." This term seems to have been first used around the turn of the twentieth century, when global racial hierarchies were introduced among Korean elites (and in East Asia more broadly) through the influx of a Western imperialist worldview. One of the earliest discussions of *injong* appeared in *Donngnip Sinmum*, one of the first Korean newspapers (published 1896–1899). In an op-ed titled "*Injonggwa Nara'ui Bunbyeol*" 인종과 나라의 분별 (Distinguishing Races and Nations), an anonymous writer echoes the German physician Johann Friedrich Blumenbach's eighteenth-century racial classifications, dividing the world's population into five different races: Mongolians (yellow), Caucasians (white), Africans (black), Malays (brown), and Americans (red). The anonymous writer reflects on Western racial hierarchies that regard certain races as superior to others, arguing that "one should ponder why a certain race is respected while certain others are not, despite the fact that people of all races share common traits such as love, hate, and rejoicing with one another."[11] Rather than identifying certain races as inherently superior to others, the writer instead ties racial identities to nation-states' civilizational advancements, dividing them into four classes: truly-enlightened, half-enlightened, not-yet-enlightened, and barbaric. Such a relationship between race and civilization becomes the basis on which the Korean writer argues that Koreans, as a part of the "yellow" race, can and should strive to reach a higher level of enlightenment to compete with other races. Evincing a clearly racist agenda, however, the author argues that so-called "blacks" and "reds" are exempt from this competition, because they are "still part of humanity but not worth mentioning."[12]

Such racial perceptions that privileged fairer skin tones over darker ones aligned with an already existing class system that Koreans had subscribed to for centuries, especially during the late Chosun period (1392–1895). This system found virtue in learned intellectual men, who due to their lack of outdoor activity had fairer skin than those who worked outdoors in agriculture.[13] In other words, physical appearance, especially the color of one's skin, had long been considered one way of ascribing virtue to individuals in Korean society. Skin tone already suggested the individual's socioeconomic status, along with other, more visible and material markers. This specific hierarchy that existed in pre-twentieth-century Korean society was based on a class system, and certain physical and cultural markers—whether skin color, articles of clothing, or certain mannerisms—enabled one to read and categorize people into socioeconomic groups. Given this history, when the concept of "race" was first introduced and associated with physical markers, most prominently skin color, race was subsumed under the already-established systems of class in Korea. This conflation of the two understandings of race— one as an ideology of biological difference and the other as a class marker— persisted throughout Korea's subsequent interactions with non-Koreans. It was applied to white missionaries at the turn of the twentieth century, to Japanese colonizers during Japan's occupation of Korea from 1910 to 1945, and to US soldiers stationed in Korea after World War II. It continues to persist today as immigrants and expats of different racial and ethnic backgrounds and their supporters speak up against explicit and implicit racism in Korean society, as discussed at the beginning of this chapter.[14]

In the 1990s, due to the rise of globalization, a greater influx of immigrant workers, and increases in interracial marriage, Korea experienced the growth of immigrant communities in both urban and rural areas. These communities began demanding that they should have rights as legitimate participants in Korean society without having to somehow "become" Korean.[15] To many Koreans, who took pride in the long-standing yet deeply misguided belief in their racial and ethnic homogeneity, these growing communities of foreigners posed important questions to the public and to policymakers regarding who could and should be considered "Korean" (a concept with legal, racial, ethnic, and cultural ramifications). Consequently, the Korean government and NGOs saw the need for more conscious policies to deal with *daminjok* 다 민족 (multiethnic) and *damuhwa* 다문화 (multicultural) populations that were making their lives in Korea. However, the policies have received significant criticism for the assimilationist attitudes they project, which reflect long-standing Korean attitudes toward immigrants.[16]

In the language of the government's policies, which ostensibly aim to embrace residents who are not racially and ethnically Korean, the term "race" is largely absent, replaced by terms such as "multicultural" and "multiethnic," which are less obviously based on the body. One could argue that this absence results from the fact that a majority of the immigrant population in recent years is from other Asian countries, meaning that their racial and racialized identities are lumped into the arbitrary category of "Asian," or *Hwanginjong* 황인종 (people of yellow skin). However, the absence of race in official policy language hints at a centuries-old Korean attitude that neither engages with nor acknowledges race within the Korean domestic context. Instead, race, racialized bodies, and their performance have become metonyms of culture, which are more easily dissociated from individual corporeality. They are consumed and circulated as abstract ideas, which often manifest as associations of darker skin with low(er) class and lighter skin with high(er) class. In this way, much-needed discussions regarding race and racism have been dismissed and limited to discussions of class and culture. Thus, how race and ethnicity are portrayed and performed on Korean musical theater stages must be understood as operating within a context in which one's race is dismissed and frequently conflated with, if not replaced by, a (marked) class identity.[17]

## STAGING RACIALIZED CHARACTERS IN *BBALLAE*

Considering these contexts, *Bballae* provides an interesting case to explore the conflation of race and class, especially because musical theater bears a particular cultural status in South Korea as a form of popular culture enjoyed by a rather narrow—and heterogeneous—audience, mainly limited to middle to high-income Seoul residents. As a Korean production in which non-Korean characters are performed by Korean actors, how does *Bballae* perform race and racialized identities, and how do these performances connect with musical-theater audiences?

In *Bballae*, the two main ethnic others—Solongos and Michael—are both marked as different, racialized, and othered on stage. Moreover, they are able to find a home only among characters similarly marginalized as low-class residents of Seoul. Yet, the performances of Solongos and Michael have some differences. Compared to Michael, Solongos's racialized identity serves primarily as a dramaturgical device to place him in the marginalized community of *daldongne*. In this sense, his racial otherness is portrayed as something that can be transcended through economic mobility. When Solongos and Nayoung marry at the end, in a hopeful note they vow to each other that they will work hard, make lots of money, have children, buy a house and car, and travel. In this vision, their struggles and precarious status as illegal migrant and part-time worker are temporarily relieved. This ending clearly gives the assumed heteronormative, middle-class audience a sense of neoliberal multicultural satisfaction at the thought that Solongos and Nayoung could have the freedom to pursue their lives together and escape their precarious situations. In this way, Solongos's ethnic and racial identity is subsumed under his economic identity as a familiar neoliberal subject. This process is further consolidated because Solongos does not wear any particular makeup or costume to identify him as Mongolian. The only sign of difference is that he speaks slowly with a slight accent, which can also be seen as a mark of low class or a lack of education. The portrayal of Michael's ethnic and racial identity is quite different from that of Solongos, which we can see by taking a closer look at bodily movement or choreography.

## DRAMATIZING AND CHOREOGRAPHING DIFFERENCE

Korean original musicals typically have a smaller budget and therefore a smaller physical production than imported musicals, which imposes greater constraints for producers and compels them to prioritize their needs. This pressure has often led Korean producers and musical creators to neglect choreography and privilege the literary narrative over other aspects of production. While such an attitude is less relevant in the case of larger productions, whether imported or home-grown, smaller original productions tend to minimize elaborate choreography. While recent years have seen growing awareness of the importance of movement, this was not the case when *Bballae* was first introduced in 2005.[18]

Nevertheless, meaningful choreography does appear in the cast's movements and staging, especially as they relate to the performance of ethnic, racial, and class identities. *Bballae*'s choreography—developed by Seo Jeongseon 서정선, who has experience in small-scale original musicals—emphasizes mundane movements such as sweeping the floor, running, driving or catching a bus, opening an umbrella, and doing the laundry. As a musical about the ordinary lives of economically and socially marginalized people who represent in some fashion struggles and sufferings to which the audience can relate, a choreography of mundane gestures and movements is particularly effective. This is especially true in one of the best-known scenes that appears toward the end of the musical, in which the female residents of Nayoung's house do the laundry, while singing about how they can overcome the sadness, frustration, and negativity that they face. At the beginning of this scene, Nayoung enters from stage left, dejected and limp, having been demoted for standing up to an unjust management decision. She collapses in front of the door to her room and begins bawling. Both the landlady and Heejung's Mother, who have just started doing their laundry, run to Nayoung to comfort her. Invoking the mundane movements of wringing water from a soaked bed sheet they are washing, the two women pull on either end, sweeping it over Nayoung's head and creating a whooshing sound. Their actions,

Fig. 7.1. Nayoung (played by Soyee Kwon) comes out from under the bed sheet, held by Heejung umma (played by Jihye Kim, left) and the landlady (played by Yiju Jang, right) in *BBALLAE*, 22<sup>nd</sup> Production, 2019, Seoul. Photo courtesy CH SOOBAK.

combined with the sound, enact a moment of release when Nayoung reappears from underneath the sheet.[19]

During this song and dance, Nayoung's limp form revives, almost as though her damp and wet body—expressing in material form the oppressions of a patriarchal, neoliberal society—is dried, stretched, and refreshed, prepared to take on another day. By the end of the scene, Nayoung spreads her arms into the sky with a big smile on her face. Granted, the message of the song is limited because it preaches a passive acceptance of the problems of life, with lyrics imploring one to accept the changes that occur as one's life passes through time, just as a wet sheet is dried and refreshed by the flowing wind. Moreover, this scene confirms gender norms with female characters doing laundry, a household chore associated with women, to relieve their frustration. Nonetheless, the choreography and the movements in this signature scene exhibit a sense of relief for the female Korean characters in the story.

Although their experiences are similar, Solongos experiences perhaps even more severe oppression from Korean society than Nayoung. However,

Solongos does not have a moment in which he can experience a release like his female counterpart Nayoung. This is not, however, the case with the character of Michael, Solongos's Filipino friend. In an early scene, Michael helps Solongos with his laundry, while Solongos helps Michael with his Korean. Solongos teases Michael for his lack of linguistic proficiency in Korean. In response, Michael sings a hip-hop style rap song titled "Na Hangungmal Da Ara 나 한국말 다 알아" (I Know Korean Well), in which he claims that he knows Korean well enough. Michael begins singing and dancing by himself, but is soon joined by an ensemble of apparently non-Korean characters who wear baseball caps and bomber jackets with Afro wigs. Together, they dance a few basic b-boy steps while Michael raps about the verbal and psychological abuse he experiences in Korea.

In these lyrics, Michael recites explicit and disturbing curse words that have been directed at him by his Korean co-workers and boss, along with his own pleas to them to stop. However, this song serves as a cathartic moment for Michael and the audience as he spews them out in this fast-paced rap, which culminates in a fully choreographed dance break. Here, Michael can communicate his feelings not only through words but through dance movements, which involve a combination of uprock and freestyling. While Michael's dance moves may seem out of place and not necessarily associated with his Filipino identity, the emotive implications of his rapping and dancing to a hip-hop beat are clear. Michael is portrayed as expressive, unbridled, and rebellious, as he swings his arms side to side and stomps the ground with ensemble members who seem to be his friends, singing and dancing almost as a street b-boy.

In contrast to Michael, Solongos is never given the opportunity for such expressive choreography or language. Solongos's relative constraint is evident in "Apeugo Nunmulnaneun Saram" 아프고 눈물나는 사람 (A Human with Pains and Tears), a song he sings in the second half of the production. In this scene, Nayoung and Solongos lament their shared plights as marginalized denizens of Seoul. The song follows an altercation in which Solongos and Nayoung encounter two drunk Korean men who harass Nayoung and Solongos for their respective identities. The song begins as the harassers leave and Solongos is covering Nayoung, who is on the ground because one of the men shoved her for trying to fight back. Nayoung asks, "Why are you just taking a beating [instead of fighting back?],"[20] and the song begins as Solongos's response to Nayoung. Solongos explains that he takes the beating, the injustice, because of his family back home and the debts he has for coming to Korea. He sings about how he forgets that he is also a human and that he

Fig 7.2. Solongos (played by Kiheon Kang) and Nayoung (played by Soyee Kwon) sing *Apeugo Nunmulnaneun Saram* [A Human with Pains and Tears] in *BBALLAE*, 22nd Production, 2019, Seoul. Courtesy of CH SOOBAK.

too feels pain and sheds tears. As Solongos is singing, he and Nayoung slowly raise themselves up from the ground, and they stand a few feet away from each other without much movement. Once Solongos sings his verse, Nayoung responds to explain why she too endures the injustices—because of the rent to be paid—and explains that circumstances do not get better anywhere she goes. During the chorus, the two come closer to each other, and they sing together about how they forget that they are also human. They exit stage right supporting one another as they walk, accompanied by a crescendoed underscoring of the song.

Although Solongos's lyrics reveal and speak of the plights he has experienced in Korea, this song fails to produce the cathartic effect of Michael's. One reason is that the song dramaturgically functions as a moment of bonding for the two protagonists, since it is the first duet between Solongos and Nayoung. The lyrics strengthen their bonding as they share the sufferings of economically marginalized, uprooted people in Seoul. Despite the fact that Solongos genuinely speaks of his hardships and how he needs to bear the injustice of these acts, the song's romantic purpose in the drama mutes the honest confessions of both Solongos and Nayoung. Moreover, the choreography of the scene inhibits Solongos's moment of release. During the entire scene, Solongos hardly moves. The stillness of his body speaks of an imposed constraint caused by his racial difference, but in a different way from Michael's. Because Solongos is motionless and his gestures slight, his sense of anger becomes deflated. As a result, the song effectively builds intimacy between Nayoung and Solongos, rather than releasing Solongos's anguish. While this adds to the development of the romantic plotline, it detracts from Solongos's ability to convey a moment of outward anger, self-assertion, or open condemnation of the race- and class-based prejudice he endures.

The differences in Solongos's and Michael's choreography ultimately foreshadows their different fates in the story. Toward the end of the musical, the audience finds out that Solongos is permitted to remain in Korea and continue his "Korean Dream," while Michael has already been deported. In fact, the audience learns of Michael's deportation only after he is gone, as a minor rumor of the neighborhood. The divergence in Solongos's and Michael's fates has a clear message—it shows who is and is not able to remain in the Korean community. Solongos, with his soft-spoken and gentle demeanor, does not express his dissent or frustration; as a reward, he is able to stay in Korea, win his love, and pursue a future that appears hopeful, no matter how provisional, temporary, or insecure it may in reality be.

## CONCLUSION: A STORY OF NEOLIBERAL ASSIMILATION

Even though *Bballae* is widely celebrated in the media and by the public as the epitome of Korea's multicultural strength, when analyzed through its choreography, this work undercuts the very openness that is ostensibly its strength, instead revealing the surveillance and regulation that ultimately assimilate and oppress racialized ethnic non-Koreans until they either conform to become neoliberal South Korean subjects or leave the community. The audience is given a vicarious sense of hope and satisfaction at the end of the show, when they see Solongos and Nayoung standing together on the rooftop of their *daldongne* apartment, listing goals they want to achieve together. In this scene, the rest of the cast on stage must physically look up to the couple as they congratulate and celebrate them, signaling visually their elevated status. The hopeful tone of the voices and music in this scene conveys to the audience that things will get better, that their previous sufferings led them to find each other, and that they will—might—now overcome life's struggles together. Many musicals, especially musical dramas and conventional comedies, share a similar arc, in which a protagonist expresses a desire that is then pursued and attained over the course of the narrative. In *Bballae*, the neoliberal idea of never-ending self-improvement and competition is placed within this narrative, as the protagonists, instead of basking in the glory of finding one another, choose to list more "wants" to be fulfilled, albeit here together rather than individually.

Perhaps this is exactly *Bballae's* appeal: it provides an example of an individual who successfully assimilates into South Korea's neoliberal multicultural ideology (in this case, Solongos), and it concludes with a heartfelt and sincere celebration of that individual. It is a familiar trope to the similarly-minded subjects of neoliberal multicultural ideology, and the audience can therefore relate. By the musical's end, Solongos's racially marginalized identity as an outsider is replaced by his new identity as an obedient neoliberal subject who can now stand above the other economically marginalized residents of the neighborhood. In this vision, Solongos is no longer an outsider in the community of neoliberal multicultural citizens of the world.

## CODA: *BBALLAE* IN EAST ASIA

As of 2019, *Bballae* is still one of the most popular musicals in Korea. Its twenty-second production still welcomes audiences consisting mostly of Koreans, but it now also attracts Chinese and Japanese tourists, for whom it provides Japanese and Chinese translations. In 2012, *Bballae* received a Japanese-language production in Japan, which proved to be successful, with positive responses indicating that Japanese audiences were able to relate to the struggles of marginalized characters.[21] In China, a Korean-language production toured in 2016, followed by a Chinese-language production at Dayin Theater (大隐剧院) in Beijing in 2017. The 2017 Chinese-language production almost did not happen due to rising political tensions between Korea and China surrounding the placement of a Terminal High Altitude Area Defense (THAAD) system in Korea. As a result of this tension, the 2016 Chinese tour production had been abruptly cut short, as were the preproduction preparations for the local production. However, rapid changes in the Korean political climate, with the rallies that resulted with the impeachment of then-president Park Geun Hye and inauguration of the new president Moon Jae In, is supposed to have diminished the tension. This led to the successful opening of the local Chinese production in June of 2017. The Chinese-language production was also highly successful, to the point that there was a discussion of a follow-up revival later that fall.[22]

*Bballae*'s reception in Japan and China requires further study, as responses and adaptations may reveal more about different understandings of and relationships to racialized others and the relationships among ethnicity, race, gender, class, and socioeconomic marginalization in other East Asian nation-states. However, for now, it suffices to say that both the Japanese and Chinese productions were replica productions, meaning that the audiences saw the same story about Solongos and Nayoung who live in Seoul. Considering that Solongos symbolized at the end of the story a successful example of neoliberal multicultural assimilation, I believe that the positive reception of the productions in both Japan and China hint at the spread of neoliberal multicultural ideologies in these countries.

To conclude, *Bballae* holds a unique place in the history of Korean musical theater. It is an original work that received significant love from fans and the public over more than a decade following its humble beginning as a school production in 2003. Yet, it remains the only musical that really portrays how contemporary Koreans understand race and racialized bodies in a domestic Korean context. As the show became popular, *Bballae*'s creators and cast were able to extend its experiences beyond Korea to Japan and China, in the process revealing the spread and limitations of the neoliberal ideologies embedded in a musical marketed as a story of openness and acceptance. In the past few years, Koreans have seen in the media a number of non-Koreans of different class and cultural backgrounds, many of whom confronted the lack of awareness and acknowledgement of race in Korean society. Considering that *Bballae*'s script has been updated to accommodate changing living conditions in Seoul, most notably the changing minimum wage, it will be interesting to see whether increasing awareness of race is also reflected in the show's future revivals. Until then, one can only imagine a new version of *Bballae* whose choreography reflects and helps constitute a society in which the many Solongos are no longer constrained and the many Michaels do not just disappear.

## ADDITIONAL RESOURCES

Full resolution versions of Figure 7.1 at https://doi.org/10.3998/ mpub.11521701.cmp.13 and Figure 7.2 at https://doi.org/10.3998/ mpub.11521701.cmp.14

Link 7.1: Munhwaga Junggye (Culture Report) E206.091110 (Highlights from the 2009 production of *Bballae*). Available at https://doi.org/10.3998/mpub.11521701.cmp.49

Link 7.2: Arts Avenue 2017 (Musical Bballae) from Arirang TV (English language program on musical *Bballae*). Available at https://doi.org/10.3998/mpub.11521701.cmp.50

Link 7.3: Arirang News from 2015 (Musical *Bballae* to be presented in China). Available at https://doi.org/10.3998/mpub.11521701.cmp.51

Link 7.4: *The Korea Times* article on Musical Korean Wave: Mee-You Kwon, "Musical as Next 'Hallyu'" September 18, 2012. Available at https://doi.org/10.3998/mpub.11521701.cmp.52

## Notes

1. Adjectives and descriptions associated with the non-Koreans in Korea included *Deoreobda* (dirty), *Sikkeureobda* (loud), *Naemsaega nanda* (smelly), *Musikhada* (ignorant), *Ge'eureuda* (lazy), *Doneul barkinda* (money hungry), *Jamjaejeok tereoriseuteu* (potential terrorist), and *A'ireul na'eureo palryeo'on bulssanghan saram* (a pitiful person who was sold to come to have babies). Changsoo Lee, "Naemsaenanda, Migaehada, . . . Hangukeun Chabyeol Gonghwaguk" 냄새난다, 미개하다 . . . 한국은 차별 공화국, *Segye Ilbo*, March 20, 2017. Unfortunately, this article is just a snapshot of more prevalent and blatant incidents of racism, the victims of which are more frequently darker-skinned persons who are not ethnically or racially Koreans. For more on racism in Korea, see Sang-Bok Ha, "Yellow Skin, White Masks: A Historical Consideration of Internalized Racism and Multiculturalism in South Korea" (in Korean), *Inmun Gwahak Yeongu* 33 (2012): 526–56.

2. Tamar Herman, "K-Pop Girl Group Mamamoo Apologizes for Blackface 'Uptown Funk' Performance," *Billboard*, March 6, 2017 (http://www.billboard.com/articles/columns/k-town/7710346/k-pop-girl-group-mamamoo-apologizes-blackface-performance-uptown-funk). Mamamoo is not the only pop-culture example in which Koreans have been criticized for blackface makeup. See Gil-Soo Han, "K-Pop Nationalism: Celebrities and Acting Blackface in the Korean Media," *Continuum* 29, no. 1 (2015): 2–16; Gil-Soo Han, *Nouveau-riche Nationalism and Multiculturalism in Korea: A Media Narrative Analysis* (London: Routledge, 2016).

3. Incidentally, the first commercial production of a US American-style musical that Koreans saw was Gershwin's *Porgy and Bess* in 1966. All performers wore blackface makeup, and there was little critical discussion of the practice's implications. More research is needed on performers' different relationships to blackface in K-pop

and the musical stage. However, the sociocultural backgrounds of the two are often shared. For more on the beginnings of musical theater in Korea, see Ji Hyon (Kayla) Yuh, "Modern Musicals in Asia-Korea," in the *Routledge Handbook of Asian Theatre*, ed. Siyuan Liu (New York: Routledge, 2016), 541–44; Mankyu Park, *Hanguk Musicalsa* 한국 뮤지컬사 [The History of Korean Musicals Since 1941] (Seoul: Han'ul Academy, 2011); Inkyeong Yoo, *Hanguk Musical'ui Segye: Jeontong'gwa Hyeoksin.* 한국 뮤지컬 의 전통과 혁신 [The World of Korean Musicals: Tradition and Innovation] (Seoul: Yeongeukgwa Ingan, 2009). For more on the general background of Korean theater in the last century, see Gungnip Yesul Jaryowon 국립예술자료원 *Park Yong Gu: Hanbando Leunesangseu'ui Kihoekja* 박용구: 한반도 르네상스의 기획자 [Park Yong Gu: The Producer of Korean Renaissance] (Suryusanbang, 2014); Hanguk Geunhyeondae Yeongeuk Baeknyeonsa Pyeonchan Uiwonhoe 한국 근현대 현극 백년사 편찬위원 회 [One Hundred Years of Korean Modern and Contemporary Theatre], ed. *Hanguk Geunhyeondae Yeongeuk Baeknyeonsa* 한국 근현대 연극 백년사 (Jibmundang, 2009); Hanguk Yeongeuk Hyeophoe 한국연극협회 [Hundred Years of Korean Modern Theatre History], ed. *Hanguk Hyeondaeyeongeuk baeknyeon* 한국 현대연극 백년 (Yeongeukgwa Ingan, 2009).

4. Other original musicals have featured characters of non-Korean lineage. However, often these are minor characters, such as Japanese characters in *The Last Empress* and *Hero*, which tell the stories of heroic individuals during the period of Japanese colonization in Korea; they are no more than a stereotyped tool that helps the creators highlight the story of main characters. One recent production that featured non-Korean characters as protagonists is *Pureun Nun Pak Yeon* 푸른 눈 박연 (Blue-Eyed Park Yeon). Created and first produced in 2013, it told a story of Jan Jans Weltevree, a Dutch sailor from the sixteenth century who was shipwrecked off the Korean coast on his way to Japan. It tells how he was gradually assimilated and "became" Korean, in part because he fell in love with a local Korean woman, but also because people were generally nice to him despite the initial linguistic and cultural barriers. This production's treatment of Weltevree's foreignness is much more cursory than what appears in *Bballae*, in that Weltevree's identity as a person of a different race was no more than an easy dramaturgical challenge for a story of love and loyalty. It ultimately flattens out the possibility of more subtle exploration of the character's white body evoked by the titular image of "blue" eyes.

5. For more on the Americanization of Korean culture in the twentieth century, see *Amelikanaijeisyeon: Haebang Ihu Hangukeseo'ui migukhwa* 아메리카나이제이션: 해방 이후 한국에서의 미국화 [Americanization: Americanization in Korea after Independence], eds. Dukho Kim and Yongjin Won 김덕호, 원용진 (Pureun Yeoksa, 2008).

6. For example, the title of one newspaper article reads, "Big-budgeted musicals make the big bucks." It cites the *Phantom of the Opera* as an example, stating that the production cost was 12 billion KRW (approximately US$110 million) and the profit was 19.2 billion KRW (approximately US$170 million). "Big-budgeted musicals make the big bucks" (in Korean), *Maeil Kyeongje,* March 23, 2003.

·

7. The increase in original musicals was steeper than in licensed musicals, which tended to require bigger budgets. According to Do Yoon Seol, the producer of *The Phantom of the Opera* in 2002, the musical theater industry's market capital increased from about 70 billion KRW to 200 billion KRW between 2002 and 2005. Hyeong Joong Kim, "Seol Do Yoon, Kim Yong Hyeon Daepyo 2006 Hanguk Myujikeol Jindan" 설도윤, 김용현 대표 2006 한국 뮤지컬 진단 [Producers Do Yoon Seol and Yong Hyeon Kim Diagnoses 2006 Korean Musical], *Sports Chosun*, December 30, 2005.

8. Unlike Broadway or Off-Broadway productions, Korean productions run in repertoire. Instead of an open run, productions generally open, continue for three months, close, and return after some time. As of July 2019, *Bballae* is featuring its twenty-second cast.

9. During the early 2000s, the government acknowledged the presence of many migrant workers who came to Korea (illegally and legally) as laborers, trainees, or brides from countries in central Asia, China, and Southeast Asia by making new policies to enhance their lives in Korea.

10. Those who argue that Mongolians look most similar to Koreans use research data that reveal the genetic similarities. However, such "evidence" is often misleading because they mix Mongolians with Mongoloids. Mongolians are people of Mongol descent, while Mongoloid is one of the categories of race that includes many Asians, such as Koreans and Mongolians. Chu's statement, therefore, reveals a lack of clear understanding and an underlying racial stereotyping. Don Kyu Park, "Hangugeun Mujigae'ui Nara, Meonjikateun oneuleul Teoreonae" 한국은 무지개의 나라, 먼지같은 오늘을 털어내 [Korea, A Country of Rainbows . . . Shake Off Today Like You Shake Off Dust], *Chosun Ilbo*, Apr. 16, 2008.

11. *Doknip Sinmun*, "Injonggwa Nara'ui Bunbyeol" [Distinguishing Races and Nations], April 7, 1896.

12. Ibid. It is also important to note that the anonymous writer may have subscribed to the Japanese view of race because it served their colonial expansion at the beginning of the twentieth century. Many new ideas at the turn of the century were introduced to Korea by way of Japan.

13. Nadia Kim, *Imperial Citizens: Koreans and Race from Seoul to LA* (Stanford: Stanford University Press, 2008).

14. For more on the conflation of race and class identity, see Jong-Il Lee, "An Analysis of Cases of Korean Racial Prejudice" (in Korean), *Sahoegwa Gyoyuk Yeongu* 19, no. 4 (2012): 95–120; "A Socio-Historical Approach to the Formation of Racial Prejudice in Korea" (in Korean), *Sahoegwa Gyoyuk Yeongu* 18, no. 2, (2011): 73–89; also see Gi-Wook Shin, *Ethnic Nationalism in Korea: Genealogy, Politics, and Legacy* (Stanford: Stanford University Press, 2006); and Chan Seung Park, 박찬승, *Minjok, Minjokju'ui* 민족, 민족주의 [Ethnicity, Ethnicnationalism], 2nd ed. (Seoul: Samhwa, 2010). For studies that debunk the centuries-old notion of Korean homogeneity, see Soo Il Chung, 정수일, *Hankuksokui Segye: Urineun Eoddeoke Segyewa Sotonghae Watneunga* 한국속의 세계:

우리는 어떻게 세계와 소통해 왔는가 [The World inside Korea: How Have We Communicated with the World?] (Seoul: Changbi, 2005).

15. According to a Korea Immigrations Service report, the number of foreigners staying in Korea increased from 750,000 in 2005 to almost two million by the end of 2015. For more information, see Korea Immigration Service, Churipguk, Oegukin Jeongchaek Tongye Wolbo 외국인 정책 통계 월보 [Immigration Service Statistics Report], December 2015.

16. Instead of receiving equal treatment, the non-Korean immigrants in Korea are often expected to assimilate and "become" Koreans by adopting languages and customs before they are considered to be fully incorporated as legitimate members of Korean society. Such an attitude hearkens back to the oppressive strategies of colonialism, and is more troubling when one considers that those who are from countries less developed than South Korea are more likely to receive such treatment.

17. I am indebted here to the work of Jodi Melamed, which informs much of my analysis of *Bballae* below. See Jodi Melamed, *Represent and Destroy: Rationalizing Violence in the New Racial Capitalism* (Minneapolis: University of Minnesota Press, 2011), 138.

18. It is important to note that choreography in Korean original musicals is still relatively underdeveloped, especially considering that the Korean musical theater industry has grown and expanded rapidly in the last decade or so. Proper training is lacking for those who want to develop skills to become choreographers. Also, the sheer volume of new works and the lack of awareness about the importance of choreography as an essential dramaturgical tool in musicals have hindered the development of the field until very recently. See Joon Ho Song, "Hanguk Myujikeol Anmuui Hyeonjae," 한국 뮤지컬 안무의 현재 [Current Issues of Korea Musical Choreography], *The Musical Magazine*, April, 10, 2015.

19. Musical *Bballae*뮤지컬 빨래, Minju Chu and Min Chanhong, May 23, 2015, Fifteenth Season.

20. Ibid.

21. Lee, Minseon, "Bballae, Nojima Naoto, Nakano Mana: Ilboneseo Hangukeuro Bballaehareo Wasseoyo" 일본에서 한국으로 빨래하러 왔어요 [Nojima Naoto, Nakano Mana: We Came to Do Laundry to Korea from Japan], *The Musical Magazine*, November 2012, p. 25.

22. For more complete coverage of the timeline, processes, issues, and/or implications of THAAD deployment in Korea, see Azriel Bermant and Igor Sutyagin, "Moving Forward with THAAD," *Foreign Affairs*, August, 21, 2017; Adam Taylor, "South Korea and China move to normalize relations after THAAD dispute," *Washington Post*, October 31, 2017; and Clint Work, "South Korea and China Make Amends. Now What?" *The Diplomat*, November 18, 2017.

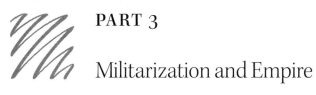

**PART 3**

Militarization and Empire

# CHAPTER 8

# Masking Japanese Militarism as a Dream of Sino-Japanese Friendship

## *Miyako Odori* Performances in the 1930s

### *Mariko Okada* 岡田万里子

Performance offers audiences a chance to dream, to escape into fantasy. Despite, or because of, their beauty, such fantasies can also serve systems of political control. This chapter explores how Japanese dance performances during the Second Sino-Japanese War were used to instill nationalism and patriotism in audiences in order to foster devotion and support for Japan's regime of radical militarism and imperialism.

Imperial Japan expanded its territorial control over Asia and Oceania from the late nineteenth century to the early 1940s. The Japanese Imperial Army annexed Taiwan in 1895 and gained control over Korea in 1910. In 1914, it put the South Sea Islands under mandate. In the 1930s, it built the puppet state of Manchukuo in northern China. Japanese imperialism terrorized all of East Asia and adjacent areas during this period. The Greater East Asia Co-Prosperity Sphere, Japan's imperial concept during World War II, was an errant policy that required an exorbitant budget and strong support from the general public. The militaristic government utilized the arts to gain the public's understanding, approval, contributions, and advocacy for this policy. Dance was especially exploited to show an idealized world that could generate the public's devotion to this common dream of a militarized nation.

This chapter describes how the Japanese state used Kyoto's traditional dance performances, which are designed to convey a cheery, naïve, and lighthearted tone, to mask its extreme aggression in China as benevolent friendship. It shows how these performances were appropriated by the state agenda and thereby became a model example of imperial Japan's use of dance as a vehicle for public indoctrination. The chapter describes the background, milieu, and contexts of this traditional dance form before focusing on one performance in particular, a 1939 children's dance, to demonstrate its use as wartime propaganda. Although the available sources do not give us a window into the impetus for such cultural propaganda—whether they were produced at the direction of state authorities or created independently by writers and choreographers—the evidence does show that it is likely to have had a strong effect on its audience.

Kyoto was the capital of Japan from the eighth to the twelfth century and again from the fourteenth to the sixteenth century. Even after the capital was moved to today's Tokyo in the early seventeenth century, this traditional city remained an important cultural center, and Kyoto's many historic buildings, arts, events, industries, and lifestyles continue to attract tourists from both inside and outside Japan today. Geisha—female entertainers who have served at banquets performing dance and music since the eighteenth century—are particularly powerful popular icons of Kyoto. The word *"geisha"* literally means "art person," and today geisha dance and music are regarded as traditional arts in Japan. Their official costume is the traditional Japanese *kimono* with wigs styled in a traditional hairstyle as well. Today's geisha train meticulously to make people feel as if they are stepping back into eighteenth-century Japan. The performative archaism of their artistic practices and refined behavior distinguishes them from other entertainers. In the 1930s, however, geisha did not foreground their traditional qualities, but rather were known for their progressive modern outlook. From their beginning in the Edo (江戸) or Tokugawa (徳川) period (1603–1868), geisha had always been popular icons, similar to later movie actresses or singers. Portraits of geisha were printed and sold, and in the twentieth century, their songs were recorded and released, incorporating them into Japan's modern commercial entertainment culture.

As icons and celebrities, geisha could also be utilized politically. Until the late nineteenth century, geisha danced at private banquets and dance-school recitals, but in general not in public performances. In 1872, the Kyoto city government organized for the first time a public geisha dance performance with the aim of drawing large crowds to the Kyoto Exposition. The Kyoto Exposition was one of the city's modernization efforts and was a huge success. The geisha public dance, called the *Miyako Odori* (都踊, literally "capital dance"), won first place in popular events during the exposition.[1] Following this success, many geisha districts, which could be found nationwide, organized their own public dance performances. Four months after the first performance, two other geisha districts are reported to have already organized their own dance performances in imitation of the *Miyako Odori*.[2] There were eight geisha communities in Kyoto, and more than half of them held public dance per-

Fig, 8.1. *Miyako Odori* in 2019. Its group dance in identical costumes has basically followed the same style since its first performance in 1872. Photo by Hayashi Photo provided by Gion Kobu Kabukai.

formances as part of the exposition.[3] From this time onward, original geisha dance performances representing the city of Kyoto became an annual event held every spring, a tradition that continues today.[4]

## DISGUISING INVASION WITH IMAGINARY FRIENDSHIP

In the 1930s, Japan was making a dash to vastly expand its empire. In September 1931, the army staged the Manchurian Incident, which it used as a pretext to invade Manchuria. Japan created a puppet regime in northern China called Manchukuo in 1932 and walked out of the League of Nations. The Sino-Japanese War began in 1937.

Kyoto's annual geisha dance performances in the 1930s reflected this militaristic climate. The themes tended to be nationalistic, with effusive praise for Japan's history and culture. A number of performance titles reflect this theme, often by using references to the rising sun, a symbol of imperial Japan. Such titles included "The Corner-Stones of the Sunrise-Land" (1933), "The Rising Sun Shines Everywhere" (1938), and "The Basis of the Dynasty" (1939).[5] A dance in the 1939 performance, entitled "Nisshi-shinkō 日支親交" or "Friendship between Japan and China,"[6] stands out for its particularly nationalistic tone and content. According to notes in the official program, the dance was divided into two scenes, using two types of accompanying music. The first half used "Aiba Shingunka 愛馬進軍歌" (The March of the Beloved Horses), and the second half used "Kōa Ondo 興亜音頭" (Dance for Asian Prosperity).[7] The march was a popular war number with lyrics and music chosen by the Army Ministry, and six different record companies released recordings of it.[8] The song describes war horses at the front, rhapsodizing on the deep bonds between soldiers and their animals. "Kōa Ondo," by contrast, names Chinese landmarks such as the Forbidden Palace and the Great Wall and the Five-Colored Flag, which represented the "five races" of Manchukuo. "Brothers, brothers, hand in hand, March, April, East Wind," is its repeated refrain. The words "brothers" and the names of the months were sung in Chinese. Since Japan is located east of China, the east wind here symbolizes Japan's influence or power. The months may have been included because the performance was held from April 1 to 30. These lyrics were clearly chosen to promote a vision of friendship between the Chinese and Japanese.

The songs used in this dance performance can still be heard on records.[9] "Kōa Ondo" was composed by Yamada Shōtarō 山田抄太郎 (1899–1970), a rising star shamisen player, who taught in the Gion district and composed the music for the annual public performance. He wrote bright, cheerful music for this song, utilizing Chinese-style melodies and a Chinese gong to match the Chinese lyrics, which were written by the famous poet Kitahara Hakushū 北原白秋 (1885–1942).[10] From these Chinese elements, the Japanese audience could conjure images of Chinese people in good spirits, which is clearly what Japan's military government wanted the public to believe. Of course, the real situation in China was anything but happy. China was in the midst of the Second Sino-Japanese War (1937–1945), which left millions of casualties on all sides. In utter contrast, the dance performance showed peaceful relationships between the two countries. Audiences listened to the friendly, sunny Chinese music and cheerful lyrics, which completely obfuscated the devastating reality of the times.

Extant documents related to this performance show that the performers in this dance were all children in training who had not yet become geisha professionals.[11] In the 1930s, girls under the age of ten were sold to districts such as Gion and trained to be geisha. As part of their study, they learned dance and music. The young girl apprentices danced in public, even before their debut as geisha. Their 1939 performance, which was shot on 16 mm film and is only 35 seconds long, is shocking because it shows little girls dancing exu-

Fig, 8.2. Child dancers in the costume modeled after the uniform of the *Kokubō fujin-kai,* Japan's National Defense Women's Association. Nisshi-shinkō 日支親交" or "Friendship between Japan and China" from 1939 *Miyako Odori.* Courtesy Gion Kobu Kabukai and Kyomai Inoue-ryu.

berantly in celebration of war.[12] In the first half of the dance, twenty bobbed-hairstyle girls wear *kappōgi* (Japanese-style aprons with sleeves) and *tasuki* (a sash to tuck up kimono sleeves), the uniform of the *Kokubō fujin-kai* 国防婦人会, Japan's National Defense Women's Association. They dance holding Japan's national flag with its rising sun image. The children in the adult women's uniforms look adorable, but strange. At the same time, the image they create is powerful; it is likely to have deeply impressed their audience.

The available sources do not tell us whether this wardrobe choice was made with the consent of that association or at its direction, or at the direction of any state authorities. What is known is that the president of the performance organization submitted a written plan for the dance, including the use of the Horse March, to Kyoto police on February 14, 1939.[13] Whether initiated from above or created organically from below and merely approved by authorities, however, the performance clearly aligned with the pervasive discourse and is likely to have elicited a strong sense of patriotic solidarity with the state and its war.

The official program indicated that a district organization had employed a choreographer from outside of the organization for the first time in its history. A famous choreographer for children, Shimada Yutaka 島田豊(1900–1984), developed the dance *Aiba Shingunka* for the first half of the child dancers' performance. Shimada had already created this dance with the same song and received great praise in the region.[14] The organizers of the *Miyako Odori* probably sought to use his fame to their advantage to gain support from the state by promoting the war effort through their productions.

The stage set for the second half of this dance depicted the front steps of the Hall of Supreme Harmony (*Taihe dian* 太和殿) within the Forbidden City in Beijing. On the stage, ten child dancers wearing Chinese *qipao* and ten child dancers in Japanese kimonos danced hand in hand in a big circle. One newspaper reviewer described it as "a beautiful scene where Chinese children and children of our country cheerfully dance together, holding their own national flags, hand in hand, celebrating our solid foundation of peace in Asia."[15] The choreography of the second half was quite simple, something one newspaper reviewer criticized.[16] However, because this dance formation was similar to the form of a well-known children's game, Kagome Kagome, it might have resonated deeply with the audience, who probably recalled this song and game from their own childhoods.[17] This impression seemed to be so strong that it made the audience feel as if they themselves had participated in a friendship dance with the Chinese children. The choreographer's use of a nostalgic children's game further magnified the joyful impression of this scene. Furthermore, the straightforwardness of the segment probably made it accessible and easily understood.

Having children dance this scene would have produced a strong impression because it was simultaneously unusual and endearing. Although *Miyako Odori* often utilized children dancers at this time, they typically played only subsidiary roles to make the main geisha dancers look better. This is the first attempt in which *Miyako Odori* featured children's dances as the main focus. The lyrics of the accompanying song were also simple, with many easy-to-learn refrains. After the performance, the record of this song was released. It is not difficult to imagine that the audience would start singing this tune on the street after leaving the show and that this dance "dream" might be believable in the form of a children's performance.[18]

## A COLLECTIVE IDEAL ON STAGE

In reality, Japanese-Chinese relations were horrific. After occupying the Chinese capital of Nanjing in December 1937, Japan faced a difficult battle and unleashed bloodshed and destruction as it continued to invade China. What the audience was shown was not reality, but a bright happy event in which children from both nations danced together in front of China's representative monument, the Forbidden City.

Before the invention of motion pictures, these performances served the same role as a news program or a documentary film today. In Japanese theater history, it is well known that theater conveyed the military situation during the First Sino-Japanese War of 1894–1895.[19] There is no known evidence that the creators of *Miyako Odori* went to the battlefields in China to gather news. However, the creators of the *Kamogawa Odori* 鴨川をどり (Kamo River Dance), a public dance performance of a geisha quarter that was a neighbor to Gion, visited the Ryūkyū Islands in 1940 to gather information about war events there, with the intention of producing a performance titled "Nanshin Nippon" (Japan Moves South).[20] Such deployments of performance to portray current events still occurred in the 1930s. While the battlefield is not the stage and, if staged, war must be stylized, the move toward glorification and idealization of the war "reality" on stage was spurred by the nationalistic and militaristic aims of performances in this period.

The *Miyako Odori* performance was not an attempt at realistic documentary representation. But was it merely a device to project the propaganda of Japan's superiority and glory and generosity? Or was it a cover for the present horrors, just a frothy way to disguise reality? Or possibly a projection of the audience's war-worn desire to see a moment of ideal harmony? If performance continued to play the role of news reporting at this moment in Japan's theatrical history, I would argue that the *Miyako Odori* in the 1930s can be thought of as a contrasting impulse. That is, news reports theoretically conveyed real events while allowing the audience to maintain some distance. *Miyako Odori* performances did not try to convey the actual situation, but instead sought to replace reality with fiction. The impulse to communicate information and the impulse to obfuscate it through re-invention and idealization are different. Instead of just hiding information, *Miyako Odori* performances sought to provide audiences with alternative images that coincided with their dreams, which were inevitably shaped both by their own desires and by state propaganda.[21]

In the 1930s, *Miyako Odori* changed focus: no longer did it focus on reality, instead showing the audience a fictional dream. Performance has always helped people escape from their burdens, but the dream shown by *Miyako Odori* was more than an escape. I would suggest that it functioned like collective memory, which contributes to national identity. The friendly relationship with China was not, needless to say, a memory, because it had not happened. It could, however, represent a collective ideal or dream. Nationalistic ideals were cleverly constructed within the performances to produce this enthusiastic collective response by audiences. In this way, these dances *produced* collective memory, even if fictionalized, in order to create national identity.

To create this collective memory, first the message of the performance was circulated through a media mix of audio records, programs, postcards, magazines, newspapers, and even newsreels. Those who did not go to the theater were  inspired by newspaper reports, magazine reviews, posters in the street, and even songs on the radio. Second, the performance functioned as a patriotic fundraising event, with donations collected for the army. They often invited the soldiers' families, disabled soldiers, and bereaved families to the performances. These special invitations were publicly reported in newspapers, which also promoted the performances, and these kinds of charitable investments proved to be of great practical use for attracting audiences. Third, the structure of the theater building also worked effectively to create a fictionalized collective memory and sense of national identity. Different from typical Western-style theaters, this theater had passage stages that cut through the audience to the stage at each side of the auditorium. Two runways ran from both ends of the main stage to the back of the audience, thus surrounding the audience with dancers on three sides. The rousing spirit of the marching music and the overwhelming atmosphere produced by the performance must have stirred the audience. These three elements—promotion in the media, the draw of charitable causes, and the immersive theatrical environment—made the performance an effective mechanism to foster a collective ideal. Dance could make an audience dream, and these modern devices assembled these dreams into a state apparatus for Japan's nationalist and imperialist propaganda.

## POPULARITY, INNOCENCE, AND OBEDIENCE

To explore the context of why the geishas' dance performances acquired such strong power to instill a fictional, nationalistic ideal in their audiences, it is important to consider the original intentions of the performances. From its inception, geisha performance was a popular event. Its purpose was to attract customers—who would also partake in other geisha entertainments—to benefit commercial districts such as Gion. The *Miyako Odori* at the Kyoto exposition, as a large public event, expanded this audience into the general public. In other words, geishas' public performance was always a purposeful event intended to pursue economic gain and expand local power. In this way, it was imbued with politics, and authorities with different goals could utilize it to their advantage.

Another important factor at work in geisha performance is the dimension of social inequality. Performers, including both geisha and traditional Japanese theater actors, belonged to a profession whose practitioners had been discriminated against and denied full citizenship status since premodern times. The belief that geisha belonged to a lowly class also functioned powerfully to reinforce national policy. Entertainers aspired to be accepted as *kokumin*, which means both "people" and "citizens."[22] Perhaps this is why geisha were very sensitive to the views of the authorities, because as disenfranchised people they needed opportunities to garner favor from those in power. They might anticipate requests from the authorities, even when the authorities did not directly order them. On the other hand, the authorities seemed to be also seeking opportunities to use performances and the popularity and influence of entertainers to help control the public. Bellicose acts staged in *Miyako Odori* performance are good examples of this system. The government's interests thus coincided with entertainers' needs and aspirations, which may have facilitated their collaboration.

In addition to this condition of facing discrimination, the geisha's appearance is another important contributing distinction. In the example of the 1939 performance, the dancers were young girls, and the whole program consisted of child dancers and young geisha. Along with the child dancers, the geisha looked innocent and nonpolitical, favorable characteristics that could be easily deployed to lower defenses and open the audiences to their charms. At the time, women did not have the right to vote in Japan, and only a few women were involved in explicitly political activities. Some geisha reported their opinions to newspapers and magazines, and some made public political speeches. They were not just passive puppets, even though their appearances made them into romanticized cultural icons of doll-like, seductive idols. Both the state and the producers appear to have utilized these appearances for their respective goals.

Geisha performances were not the only ones used to stir up loyalty during the war effort. Used in similar ways were other popular culture forms, such as war songs, war paintings, and propaganda films. Traditional theatrical performances, such as *kabuki* and *bunraku*, also presented war-related themes. But the dance performances of the geisha were special, because they could portray unrealistic scenes. To understand how dance could do this, I will describe some characteristics of Japanese traditional dance.

While almost all dance performances are accompanied by music, Japanese traditional dance, including that of the geisha, is with few exceptions accompanied not only by music but specifically by vocal music. Because the lyrics can express the context of the story or action, dance can represent concrete elements of the narrative. Unlike plays and movies, however, the context tends to be simplified because these dances are shorter and often more abstract. The dance does not have to delve into the concrete details of its theme; rather, it can use words to convey intentions and emotions beyond those expressed in the literal meaning. The lyrics of "Kōa Ondo"— which contain the line cited above, "Brothers, brothers, hand in hand, March, April, East Wind"—are a good example. This gives the idea that dance is relatively unrestrained. Some consider dance a synthesis of the advantages of other arts. Descriptive language, visualization, and oral and audio media— together with the impact of moving bodies—allow dance to occupy a special sensual and emotive place. The authorities who became aware of this at the time recognized this power of the *Miyako Odori* performances.

CONCLUSION

In the 1930s, Japan was headed toward destruction. Its armies were overextended, and its military infrastructure was deteriorating. The government hastened to use entertainment in its efforts to conceal the situation and to galvanize the loyalty of the common people. *Miyako Odori* was one of these popular and powerful entertainments. People were easily seduced and transported by the beautiful appearance of the young performers, the upbeat tunes and lyrics, and the spectacular stage settings of the performance. Further, the *Miyako Odori* established a precedent for other kinds of popular entertainment to follow, setting the stage for further exploitation of entertainment by the government during the war years.

Other types of entertainment also served the interests of Japan's wartime military authorities. The 1938 *Miyako Odori* included a dance celebrating the occupation of Nanjing and another celebrating the Anti-Comintern Pact.

Authorities also used war songs and national flags for finales. For example, the final act of the 1938 performance, under cherry trees in full bloom, displayed more than fifty gorgeously appareled dancers waving national flags that included the Nazi swastika, the fascist Italian flag with Mussolini's Roman ax, the Rising Sun (the Japanese Imperial Navy flag), and the Manchukuo flag of the Beijing puppet state with its five stripes representing the "five races."[23] Newspapers printed favorable accounts of such nationalistic dances.[24] The *Miyako Odori* was performed annually until 1943. After 1939, wartime austerity put a stop to the expensive color programs. The humbler black-and-white printed programs, however, show the titles of the performances and their individual scenes, which demonstrate *Miyako Odori*'s continued subservience to military authorities.[25]

To conclude, *Miyako Odori* and other dance performances by geisha communities excelled as political propaganda because they made spectators dream. The system was reinforced by its popularity, the innocent appearances of geisha and child dancers, and its poetic lyrics. Discrimination against entertainers also worked to support propaganda aims. In the 1930s, stage performance was about to be replaced by a new entertainment, talkie films. In terms of the power of circulation, stage performance was no match for film. Thus, as it lost its role as a news medium, the stage explored other opportunities to survive. Under the militaristic climate of the times, *Miyako Odori* found a way to sustain itself, by selling beautiful dreams to mask the horrors of war.

ADDITIONAL RESOURCES

Full resolution versions of Figure 8.1 at https://doi.org/10.3998/mpub.11521701.cmp.15 and Figure 8.2 at https://doi.org/10.3998/mpub.11521701.cmp.16

Link 8.1: Kyoto Tourism Site. Available at https://doi.org/10.3998/mpub.11521701.cmp.53

Link 8.2: Miyako Odori Official Site. Available at https://doi.org/10.3998/mpub.11521701.cmp.54

Link 8.3: Records of "Aiba Shingunka" and "Kōa Ondo" in the Historical Record Collection at the National Diet Library. Available at https://doi.org/10.3998/mpub.11521701.cmp.55

## Notes

1. "Kyōto Nigiwai Mitate" 京都賑見立, 1873; Yoshida Mitsukuni 吉田光圀 "Kyōto no Hakurankai" 京都の博覧会, Hayashiya Tatsusaburō 林屋辰三郎et al., eds., *Kyōto no Rekishi* 京都の歴史 (Tokyo: Gakugei Shorin 学芸書林, 1975), 125, fig. 45.

2. *Kyoto Shinbun*, no. 35, July 1872, reported that geisha in Asuwa, Fukui (150 km from Kyoto), started a dance performance called "Asuwa Odori" in imitation of Kyoto's *Miyako Odori*. In Shimomiyajima, Hiroshima (400 km from Kyoto), a similar performance was held.

3. According to the official city of Kyoto document "Yūsho Kiji" dated November 1873, Kyoto had eight licensed geisha districts. Kyotofuritsu Sōgōshiryōkan 京都府立総合資料館, *Kyōtofu Hyakunen no Shiryō 4 Shakai hen* 京都府百年の資料 社会編 (Kyōto: Kyōto Prefecture, 1972), 484–85. Tanaka Ryokko mentions five public performances: Gion, Shimogawara, Ponto-chō, Miyagawa-chō, and Shimabara. Tanaka Ryokkō 田中緑紅, *Kyō no Buyō* 京の舞踊 (Kyōto: Kyō o Kataru Kai, 1963), 43–62, 70–80, 86.

4. Today, there are five geisha quarters in Kyoto, and all of five quarters organize their public annual dance performance. Among them the most popular performance has always been the *Miyako Odori* performance held in the geisha district of Gion, the most famous quarter and one that has served as the setting of many novels and films. Mizoguchi Kenji's 1936 film *Sisters of the Gion* is one of the most famous films about the district. Arthur Golden's bestselling 1997 novel *Memoirs of a Geisha* is also set here. *Gion no Kyōdai* 祇園の姉妹 directed by Mizoguchi Kenji 溝口健二, Daiichi Eiga, 1936, film. Arthur Golden, *Memoirs of a Geisha* (New York: Random House, 1997). Without exception the *Miyako Odori* performance has been choreographed by a unique, all-female dance school, the Inoue ryû (井上流), that has exercised strong control over geisha dance in this district. Due to the popularity of the annual event, many materials still exist, including pictures, postcards, official programs, lyrics, dance scores, photo books, newspaper reports, records, films, and reviews in magazines. It was also possible to interview retired geisha about their dance performances in the first half of the twentieth century. Films, above all, proved to have the greatest impact, and in 1999, I organized a study group to explore them in detail. We published a report on films and dance studies of the performances, which serves as the basis for this chapter. Nagata Toyoomi 長田豊臣, *Mukei Bunkazai to Kiroku Hozon: Miyako Odori no Jurokumiri Eiga o Daizai toshite* 無形文化財と記録保存: 都をどりの十六ミリ映画を題材として (Kyoto: Ritsumeikan University, 2001).

5. English titles in 1933 and 1938 were printed in the official programs of *Miyako Odori*. Since there were no English translations of the entire title in the 1939 program, the title "The Basis of the Dynasty" is translated by Mariko Okada based on explanatory notes of the official program. Its original title was "Kenmu no Minamoto 建武の源." Program for *Miyako Odori* at the Kaburenjō Theater, Kyoto: Kabukai. Playbill, 1933, 12; program for *Miyako Odori* at the Kaburenjō Theater, Kyoto: Kabukai. Playbill, 1938, 23; program for *Miyako Odori* at the Kaburenjō Theater, Kyoto: Kabukai. Playbill, 1939, 13.

6. Program for *Miyako Odori* at the Kaburenjō Theater, Kyoto: Kabukai. Playbill, 1939, 23, 44.

7. Program for *Miyako Odori* at the Kaburenjō Theater, Kyoto: Kabukai. Playbill, 1939, 44, 64.

8. Kurata Yoshihiro 倉田 喜弘, *Nihon Rekōdo Bunkashi* 日本レコード文化史 (Tōkyō: Tōkyō Shoseki, 1980), 204–6; Morimoto Toshikatsu 森本敏克, *Rekōdo Hayariuta* 音盤歌謡史：歌と映画とレコードと (Kyōto: Shirakawa Shoin, 1975), 142–43.

9. Several records of "Aiba Shingunka" can be found in archives and private collections. A record of "Kōa Ondo" documented the performance of geisha in Gion. Both are found in the Historical Record Collection at the National Diet Library (http://rekion.dl.ndl.go.jp/). Writer and composer names are printed on the record labels as well as in the official program. Program for *Miyako Odori* at the Kaburenjō Theater (Kyoto: Kabukai. Playbill, 1939), 13; Kyōto Gion Kōbu Geigi-ren "Kōa-ondo," Victor PR163, 1939.

10. Program for *Miyako Odori* at the Kaburenjō Theater, Kyoto: Kabukai. Playbill, 1939, 13; Kyōto Gion Kōbu Geigi-ren "Kōa-ondo," Victor PR163, 1939.

11. Ten names for Chinese girls and ten names for Japanese girls are listed in the official program. Their names are different from the professional names of geisha. They are the real names of girls who were training to be geisha. The film also shows younger girls dancing in this scene. A retired geisha also mentioned that girls in training used to appear on the *Miyako Odori* stage in the 1930s.

12. This film is in the possession of the headmaster of the Inoue School of Dance.

13. "Miyako Odori ni Kensetsu-chō" 都をどりに建設調, *Kyōto Hinode Shinbun* 京都日出新聞, February 15, 1939, 3.

14. Ōnishi Hidenori 大西秀紀, "Miyako Odori Kanren no Rekōdo" 都をどり関連のレコード; Nagata Toyoomi 長田豊臣, *Mukei Bunkazai to Kiroku Hozon: Miyako Odori no Jūūrokumiri Eiga o Daizai toshite* 無形文化財と記録保存：都をどりの十六ミリ映画を題材として (Kyoto: Ritsumeikan University, 2001), 178–80. Presentations of the song took place in multiple cities after its release on January 15. In Kyoto, the event took place at Gion on February 5, 1939. The finale included Shimada's children's dance. Ōnishi has suggested that this event may have triggered the district to ask Shimada to choreograph that year's *Miyako Odori*.

15. "Meibutsu Miyako Odori mo Kōa no Haru o Kotohogu" 名物"都をどり"も興亜の春をことほぐ, *Kyōto Hinode Shinbun* 京都日出新聞, April 19, 1939, 3.

16. "Kenmu no Minamoto: Kotoshi no Miyako Odori Inshōki" 建武の源：今年の"都踊"印象記, *Kyōto Hinode Shinbun* 京都日出新聞, April 17, 1939, 3.

17. Kagome Kagome is a Japanese children's game accompanied by a song of the same title. It appears to be quite old—lyrics closely resembling those of the song have been found in an eighteenth-century document. One player sits covering eyes with hands. The other children join hands and walk in a circle around the player, singing the song for the game. When the song finishes, the player tries to name the person standing behind the player. If the guess is correct, the person behind exchanges places with the first player. The recorded dance did not have the children sitting in the center of the circle, but dancing in a circle reminds people of this game.

18. This has a precedent in 1934. The dance song "Gion Ondo," or "Gion Dance Song," was used in *Miyako Odori* and later released as a record. Hayasaki Haruyū 早崎春勇 (1909–?), a famous Gion geisha, wrote that she remembered everyone singing this song in the streets after the show. Hayasak Haruyū 早崎春勇, *Gion Yoi Banashi* 祇園よいばなし (Kyoto: Kyoto-shoin, 1990), 36–37.

19. Kawakami Otojirō 川上音二郎 (1864–1911) is very famous for his war dramas. He visited the field to gather information and developed performances based on his experiences and observations after returning to Japan. Joseph L. Anderson, *Enter a Samurai: Kawakami Otojirō and Japanese Theatre in the West* (Tucson, AZ: Wheatmark, 2011), 24–26.

20. A newspaper reported that the organizers of the performance traveled from Kyūshū to Ryūkyū island to take in its local dance, and as a result the performance completely changed its style. "Kamogawa Odori" 鴨川をどり, *Kyōto Nichinichi Shinbun*, May 12, 1940, 3.

21. When I showed the film to retired geisha in 1999, two of them told me about scene IV of the 1938 *Miyako Odori*, which depicted the Nanjing occupation. They still remembered the scene, and that spectators applauded enthusiastically, in tears. This scene is another example of stylized war. Since this act was not performed by dancers but instead used music and varied scenery, I do not analyze it in this chapter. However, the reaction of the spectators shows that the act was carefully produced to accord with people's desire.

22. In 1915, when Emperor Taisho ascended the throne, there was an argument about whether geisha can celebrate or not. In the *Yomiuri Newspaper* issued on October 29, 1915, there was a headline reading "Geisha were not rejected in Nagoya. They are equally citizens." This headline shows the ongoing discrimination geisha faced and their struggle for citizenship.

23. These were shot on 16 mm film, now possessed by the Inoue School, and these elements were explained in the official program. Program for *Miyako Odori* at the Kaburenjō Theater, Kyoto: Kabukai. Playbill, 1938, 23.

24. "It would be extremely meaningful for the audience to sing the Patriot March together, waving flags of the Anti-Comintern Pact nations, at the last scene in Heian Shrine, though it is highly unlikely that audiences would not join in the chorus." "Gunkoku no haru o utau, Miyako Odori mo ato isshūkan, Jūnenrai minu ōatari, Kyokkō Henki, kotoshi no Miyako Odori" 軍国の春を謳ふ 都踊もあと一週間 十年来見ぬ大当り旭光遍輝 ことしの都をどり, *Kyoto Hinode Shinbun* 京都日出新聞, April 25, 1938, 3.

25. Printed on the programs in 1942 and 1943 were such warlike phrases as "Susume Ichioku Hinotama da 進め一億火の玉だ (Go, hundred million balls of fire! )," "Tatakainukō Daitōa-sen 戦い抜こう大東亜戦 (Fight out the Greater East Asian War!)," "Katte kabuto no o o shimeyo 勝って兜の緒を締めよ (Tighten helmet even after victory)," and "Uchiteshi yamamu 撃ちてし止まむ (Shoot to destroy!)." These programs are rectangular single sheets of paper with double-sided printing. They are 18.3 cen-

timeters by 53.0 centimeters, a traditional Japanese paper size. The programs printed a list of performers, lyrics, and scene explanations; the elements of performances
conformed to the wartime situation. This simple style of program is seen throughout
history, and such programs have been used as advertising flyers. Program for *Miyako
Odori* at the Kaburenjō Theater, Playbill, 1942; program for *Miyako Odori* at the Kaburenjō Theater, Playbill, 1943.

# CHAPTER 9

# Imagined Choreographies

## Itō Michio's Philippines Pageant and the Transpacific Performance of Japanese Imperialism

*Tara Rodman*

In 1944, the Japanese modern dancer and choreographer Itō Michio 伊藤 道郎 (1893–1961) drew up plans for a national festival pageant in the Philippines. The proposal envisioned an episodic chronicle of Filipino history culminating with the nation's independence from American rule, the event the festival was intended to celebrate. This pageant, which has gone almost entirely unacknowledged in scholarship on Itō, presents three challenges to the dance historian—challenges that help explain this critical silence.[1] First, the pageant's massive scope and propagandist content make it seem inconsistent with Itō's best-known works, which were lyrical, abstract, and small-scale. Second, it implicates Itō as a collaborator with Japan's wartime military government. And, finally, it never happened.

This essay argues that it is precisely by attending to an unrealized project such as the Philippines pageant that a crucial facet of Itō's career becomes visible: across his career in Europe, the United States, and Japan, he sought to choreograph ways of being in community that could transcend geography, race, and regime. This investment in embodied community crystalized in his proposal for the Philippines pageant, but it emerges as a distinct thread winding through his earlier experiences and artistic work. Moreover, I propose that attending to the history made visible by focusing on the unrealized project, in turn, offers a way to imaginatively access Itō's investment in embodied community. That is, tracing Itō's career-long engagement with the pageant form, civic performances, and mass choreography, alongside the planning documents he authored, provides a wealth of material with which to imagine what Itō imagined. If choreographic reconstruction is a mainstay of dance studies, honed to recover past performances, what I propose here is an extension of that methodology to events that never occurred—imagined reconstruction—to access performances that, though never actualized on stage, represent significant events in our understanding of dance history.

## CHOREOGRAPHIES OF COMMUNITY

Itō is best known for his participation in the 1916 dance drama *At the Hawk's Well*, a collaboration with the poets W. B. Yeats and Ezra Pound. Performed twice, in private London drawing rooms (though Itō repeatedly remounted the production in New York, Los Angeles, and Tokyo), it is recognized as paradigmatic of a European modernist penchant for the obscure, the poetic, and the antitheatrical. Itō's subsequent solo choreography, of pieces such as the moody *Tone Poem I* and *II*, or *Pizzicati*, a playful shadow dance, cemented his reputation as a choreographer of compact, lyrical, and allusive works. Group choreographies, such as the solemn *Ecclesiastique*, and even his large-scale pieces staged in the Hollywood and Rose Bowls in the 1930s, used classical or literary themes to inspire abstract group movements. It is for these pieces that Itō has been claimed as "a forgotten pioneer" of modern dance in both Japan and the US.[2] But alongside this strain of concert dance choreography, we can also find in Itō's biography a persistent interest in the power of embodied movement to invoke a sense of community. A narrative highlighting Itō's engagement with choreographed community runs parallel to the more standard accounts of his career and is crucial to understanding his plans for the Philippines festival pageant.

Shortly after arriving in Europe, Itō enrolled in the Jaques-Dalcroze Institute for Eurythmics in Hellerau, Germany. The year he spent there (1913–14) established both the basis for his own choreographic vocabulary and his belief in the potential of bodies moving in unison to communicate a powerful sense of communality. The core of Émile Jaques-Dalcroze's method consisted of twenty arm movements that allowed students to express musical rhythms in their bodies. Echoing this training, within a few years after leaving Hellerau, Itō had developed his own technique, consisting of two movement sequences, each made up of ten poses, that a dancer could move through, rearrange, and use as the basis for original choreography.[3]

In addition to this choreographic technique, Hellerau was also the source of the artistic and political ideals that guided much of Itō's career and influenced his plans for the Philippines pageant. While the Dalcroze method itself, with its emphasis on restoring natural rhythms through bodily movement, provided a great deal of this ideological emphasis, so too did two mass

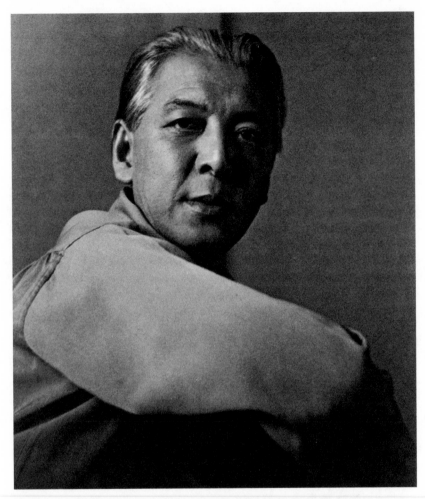

Fig, 9.1. Michio Itō, October 1938, California. Photo by Johan Hagemeyer, from the Johan Hagemeyer photograph collection, BANC PIC 1964.063 Ito, Michio :005—PIC, © The Regents of the University of California, The Bancroft Library, University of California, Berkeley.

productions that took place around the period of Itō's study there. In 1912 and 1913, the Dalcroze Institute hosted summer festivals, featuring lecture demonstrations, tours of the school, and most famously, a production of Gluck's *Orpheus and Eurydice* staged by Jaques-Dalcroze and Adolphe Appia. For the opera's spectators, Jaques-Dalcroze's innovations, particularly in the crowd scenes, made an unforgettable impression. As the conductor Ernest

Ansermet recalled, "The students formed several groups of Spirits. They took imperceptible movements to the music, inclinations of the head, liftings of the arms; they passed hardly touching the ground, weightless, and Orpheus crossed their groups without disturbing them, the groups reforming behind him."[4] With the briefest of movements, the group arrangements communicated a sense of replete motion, and emotion. Indeed, the expression and eliciting of an emotional response were central to Jaques-Dalcroze's goal of creating a correspondence between space, music, and movement. As he wrote to his sister during rehearsals, "For the finale, I found a gesture for the crowd so extraordinary that everyone trembled and this single gesture will awaken the sensitive to be moved."[5] This production crystalized the dual promises of the Dalcroze method—that it could simultaneously produce art of high artistic merit and serve as a form of corporeal repair for individuals, and for society as a whole.

In the summer of 1914, Jaques-Dalcroze staged a mass history pageant in Switzerland to celebrate the centennial of the Geneva Republic's entry into the Swiss Confederation. As Percy B. Ingham described it, "In the first act, lasting close on an hour, tableaux vivants illustrating the history of Geneva from remote times down to 1814 were shown as a background, while the 50 metre wide stage was filled by three to four hundred rhythmic pupils who gave plastic expression to the music, itself appropriate to the scenes shown in the background."[6] Spectators for the event reportedly numbered 6,000; they sat facing the stage, whose back wall could roll up to reveal Lake Geneva and the Swiss countryside.[7] The Geneva Festival thus offered another demonstration of the unifying power of mass performance, this time very clearly in service of producing a sense of national community. Notably, Itō was not present at either of these events. The *Orpheus* occurred right before Itō arrived at the school, while the Geneva pageant, of course, took place in Geneva—which not only made it difficult for students to see, but precluded the organization of a festival at the school in Hellerau that year. Itō's affective sense of absence from these two events is evident in his efforts to recreate the Hellerau experience again and again throughout his career, and perhaps helps to explain his abiding interest in large-scale choreographies of communality thereafter.

In the US, where Itō moved at the end of 1916, the broader phenomenon of choreographies of mass movement coalesced into what is known as the American Pageant Movement, in which the pageant was embraced as a form geared to the expression of American democracy. American modern dance, in particular, shows evidence of the influence of this movement—Ruth St. Denis, Isadora Duncan, Doris Humphrey, and Lester Horton all choreographed or participated in pageants. Moreover, modern dancers shared several ideological and thematic characteristics with pageant devisers: an embrace of mythohistoric themes, an emphasis on the value of the amateur performer, and a belief in movement as an expressive mode of spiritual truth.

Itō repeatedly experienced, participated in, or worked alongside pageant and other large-scale, communitarian productions in the US. In 1919, he appeared with his former teacher, the opera singer Miura Tamaki, in a pageant, *Call to Commerce, Business, and the Professions*, staged as part of the World Peace Festival held in Washington, DC, on the first Fourth of July following the end of World War I.[8] And in 1928, Itō appeared in a program, "Orchestral Dramas," organized by the progressive arts patrons Alice and Irene Lewisohn, which included Ernest Bloch's *Israel*, a massive dance-drama symphony that staged supplicants praying at the Wailing Wall, culminating in a scene of revelation.[9] In Los Angeles, where Itō settled in 1929, he staged his own large group works, which he called "Dance Symphonies." Staged in the area's large open-air Bowls, which had all been constructed specifically as spaces for community performance, the dances were seen by thousands of spectators.[10] They thus called into being a sense of active, embodied community, which was enhanced by the fact that many of the dancers were young, local Californians.

In these California projects, the meanings of communality generated through the sites of performance and casting of local dancers were magnified by Itō's techniques of staging, which relied on large groupings and the creation of colorful stage pictures to communicate a sense of vibrant unity. For example, in 1930, Itō staged a version of the "Polovtsian Dances" section of Alexander Borodin's *Prince Igor*. A critic writing for the *Hollywood Citizen News*, noting the overflowing audience and standing ovation given the performance, observed, "The ensemble was particularly fine, and parti-colored costumes that enabled instantaneous change of colored patterns according to the angle presented by the dancers were exceptionally effective."[11] The striking visual effect of using the dancers' bodies en masse to create color impressions was echoed in a choreography reliant on large group arrangements to magnify the dramatic impact. A sketched silhouette of one scene, published in the *Los Angeles Evening Herald*, shows opposing groups of male and female dancers; each side essentially performs one uncomplicated motion in unison, but with enough variation in arrangement, level, and direction to create an overall sense of vivid action. The newspaper joined this illustration with a close-up photograph of two of the featured soloists, the fencer Ralph Faulkner (who was married to choreographer and dance-studio owner Edith

Fig. 9.2. *Prince Igor* at Hollywood Bowl. *Los Angeles Evening Herald,* August 14, 1930. Artist and photographer unknown. Courtesy Los Angeles Philharmonic Archive.

Jane), and Louise Glenn, a local dancer known for her acrobatic agility. Their pose—dramatic and arresting in both form and facial expressions—suggests how soloists would have emerged out of the group, juxtaposed against its choreographic unity to embody moments of heightened emotion. Such staging, which placed so much emphasis on simple gestures and pictorial effects rather than dancerly virtuosity, invited the audience to affectively join in the activity of expressive community dance, offering movement as an accessible way to feel—and produce—a sense of community.

From its early seeds at the Dalcroze Institute, Itō's belief in the renovating power of dance intensified during his time in the US, and he repeatedly imagined ways to expand this belief out of the studio and onto the world stage. A 1928 article in the *New York Tribune* opened, "Michio Ito, it is said, once went down to Washington to see President Harding concerning a theory for world peace. It was quite simple, merely: Let each great nation yield up the price of a battleship and let the combined sums be applied toward the foundation of an international dance academy. Mr. Ito practically guaranteed that this would end war, so strong was and is his faith in his art."[12] The same anecdote appears in Itō's postwar memoirs, and although, like many of his narratives, it was probably fabricated, it displays his quixotic but earnest faith in the power of dance as an embodied political activity that could remake human relations, on a sociopolitical, indeed, global scale. Precisely because mass pageants seemed to materialize this commitment through their incorporation of individuals into unified movement in service of an embodiment of community, they appealed to Itō as a performative instantiation of his deepest beliefs about dance.

Itō's involvement in choreographies of American community seemed to suddenly end on December 7, 1941, the day of the bombing of Pearl Harbor. The FBI raided Itō's Los Angeles home and sent him to a series of Department of Justice camps, where he was interned as an enemy alien for nearly two years.[13] In 1943, Itō was granted repatriation, and he returned to Japan by the end of the year. Back in Tokyo, he threw himself into activities on behalf of the Japanese war effort and imperial administration, performing the national loyalty expected—and suspected—of him. Itō focused his efforts on founding the Greater East Asia Stage Arts Research Institute (大東亜舞台芸術研究所), an organization intended to mobilize performing artists across the Japanese Empire—known officially at the time as the core part of the Greater East Asia Co-Prosperity Sphere. Although Japan was mobilized for total war, Itō's homecoming and organizational efforts reintegrated him into a network of social, artistic, and political ties after he had lived out of the country for over two decades. High-ranking government and army officials, who had also provided financial assistance while Itō was in California, again offered him funding and a furnished apartment. Meanwhile, a friend's abandoned beauty parlor served as the Institute's office and rehearsal space; Itō also used it for his newly established dance studio.[14] Itō enlisted the participation of prominent artists and intellectuals, such as the composer Yamada Kōsaku, playwrights Kishida Kunio and Kubota Mantarō, and scholar of Indian literature and Sanskrit, Tsuji Naoshirō, who all joined the Institute's advisory board.

That Itō's project was supported by the government and military, even at such a late stage of the war, reflected the fact that his proposal complemented other cultural propaganda activities carried out across Japan's empire. In 1941, a new policy of cultural propaganda, based on the Nazi *propaganda Korps*, called for battalions of civilian *bunkajin* (men of culture) to be attached to Japan's armies in Southeast Asia. These writers, painters, musicians, filmmakers, and other culture makers had the responsibility of persuading indigenous populations to willingly join in the creation of a new Asia envisioned by Japanese leaders. Theater and dance became active spheres for this propaganda work, as writers such as Takeda Rintarō and Kon Hidemi organized theatrical productions in Indonesia and the Philippines in the service of Japan's imperial agenda.[15]

Itō's choice of the Philippines as the site of his festival followed these models of policy and practice and reflected its status as a major site of military and cultural contest during the Pacific War. The Philippines had been a Spanish and then a US colony until, on December 8, 1941, Japan invaded it in a series of battles that lasted through May 1942, subsequently occupying the country until the summer of 1945. During this period, the Philippines, like Burma, occupied an ambiguous category in Japan's Co-Prosperity Sphere. To perpetuate the claim that Japan's imperialism served a broader, nobler goal of Pan-Asianism, Japan granted the Philippines independence in October 1943. In reality, however, administration and military conditions were in Japanese control, but carried out through local officials. This arrangement was meant to exemplify the idea behind wartime Japan's vision for a New Order in Asia, in which Asian nations, free from Western dominion, were united in partnership under Japanese leadership.

Ultimately, the overall conditions of war and the US firebombing of Tokyo in the spring of 1945 severely curtailed the Institute's activities. Indeed, Itō was only able to mount one production, a Takarazuka-style revue, before he fled with his family and students for safety to the countryside. As a result, the Institute existed primarily on paper, in a series of thirteen documents that Itō drew up. Two of these were submitted to the Greater East Asia Ministry, while the rest—including the one outlining the Philippines pageant—remained in his private possession.[16] These papers fill in the narrative gap in his career occasioned by the war. But they also document how Itō's act of allegiance to imperial Japan offered an opportunity for him to work toward a production of embodied community that in scope and political meaning would fulfill his long-standing belief that choreography might remake the world.

## IMAGINING THE IMAGINED PAGEANT

The documents that remain as evidence of Itō's vision for the Philippines pageant offer only spare hints of what he intended. To write about a production that existed only within Itō's imagination, then, I resort to my own imagination, acknowledging, in the process, the vast spaces of time, geography, and identity that I cannot traverse, and that I do not try to occupy. This is what I see:

The festival was supposed to take place in Manila. However, like the Geneva pageant, and like the Dalcroze Institute itself, I imagine that Itō envisioned a location slightly removed from the city, where nature asserted itself as part of the backdrop—and was thus incorporated as a national property. I picture the ground cleared for a stage with two levels of platforms and sets of ramps and stairs on both sides. The playing space would be both this explicit stage and the cleared area running into the audience, so that spectators would feel the depicted history as their own. Reflecting Adolph Appia's contributions to the Hellerau experiments, when performers massed themselves on this stage, the lines and shadows created by their movement would transform their bodies into an additional source of architecture, molding the empty air into meaningful space.

Itō embraced the pageant genre, both during his time in the US and after his return to Japan, for its capacity to enact a performative instantiation of national community. This ideological work was woven into Itō's vision for the Philippines pageant's dramaturgy, its participants, and the process of its creation. For instance, the pageant's content consisted of an episodic presentation of the history of the Philippines up to independence:

> "... before the Spaniards came, then the era of Spanish rule, the era of American rule," and then, "under the Great East Asia war, the four stages of the era of the construction of a new Philippines ... the tyrannical rule of Euro-American colonial dominion, the growth of a national (*minzoku*) sentiment among the Filipino people, the history of the hardship of the independence movement, and the awakening of the Greater East Asia Co-Prosperity Sphere through which, with Japanese support, independence was achieved."[17]

The episodic structure, presuming an ignorant spectator, presented history as teleological drama. In Itō's dramaturgy, the stages of imperial dominion by Western nations proceeded as installments culminating in the inevitable scene of independence. The pageant's content thus imparted educative significance to an explicitly bookended narrative, whereby the nation's history became familiar and preordained.

I imagine that each stage in this national history would be a scene beginning and ending in a tableau vivant, as had the Geneva pageant. Each scene would include representational pantomime along with more abstract choreography to suggest the emotional import of the action. I imagine that, as Itō had done in his California dance symphonies, the hundreds of members of the movement chorus would have been broken into smaller groups. Each group would perform its own simple, graphic choreography in unison, while complementing the others, alternately filling the space with a sense of massed movement and stilled presence. As in the *Orpheus* at Hellerau, protagonists would emerge out of these groups, with the collectivity reforming behind them. And, true to Itō's Dalcrozian training, there would be close correspondence between the pageant's dramaturgy, the performers' rhythmic movement, and the music, to induce strong emotion in the spectators.

The national pedagogy achieved by the pageant's content was complemented by its participants and production process. Itō called for the festival activity to be led and carried out by locals: "Filipino writers, musicians, actors, dancers and so on will be mobilized and trained, from the drawing up of scripts to the entire creative process, so that as much as possible is done by Filipinos themselves. . . . This plan's chief executive should, of course, be Filipino, a local member of the cultural elite [*bunkajin*], who can directly make contact with artists, as it is essential that they make the final decisions."[18] Highlighting the abundant artistic, cultural, and organizational capacity of the local populace, Itō emphasized the notion that community participation was essential to the performative staging of national collectivity. I imagine that, as had been the case in California, Itō particularly saw this as an opportunity to train young local dancers, who could then perform solo interludes within the program, demonstrating in their artistic presence the corporeal potential of Filipino youth.

Just as surely as the proposal envisioned a choreography of Filipino national collectivity, however, it disclosed Itō's position as a subject of Japan. Indeed, lurking behind the pageant's nationalist framework was the offstage presence of imperial Japan. And in Itō's plans, the pageant's anticipated expression of national allegiance doubled as an expression of colonial allegiance. Thus, Itō writes that the Institute would "sponsor the artistry of stage artists from every area of Greater East Asia and, at the same time, encourage awareness of themselves as independent peoples, with their hands raising up the New East Asian Culture, with deep emotion for both the 'sun' and 'Japan.'"[19] In this formulation, local Filipino "awareness of themselves as independent peoples" overlaps with, and even engenders a "deep emotion" for, imperial Japan, the presence of which is doubled in the reference to "Japan" and to its national symbol, the "sun." To express this coupling of national and

colonial identification, I imagine elements of Itō's own choreographic repertoire and method repurposed for this moment. Perhaps he would have used a
straightforward sequence of codified positions from his technique, in which
the arms, raised overhead but bent at the elbows, move through a flourish
with the hands. Performed with the dancers' faces beatifically lifted upward,
the scripted sentiment "with deep emotion for both the 'sun' and 'Japan'"
would be corporealized in broadly legible movement, as the abstract positions of the Itō technique became explicitly representational. Itō's plan for
the pageant thus always called for the simultaneous performance of two different collective identities—that of the Philippines as a nation, as well as that
of the Pan-Asian spirit unified under the protective sphere of Japan's Greater
East Asia.

## GLIMPSING THE PAN-ASIAN IMAGINARY

My imagined reconstruction of Itō's imagined Philippines pageant draws
together details of his technique, his dance education, and his past encounters with other pageant events to produce a description of an event that
occurred only in Itō's mind. Much of this effort coheres with the collection
and continuing project of *Imagined Theatres* organized by Daniel Sack.[20] As
Sack describes it, the appeal of the invitation of an imagined theater is its
promise to go beyond the possible, to exceed limits—theatrical, physical,
social, political—via recourse to the capaciousness of the disembodied and
unrealizable. Itō's Philippines pageant, like Sack's "imagined theatres," was
not possible; the deteriorating conditions of the war made such an expendi-
ture of human and material resources fundamentally unthinkable. And yet,
unlike the theaters gathered under Sack's rubric, the pageant was also by no
means impossible. Indeed, Itō's prior experiences with the pageant form had
consistently demonstrated surprising allocations of funds, time, and people
to such grandiose projects. Indeed, the origin of his dance education and of
his wartime proposal—the pageants and festivals connected to the Dalcroze
Institute at Hellerau—were themselves extraordinary instantiations of the
attainability of such visions. Indeed, even as it would seem a wasteful absurdity, the rapacious needs of a wartime empire to justify itself had authorized
and seen to fruition many other similar efforts of performance propaganda.

Itō's proposal for the Philippines pageant, then, anticipated the project's
failure at the same time that it took seriously the possibility of its enactment—
and even more so, took seriously the significance of its ideological promise.
For what is striking about Itō's proposal is the way it ties Japan's imperial

agenda to his own fervent belief that choreography might remake the world by calling into existence a sense of embodied collectivity. This was a belief that was foundational to the Life Reform Movement enacted at Hellerau and to the origins of early modern dance in both Europe and the US, in which Itō was a direct participant. In the dislocations and reversals in status that marked his experience of the Pacific War, Itō picked up the thread of this belief in the ideology of Pan-Asianism.

Though the ideology of Pan-Asianism ultimately came to be seen as an apologia for Japan's imperialism, it had several different strains and various supporters from countries across Asia, especially in the early twentieth century.[21] Certainly, Itō was not alone in desiring the creation of artistic forms that were rooted in various Asian traditions and could affectively represent a sort of Pan-Asian aesthetic community. For example, Choe Seung-hui, a Korean dancer trained by Itō's friend Ishii Baku, similarly devoted herself during the war to devising new modern dance forms that she called "Eastern dance."[22] For Itō, the ideology seemed to be a clear successor to the ideals he had imbibed at Hellerau, in that it articulated a dissolving of national boundaries in favor of a vision of communitarian connection. It was thus no accident that Itō selected as the founding principle of his Greater East Asia Stage Arts Research Institute one of the dicta enunciated at the Greater East Asia Conference, held in Tokyo on November 5 and 6, 1943: "Every country of Greater East Asia, mutually respecting each other's traditions, and expanding the creativity of every people [*minzoku*], will uplift the culture of Greater East Asia."[23] In this formulation, artistic tradition and creativity stood as the basis for a reorganization of social and political boundaries. Like Itō's vision for the Philippines festival pageant, this notion coupled the violent reality of Japan's imperialism with the allure of an imagined world, in which choreography might call into being new bodies of community.

The troubling utopianism of this vision epitomizes a much broader phenomenon by which numerous Japanese artists and intellectuals were drawn to their nation's imperial project. As historian Louise Young has observed, "Because such imperial projects were multidimensional, the mobilization of support among their divergent interests required an inclusive vision that promised something for everyone."[24] The promise offered by the idea of empire and Japan's New Order in Asia was effective because it was capacious enough to appeal to many different groups, whose own individual yearnings seemed to find an outlet in the opportunities presented by colonial expansion. While Young writes of the business leaders, military personnel, and intellectuals who supported the colonial agenda in Manchuria, the same was true of many Japanese artists, motivated to commit their talents to efforts aimed at regions across the empire. The imagined status of Itō's pageant crystallizes this pervasive phenomenon, in which an individual's own private dreams could be tied to those of the empire, suddenly articulated as not merely personal, but as serving a broader social, regional community. The appeal of this vision was thus precisely how it transformed individual desires into national-imperial ones.

The personal idealism underlying Itō's and many others' involvement in the extraordinary violence of Japan's imperial project is what enabled many individuals to connect their prewar lives to their experience during the war, and to do so again during the Allied Occupation that followed the end of the war in 1945. Moreover, seeing the ways in which private ideologies structured this kind of continuity helps to reveal differences in mid-twentieth-century imperialisms and authoritarianisms. While it has become a standard part of dance historiography to acknowledge how early modern dance in Germany helped sow seeds for its turn to fascism—and many dancers' collaboration with the Third Reich—that particular continuity is not predetermined across national borders. That is, simply because Itō was exposed to ideas and bodily practices in Germany that contributed to German fascism does not categorically mean that he was destined to contribute to Japan's authoritarianism. Across thirty years and three continents, these ideas—and the bodily practices they engaged—shifted, taking on new physical manifestations and different ideological dimensions. It was within the distinct political circumstances of East Asia as a region of varied global and interregional imperialisms that Itō's own choreographic commitments manifested as part of the imperial imagination.

## ADDITIONAL RESOURCES

Full resolution versions of Figure 9.1 at https://doi.org/10.3998/ mpub.11521701.cmp.17 and Figure 9.2 at https://doi.org/10.3998/ mpub.11521701.cmp.18

Link 9.1: A website run by Itō's granddaughter. Available at https://doi. org/10.3998/mpub.11521701.cmp.56

Link 9.2: A documentary about Itō available online, produced by Repertory Dance Theatre. Available at https://doi.org/10.3998/mpub.11521701.cmp.57

Link 9.3: Trailer for another film, by the Los Angeles Dance Foundation. Available at https://doi.org/10.3998/mpub.11521701.cmp.58

## Notes

Research for this essay was supported by grants from the Fulbright IIE (Japan) and the Nippon Foundation. Thanks as well to Jordana Cox, Katherine Zien, and Jesse Wolfson for comments on drafts of the essay, to Isabelle Smeall for image assistance, and to Emily Wilcox and Katherine Mezur for their tremendous work on this volume.

1. Fujita Fujio, who has written a popular biography of Itō in Japanese, is the sole exception. Fujita Fujio 藤田冨士男, *Itō Michio Sekai wo Mau: Taiyou no Gekijo wo Mezashite* 伊藤道郎、世界を舞う：太陽の劇場をめざして [Itō Michio Dancing the World: Aiming at a Theatre of the Sun] (Musashino Shobō, 1992); and *Daitoua Butai Geijutsu Kenkyuusho Kankei Shiryou* 大東亜舞台芸術研究所関係資料 [Greater East Asia Stage Arts Research Institute Related Documents], ed. —(Fujishuppan, 1993).

2. See, for example, Helen Caldwell, *Michio Ito: The Dancer and His Dances* (University of California Press, 1977); Mary Fleischer, *Embodied Texts: Symbolist Playwright-Dancer Collaborations* (Rodopi, 2007); Takeishi Midori 武石みどり, *Itō Michio no Nihonteki Buyou* 伊藤道郎の日本的舞踊 [Itō Michio's Japanese Dance] (Tokyo Ongaku Daigaku Kenkyū Kiyou, vol. 24, 2000), 35–60; and —-, *Japanese Elements in Michio Ito's Early Period (1915–1924): Meetings of East and West in the Collaborative Works*, edited and revised by David Pacun (Gendaitosho, 2006). Pushing against this characterization, in different ways, is the work of Yutian Wong, Carol Sorgenfrei, and Carrie Preston: Yutian Wong, "Artistic Utopias: Michio Ito and the Trope of the International," in *Worlding Dance*, ed. Susan Leigh Foster (Palgrave Macmillan, 2009), 144–62; Carol Sorgenfrei, "Strategic Unweaving: Ito Michio and the Diasporic Dancing Body," in *The Politics of Interweaving Performance Cultures: Beyond Postcolonialism*, eds. Erika Fischer-Lichte, Torsten Jost, and Saskya Iris Jain (Routledge, 2014), 201–22; Carrie J. Preston, *Learning to Kneel: Noh, Modernism, and Journeys in Teaching* (Columbia University Press, 2016).

3. For a more detailed discussion, see Mary-Jean Cowell, with Shimazaki Satoru, "East and West in the Work of Michio Ito," *Dance Research Journal* 26, no. 2 (October 1994).

4. Quoted in Selma Landen Odom, "Choreographing *Orpheus*: Hellerau 1913 and Warwick 1991," *Dance Reconstructed: Conference Proceedings* (1993), 130.

5. Quoted in Odom, "Choreographing *Orpheus*," 129.

6. Percy B. Ingham, "The Method: Growth and Practice," *The Eurythmics of Jaques-Dalcroze* (Small, Maynard & Co, 1918), 40–41.

7. Richard C. Beacham, *Adolphe Appia: Artist and Visionary of the Modern Theatre* (Harwood Academic Publishers, 1994), 108.

8. "Celebration of Fourth to Outstrip All," *Washington Times*, June 29, 1919.

9. "Symphony with Stage Action at Manhattan," *New York Herald Tribune*, May 5, 1928.

10. Naima Prevots, *American Pageantry: A Movement for Art and Democracy* (UMI Research Press, 1989); Prevots, *Dancing in the Sun: Hollywood Choreographers, 1915–1937* (UMI Research Press), 1987.

11. Richard Drake Saunders, "Prince Igor," *Hollywood Citizen News*, August 16, 1930.

12. Mary F. Watkins, "The Dancers," *New York Herald Tribune*, May 6, 1928.

13. He was held at Fort Missoula in Montana, Fort Sill in Oklahoma, and Camp Livingston in Louisiana, and after being granted his request for repatriation, at a facility in Santa Fe, New Mexico. World War II Japanese Internee Cards, National Archives. See also Kevin Riordan, "Performance in the Wartime Archive: Michio Ito at the Alien Enemy Hearing Board," *American Studies* 55, no. 4 (2017).

14. At night, Itō's younger brother, the director Senda Koreya, recently released from prison for communist beliefs and prohibited from working in the theater, secretly used the space for rehearsals for the newly founded theater group, the *Haiyu-za* (俳優座). Senda Koreya 千田是也, *Mo hitotsu no shingekishi* もう一つの新劇史 [One More History of Shingeki] (Chukuma Shobo, 1975).

15. See Matthew Isaac Cohen, *Inventing the Performing Arts: Modernity and Tradition in Colonial Indonesia* (University of Hawai'i Press, 2016); Mark Ethan, "The Perils of Co-Prosperity: Takeda Rintarō, Occupied Southeast Asia, and the Seductions of Postcolonial Empire," *American Historical Review* 119, no. 4 (2014). Faye Yuan Kleeman, *In Transit: The Formation of the Colonial East Asian Cultural Sphere* (University of Hawai'i Press, 2014); Samuel L. Leiter, "Wartime Colonial and Traditional Theatre," in *A History of Japanese Theatre*, ed. Jonah Salz (Cambridge University Press, 2016), 251–63; Sang Mi Park, "Wartime Japan's Theater Movement," *WIAS Research Bulletin* 1 (2009). Motoe Terami-Wada, "The Japanese Propaganda Corps in the Philippines: Laying the Foundation," in *Japanese Cultural Policies in Southeast Asia during World War 2*, ed. Grant K. Goodman (St. Martin's Press, 1991), 173–211; Yoshida Yukihiko, "National Dance under the Rising Sun, mainly from National Dance, Buyō Geijutsu and the Activities of Takaya Eguchi," *International Journal of Eastern Sports and Physical Education* 7, no. 1 (October 2009).

16. These documents are held at Waseda University's Tsubouchi Memorial Theatre Museum, Senda Koreya Archive, hereafter, GEA.

17. GEA #7.

18. Ibid.

19. Ibid.

20. Daniel Sack, ed. *Imagined Theatres: Writing for a Theoretical Stage* (Routledge, 2017).

21. Eri Hotta, *Pan-Asianism and Japan's War, 1931–1945* (Palgrave Macmillan, 2007); Sven Saaler and J. Victor Koschmann, eds., *Pan-Asianism in Modern Japanese History: Colonialism, Regionalism and Borders* (Routledge, 2007).

22. Emily Wilcox, "Crossing Over: Choe Seung-hui's Pan-Asianism in Revolutionary Time," 무용역사기록학 (*The Journal of Society for Dance Documentation and History*) 51 (December 2018): 65–97. See also Suzy Kim, this volume.

23. GEA #2.

24. Louise Young, *Japan's Total Empire: Manchuria and the Culture of Wartime Imperialism* (University of California Press, 1998), 239.

# CHAPTER 10

# Exorcism and Reclamation

## Lin Lee-chen's *Jiao* and the Corporeal History of the Taiwanese

*Ya-ping Chen* 陳雅萍

From deep in the space on the stage of the National Theatre in Taipei, out of the darkness shrouded in thin mist, emerges a procession of figures in silhouette. It proceeds in the dim lights at an extremely slow and measured pace toward the audience, undulating gently and perfectly in tune with the delicate singing of a female voice chanting the ancient melody of *Nanguan* 南管, a form of classical music of the Han people 漢人 practiced in Taiwan, southern China, and Southeast Asia. As the line of procession approaches the audience, it becomes clear that at the front is a deity-like figure covered in layers of embroidered gowns and wearing an elaborate crown, whose expressionless face is painted heavily in white like a wooden mask. The solemn procession advances in slow dipping steps that bounce back softly with the circular flow of breathing and highly concentrated inner energy in the dancers' bodies.

This is the scene "Rising" (*Xian xiang* 獻香) from the evening-length work *Jiao* 醮 (*Miroirs de Vie*/Mirrors of Life) created by Taiwanese choreographer Lin Lee-chen 林麗珍 (b. 1950).[1] In stark contrast to the extremely slow and sustained flow of quiet energy described above, the episode "Agitation" (*Luhua* 蘆花) from the same dance is characterized by intense muscularity punctuated by outbursts of spasmodic force full of raw energy. Men stride forcefully, taking large aggressive steps or crawling on all fours like insects or beasts in battle. They challenge each other with twisting, arching, extending, and twirling postures that push their bodies into all sorts of contorted shapes, or even shake violently as if possessed by some supernatural or animalistic spirits.

The intense physicality and heightened mental concentration of the dancers, conveyed through the polarized modes of extreme expression depicted above, were unprecedented on dance stages in Taiwan when this work premiered in 1995.[2] Some critics praised *Jiao* as a phenomenal achievement in its creation of a profound corporeal form rooted in the cultural memory and spiritual structure of the land and its history.[3] Others criticized some sections of it as being too "raw" and not choreographically formulated enough to be a successful work of dance art.[4] Inspired by the unique presence of the dancers' physical and spiritual strength in *Jiao*, this chapter aims to examine the choreographic embodiments not only within the framework of the dance's cultural and ritualistic references, but in the context of the corporeal history of twentieth-century Taiwan. On the one hand, I argue that the inner-focused breathing and the quality of meditative movement of the dancers in quiet episodes like "Rising" resensitized the mental-physical sensibilities of its Taiwanese audience in the mid 1990s, who had been deprived of a true ownership of their own bodies by the trenchant control of Taiwan's martial-law state, which only started to thaw in the late 1980s. On the other hand, I suggest that the animalistic energy released in the spasmodic excitement of the flesh, especially through evocations of the physical image of *jitong* 乩 童 (spiritual mediums in Taiwanese folk religions) in scenes like "Agitation," exorcized metaphorically the phantom of past history, the suppression of the living body by the dictatorship of militarized culture that had haunted Taiwan society for more than half a century.

As a Taiwanese child growing up in the era of martial law (1949–1987) who came of age at the time when Taiwan society was undergoing a transition from autocratic rule to democracy, I experienced personally and bodily the military indoctrination of state ideology imposed by the Kuomintang regime (the Chinese Nationalist Party, commonly known as the KMT) through everyday life in school. This included strict hair and uniform regulation under the watching eye of military officers (*jiaoguan* 教官) stationed on campuses and compulsory military exercises as part of every high school's curricula. The lifting of martial law in 1987 ushered in political and social changes gradually, but forty years of thought and body control did not dissipate easily. If, as Judith Butler analyzes in *Frames of War,* "The 'being' of the body . . . is always given over to others, to norms, to social and political organizations that have developed historically," then correspondingly there exists the "regulation of affect" since "what we feel is in part conditioned by how we interpret the world," or what Butler calls the "frame of interpretation."[5] The effects of militarized culture in Taiwan from the Japanese colonial era (1895–1945) to the postwar KMT martial-law rule (1949–1987) formed a particular ontology of the body and its accompanying circuit of affect within a framework of militarization. With its premiere in 1995, eight years after the end of martial law, *Jiao* was implicitly in conversation with this Taiwanese bodily history.

## MILITARIZED CULTURE AND THE CORPOREAL HISTORY
## OF THE TAIWANESE

Due to the war on terrorism in the new millennium and its broad impact on the daily life of many populations in both war zones and locations not directly under threat, scholars have paid increasing attention to the effects of war on individual psyches, the social fabric, and cultural production on local, national and global levels. Such a phenomenon of "total militarization," in the words of Sara Brady and Lindsey Mantoan, subsumes us in both obvious and insidious ways into a worldview that privileges a belief in hierarchy, obedience, and the use of force. In other words, it results in the performance of "dehumanization" not only through military mechanisms but also in daily life, where civilians are less recognized as "private citizens" than as "subjects of surveillance and counterinsurgency."[6]

Looking back at history, "total militarization" was the reality of many Asian societies during much of the twentieth century due to their colonial histories and the rule of dictatorial regimes in the Cold War era, though the degrees of severity and cruelty varied in different regions and during different times. Sociologist Huang Ching-lin 黃金麟 traces the genealogy of military governance of the Taiwanese to two origins. One is the militarization of Taiwan society in the later stage of Japanese colonial rule, which began in 1937 when Japan launched its full-scale invasion of China and intensified in 1941 after the Japanese imperial navy advanced into the South Pacific. Not only were training camps established all over Taiwan for recruiting Taiwanese youths into "voluntary" military services, military exercises also became compulsory for high school students of both genders after 1941.[7] Two recently recovered and restored documentaries produced by the governor-general of Taiwan during World War II, *Civilian Dojo* 國民道場 and *Taiwanese Youth Corp for the Nation* 台灣勤行報國青年隊, record images of ritual-like drills of physical-mental militarization aimed at converting Taiwanese youths into imperial soldiers ready to sacrifice for the Japanese nation and emperor.[8] In this climate of war and colonialism, unquestioned respect for hierarchy and absolute obedience to the imperial Japanese military state authorities constituted the moral obligation of every Taiwanese subject.[9]

The other line of genealogy, according to Huang, can be traced to the advocating of "military citizenship" (*junguomin* 軍國民) by Chinese intellectuals in early-twentieth-century China, which aimed to turn every citizen into a potential soldier through modern military training to strengthen the ailing Chinese nation besieged by foreign aggressors.[10] The idea was made into a national policy when the KMT government, then based in mainland China, passed the "Scheme for Implementing Military Training in Secondary Schools and Beyond" in 1928. After the KMT was ousted from mainland China by the Chinese Communist Party (CCP) in 1949, it transplanted its military training policy to Taiwan, where it further reinforced the policy for the double purposes of continuing the civil war against the CCP and exerting internal control to reassure its absolute rule over the island of Taiwan. Hence, though the Taiwanese were liberated from five decades of Japanese colonialism after the end of World War II in 1945, military governance of their minds and bodies continued uninterruptedly into the new era ruled by the KMT.

Two important measures constituted Taiwan's military governance in the postwar era: general conscription of male adults and compulsory military training (*junxun* 軍訓) for high school and college students aged twelve to twenty-two. The goal was to make civil society part of the impending "total war" against the communists by "uniting soldiers and citizens as one force" (*junmin yiti* 軍民一體). Huang further elaborates,

> Military indoctrination became a normal part of political governance. Not only did the KMT habitually use the method to manage all levels of schools, the principal, director of discipline, military officers, and teachers at every school employed the same measures to manage students. After the network of governance was in place, students also followed the same discipline for self bodily management. The reliability of the above practice was the primary condition for *normalizing* military indoctrination in Taiwan.[11] (emphasis added)

In addition to strict regulation of students' physical appearance, military governance was most effectively carried out by means of the physical discipline of bodily postures and behaviors, as exemplified by required gatherings every morning for national flag hoisting and national anthem singing, as well as drilling exercises in military training courses.

On the societal level, the implementation of martial law in 1949 subjected Taiwan society to panoptic surveillance and strict control by the state machine, a situation described by Huang as "the antagonization of society" (*ditihua shehui* 敵體化社會). The loss of the mainland to the CCP, the five decades of Japanese rule on the island, and the KMT's need to exercise absolute control of its last remaining territory politically, socially, and economically all contributed to the garrison state governance in Taiwan, which earned the name of "White Terror" (1949–1991), with its most intensive years spanning the 1950s to the early 1980s.[12] In addition to thousands of cases of political persecution under often-fabricated charges of treason or being communist spies, the notorious Garrison Command Headquarters (*jingbei zongbu* 警備總部) exercised severe censorship on speech, thought, publications, public gatherings, and all forms of civic expression.[13] The permeating ambience of political witch-hunts not only intimidated people from social engagement, it resulted in the internalization of self-censorship of one's own body, thought, and even interpersonal relationships. The layers upon layers of bodily encoding by external regulations and internalized self-governance grew into an omnipresent phantom haunting the Taiwanese people for more than four decades.

The combined effects of the above policies were the instrumentalization of bodies by the state on the one hand, and on the other the deprivation of peoples' sense of ownership of their own bodies, their physical appearance and capacity as well as their sensuous ability and desire. Such a pervasive framework of militarized culture effectively formulated people's consciousness and their sense of self and as a result conditioned their ways of perceiving and interacting with the world.

## *JIAO* AND THE INSPIRATION OF *ZHONGYUAN JI*

Seen in retrospect, the heightened existential intensity of the body in *Jiao* resonated with a surge of preoccupation with the visceral reality and corporeal history of bodies in the arts in Taiwan during the 1980s and '90s. Images of traumatized bodies appeared as subject matter in works by Taiwanese visual artists such as Chen Chieh-jen 陳界仁 and Wu Tien-chang 吳天章, where the bodies served as a metaphoric reservoir for memories about Taiwan's colonial past and decades of garrison state rule under martial law. Likewise, in Taiwan's Little Theatre Movement, which emerged in the mid-1980s, bodily actions replaced verbal texts as the most important medium of expression to release suppressed energy and excavate the tabooed history of martial-law bodies.

Lin Lee-chen's choice of the title and subject matter of "*jiao*" is no coincidence. The word refers to rituals of the Taoist religion 道教, which are held for the purposes of worshiping deities, exorcism, or appeasing and consoling the dead. Lin's choreography is a ritualistic dance theater inspired by the rites of *Zhongyuan Ji* 中元祭, a festival of Taoist-Buddhist origin commemorating and entertaining homeless ghosts who died unnatural deaths or in foreign lands, with religious ceremonies and feasts of food and drinks. Because of the many untimely and violent deaths in the course of Taiwan's settlement, the *Zhongyuan Ji* has carried special significance to the Taiwanese through time and has been celebrated more enthusiastically on the island than in mainland China, where it originated.

Though the festival takes place all over Taiwan, nowhere has it been more grandiosely and devotedly celebrated than in Lin's hometown, Keelung, a strategic harbor city located at the northeastern tip of Taiwan. Due to the occurrence of "*Zhang Quan pin*" 漳泉拼, large-scale armed fights between immigrants from Zhangzhou and Quanzhou in Fujian province in southern China, as well as the many battles fought between foreign invaders and local settlers in the city's past, the *Zhongyuan Ji* became the most important festivity in Keelung, where it is traditionally celebrated for the whole seventh month on the lunar calendar. Moreover, since many of its inhabitants earn their living on the dangerous sea, the festival relates strongly to the daily life and emotional world of local communities, especially fishing villages, where Lin grew up. Lin stresses the close ties between the creation of *Jiao* and her hometown, its history, and the collective memories of its inhabitants structured in local religious practices.[14]

The process of militarization in Taiwan described earlier was inextricably interlocked with the KMT government's sinocentric cultural policy and education system, which suppressed Taiwan's history and marginalized local cultures and memories. For a long time, even personal memories of the Taiwanese who lived under Japanese rule or suffered from the effects of "White Terror" were taboo, not only in public but in private life. During the late 1980s and 1990s, intellectuals and artists, as well as political opposition forces, viewed and used folk religious ceremonies and iconographies as important means for reclaiming local cultural identification to counter the KMT's sinocentrism and to recover community memories amid rapidly expanding capitalist urbanism. Among all the religious festivals, the *Zhongyuan Ji* was particularly symbolic due to the taboo subjects of death and wandering ghosts, as well as the accompanying messages of redemption and compassion. These subjects resonated in subtle yet profound ways with the political history of the "White Terror" era and were sometimes metaphorically transformed into contemporary interpretations to exorcize the ghosts of dictatorship and to seek redemption for the victims of political and economic oppression.[15]

## "RISING" AND "RECOLLECTION"—RECLAIMING THE LIVING BODY

Though the theme and content of *Jiao* do not address the political history of Taiwanese bodies directly, I argue that the corporeal expressions Lin choreographed were, in a profound way, therapeutic or exorcistic counteractions to the subjugated and instrumentalized bodies formed by the militarized culture. The premiere of *Jiao* was composed of twelve episodes, which began with the rite of purification by a senior Taoist priest on the stage transforming the theater space into a ritual site, and ended with the ceremony of burning a paper house for the wandering ghosts, an important part of the *Zhongyuan Ji* in Keelung. Within this ritualistic framework, Lin probed deeply into the psychological reservoir embedded in the visceral corporeality of the dancers and recreated a spiritual cosmology on stage through the extraordinary intensity of the dancers' physical presence, bodily actions, and mental concentration.

In the scene "Rising" described earlier, Lin forsakes the horizontal presentation conventionally seen on the proscenium stage and removes the backdrop to utilize the depth of the stage space to conjure up the image of a line of the dead traveling from the underworld. The deity-like figure at the front resembles the image of the sea goddess Mazu 媽祖 (played by Chang Hui-yu 張惠玉), the most popular and widely worshiped deity in Taiwan. She carries a bunch of burning incense at her chest and is followed by a man holding high above her a large paper lantern written with the character *jiao*. At his heels, two other men escort the procession, one clenching a strand of bronze bells in a raised hand and the other bearing a tall bamboo pole, the object for summoning wandering ghosts at the *Zhongyuan Ji* ceremonial sites.

This mysterious line walks at an extremely slow and measured pace perfectly in tune with the refined melody of the *Nanguan* singing. With their knees remaining slightly bent and paying absolute attention to a circular flow of breathing, the dancers advance in a rhythm of walking with slow dipping steps simulating the undulation of the sea, over which Mazu leads the spirits of the dead to join the living in the *Zhongyuan Ji* ceremony. At the same time, the image of the procession evokes the memory of the ancestors' journey across the Black Water to settle on Taiwan centuries ago. In those dangerous voyages, Mazu was worshiped as the guardian deity for safe journeys. Writer Yuan Chiung-chiung 袁瓊瓊 reflected on the effect of this solemn march in 1995: "That slow and unhurried procession must be reminding us ... that it is the line from which we came and to which we belong and will one day return. [They are] gods and also humans, ancestors and also us."[16]

The deep physical and affective empathy between the performers/characters and the audience described by Yuan was achieved through Lin's unusual treatment of the dancers' corporeal presence and her method of choreography. The most important movement in *Jiao* is "walking," and the underlying strength giving substance to every minute detail in the movement is "breathing." Every training session at the Legend Lin Dance Theatre begins with an exercise of meditative breathing called *jingzuo* 靜坐 (meditative sitting), in which the practitioner engages in cycles of long deep breathing that initiates in the lower abdomen (*dantien* 丹田) and extends continuously upward along the spine to the tip of the head, then gradually collapses downward along the vertebra while the practitioner slowly exhales. Another core training section is *jingzou* 靜走 (meditative walking), in which the practitioner, with the body centered and knees slightly bent, puts one foot forward, touches down at tip-toe, and then presses the bottom of the foot inch by inch onto the floor, while shifting the center of the weight forward before taking another step.[17]

The scene "Rising" is a theatrical reenactment of the meditative practices of "walking" and "breathing," two of the most fundamental actions of human beings, within the ritualistic framework inspired by the *Zhongyuan Ji*. The intense body-mind concentration aims to awaken a deep sensibility regarding the living body, our own as well as those of other beings. Countering the suppression of corporeal sensibility and the accompanying anti-empathetic affect cultivated by the antagonized society of Taiwan after four decades of martial law, the prolonged rhythm of walking and the continuous flow of deep breathing in "Rising" reclaimed for the performers and the audience alike a deep feeling of a shared sense of life. Butler talks about how the "simple, almost primeval, arithmetic of breathing in and out" constitutes the ultimate source for expressions about living and longing in poems by Guantánamo detainees.[18] When the inhaling and exhaling of the body is made into the cadence of poems, it reveals the vulnerability of the breathing body under subjugation while at the same time trying to establish connection to the world by sharing the primeval breath with others. This sense of the "shared precariousness of life," based on the corporeal needs and desires common to our bodies, forms the fundamental condition of our responsiveness to others and our ontological existence.

At the end of the solemn procession appears a silk screen escorted by two files of young women. Behind it walks a solo woman (played by Yu Chiu-yueh 于秋月), who later in the scene "Recollection" (*Yaoxiang* 遙想) is joined by a man (played by Liu Jen-nan 劉仁楠) emerging out of the darkness upstage for an exquisite duet full of subdued passion. Four female attendants, each carrying a tall reed stalk, enter and position themselves at four corners center stage to form a symbolic universe and a secluded space for the couple. After they slowly approach each other and kneel down face to face, the woman, holding the ends of a silk shawl at her chest, bends forward far down to the ground while the man leans above her. To the sobbing tune of a single flute,

Fig. 10.1. Still from a 2006 performance of "Recollection" from *Jiao* (1995) at the National Theatre in Taipei. The dancers are Lee Shen-tzu 李聲慈 and Lee Ming-wei 李銘偉. Photo courtesy Legend Lin Dance Theatre.

they pause for a while in this posture of bowing deeply to each other. Suddenly, the woman opens her shawl and the couple's nude torsos, now gently touching each other, begin moving extremely slowly together in a circle. As the woman, leaning to one side, arches her head deeply backward, the man glides his right hand over her hip to tenderly grasp her left wrist. This is the only moment when their hands are ever in contact. Later, the man flips the shawl in the air and places it around the woman's bare back before leaning backward to an almost lying position. In the dimming stage lights, the woman prostrates herself quietly over him as the shivering reed stalks shed tiny blossoms over them like dropping tears.

The stark contrast between the woman's porcelain-white torso and the man's darkly tanned body makes the couple the embodiments of *yin* and *yang*—the principles of femininity and masculinity in the Taoist cosmos, death (*yin jie* 陰界) and life (*yang jie* 陽界). Carried out at an extremely slow pace, the duet is sustained by a continuous flow of quiet breathing and subdued energy, which is uninterrupted even at the transitions between the dancers' movements. The sudden release of energy in the flipping of the shawl conveys an undercurrent of strong feelings beneath the surface of restrained quietness. In this exquisite synergy of meditative serenity and corporeal sensuality, the choreographer's intention goes beyond the depiction of ordinary love between a man and a woman. Lin remarked in 1995 that her choice to refrain from the use of arm gestures was to return the body to its primeval "animalistic state in nature," a prerational, presocialized existence dominated by the unmediated sensual experience of touch. The intermingling of *yin* and *yang* symbolized by the duet was to convey a harmonious state of coexistence between living beings, between humankind and nature; the inspiration was the deep impact Lin felt when witnessing the abundance of life energy in the hundreds of insects moving and thriving amid reed stalks in the wilderness of Taiwan.[19]

The subdued yet profound depiction of passion in the sensual intimacy of this duet heightened viewers' perception of the sensuous and emotional capacities of bodies. Moreover, the encounter between the living and the dead in the narrative of the dance not only reminded us of the precariousness of life, it introduced a temporal/historical dimension to our circuit of affective responsiveness by bringing corporeal memories of the past into encounters with the present. Seen in the context of the erasure of personal and collective memories by the brutal force of political persecution and intimidation under martial law, the scene "Recollection" resonated in broad and deep ways with the histories and memories of Taiwanese audiences.

## "AGITATION" AND "POSSESSION"—EXORCISING THE ANTAGONIZED SELF

Throbbing drumbeats and chiming bells usher in several men who stride in large steps from different directions across the stage. Wearing red headbands and loincloths, they grip reed stalks in their hands while striding, or bite them between their teeth while crawling on all fours like beasts or insects in the wilderness. Two of the men position themselves across from each other like foes in a duel. Bending their torsos forward and then straightening them up, the two men shake their whole bodies violently before twisting, arching, extending, and twirling themselves into all sorts of contorted shapes. While the two men challenge each other into more and more intense physical actions, the other men further excite them with quivering reed stalks and deep cries of "he." Performed to rapid drumbeats, the men's muscular tension accumulates higher and higher within their bodies until it erupts at the pounding strikes of the percussion and then re-accumulates again for an even more powerful eruption at a later moment. Inspired by the "*Zhang Quan pin*" battles in the local history of Keelung, the scene "Agitation" draws on images from the natural environment and religious culture of Taiwan. Reeds grow in abundance along riverbanks across the island, the sites for many of the ancient conflicts over water resource or land. The agitated physicality of the men evokes the body image of *jitong* in Taiwanese folk religions, who perform dangerous acts while being possessed by deities or other supernatural beings.

The following episode, "Possession" (*Yinhuo* 引火), further explores metaphorically the physical and spiritual power of the *jitong* image. A man carries in an oversized gown hung at the top of a tall bamboo pole symbolizing *Lao Da Gong* 老大公—the name for the collective spirits of the men who fell in "*Zhang Quan pin*" and the ghost-gatekeeper in the legend of the Keelung *Zhongyuan Ji*. Under the looming shape of *Lao Da Gong*, three men—one carrying reed stalks, another a bunch of burning incense, and the third a strand of bronze bells—budge forward tightly together (played by Ku Che-cheng 顧哲誠, Liu Jen-nan 劉仁楠, and Chai Tian-cheng 翟天成). They stamp heavily on the ground and shake their bodies violently to the pulsating rhythm of the chiming bells. Then, the man with bronze bells crawls between the opened legs of the other two, who groan and push their pelvises forcefully as if to help him along the narrow path. Wriggling and moaning as if in great pain, he inches forward like a newborn struggling to enter the world, and then inches backward to reverse the passage. After this symbolic journey of birth and death, he is lashed relentlessly by the man with reed stalks. As the bells chime louder and louder and the men's growling reaches higher and higher, the muscular tension in their quivering bodies builds up to an explosive point when at an orgiastic moment the lashed man collapses to the ground, moaning helplessly like a dying animal gasping for the last breath of life in the dimming lights. The sobbing sound of a Taiwanese flute (*yamudi* 鴨母笛) is heard traveling across the dark stage, its long deep tune of breath seeming to console all the wounded spirits who have fallen unwillingly.

The image of flogging recalls the ritualistic flagellation carried out by *jitong* in folk religious rites, in which the spiritual mediums work themselves into a trance through unrestrained shaking of their bodies and often perform self-inflicted torture to demonstrate the power of the deities who possess them. In "Possession," violent shaking was also used to achieve the extraordinary mental and physical condition the choreographer desired. On the one hand, it enacted a primordial state of existence bursting with animalistic vigor in which one seemed to be merged with the life-giving-and-destroying force of

Fig. 10.2. Still from a 2006 performance of "Possession" from *Jiao* (1995) at the National Theatre in Taipei. The dancers are Chen Chi-shun 陳啟順, Lee Ming-wei 李銘偉, Cheng Chieh-wen 鄭傑文, Tsai Che-Jen 蔡哲仁. Photo by Chin Cheng-tsai 金成財 courtesy Legend Lin Dance Theatre.

nature. On the other hand, the symbolic flogging and the final exhaustion of the flesh implied a rite of exorcism, which cleansed and expelled the psychological traumas and corporeal coercions inscribed on the collective body and memory of Taiwanese people, an antagonized self both shaped and haunted by the garrison state rule until the early 1990s.

## Jiao *as a Healing Encounter*

"In a certain sense, the dancers became a kind of *lingmei* 靈媒 [spiritual mediums] in *Jiao*," said Lin in 1995.[20] In other words, they had to give up their ordinary selves to enter another state of being by offering themselves as vehicles for the experiential and emotional conditions of others. In this regard, the ritual theater of *Jiao* resonated in profound ways with the belief and practice of the "healing encounter" (*liaoyu* 療遇) in Taiwanese folk shamanism (*wu zongjiao* 巫宗教), which seeks to remedy unfulfilled wishes and restore lost relationships through rituals of encountering.

One such shamanistic practice is *qianwang* 牽亡, "a folk practice for the deceased's family to call the dead spirit to come to presence by means of possessing a spiritual medium."[21] It is carried out through memories of the dead and reenacted dialogues between the shaman, who is believed to be possessed by the dead, and the deceased's family members, thus creating what psychologist Yu Te-huei 余德慧 calls "an 'as if' world still there" (*diannian shijie* 惦念世界).[22] The reencountering serves as a form of consolation, where psychotherapy takes effect and a cultural healing space is created. Yu elaborates:

> We place focus on how to explain the mental state of human beings from the perspective of a lost relationship due to death, [and] how people take action by reconnecting and reencountering [the dead] to amend those gaps.... *The lost relationship is restored as a relationship in recollection through reenactment.*... The recollection is founded on the logic of myth, symbol, and poetics.[23] (emphasis added)

If *Jiao* could be understood as such a ritual of "healing encounter" enacted between the dancers/spiritual mediums and the spectators, its premiere in 1995 restored for the Taiwanese certain important relationships that had been interrupted by the political and social circumstances of the postwar era: the collective memories of suppressed political traumas and local histories, the emotional attachments embedded in the customs and religious practices of one's homeland, and the ownership of one's body and all its sensorial capacities connecting one to others and to the world.

One of the most enduring effects of Taiwan's militarized culture was the regulation of affect by visible and invisible forces. Countering the sensorial inertia and corporeal coercion of the martial law bodies, *Jiao* provided a different framework for interpreting this existential relationship, that of coexistence and interdependency. By arousing corporeal empathy with and affective compassion for the characters in the dance, both the living and the dead, *Jiao* reminded its audience of the shared vulnerability of all beings. These bodies in the liminal time and space of ritual encountering advocated a "politics of affect" that sought the possibilities of passionate encounters between lives by embracing fully the desires, longings, and responsiveness of corporeal reality.

## ADDITIONAL RESOURCES

Full resolution versions of Figure 10.1 at https://doi.org/10.3998/mpub.11521701.cmp.19 and Figure 10.2 at https://doi.org/10.3998/mpub.11521701.cmp.20

Link 10.1: Excerpts from *Jiao* (*Miroirs de Vie*/Mirrors of Life) performed by a new generation of dancers at the National Theatre in Taipei in 2006. Available at https://doi.org/10.3998/mpub.11521701.cmp.59

Link 10.2: Trailer for *The Walkers*, a documentary on the Legend Lin Dance Theatre. Available at https://doi.org/10.3998/mpub.11521701.cmp.60

Link 10.3: The official Facebook page of the Legend Lin Dance Theatre. Available at https://doi.org/10.3998/mpub.11521701.cmp.61

Link 10.4: Review by Chen Ya-ping in *Biaoyan Yishu*, No. 33 (1995) (in Chinese). Available at https://doi.org/10.3998/mpub.11521701.cmp.62

Link 10.5: Review by Lu Chien-ying in *BiaoyanYishu*, No. 33 (1995) (in Chinese). Available at https://doi.org/10.3998/mpub.11521701.cmp.63

Link 10.6: Article by Chang Wei-lun in *Biaoyan Yishu*, No. 30 (1995) (in Chinese). Available at https://doi.org/10.3998/mpub.11521701.cmp.64

## *Notes*

1. Lin Lee-chen is an internationally acclaimed choreographer known for her trilogy of epic-scale ritual dance theater: *Jiao* 醮 (*Mirrors of Life*), *Huashenji* 花神祭 (*Anthem to the Faded Flowers*), and *Guan* 觀 (*Song of Pensive Beholding*). She founded the Legend Lin Dance Theatre 無垢舞蹈劇場 in 1995.

2. *Jiao* has been restaged several times after 1995. The analysis in this chapter is specifically about the premiere version based on the author's attendance of a live performance then, reviews written at the time, and a video recording of that version.

3. Wang Mo-ling 王墨林, "Shenti yu kongjian de yuanxing: shilun Lin Lee-chen *Jiao* de xingshi" 身體與空間的原型:試論林麗珍《醮》的形式, *Taiwan wudao zazhi* 台灣舞蹈雜誌, no. 13 (1995): 81–82. Chen Ya-ping 陳雅萍, "Qianshi jinsheng, yiduan shikong mianyan de wujin duihua" 前世今生，一段時空綿延的無盡對話, *Biaoyan Yishu* 表演藝術, no. 33 (1995): 89–90.

4. Lu Chien-ying 盧健英, "Jiao, yizhi tigong xuduo sikao yiti de wudao" 醮，一支提供許多思考議題的舞蹈, *Biaoyan Yishu* 表演藝術, no. 33 (1995): 88–89.

5. Judith Butler, *Frames of War: When Is Life Grievable?* (London: Verso, 2016), 2, 41.

6. Sara Brady and Lindsey Mantoan, "Introduction: In the Absence of the Gun: Performing Militarization," *Performance in a Militarized Culture* (New York: Routledge, 2018). See also Gay Morris and Jens Richard Giersdorf, *Choreographies of the 21st Century Wars* (New York: Oxford University Press, 2016).

7. Huang Ching-lin 黃金麟, *Zhanzheng, shenti, xiandaixing* 戰爭、身體、現代性 (Taipei: United Daily Press, 2009).

8. National Museum of Taiwan History 國立台灣歷史博物館, *Piange zhuandong jian de Taiwan xianying* (DVD & booklet) 片格轉動間的台灣顯影 (Tainan: National Museum of Taiwan History, 2012 [2008]).

9. At the end of the Japanese colonial rule, the population in Taiwan was about six million, including 150,000 Taiwanese indigenous peoples and 500,000 Japanese. The rest were mostly Han people who had immigrated from mainland China since the seventeenth century. The Japanese employed a separate policy of rule for the indigenous peoples and recruited them for the most dangerous missions in the Southeast Asian jungles during the war.

10. Huang Ching-lin 黃金麟, *Lishi, shenti, guojia: xiandai zhongguo de shenti shengchen, 1895–1937* 歷史、身體、國家:現代中國的身體生成 1895–1937 (Taipei: United Daily Press, 2005).

11. Huang, *Zhanzheng, shenti, xiandaixing*, 149. All translations from Chinese texts are the author's.

12. When the war ended, the Japanese in Taiwan were repatriated, while a large wave of Chinese immigrants, estimated at about 1.2 million, arrived with the KMT in around 1949. They suffered as much as the native Taiwanese from the "White Terror," including severe punishments for such simple acts as attempting to contact family members and relatives remaining in mainland China.

13. Censorship was comparatively loosened in the 1970s; yet the large-scale arrest of political dissidents in the 1979 Kaohsiung Formosa Incident and its aftermath marked another climax of the "White Terror" era.

14. Chen Hsin-yi 陳芯宜, *Xingzhe* 行者 (DVD & booklet) (Taipei: Walkers Image, 2015).

15. Gu Nian Miao People's Workshop 姑娘廟民眾工作室, *Tien, Di, Ren, Shen, Gui.* 天地人神鬼 (Taipei: Qianwei Publisher, 1994).

16. Yuan Chiung-chiung 袁瓊瓊, "Cong heliu dao haiyang—guanyu wuzuo Jiao ji qita (I, II & III)" 從河流到海洋—關於舞作《醮》及其他 (I, II, & III), newspaper clippings from the collection of the Legend Lin Dance Theatre (1995).

17. This description is mainly based on the author's personal experience in the Legend Lin Dance Theatre's body awareness courses for noncompany practitioners.

18. Butler, *Frames of War*, 60. Guantánamo detainees are captives of war imprisoned by the US military in the Guantánamo Bay Detention Camp. In 2007, a collection of smuggled-out poems by Guantánamo detainees, who were tortured, was published.

19. Lin Lee-chen 林麗珍, personal interview with the author, May 25, 1995.

20. Lin, personal interview.

21. Yu Te-huei 余德慧, *Taiwan wuzongjiao de xinling liaoyu* 台灣巫宗教的心靈療遇 (Taipei: Psygarden Press, 2006), 137.

22. Yu, *Taiwan wuzongjiao de xinling liaoyu*, 137.

23. Yu, *Taiwan wuzongjiao de xinling liaoyu*, 21.

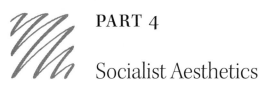

PART 4

Socialist Aesthetics

# CHAPTER 11

# Choe Seung-hui Between Classical and Folk

## Aesthetics of National Form and Socialist Content in North Korea

*Suzy Kim*

Despite subtle differences, the "traditional" fan dance is performed in both North and South Korea as part of their cultural heritage. Women, often in groups but at times solo, step gingerly into various formations even as they briskly whip open and shut a pair of folding fans to extend and accentuate their arms. Such adaptations are commonly attributed to the legacy of Choe Seung-hui (Ch'oe Sŭng-hŭi 최승희 1911–1969). Less well known are her striking poses as a woman warrior performing the sword dance as she pirouettes and leaps with a double sword to vanquish her oppressors in a narrative dance-drama that fused classical ballet technique with folk motifs. Dressed in colorful costumes with long flowing sleeves and skirts that drew on folk culture, Choe's dance-dramas were just as instrumental as the fan dance in setting the foundation for "revolutionary" dance performances in North Korea.

Hailed for adapting traditional dance for the modern stage, Choe Seung-hui became the first Korean dancer to achieve global fame, touring the United States, Latin America, Europe, and Asia at a time when the sovereignty of Korea was tenuous due to its colonial occupation by Japan (1910–1945). Her celebrity as the "dancer of the Orient" thus closely intersected with Imperial Japan's own ambition to assimilate Korea, leading to charges of collaboration when Japan was defeated at the end of World War II. Complicating her status even further, a divided Korean peninsula has left mixed legacies of her artistic contributions in North and South Korea. After Korea was divided by the Allied powers soon after gaining independence at the end of World War II, Choe settled in North Korea, relegating her to persona non grata status in the South. In the 1960s, she fell out of favor in the North, too, and neither the North nor the South gave her proper recognition until decades later with the thaw of the Cold War. In the late 1980s the ban on North Korean materials in the South was partially lifted with the end of military rule. In the early 1990s

계월향 (최승희 분)

Fig. 11.1. Choe Seung-hui dressed in role of Kye Wŏlhyang in the eponymous titled dance-drama, 1961. Source: "人氣 스타—崔承喜와 桂月香," 新生活 Sinsaenghwal May 1961 (no. 51), p. 35–37 available at the Library of Congress.

in the North, its leader, Kim Il Sung, began publishing his memoir, which included references to Choe, crediting her as the founder of modern dance in Korea. As a result, not only does Choe's personal biography capture the currents of modern Korean history, but the aesthetic choices she faced and ultimately made were shaped by the contradictions and supposed binaries attributed to these currents—between so-called tradition and modernity, East and West, North and South, nationalist and socialist—no matter how slippery these categories could be in reality.

Since the revival of popular and scholarly interest in Choe Seung-hui, a growing number of biographies have been published in Korean, as have more academic analyses of her work in both English and Korean sources, particular attention being paid to her formative period in the 1920s and 1930s.[1] Rather than focus on Choe per se, this chapter aims to assess her role in the development of dance in North Korea as an example of socialist realist aesthetics. I analyze her theorization of form in terms of both ballet technique and folk dance, navigating the politics of aesthetics as shaped by the debates surrounding "high" (elite) versus "low" (mass) art. The chapter concludes by illustrating how Choe's dilemma was ultimately resolved through a renewed commitment to folk dance as the quintessential embodiment of both national form and socialist content.[2]

## ART IN THE "AGE OF PEOPLE'S CREATION"

Previous studies of Choe's earlier career have described her successful adaptation of traditional Korean dance as a form of tactical Orientalism—an attempt at an alternative modernity through the exotic embodiment of a superior East over the West.[3] However, Choe's contribution to the development of dance in North Korea illustrates the extent to which her dance should be seen in continuity with developments in the history of twentieth-century aesthetics, specifically the issues Walter Benjamin so eloquently laid out in his 1936 essay, "The Work of Art in the Age of Mechanical Reproduction." As Emily Wilcox shows in regard to modern Chinese dance, the major aesthetic preoccupation for artists of nascent countries emerging out of colonial and semicolonial status centered on questions of form rather than content.[4] Instead of experiments in abstract form or a strict adherence to formalism, however, form was sought in the interstices of everyday life, because the question of form was so closely intertwined with questions of national identity.

In reaction to the homogenizing forces of industrialization, the beginning of the twentieth century saw a major preoccupation with "folk" and the varied possibilities offered by its diverse forms.[5] In the heyday of nation-building, the term came to increasingly represent the general populace, going beyond concerns of simply preserving the past, to discover everyday practices of the common people as a new form of national culture. From the early exposition by Stalin, "Marxism and the National Question" (1913), to the later incorporation of minority nations in the multiethnic state construction of the Soviet Union and the People's Republic of China, folk culture received widespread attention. Choe was praised for her adaptation of folk-dance rhythms for the modern stage, and one of her lasting contributions to Chinese dance was a conceptual distinction between the "folk," identified with peasants and agrarian culture in performances such as the masked dances, and the "classical," identified with elite urban culture represented by the fan dance.[6]

While the attention to "folk" was certainly global in scope, as Philipp Herzog shows in the case of Estonia, folk culture as representative of nationalism was subsumed under the Soviet cultural policy when Estonia became part of the Soviet Union in 1944. This accorded with the principles of socialist realism, which saw folk culture as the source of art for its collective expression of communal living. Such attention to folk culture was not limited to socialist realist dogma, however; it later became part of the global countercultural movement in the 1960s. Rather than strictly separating the different artistic fields as in the classical arts, the new amateur art system open to mass participation combined dance with music, song, and theater that went hand in hand with folk traditions. In other words, a new valorization of folk culture and the incorporation of peasants as artists allowed a general democratization of the arts, in terms of both how art came to be defined and who had the resources to produce it. Folk dance was a major component of this amateur art system precisely because it was "relatively apolitical compared to other genres that were based on textual messages."[7] As such, it became an important way to demonstrate national culture and cultivate "friendship among the peoples," embodying the socialist realist epithet "national in form, socialist in content."

On Korea's liberation from Japanese colonial rule in 1945, dance circles and other mass culture and arts circles flourished throughout the North, and in March 1946, the North Korean Literature and Arts Union was founded, including the Dancers Union.[8] Saddled with her two young children and living in China at the time of Korean liberation, Choe did not return to Korea until July 1946. But when she arrived in her native Seoul, criticisms of her pro-Japanese collaboration began to resurface. In an interview she gave with reporters on her arrival in Seoul, she announced that she planned to work on developing a form of "Korean ballet" (*K'orian palle* 코리안 발레), which was roundly criticized as opportunistic. Detractors railed that "she danced Japanese dances under the Japanese and now that they are defeated, she wants to dance Western dances."[9] Her reference to Korean ballet was misunderstood as Western dance, whereas Choe probably meant a form of dance-drama (*muyonggŭk* 舞踊劇), much like the Chinese Opera she had been studying in China. Dance-drama was to become her major legacy, as well as the core of the challenges she faced in the history of North Korean dance as described below. With the lifting of Japanese censorship, grievances and sharp denunciations were now aired in public, and Choe opted to follow her socialist husband to North Korea.

According to a 2012 North Korean biography, Choe received a letter of invitation from North Korean leader Kim Il Sung soon after her arrival in Seoul.[10] Despite the strong anticolonial rhetoric, North Korea proved much more tolerant of colonial-era intellectuals, artists, and educators, not only because of the historically lower population compared to the rich rice-producing centers in the South, but also due to Kim Il Sung's united-front strategy, which sought to rally the majority against the minority of landlords and collaborators who had actively supported the colonial apparatus. With her arrival in Pyongyang, a rare three-story building with a view of the Taedong River became the Choe Seung-hui Dance Institute (*Ch'oe Sŭng-hŭi muyong yŏnguso* 최승희무용연구소), fitted with student dormitories, offices, and a dance hall.

Her school was to become a permanent institution in North Korea, receiving the status of a national school in 1953. There were several name changes since its founding; it became the National Dance Academy (*Kungrip muyong hakkyo* 국립무용학교) in 1956, the Pyongyang Arts University (*Pyongyang yesul taehak* 평양예술대학) in 1965, and finally the Pyongyang Music and Dance University (*Pyongyang ŭmak muyong taehak* 평양음악무용대학) in 1972.[11] With Choe's fame, her first class enrolled forty students in the fall of 1946, and she quickly garnered the most prestigious posts in her field.[12] She was named chair of the Central Committee of the Korean Dancers Union (*Chosŏn muyongga tongmaeng* 조선무용가동맹), a position she held until her death in 1969 except for a brief hiatus when she was politically censured, and she was also named president of the National Dance Theater. She gained political status too, being elected as representative to the Provisional People's Committee (to become the Supreme People's Assembly) of North Korea in the first election of November 1946.[13]

In 1957, North Korea celebrated the thirty-year anniversary of Choe's debut with great fanfare. She was awarded a national medal with full coverage in newspapers, magazines, and radio, and her work was lavishly praised.[14] This was when Choe began publishing some of her most important texts, including the two-volume *Basics of Korean National Dance* and *Collection of Dance-Drama Scripts*, both issued in 1958, and the *Basics of Korean Children's Dance*, published in 1964.[15] The dance circles created after liberation came together to compete in the National Arts Festival (*Chŏnguk yesul ch'ukjŏn* 전국예술축전); they were often reviewed by Choe Seung-hui herself. In one such review, Choe linked the creativity of labor from everyday life with artistic creativity, praising the work of the working masses and students, who were independently creating great works of art.[16] Calling this the "age of people's creation," Choe credited the party's cultural policy for raising the people's aesthetic level and fostering artistic works. She defined beauty as a life of creative work, peopled by those moving forward and upward toward things "newer, greater, and more radiant, toward true communism."

## POLITICS OF AESTHETICS

In the early twentieth century, even as dance became a "modern" art form with its avowed aim of self-expression, dancers were at the mercy of the consumer public insofar as dance was mediated by capital for its production.[17] Choe had certainly experienced this throughout her US tour in 1938 and 1940, when she was dismayed by what she perceived to be the "vices of blind faith in the audience, even by the critics."[18] In their efforts to "overcome" such ravages of modernity, Korean intellectuals faced two choices. While conservative thinkers sought to find Korean roots in Korea's elite literati culture of the Chosŏn dynasty (the last Korean dynasty before Japanese occupation), leftists were motivated to look elsewhere. As Yi Chu-mi astutely observes, rather than defining "Koreanness" through a conservative appeal to past traditions, they sought a "Korea specific strategy" in the struggle against imperialism toward a progressive future.[19] Eschewing elite cultural forms such as *sijo* poetry or *p'ansori* song as the source of Koreanness, starting in the 1930s Choe had looked to local folk traditions such as the masked dances of the peasants, shaman dances, monk dances, and *kisaeng* (courtesan) dances for inspiration.[20] As a result, there was already an affinity between Choe's dance form derived from folk culture and the North Korean aesthetic application of socialist realism.

With her proven ability to fuse diverse elements, Choe again excelled, this time throughout the Soviet-led socialist bloc with the support of the North Korean government. Her dance troupe won first place at the inaugural World Festival of Youth and Students held in August 1947 in Prague.[21] Even in the midst of the Korean War (1950–1953), Choe and her dancers were able to participate in the third World Festival of Youth and Students in 1951 in Berlin, to be followed by a three-month tour to Poland, Czechoslovakia, Hungary, Romania, and Bulgaria.[22] Throughout Choe's career, she never missed competing in these festivals, which were held every other year. By the time of the sixth World Festival of Youth and Students in 1957, Choe's company had toured China, Mongolia, Vietnam, the Soviet Union, Bulgaria, Romania, Albania, and Czechoslovakia leading up to the festival, gaining accolades from such famed Russian artists as ballet dancer Galina Ulanova and dancer and choreographer Rostislav Vladimirovich Zakharov.[23] Attesting to such critical acclaim, Choe's production of the dance suite *Song of Peace* (P'yŏnghwa ŭi norae 평화의 노래) won first place for the Peace Prize at the 1957 festival.[24]

Much can be gleaned about the politics of aesthetics in North Korea by examining the significance placed on Choe in North Korean sources. Choe's 2012 biography begins, like so many North Korean publications, with a quote from Kim Il Sung. In his memoir, Kim had described Choe's significance to Korean dance in this way:

> The 1920s and 1930s were a time when there was a wellspring of fierce attempts to develop our own elements in the fields of literature and the arts, preserving our sense of *minjok* (ethnic nation)[25] amid the turbulent influx of outside forces. It was at this time that Choe Seung-hui succeeded in modernizing Korean dance. She contributed to laying the foundation for the development of modern Korean dance by going deeply into the dances of the people, monks, shamans, *kisaeng*, and court dances to discover one-by-one the elegant dance rhythms filled with our people's sentiment (*uri minjokjŏk chŏngsŏ* 우리 민족적 정서).[26]

Until that time, Kim noted, Korean dance had not reached the modern theater, even though singers and instrumentalists had done so. It was only once Choe's creative dances appealed to modern sensibilities that dance was able to take to the stage along with the other arts.[27]

Despite praise, however, Choe's continued performance of solo dances came under scrutiny after her move to North Korea for lacking "mass appeal (大衆性) and realistic content," and she was encouraged to follow the other arts in creating "spirited works singing the efforts of workers and farmers to increase production."[28] Urged to create group dances rather than solos or duets because "group dances are better to watch and enable the training of many dancers to quickly develop the dance arts," political currents pushed Choe to develop song and dance "appropriate to our people's aesthetic tastes (*migam* 味感)."[29] Collective dance portraying the realities of peasant life with references to anticolonial partisan struggle took precedence over individual creative expression.

In confronting such critiques, Choe faced one of the major debates to emerge with the rise of mass culture in the twentieth century: the relationship between art and popular culture, or "high" and "low" art. Her biography affirms the socialist realist principle that "artists should strive to serve the working people . . . creat[ing] dances that reflect the sentiments (*chŏngsŏ* 정서) and everyday emotions (*saenghwal kamjŏng* 생활감정) of our people."[30] To do so, dancers had to be willing to go directly to the scenes of people's lives to learn their thoughts and desires. Choe herself had done so during the colonial era to learn about local folk culture, which she adapted in her dances. The biography points out that Choe had insisted from early in her career that dance must not be a form of entertainment (*yuhŭng* 유흥) or hobby (*hŭngmi* 흥미), and she strove to elevate the artistry of her dance even while she challenged formalism toward new forms of dance.[31]

While political ideology and party policies undeniably became wedded to the creative process in North Korea, party agenda often went hand in hand with Choe's own ambitions, one of which was to develop Korean ballet, combining ballet technique with narrative dance-drama. Ballet not only represented artistic superiority in the "Soviet Union's *mission civilisatrice* . . . to create *k'ultura*," but it had a long history in dance as a demonstration of virtuoso bravura.[32] Choe's ambition as a dancer and choreographer to master ballet technique is therefore not surprising. Her second dance-drama reflected this convergence of ballet with folk motifs. The *Story of Sado Castle* (Sadosŏng ŭi iyagi 사도성의 이야기) was performed in 1955 on the ten-year anniversary of Korea's liberation. Set in ancient times during the Silla dynasty (668–935 CE), the plot features a strong female protagonist fighting the injustices of a class system that oppresses the commoners, who are portrayed as the true historical subjects, embodying dignity and virtue. Featuring Choe's famous sword dance, the central character as a "courageous woman warrior" (*ssikssik'an nyŏjangbu* 씩씩한 녀장부) deftly handles a double sword in both hands as she twirls and spars against her opponents.[33] Due to elaborate set designs and colorful costumes, which must have benefited from Choe's earlier study of Chinese Opera, both of her first two dance-dramas were hugely successful. The earlier *Song of Panya Wŏlsŏng* (반야월성곡) was staged in Beijing in December 1949 for the Asian Women's Conference, and then in the Soviet Union and Eastern Europe in 1950, while the *Story of Sado Castle* was recorded on film with newly imported Soviet technology to become the first color film in North Korea.[34] In contrast to her earlier solos and duets, Choe had incorporated group dances with folk narratives that would appeal to mass audiences.

Upon Choe Seung-hui's return from a five-month tour of the Soviet Union between 1956 and 1957, the North Korean party newspaper *Rodong Sinmun* highlighted the experimental incorporation of ballet technique for male dancers in the *Story of Sado Castle*. Pointing to the successful tour as proof of her effective introduction of classical ballet into Korean dance, Choe resolved to "chew on the classic ballet elements over and over until they become part of our flesh so that our national ballet should become more beautiful and full."[35] But as artists debated the form best suited for the socialist age, ballet itself was fraught with controversy even in the Soviet Union. Avant-garde experiments led to *drambalet* that incorporated pantomime and dramatic theater, blending music, song, and dance, whereas a later generation of choreographers called for a renewed focus on strict balletic form.[36] Choe herself wrestled with the question of form in developing her dance-drama.

As Choe's husband An Mak (안막) came under fire and was purged in the 1958 factional challenge against Kim Il Sung, Choe's dance was increasingly embroiled in the politics of aesthetics over how to articulate national form with socialist content. For example, her 1958 work, *Unrim and Okran* (Unrim kwa Okran 운림과 옥란), later revised as the *Legend of Okryŏn Pond* (Okryŏnmot ŭi chŏnsŏl 옥련못의 전설), came under attack for the lack of "Korean flavor" in the accompanying music. Decrying the "smaller number of Korean instruments and an increased proportion of loud brass instruments," critics complained that "the musical accompaniment consisted of thick metallic music that grated the ear, instead of the soft and gentle melodies with Korean flavor (*Chosŏn mat* 조선맛)."[37] Choe incorporated music as an integral part of her dance compositions and, reflecting the hybridity of her dances, melded traditional Korean instruments with Western orchestral music to create new sounds, modifying Korean instruments to accommodate the stage.[38]

While there is no doubt that such criticisms came about in the context of the 1958 factional conflict, the critique was not arbitrary. The basic points of contention can be traced aesthetically. First and foremost, Choe was enmeshed in the long-standing question about the meaning of art in the "age of people's creation," as she herself had framed the issue: how to elevate artistic bravura to the highest levels even as the arts were opened to mass participation. Choe's attempt to combine the "high" art of ballet with Korean folk dance in a step toward a new form of dance-drama was ultimately stymied by the preoccupation with national form. The appeal to "Korean flavor" signaled the beginnings of North Korean nationalism in the form of the Juche ideology that was to become the defining feature of North Korean politics and art after Choe's death.[39]

## BETWEEN CLASSICAL BALLET AND FOLK DANCE

Despite the beginning of her decline after 1958, Choe continued to publish prolifically throughout the 1960s, expanding on and perfecting her dance philosophy. She emphasized her role in crafting dance-drama as a new dance form and shaping the socialist content of contemporary dance in North Korea. Choe noted how many varieties of group dances were now a part of Korean dance-dramas thanks to her work, "brilliantly illustrating the power and beauty in our people's lives through the joy felt by the many characters in the creative process of collective labor."[40] Ruminating on the challenges of writing dance-drama scripts, Choe emphasized the role of artists in "continually examining everyday life to find what is beautiful, for what is patriotic, heroic, and revolutionary, in order to turn what is beautiful in life into what is beautiful in art."[41] She concluded that the narrative conflict depicted in the script must be based on real life, or it cannot embody a true sense of drama, violating the principles of socialist realism.

In line with socialist realist methods, Choe wrote extensively about the importance of observing ordinary everyday life for artistic inspiration. In two of her most insightful texts, Choe detailed her thoughts on this process. In a 1962 journal article in *Chosŏn Yesul* (조선예술 Korean Art) titled "Artistic skill and artistic training" (*Yesuljŏk kiryang kwa yesuljŏk yŏnma* 예술적 기량과 예술적 연마), Choe forcefully rejected arguments for autonomous art, or *l'art pour l'art*. Rather, she wrote, "artistic skill must enliven the artist's creative intention to depict truthfully, profoundly, and clearly the everyday life and human characteristics as required by the creative methods of socialist realism."[42] She went on to define true artistry as "the ability to move millions of people by wonderfully turning life truths into artistic truths, and the beauty of life into the beauty of art."[43] Choe then explained what kind of national form must be joined with such socialist content. In a 1965 article also in *Chosŏn*

*Yesul* titled "Artistic tradition and artistic creation" (*Yesuljŏk chŏnt'ong kwa yesuljŏk ch'angjo* 예술적 전통과 예술적 창조), Choe clarified that looking to the past does not mean relying on it or imitating it. Rather, she argued that the past is a resource "to improve on what is weak, to shape what is rough, to revive what is lost, and to make what does not exist in order to bring artistic innovation to meet the aesthetic demands of our age."[44] Defining artistic innovation as the creation of something *new* on the basis of past artistic traditions, she insisted that the new had to be better than the old; mere novelty could not constitute true artistic innovation.

So what was modern Korean dance for Choe? She combined her theorization of socialist aesthetics of the everyday with national form to identify folk dance as the core. According to Choe, dance movements reflect people's labor practices and everyday movements particular to their culture and environment.[45] For example, she pointed to the traditional Korean socks (*pŏsŏn* 버선) with their upturned front ends, which caused people to walk with their toes slightly raised, resulting in distinctive Korean dance steps that lead with the heel gliding across the stage, in contrast to the ballet pointe.[46] Placing importance on the skillful use of Korean clothes as costumes that shaped the dance movements themselves, Choe highlighted everyday movements such as the handling of hair ribbons (*taenggi* 댕기), the gathering and whisking of the skirt (*ch'ima* 치마) and jacket (*turumagi* 두루마기), and the tossing off of long sleeves (*hansam* 한삼) or scarves, as expressions of Koreanness in dance.[47] She singled out her sword dance, drum dance, and fan dance as the best examples of such practices.[48]

These principles of Korean dance in North Korea have come to be attributed to its political leaders; however, Choe's own writings between the 1950s and 1960s show that she set the standard. As confirmed by trained dancers Kim Ch'ae-wŏn and Paek Hyang-ju's scholarship on Choe's continued legacy, instead of Choe following instructions, her aesthetic philosophy was appropriated by the political leadership as the authoritative model for the development of Korean dance in North Korea after her death in 1969.[49] The idea to fuse different genres of dance began early in her career, reinforced by her 1930s world tour when she came directly into contact with folk dances in Latin America and Europe. Choe continued such forays with her founding of the Oriental Dance Institute in Beijing in the 1940s, and again devoted time to the task in China during the Korean War. In a lecture delivered to Chinese dancers in 1951 and published in 1954 under the title "Discussion of problems in the creation of dance" (*Muyong ch'angjak ŭi che munje rŭl ronham* 무용창작의 제문제를 론함), Choe argued, "not only do we need to know about Ori-

무용극 《계 월향》을 지도하는 최 승희.

Fig. 11.2. Choe Seung-hui preparing dancers for dance-drama *Kye Wŏlhyang*, 1961.
Source: "人氣 스타—崔承喜와 桂月香," 新生活 Sinsaenghwal May 1961 (no. 51), p.
35–37 available at the Library of Congress.

ental dance, but we must be familiar with Chinese traditional dance, dance of
the Soviet Union, and Western dance ( for example ballet). Only after knowing and mastering such dances and gaining the knowledge and training on
the basics can one expect one's body to move freely and intentionally, and be
able to express complex and varied emotions through the body's rhythms."[50]
Defying conventional boundaries between traditional and modern, or East
and West, against critics who dismissed her work as mere adaptation at best
or decoration at worst, Choe's dance philosophy stressed as the very definition of dance the primacy of the body and mastery over it in order to properly

capture human emotion through bodily rhythms and movements. However, the problem of fusing ballet technique with Korean dance continued to plague Choe throughout the 1950s. During the five-month tour in 1956–57 to the Soviet Union and Eastern Europe, Choe viewed seventeen different ballet and opera performances, including *Swan Lake, Sleeping Beauty, Bronze Horseman,* and *Spartacus.* Upon her return, she reported that her troupe's performance of *Story of Sado Castle* including ballet movements for the male dancers was well received, but that the task of "harmoniously combining Korean dance with classical ballet that is so contrary to our dance" presented a "very difficult problem."[51] This dilemma was ultimately settled by Choe's renewed commitment to folk dance in the 1960s, as shown in her writings. Choe's dance theory claimed folk culture as the most fitting art form of the everyday, aligning with socialist realism that treated art as originating from and appealing to the popular masses.

CONCLUSION

With the consolidation of Kim Il Sung's power after the defeat of two factional challenges in 1958 and then in 1967, his 1930s partisan history began to take precedence over folk aesthetics. This new outlook clashed with Choe's views, which she maintained in her publications throughout the 1960s. Until then, politically themed works were joined by those related to the folk arts, at which Choe excelled. But at the Central Committee meeting of the Korean Dancers Union in December 1964, such folk motifs were replaced by an increasing emphasis on political themes, thereby sidelining Choe with her continued insistence on folk dance in her writings.[52] In effect, her ideas about Korean tradition rooted in the folk arts clashed with the new sense of tradition rooted in Kim Il Sung's anticolonial struggle, and the halo around Choe's reputation was denounced as elitist, to be replaced by a more collectivist creative process.[53]

Ultimately her downfall coincided with the 1967 purge of a second challenge to Kim Il Sung, when his rivals were removed from power under allegations of "bourgeois thought, revisionism, feudal Confucianism, dogmatism, toadyism, factionalism, regionalism, and other such antirevolutionary tendencies."[54] Choe was criticized under similar charges, as dance became a group activity (*sojo hwaldong* 소조활동) under the amateur art system rather than a form of "high" art. With Choe gone from the scene and Kim Jong Il's emergence as the primary figure in the arts in his bid for eventual succession to his father's leadership, dance-dramas were now considered a form borrowed from classical ballet, to be replaced by revolutionary operas in the style of *Sea of Blood* (*P'ibadasik hyŏngmyŏng kagŭk* 피바다식 혁명가극), a genre attributed to Kim Jong Il.[55] In its November 1969 issue, *Chosŏn Yesul* editorialized that "without songs to clearly deliver the ideological content, dance-dramas were unable to fully and powerfully depict the enormity of real life," since past dance-dramas were based on legends, myths, and fables dealing with feudalistic ethics and morals.[56] Instead, the editorial continued, the newly created revolutionary operas would overcome the weaknesses of the past and illustrate the revolutionary reality in the present.

However, even under criticism, Choe's influence in the creation of basic Korean dance movements was to have a lasting place in North Korea. While her name was left out of official discourse until the 1990s, Kim Jong Il's writings on the art of dance continued to emphasize the importance of basic dance movement training, which was largely based on the system Choe created. A 1992 treatise attributed to Kim Jong Il essentially followed the basic principles of dance laid out by Choe more than three decades earlier. Like Choe, the treatise emphasized the importance of creating dance movements out of people's everyday lives, highlighting folk dance movements as a way to cultivate national dance.[57] Indeed, the use of folk songs and fables to create folk dances was now encouraged as "the varied movements and postures in everyday life including work life have their own national characteristics that can most clearly be demonstrated through dance."[58] At the same time, adaptations of traditional dances should not be excessively modernized to meet people's aesthetic expectations, he warned. Indirectly referring to Choe's incorporation of classical ballet in the creation of Korean dance-dramas, Kim Jong Il disparaged past dance-dramas as copies of Western dance-dramas "without adapting it in our style (*urisik ŭro mandŭlji mot'ago* 우리식으로 만들지 못하고)."[59] Instead of such "blind" following of Western styles, he advocated the creation of "new dance-dramas in our style" (*urisik ŭi saeroun muyonggŭk* 우리식의 새로운 무용극) such as *Sea of Blood*, incorporating aesthetic trends from other countries in accordance with "our own ideological and modern sentiments" to fit with the people's aesthetic tastes.[60] Regardless of such attempts to sideline Choe, the stress on the importance of folk dances, dance scripts, and collaboration between set design, music, props, and costume to create a comprehensive dance form was a reiteration of Choe's own career and writings.[61]

With the revitalization of folk dances as a way to diversify the creation of new dance forms, the 1990s saw a concerted attempt to catalog and systematize newly discovered folk dances, and some of Choe's dances reemerged. The *Story of Sado Castle* (1954) was reportedly remade as the *People of Pyongyang Castle* (1997), later restaged under its original title in 2011 during the centennial celebration of Choe's birth.[62] The return to folk arts as Choe had advocated also coincided with the crisis of socialism that ultimately led to the dissolution of the socialist bloc, driving North Korea toward a far more insular posture, as embodied in the slogan Our Style Socialism (*urisik sahoejuǔi* 우리식 사회주의).[63] While renewed nationalism may be expected with the waning of international socialism, this chapter underscores the role of "socialist content" with its emphasis on everyday practices wedded to "national form" in establishing folk as a definitive aesthetic genre in North Korean dance.

This history of Choe Seung-hui is significant because she is so subversive. Not only does she reverse the usual Chinese hegemony over Korea to show how a Korean dancer shaped Chinese traditional dance, but restoring her place in North Korean history also challenges conventional scholarship on North Korea that centers the "Kim dynasty" as a form of Confucian patriarchy from which all things emanate. In such a frame, different aspects of North Korean culture, from stage performances and films to military parades and mass games, are lumped together under the rubric of propaganda that functions to both shape reality and control the daily lives of North Koreans, ironically reinforcing the notion of an all-powerful state.[64] This chapter disrupts the usual reading of North Korean publications to compare multiple sources across time, uncovering how ideas first advanced by Choe were eventually appropriated as the official line. Such a method rejects a simple distinction between the disciplinary powers of the state and the parameters for individual choices. All choices—creative or otherwise—are made within given rules, and Choe's aesthetic choices were no different. She had to negotiate binary worlds in which she lived, confronting immense challenges. Although the story of her expert navigation may appear seamless, this is so only in hindsight as folk aesthetics has proven durable, enabling her resuscitation in both Koreas.

## ADDITIONAL RESOURCES

Full resolution versions of Figure 11.1 at https://doi.org/10.3998/mpub.11521701.cmp.21  and Figure11.2 at https://doi.org/10.3998/mpub.11521701.cmp.22

Video Clip 11.1: Choe Seung-hui and ensemble in *The Story of Sado Castle,* North Korea, 1956. Accessible at https://doi.org/10.3998/mpub.11521701.cmp.65

Video Clip 11.2: Choe Seung-hui teaching dance in Pyongyang. Accessible at https://doi.org/10.3998/mpub.11521701.cmp.66

Video Clip 11.3: Choe Seung-hui in Moscow World Youth Festival, 1957. Accessible at https://doi.org/10.3998/mpub.11521701.cmp.67

Video Clip 11.4: Choe Seung-hui Korean dance teaching curriculum, produced in North Korea, 1962. Accessible at https://doi.org/10.3998/mpub.11521701.cmp.68

Link 11.1: Compilation of Choe Seung-hui dance film footage, 1930s-1950s. Available at https://doi.org/10.3998/mpub.11521701.cmp.69

Link 11.2: North Korean-Soviet coproduction dance film from 1950s featuring Choe's daughter An Seonghui. Available at https://doi.org/10.3998/mpub.11521701.cmp.70

## Notes

* I have followed Revised Romanization for Choe's name to reduce diacritical marks but have kept the McCune-Reischauer system throughout the chapter. All translations of Korean into English are mine. I'd like to express my deep gratitude to Emily Wilcox and Katherine Mezur for their encouragement and support in writing this chapter.

1. While this list is not meant to be exhaustive, in addition to the materials cited in the rest of the essay, publications in Korean include Chŏng Pyŏng-ho 정병호, *Ch'umch'unŭn Ch'oe Sŭnghŭi—segye rŭl huiŏjabŭn Chosŏn yŏja* 춤추는 최승희—세계를 휘어잡은 조선여자 (Seoul: Ppuri kip'ŭn namu, 1995); Yu Mi-hŭi 유미희, "Pukhan muyong yesul kwa yŏsŏng haebang 북한무용예술과 여성해방, *Hanguk muyong kyoyuk hakhoeji* 한국무용교육학회지 , vol. 9, no. 1 (1998): 153-71; Ch'oe Sŏng-ok 최성옥, "Haewoe kongyŏn i Ch'oe Sŭnghŭi ŭi yesul segye e mich'in yŏnghyang 해외공연이 최승희의 예술 세계에 미친 영향," *Hanguk muyong kirok hakhoe* 한국무용기록학회, vol. 20 (2010): 107-33; Tong Kyŏng-wŏn 동경원, "Ch'oe Sŭng-hŭi muyong yŏngu: chakp'um punsŏk mit kongyŏn yesulsajŏk iŭi rŭl chungsim ŭro 최승희무용연구: 작품분석 및 공연예술사적 이의를 중심으로," *Hanguk yesul yŏngu* 한국예술연구9 (June 2014): 151-205; and in English, Young-Hoon Kim, "Border Crossing: Choe Seung-hui's Life and the Modern Experience," *Korea Journal* (Spring 2006): 170-97; Sang Mi Park, "The Making of a Cultural Icon for the Japanese Empire: Choe Seung-hui's U.S. Dance Tours and 'New Asian Culture' in the 1930s and 1940s," *positions* 14, no. 3 (Winter 2006): 585-626; Judy Van Zile, *Perspectives on Korean Dance* (Middletown, CT: Wesleyan University Press, 2001) and "Performing Modernity in Korea: The Dance of Ch'oe Sŭng-hŭi," *Ko-*

*rean Studies*, vol. 37 (2013): 124–49; Faye Yuan Kleeman, *In Transit: The Formation of the Colonial East Asian Cultural Sphere* (Honolulu: University of Hawai'i Press, 2014); and Emily Wilcox, "Crossing Over: Choe Seung-hui's Pan-Asianism in Revolutionary Time," 무용역사기록학 (*The Journal of the Society for Dance Documentation and History*) 51 (December 2018): 65–97.

2. This is a reference to the concept "national in form and socialist in content" first articulated in a speech by Stalin. See J. V. Stalin, "The Political Tasks of the University of the Peoples of the East," speech delivered at a meeting of students of the Communist University of the Toilers of the East (May 18, 1925) available at https://www.marxists.org/reference/archive/stalin/works/1925/05/18.htm (accessed August 11, 2016).

3. See for example Sang Mi Park, Judy Van Zile, and Faye Yuan Kleeman.

4. After her return from her world tour (1937–40), Choe Seung-hui spent much of the remainder of World War II in China, where her most important work was the opening of the Oriental Dance Institute in Beijing in 1944. Here she played a central role in systematizing dance adapted from Chinese Opera. For discussion of Choe's influence in the creation of a new Chinese dance vocabulary based on Peking opera and Kunqu, which led to the dance style known as Chinese classical dance, see Emily Wilcox, *Revolutionary Bodies: Chinese Dance and the Socialist Legacy* (Oakland: University of California Press, 2019).

5. For a definition of folk, see https://www.merriam-webster.com/dictionary/folk, and for the statistics on use of the term over time, see https://books.google.com/ngrams/graph?year_start=1800&year_end=2008&corpus=15&smoothing=7&case_in|sensitive=on&content=folk&direct_url=t4%3B%2Cfolk%3B%2Cc0%3B%2Cs0%3B%3Bfolk%3B%2Cc0%3B%3BFolk%3B%2Cc0%3B%3BFOLK%3B%2Cc0

6. Wilcox, *Revolutionary Bodies*, chapter 2.

7. Philipp Herzog, "'National in Form and Socialist in Content' or Rather 'Socialist in Form and National in Content'?: The 'Amateur Art System' and the Cultivation of 'Folk Art' in Soviet Estonia," *Nar. umjet* 47, no. 1 (2010): 115–40 [125].

8. Chŏng Chi-su 정지수 and Pak, Chong-sŏng 박종성, "Haebang hu muyong yesul ŭi paljŏn 해방후 무용예술의 발전," in *Pitnanŭn uri yesul* 빛나는 우리 예술 (Pyongyang: Chosŏn yesulsa, 1960), 281–332 [286].

9. Yi Yŏng-ran 이영란, *Ch'oe Sŭng-hŭi muyong yesul sasang* 최승희 무용 예술 사상 (Seoul: Minsogwŏn, 2014), 74.

10. Pae Yun-hŭi 배윤희, *T'aeyang ŭi p'um esŏ yŏngsaeng hanŭn muyongga* 태양의 품에서 영생하는 무용가 (Pyongyang: Munhak yesul ch'ulp'ansa, 2012), 12.

11. Yi, *Ch'oe Sŭng-hŭi muyong*, 74.

12. Pae, *T'aeyang ŭi p'um*, 43.

13. For details about the election and the importance of the "everyday" in the foundation of North Korea, see Suzy Kim, *Everyday Life in the North Korean Revolution, 1945–1950* (Ithaca, NY: Cornell University Press, 2013), especially chapter 3.

14. Pae, *T'aeyang ŭi p'um*, 127.

15. Choe Seung-hui 최승희, *Chosŏn minjok muyong kibon* 조선민족무용기본

(Pyongyang: Chosŏn yesul ch'ulp'ansa, 1958); Choe Seung-hui 최승희, *Muyonggŭk tae-bonjip* 무용극 대본집 (Pyongyang: Chosŏn yesul ch'ulp'ansa, 1958); Choe Seung-hui 최승희, *Chosŏn adong muyong kibon* 조선아동무용기본 (Pyongyang: Chosŏn munhak yesul ch'ongtongmaeng ch'ulp'ansa, 1964).

16. Choe Seung-hui, "Inmin ch'angjak ŭi sidae 인민 창작의 시대," *Munhak Sinmun* 문학신문 (October 27, 1961), 3.

17. Yi Chu-mi 이주미, "Ch'oe Sŭng-hŭi ŭi 'Chosŏnjŏk in kŏt' kwa 'Tongyangjŏk in kŏt'" 최승희의 '조선적인 것'과 '동양적인 것', *Hanminjok munhwa yŏngu* 한민족문화연구 23 (November 2007): 335–359 [336].

18. Sŏng Hyŏn-kyŏng 성현경, ed. *Kyŏngsŏng elittŭ ŭi manguk yuramgi* 경성엘리트의 만국유람기 (Seoul: Hyŏnsil munhwa yŏngu, 2015), 86.

19. Yi, "Ch'oe Sŭng-hŭi ŭi 'Chosŏnjŏk in kŏt,'" 340.

20. Yi, "Ch'oe Sŭng-hŭi ŭi 'Chosŏnjŏk in kŏt,'" 341.

21. Pae, *T'aeyang ŭi p'um*, 155.

22. Pae, *T'aeyang ŭi p'um*, 158.

23. Pae, *T'aeyang ŭi p'um*, 160.

24. Pae, *T'aeyang ŭi p'um*, 120.

25. Minjok (民族) has been variously translated as "people" or "nation." A neologism imported through China and Japan at the turn of the century akin to the German *volk*, it coincides with the rise of the modern nation-state and nationalism in East Asia. I have kept the original terminology in some instances when it was difficult to make an exact translation. Depending on the context, I have also used "our" or "Korean" in addition to "people" and "nation."

26. Pae, *T'aeyang ŭi p'um*, 1.

27. Pae, *T'aeyang ŭi p'um*, 164.

28. Pae, *T'aeyang ŭi p'um*, 59.

29. Pae, *T'aeyang ŭi p'um*, 46.

30. Pae, *T'aeyang ŭi p'um*, 55.

31. Pae, *T'aeyang ŭi p'um*, 57.

32. Kristen Elizabeth Hamm, "'The Friendship of Peoples': Soviet Ballet, Nationalities Policy, and the Artistic Media, 1953–1968" (MA thesis, University of Illinois, Urbana-Champaign, 2009), 3.

33. Choe Seung-hui 최승희, *Muyonggŭk taebonjip* 무용극 대본집 (Pyongyang: Chosŏn yesul ch'ulp'ansa, 1958), 53.

34. Pae, *T'aeyang ŭi p'um*, 68–71, 109.

35. "Choe Seung-hui muyong yŏn'guso ŭi kwihwan kongyŏn sŏnghwang 최승희 무용 연구소의 귀한 공연 성황," *Rodong Sinmin* 로동신문 (February 4, 1957), 3.

36. Hamm, "The Friendship of Peoples," 11–20.

37. Pae, *T'aeyang ŭi p'um*, 125.

38. The practice of modifying and improving traditional instruments, which Choe began in the 1950s, became part of state policy in November 1964, eventually becoming a central part in the production of the revolutionary operas *Sea of Blood* (1971) and

*The Flower Girl* (1972). See Kim Ch'ae-wŏn 김채원, *Ch'oe Sŭng-hŭi ch'um: kyesŭng kwa pyŏnyong* 최승희 춤: 계승과 변용 (Seoul: Minsogwŏn, 2008), 170.

39. While Juche (主體) is often translated as "self-reliance" by those inside and outside North Korea, it is *not* a neologism unique to North Korea as some have mistakenly assumed, but has been in Korean usage since the early twentieth century to denote subjectivity, or "master of self," to parse the Sino-Korean characters.

40. Choe Seung-hui, "Muyonggŭk yesul kwa muyonggŭk wŏnbon 무용극예술과 무용극 원본," *Munhak Sinmun* 문학신문 (March 16, 1965), 3.

41. Choe Seung-hui, "Muyonggŭk wŏnbon changjak eso ŭi kibon munje 무용극원본 창작에서의 기본문제," *Munhak Sinmun* 문학신문 (April 23, 1965), 3.

42. Yi Ae-sun 이애순, *Ch'oe Sŭng-hŭi muyong yesul munjip* 최승희무용예술문집 (Seoul: Kukhak charyowŏn, 2002), 78.

43. Yi, *Ch'oe Sŭng-hŭi muyong yesul munjip*, 79.

44. Yi, *Ch'oe Sŭng-hŭi muyong yesul munjip*, 72.

45. Choe Seung-hui, "Chosŏn muyong tongjak kwa kŭ kibŏp ŭi ususŏng mit minjokjŏk t'ŭksŏng 조선무용동작과 그기본의 우수성 및 민족적 특성," *Munhak Sinmun* 문학신문 (March 25, 1966), 4. The article was published serially across four issues from March 22 to April 1, 1966.

46. Choe Seung-hui, "Chosŏn muyong tongjak kwa kŭ kibŏp ŭi ususŏng mit minjokjŏk t'ŭksŏng 조선무용동작과 그기본의 우수성 및 민족적 특성," *Munhak Sinmun* (March 29, 1966), 4.

47. Choe's formulation parallels theories of the Laban School developed by dance theorist Rudolf Laban (1879–1958), who saw dance as representative of movements in everyday life. Laban's theory was put to the test by folklorist and ethnomusicologist Alan Lomax, who developed a method to analyze dance called *choreometrics*, concluding that "dance is composed of those gestures, postures, movements, and movement qualities most characteristic and most essential to the activity of everyday, and thus crucial to cultural continuity." Alan Lomax, Irmgard Bartenieff, Forrestine Paulay, "Dance Style and Culture," in *Folk Song Style and Culture* (Washington, DC: American Association for the Advancement of Science, 1968), 224.

48. Choe Seung-hui, "Chosŏn muyong tongjak kwa kŭ kibŏp ŭi ususŏng mit minjokjŏk t'ŭksŏng 조선무용동작과 그기본의 우수성 및 민족적 특성," *Munhak Sinmun* 문학신문 (April 1, 1966), 3.

49. Kim, *Ch'oe Sŭng-hŭi ch'um*, 61; Paek Hyang-ju 백향주, "Ch'oe Sŭng-hŭi <Chosŏn minjok muyong kibon> ŭi hyŏngsŏng kwa pyŏnhwa 최승희 '조선민족무용기본'의 형성과 변화" (MA thesis, Korean National University of Arts, 2006).

50. Yi, *Ch'oe Sŭng-hŭi muyong yesul munjip*, 123.

51. Yi, *Ch'oe Sŭng-hŭi muyong yesul munjip*, 190. See also "Ch'oe Sŭng-hŭi muyong yŏnguso ŭi kwihwan kongyŏn sŏnghwang 최승희무용연구소의 귀한 공연 성황," *Rodong Sinmun* 로동신문 (February 4, 1957), 3.

52. Paek, "Ch'oe Sŭng-hŭi," 51.

53. Paek, "Ch'oe Sŭng-hŭi," 52–53.

54. Paek, "Ch'oe Sŭng-hŭi," 54.

55. For more details on the development of the revolutionary operas in the style of *Sea of Blood*, see Suzy Kim, "Mothers and Maidens: Gendered Formation of Revolutionary Heroes in North Korea," *Journal of Korean Studies* 19, no. 2 (Fall 2014): 256–90.

56. Paek, "Ch'oe Sŭng-hŭi," 87.

57. Kim Jong Il 김정일, *Muyong yesullon* 무용예술론 (Pyongyang: Chosŏn rodongdang ch'ulp'ansa, 1992), 6.

58. Kim, *Muyong yesullon*, 32, 35.

59. Kim, *Muyong yesullon*, 46.

60. Kim, *Muyong yesullon*, 50.

61. Kim, *Muyong yesullon*, 8.

62. For reference to the 1997 production, see Paek, "Ch'oe Sŭng-hŭi," 111, and for footage of the 2011 production, see DVD, *T'aeyang ŭi p'um esŏ yŏngsaeng hanŭn muyongga* 태양의 품에서 영생하는 무용가 (Pyongyang: Mokran Video, 2012).

63. Paek, "Ch'oe Sŭng-hŭi," 113.

64. Suk-Young Kim, *Illusive Utopia: Theater, Film, and Everyday Performance in North Korea* (Ann Arbor: University of Michigan Press, 2010), 11–16. The most pernicious way the performative creeps into the study of North Korea is to render it a Potemkin village, in which "North Korea" becomes theatrical and fictional, fake and illusive, simply staged for the self-glorification of the leader (p. 264). Rather than using the same aesthetic criteria to evaluate North Korean performances, theatricality itself becomes a form of critique of North Korea's concern for appearances above people's welfare (p. 277).

# CHAPTER 12

# The Dilemma of Chinese Classical Dance

## Traditional or Contemporary?

*Dong Jiang* 江东

Traditional or contemporary? Throughout its history, in theory and in practice, this argument has followed the evolution of Chinese Classical Dance (*Zhongguo gudianwu* 中国古典舞, hereafter CCD). CCD is a dance style that emerged just over half a century ago, so given the long history of Chinese dance, it is a very young form to represent THE Chinese dance. Over its sixty or so years of development, CCD has had a tumultuous evolution, with positive and negative influences from events, artists, and those in power. There are people who love it and use it, and others who judge it and criticize it. Those who love it tend to believe that CCD was invented as a powerful idea to strengthen the Chinese spirit in dance, while those who criticize it argue that it has a problematic connection to foreign concepts and methodologies. Thus, through its process of growth over the last half-century, CCD and the artists who have embraced its development have gone through a difficult and critical period of experimentation, with every step being scrutinized and judged. The critical question for creators, audiences, and critics has always been: should CCD be traditional or contemporary?

Why is this traditional-or-contemporary issue so vital to the development of CCD? Before answering, I will explain the background to this dilemma, which continues to have far-reaching effects on the evolution of CCD today.

Since the founding of the People's Republic of China (PRC) in 1949, Chinese Dance has played an active and popular artistic role in Chinese social and political life; it has been regarded as a very serious art form, one of those that is supported fully by the government.[1] Historical studies document the long history of dance in China, starting from thousands of years ago. They show that Chinese dance in its historical sense can be regarded as a long river, which has experienced periods of both strength and weakness.[2] Today, we cut this river into two parts: the ancient and the present, with the dividing line in the early twentieth century.

Ancient Chinese dance has a complex history with many parts, corresponding to China's successive dynasties. Wang Kefen 王克芬 (1927–2018), a preeminent historian of Chinese dance, has published numerous books on ancient Chinese dance, some of which have also been translated and published in English.[3] Her work shows the remarkable range of dance styles practiced, for example, in the Zhou dynasty (1121–221 BCE), the Han dynasty (202 BCE–220 CE), and the Tang dynasty (618–907 CE), with the Tang often regarded as its peak. While there is rich documentation of these dances in the historical record, almost none of those ancient dance forms exist today. A few years ago, on a visit to Tokyo, I saw a performance of *Gagaku* 雅乐, a set of court dances from ancient China that are now well preserved in Japan, Korea, and Vietnam. Many believe these dances can be traced to the Tang dynasty. While these dances have been preserved abroad, there are few such preserved performance traditions in China, our own country. Standing in the present point of the river, we may feel awkwardness and pity that we are far from our ancient dances and can only regret that our old dancing forms disappeared long ago. However, from another perspective, these dances did not disappear, but enriched subsequent performance traditions, such as *xiqu* (戏曲), Chinese Traditional Opera.[4]

There are many varieties of Chinese Traditional Opera, which take their names from the geographical regions where they are popular: opera from Sichuan is called Chuan Opera (*Chuanju* 川剧); opera from Beijing is called Beijing Opera or Peking Opera (*Jingju* 京剧), etc.[5] With a development history of several centuries, these Chinese Traditional Operas synthesized nearly all performing genres—including dance, music, drama, and acrobatics—combining them into a total aesthetic system within each operatic form. So, for about 1,000 years, the art of dance in China became integrated into the traditional opera system, causing it to lose its status as an independent art form.[6]

During the early twentieth century, dance reemerged as an independent art form separate from Chinese Traditional Opera, with a strong connection to Western dance styles. New dance forms were appearing at this time in different places around the world due to radical changes in industry and society. These developments introduced new ideas to China, where dance was rarely thought of as an independent, serious art form. Three individuals stood out in this early period of early twentieth-century Chinese dance history: Ms. Yu Rongling 裕容龄 (1882–1973), a dancer in the Qing dynasty court who studied modern dance in France with Isadora Duncan; Mr. Wu Xiaobang 吴晓邦 (1906–1995), a pioneer of Chinese new dance who studied modern dance in Japan; and Ms. Dai Ailian 戴爱莲 (1916–2006), considered the mother of Chinese dance, who was born in Trinidad and studied ballet and modern dance in England.[7] Although their backgrounds were different, all three studied Western dance styles, such as ballet and modern dance, in foreign countries. Through their efforts and those of others, Chinese society became familiar with this new form of dance art with its movement languages and styles, including modernism and realism. This movement pushed Chinese dance into a brand-new era, with innovative dance forms, known by a variety of different names, such as "New Dance" (*xinxing wuyong* 新兴舞踊), "National Dance" (*minzu wudao* 民族舞蹈), "Chinese New Dance" (*Zhongguo xin wudao* 中国新舞蹈), and others. After 1949, when the PRC was established as a new nation, many dancers started careers, supported by the new government, in newly established dance companies, schools, and research institutes. The new dance culture started to boom. It was also during this period that the new genre of CCD emerged.[8]

Since the early PRC, many decades have passed, with subsequent transformations in Chinese dance. As a whole, dance history in the PRC era can be organized into three stages, divided by the period known as the Cultural Revolution (*Wenhua da geming* 文化大革命), which took place from 1966 to 1976. I would like to briefly examine the development of Chinese classical dance through each of these three stages—before, during, and after the Cultural Revolution. Then I will focus on the dilemma of the traditional and the contemporary as it has shaped CCD since the 1980s.

## CHINESE CLASSICAL DANCE BEFORE THE CULTURAL REVOLUTION

In the years following 1949, China entered a new epoch, and the young nation started to construct a new country, what many called "new China." Everything was new, and art was regarded as a useful component and a spiritual factor in the development of Chinese socialism. For this reason, artistic activities were greatly encouraged and supported by the new government. During this time, China's new dance culture was established on a foundation laid in large part by Wu Xiaobang and Dai Ailian. On the stage of the new China, experiments were welcomed and moved in the direction of exploring new forms for Chinese dance styles. With the founding of the Chinese Association of Dance Workers (later renamed the Chinese Dancers' Association) in 1949, for example, the new state officially sponsored dance as part of national culture.

The issue of training became a central problem in the early PRC dance boom. Western ballet, an already mature dance style, was borrowed as one method for training Chinese dancers. At the same time, Chinese dance professionals began to experiment with new dance training systems, one of which came to be called Chinese Classical Dance. CCD built on the movement practices of Chinese Traditional Opera and martial arts (*gongfu* 功夫). Training systems were also developed based on various styles of Han folk dance and the dances of non-Han nationalities, such as Korean, Mongolian, Tibetan, and Uyghur. By the mid-1950s, CCD, Han folk dance, and minority dances were required components of Chinese Dance training in most professional dance schools and training programs.

Based on this training model, we can get a sense of China's dance culture of the 1950s and early 1960s. The Beijing Dance School (*Beijing wudao xuexiao* 北京舞蹈学校, now the Beijing Dance Academy), established in 1954 as China's first independent professional dance conservatory, had two sections, one for ballet and the other for Chinese Dance. The ballet section, which included both classical ballet and character dance, was led by Russian ballet teachers from the Soviet Union.[9] The Chinese Dance section was also divided into two parts: Chinese Classical Dance and Chinese Folk Dance (*Zhongguo minjian wu* 中国民间舞). Chinese instructors, who came from all over China, directed these sectors. Schematically, China's dance education of the time can be said to form a triangle comprising three dance forms: Chinese Classical Dance, Chinese Folk Dance (including both Han and minority dances), and ballet. Under the Ministry of Culture, four national-level state dance companies were founded between 1951 and 1959 that corresponded to these categories: the Chinese National Opera and Dance Drama Theater (*Zhongguo geju wujuyuan* 中国歌剧舞剧院), the Central Song and Dance Ensemble (*Zhongyang gewutuan* 中央歌舞团), the Central Nationalities Song and Dance Ensemble (*Zhongyang minzu gewutuan* 中央民族歌舞团), and the Central Ballet of China (中央芭蕾舞团).[10] This three-part vision lasted, with some additions, until the mid-1960s.[11]

Among the three dance forms, CCD in particular was given the important task of establishing a distinctly Chinese school of dance technique. As discussed above, ancient Chinese dances had not been directly passed down as independent dance forms. Instead, ancient dance was transmitted only through other types of performance, such as Chinese Traditional Opera, martial arts, or folk dances. CCD was first developed by extracting the movement practices from Chinese Traditional Operas, especially from Peking Opera and Kunqu 昆曲. From my perspective, this philosophy and methodology made sense at the time. However, the Russian ballet influenced its process, planting a seed for problems later criticized by some Chinese dance practitioners and scholars.[12]

Within this pre–Cultural Revolution period of CCD history, one of the more prominent dance performers was Chen Ailian 陈爱莲 (b. 1939), a dancer from Shanghai educated in the first class of students at the Beijing Dance School. After receiving thorough training in the newly created experimental CCD method of the 1950s, Chen won four gold prize awards at the World Festival of Youth and Students dance competition in Finland in 1962, the first such major award for CCD on the international stage. Her signature dance at this time was the CCD solo *Spring, River, and Flowers on a Moonlit Night* (*Chunjiang huayueye* 春江花月夜), premiered in 1957.[13] Chen continued to dance in the post–Cultural Revolution period and is regarded as one of the best CCD dancers of all time. Even in her late seventies, Chen is amazingly still actively performing on stage. Her dancing emphasizes the aesthetic characteristics that came to define CCD during the 1950s and early 1960s, and it is still taken to be iconic of CCD today.

During this pre–Cultural Revolution period of Chinese dance history, the question of whether CCD was traditional or contemporary was not an important question for dance professionals in China. At that time, artists were more concerned with how to develop this new dancing style. For them, the development of CCD was a conscious choice to search for a distinctly Chinese movement system, with minimal Western influences, through the process of creating a new dance form.

## CHINESE CLASSICAL DANCE DURING AND AFTER THE CULTURAL REVOLUTION

Chinese dance historians today regard the ten years of the Cultural Revolution as a disaster to all professional careers, including dance. The two Chinese ballets that formed two of the eight "Model Plays" (*Yangbanxi* 样板戏) of the time were the *Red Detachment of Women (Hongse niangzijun* 红色娘子军, premiered in 1964) and the *White-haired Girl (Baimao nü* 白毛女, premiered in 1965). These dances became the political tools and symbols of the Cultural Revolution and were used to popularize the revolution's ideals throughout the country. Through exposure to these two ballets, millions of people were swept up in this new style of dancing.

While creating these two ballets, Chinese dancers tried to add some Chinese elements to the foreign dance style. Even today, we can still sense this obvious and ambitious experiment. The choreographers used some movements from CCD and Chinese Folk Dance in their choreography, and they viewed this method as an important way to reform ballet through Chinese experiments. At the same time, however, both CCD and Chinese Folk Dance were suppressed and kept from developing during this decade-long period.

With the end of the Cultural Revolution in 1976, China began a process of reform in many areas of society, which included a new openness to Western culture. The artists of the dance culture that had been developed in the pre–Cultural Revolution period resumed development of those forms and more. Soon, the triangular system was extended to include two additional forms—Chinese Contemporary Dance (*Zhongguo dangdai wu* 中国当代舞) and Modern Dance (*Xiandai wu* 现代舞). These, together with Chinese Dance and ballet, form the main framework of the Chinese concert dance scene that persists today.

In this new period of development after the Cultural Revolution, Chinese dance professionals returned to the question of whether or not CCD could establish a distinctly Chinese dance style, or a national dance form. Reviewing some of the debates that erupted in this period helps to lay the groundwork for understanding how this debate drives creation and scholarship in the field of CCD today.

An issue that had always existed in this field, even in its early years, was how CCD should be created. At first, dance professionals were excited to create a new Chinese dancing style. The name "Chinese Classical Dance" was coined by the famous Peking Opera actor, Mr. Ouyang Yuqian 欧阳予倩 (1889–1962). In the early 1950s, Ouyang served as the first president of the China Central Drama Academy and helped guide the early development of Chinese dances before the Beijing Dance School was established. At this time, the aesthetics of the CCD movement system were very similar to the movements appearing in Peking Opera and Kunqu. Later, many experts even called it "Traditional Opera–Style Chinese Classical Dance" (*Xiqu pai Zhongguo gudianwu* 戏曲派中国古典舞), to distinguish it from later forms that were not based on Traditional Chinese Opera movement. However, by the late 1950s, CCD had come to be influenced by Russian ballet, because many believed that ballet training was anatomically scientific and that elements of ballet training could shorten the time required when using CCD to train a professional dancer. During the early PRC years of the late 1950s, this was an urgent task, because the country was so desperately in need of dancers. Soon after it came into being, the new CCD system was already being used to train the first group of Chinese professional dancers, such as Chen Ailian. Thus, by the end of the 1950s, dance teachers were under tremendous time pressure: they were creating CCD and implementing it in the classroom at the same time. In this context, some saw adopting elements of ballet training into the CCD curriculum as a useful shortcut.

This new form was designed with a focus on training, which led to many new criticisms. Some scholars argued that CCD was only useful for training but did not constitute a choreographic form for expressing the special characteristics of the Chinese spirit. With this idea in mind, after the end of the Cultural Revolution in the late 1970s two core early founders, who were then professors at the Beijing Dance Academy—Ms. Li Zhengyi 李正一 (b. 1929) and Mr. Tang Mancheng 唐满城 (1932–2004)—began to restructure CCD with some new ideas. First, they reinforced its Chinese characteristics and created a new movement system called Body Rhyme (*shenyun* 身韵). This new system paid special attention to the "cultural" quality of the movements. Their efforts served as a major supplement to the former training system,[14] creating a more fluent look with the flavor of martial arts. The Body Rhyme curriculum influenced a new generation of students, leading to new dances created and choreographed in accord with this new movement system. A famous example is the CCD co-ed group dance *Yellow River* (*Huanghe* 黄河), premiered in 1988. The movement vocabulary employed in this dance is largely derived from the Body Rhyme curriculum. Audiences loved this new piece, and it was incorporated as a repertoire work in the CCD Department at the Beijing Dance Academy. Unexpectedly, however, *Yellow River* later led to another debate, because experts saw its contemporary concept and image as being too prominent. These critics felt the piece had moved too far away from traditional aesthetics, and they denied its status as Chinese Classical Dance, calling it Contemporary Dance.[15]

At around the same time, the now very famous choreographer Mr. Chen Weiya 陈维亚 (b. 1956) created new works that many Chinese dance critics deemed to be representative of a new post–Cultural Revolution era of CCD. Chen emerged as an important choreographer in the 1980s and initially choreographed works using recognizable CCD movement language and features, based on movement vocabularies developed through the CCD curriculum and repertoires of the 1950s and early 1960s, as well as the new Body Rhyme movement system. At that time, many regarded him as a voice for CCD in the new age. From Chen's dances, such as *The Return of Mulan* (*Mulan Gui* 木兰归, 1987) and *The Soul of Qin Warrior Soldiers* (*Qinyong Hun* 秦俑魂, 1984), audiences could see a very clear CCD vocabulary. The tone of the choreography followed the rules established before the Cultural Revolution, showing that Chen in fact inherited CCD's accomplished tradition. For this reason, critics accepted his dances as extensions of the CCD style.

Although choreographers like Chen Weiya were seen as signs of CCD's second prosperous boom, others were nevertheless antagonistic toward the new repertoires and asked whether CCD should pursue a more classical form that was less contemporary. This question created a compelling challenge in the dance world, leading to heated debates in the CCD field. This phenomenon continued in the 1990s and was finally resolved with the new works of a young choreographer, Ms. Tong Ruirui 佟睿睿 (b. 1977). Tong's solo choreography *Fan as a Brush* (*Shanwu danqing* 扇舞丹青) premiered in 2000, danced by female Chinese classical dance artist Wang Yabin 王亚彬 (b. 1984). This dance brought a major shift to the CCD arena; it had a new, more poetic and elegant style. It seemed to once again point to a new direction for the future of CCD. After many people saw this dance, the argument of tradition vs. contemporary seemed to be temporarily resolved, because this dance offered hope of a style that could incorporate both.

This new dance made people think of new questions, however: What exactly is CCD? What could a CCD piece look like? With rapid transitions in the political and economic sphere and changes in social circumstances, the choreographer's concept changed, as did the public's expectations. Critics once again began to ask if we could create a CCD dance with a modern idea. At this time, many new pieces appeared that expressed young choreographers' new visions. To them, CCD was an old form created by an earlier generation. They hoped they could choreograph new works with their own ideas for the new era. With this intention, the turn of the twenty-first century witnessed the emergence of a new generation of promising young choreographers, such as Mr. Zhao Xiaogang 赵小刚 (b. 1975), Mr. Zhang Yunfeng 张云峰 (b. 1972), and Mr. Hu Yan 胡岩 (b. 1980), among others.

Zhang Yunfeng's new choreography, titled *Goodbye, Cambridge* (*Zaibie Kangqiao* 再别康桥) and danced by male CCD performer Wu Weifeng 武巍峰 (b. 1980), presented an extreme answer to this question. Though the movements he used in the dance were mostly from CCD, the whole structure of the piece reflected a modern dance sensibility. Many interpreted it not as a work of CCD, but rather as a modern dance with some CCD movements. Yet the dance was only performed by CCD dancers, not by modern dancers, who in China usually remained in their own community. With this piece, CCD totally changed its nature.

No matter how intense the critics' arguments became, the audience and young students of CCD ignored them, and they show their love of these new works even in the face of critical debate. Thus, I suggest that amid the arguments, CCD continues to change gradually but firmly because of these strong

Fig. 12.1. Wang Yabin performing Chinese classical dance solo *Fan as a Brush*, premiered in 2000 and choreographed by Tong Ruirui. Photo by Ye Jin 叶进 courtesy of the photographer.

and visionary dancers, choreographers, and critics. I consider that the debate itself motivates the artists, pushing them to develop critical and creative methods. The controversies generated within the debates about CCD also add to the field's energy.

## OTHER DEVELOPMENTS:
## DANCE DRAMAS, COMPETITIONS, AND NEW APPROACHES

The developments described above mainly grew out of the Opera-based and Body Rhyme schools of CCD that developed out of the Beijing Dance Academy curriculum. Presently, that Academy continues to be the main center for training CCD experts for all of China. After graduating from the Academy, students go on to teach in other parts of the country; thus, those trained in CCD at the Academy shape CCD throughout China.[16] However, if we examine other aspects of CCD beyond education and training, we will see that other developments have been taking place alongside these curricular projects.

The first development has to do with large-scale productions known as "dance drama" (*wuju* 舞剧). From its beginnings, the proponents of CCD envisioned it as a national form, comparable to those of neighboring countries such as India, Myanmar, Japan, and Korea. Apart from training Chinese dancers, there was a parallel movement to create full-scale narrative dance works using the new CCD movement vocabularies. The Chinese National Opera and Dance Drama Theater, established in 1951, was one of the groups leading this dance drama project. Most of the Chinese dance dramas made by this and other dance companies during the 1950s and early 1960s used CCD as a dominant vocabulary. And this was also the case during the revival of CCD after 1976. Eventually, however, a paradox emerged in this dance drama style. Most dance ensembles that produce Chinese dance dramas also perform other dance styles, and in their works CCD often blended into other dance genres. In other words, very few dance drama ensembles perform and maintain a "pure" CCD dance drama style. After many years, the early love and high expectations for CCD have faded, especially as more dance styles drive the market and gain popularity. I think that CCD dance drama artists must deal with this process of diversity and assimilation, and consider what they want to preserve or remove and what they want to expand or limit in their CCD repertoires and new works.

National dance competitions are the second national phenomenon shaping the direction of CCD and its artists. Competitions at multiple levels have long driven the new innovations in CCD. Among China's major dance competitions, four are most important for the field of CCD: the National Dance Competition, the Lotus Cup Dance Competition, the Peach and Plum Cup Dance Competition, and the CCTV Dance Competition. Each competition targets specific practitioner communities and types of entries. For example, the National Dance Competition, held by the Ministry of Culture every two years, is open to all professional dancers, and it grants awards in two areas: choreography and performance. The Lotus Cup Dance Competition, held by the Chinese Dancers' Association, also takes place every two years. This award covers a large range of dance styles and types and awards according to the categories of different dance forms. The Peach and Plum Cup Dance Competition, which was started by Beijing Dance Academy but later taken over by the Ministry of Culture, takes place once every three years. Only students can participate because it is designed as a competition among the dance academies. Finally, the fourth is sponsored by CCTV (China Central Television) and takes place every two years. It is open to all, professionals and amateurs.

Because of its focus on conservatory students, the Peach and Plum Cup Dance Competition (*Tao li bei wudao bisai* 桃李杯舞蹈比赛) has a strong impact on the development of CCD. Many of the young choreographers and dancers mentioned above have staged their work and developed their reputations through participation in this and other national-level competitions. In the last several years, however, the PRC government has developed a new standard for competitions, which has caused many of them to be cancelled. For this reason, among the above four, only the Lotus Cup Dance Competition continues as usual. Fewer competitions could mean there is less incentive to produce new works, which might lead to a halt in the persistent boom that CCD has experienced in recent decades. Certainly, the role of the PRC government must also be considered as an active influence on the CCD in terms of support and direction. Further, the competitions serve as catalysts for public interest, and any reduction in televised performances could cause a disconnect between CCD innovations and nonprofessional communities.

Apart from the two structural issues above, individuals within and outside the CCD field have developed completely new schools of CCD during the post–Cultural Revolution period since 1976. These include Beijing-based Mr. Sun Ying 孙颖 (1929–2009), creator of what is known as the Han-Tang style of CCD, Lanzhou-based Ms. Gao Jin-rong 高金荣 (b. 1934), who has been central in promoting the Dunhuang (敦煌) style of CCD, and Taiwan-based Ms. Liu

Feng-xue (also written Liu Feng Shieh or Liu Feng-shueh) 刘凤学 (b. 1925), founder of the Tang dynasty style, which she also calls Neo-Classical Dance (*xin gudianwu* 新古典舞).

Sun Ying was one of the founding developers of the CCD program at the Beijing Dance School in the 1950s. However, he was not satisfied by its goal and direction, and when he had his chance, he took a different path. From the very beginning, Sun disagreed with the CCD creators' focus on Chinese Traditional Opera. He suggested that CCD should reach further back into history by looking at dances of the Han or Tang dynasties. Since this suggestion was not an easy one to realize at the time, it was not taken seriously. That was the first reason for his later rebellion.[17]

Apart from his opposition to Chinese traditional opera, Sun also opposed the use of movements of Western ballet in CCD. He believed that CCD should be a Chinese dance style, and his ideal was supported by Dai Ailian. Beginning in the 1980s, Sun staged works using a new movement system, which became known as the Han-Tang style within CCD. Sun's choreography *Ta Ge* 踏歌, which won a gold prize in the Lotus Cup Dance Competition in 1998, attracted major attention to Sun's approach. Following his death in 2009, his students have continued his legacy, showing that they value his experiments and that they will continue to use his Han-Tang style, enriching the complex aesthetic diversity of Chinese Dance.

Meanwhile, in the northwestern area of China (formerly the Silk Road), another new approach to CCD known as the Dunhuang style also emerged in the post–Cultural Revolution period. This style refers to the Dunhuang Mogao grottoes, where hundreds of dancing scenes were painted during the first millennium CE. A dance drama staged in 1978 called *Flowers and Rain on Silk Road* (*Silu huayu* 丝路花雨) won national awards and drew attention to this newly developed dance style.[18] By imitating the gestures of dancers depicted in the wall paintings of the Mogao grottoes, dance artists carefully designed and invented a movement system with a completely new dance vocabulary and aesthetic.[19] This form is taught today both at BDA and in the Lanzhou Dance School in Gansu province. Gao Jinrong, former principal of the Gansu Art School, is the representative figure in this form. Gao, now in her eighties, continues to work in Lanzhou while Shi Min 史敏 (b. 1964), originally also from Lanzhou, leads the development of the style through her teaching at Beijing Dance Academy.

In China today, the three styles just discussed—Body Rhyme/Chinese Traditional Opera, Han-Tang, and Dunhuang—are regarded as the three primary schools of CCD. Apart from these, new ambitions to construct Chi-

Fig, 12.2. Students from the Beijing Dance Academy performing a group dance created for the 2009 revival of Han-Tang style dance drama *Tongque Ji* 铜雀伎 (originally premiered in 1985), choreographed by Sun Ying. Photo by Ye Jin 叶进 courtesy of the photographer.

nese classical dance styles have led to the emergence of other new styles and experiments, such as the Nanjing-based Kun-style dance (*Kun wu* 昆舞), and others. Liu Jian 刘建 (b. 1956), a professor at Beijing Dance Academy and a core scholar in the Chinese dance studies field, believes that the most ideal situation for CCD is to continue to multiply, representing different epochs and regions through diverse dance styles.

Outside the mainland, dance artists in Taiwan have also experimented with creating new dance forms inspired by ancient dances. The most important pioneer of these is Liu Feng-xue. In her early nineties, Liu continues to conduct research and lead her company, which is based in Taipei. Liu was born in northeast China and moved to Taiwan before 1949. In Taiwan, she mentored many young dancers. Liu received her PhD at the Laban Center in London when she was sixty years old, setting a positive example for other aspiring dance scholars. As a result, many of her dances are recorded in Laban dance notation.

Liu spent years of hard work doing her research on Tang-style dance. She stayed in the Japanese royal court in Tokyo for several years to research the Chinese ancient documents stored there, many of which we could not find in China. She learned Japanese *Gagaku*, which was believed to come directly from China in the time of the Tang dynasty. Liu has reconstructed four large pieces and four small pieces of Tang dynasty dances so far. Although it is never possible to recover a dance from the past, I believe Liu's dances have a faithful resemblance to ancient dance styles. Through further academic research work and experiments, Liu, Sun, Gao, and others have allowed us to come closer and closer to ancient dance traditions. I have a great respect for these activities, as do other dance scholars across China. There are many historical dance reconstruction activities taking place in China today, using a wide variety of historical source materials, from Han brick paintings to Silk Road grottos to court ritual notation books.

CONCLUSION

Dance artists in China have worked very hard to invent a dance form with a strong and distinct Chinese style, since no ancient dances as independent art forms survived in early twentieth-century China. The Chinese dancers in the post-1949 era always hoped to find a way to express an artistic spirit of their own. Thus, when they designed CCD, no one doubted its legitimacy. And the early CCD created excellent dances, which the public hoped they would keep developing.

Deep and fundamental changes in society transformed the context for dance artists and led to further reinventions of CCD. During the 1980s, CCD dancers started to confront challenges that led both artists and the public to doubt its value and direction, especially its relationship to Western dance forms such as ballet and, later, modern dance. New choreography continued to raise new debates—did an artist go too far in a new piece and lose the accepted aesthetic character of CCD? Eventually, the debates among critics centered on the issue of whether a work was traditional or contemporary. Ultimately, this judging and questioning of traditional or contemporary elements in a dance has now become a standard for CCD's development among dance artists and critics. I do not think this is a bad thing, to continue to debate and discuss CCD developments, because it enlivens and enriches critical and creative dance studies in China. The argument over traditional or contemporary is like a ruler or a mirror that can provide artists with corrections at the right moment. Debate is of course good for artistic development. In China we have a saying: the fire burns higher when everybody adds wood to it. As a result, thanks to these transformations and debates, CCD remains a vital and creative force in China's concert dance scene, with dance artists and their publics involved in its future experiments and provocations.

ADDITIONAL RESOURCES

Full resolution versions of Figure 12.1 at https://doi.org/10.3998/mpub.11521701.cmp.23 and Figure 12.2 at https://doi.org/10.3998/mpub.11521701.cmp.24

Link 12.1: Chen Ailian performing "Spring, River, and Flowers on a Moonlit Night," 1959. Available at https://doi.org/10.3998/mpub.11521701.cmp.71

Link 12.2: Excerpt from Chinese classical-style dance drama *Magic Lotus Lantern*, 1959. Available at https://doi.org/10.3998/mpub.11521701.cmp.72

Video Clip 12.1: Wang Yabin performing "Fan as a Brush" (*Shanwu danqing*). Accessible at https://doi.org/10.3998/mpub.11521701.cmp.73

Video Clip 12.2: Students from the Beijing Dance Academy performing *Ta Ge*. Fulcrum_Vid12_02_Jiang. Accessible at https://doi.org/10.3998/mpub.11521701.cmp.74

Link 12.3: Official website of the Neo-Classic Dance Company of Taiwan. Accessible at https://doi.org/10.3998/mpub.11521701.cmp.75

## Notes

1. Chinese Dance (*Zhongguo wu* 中国舞) is an umbrella term that includes multiple dance genres, one of which is Chinese Classical Dance. For histories of this genre in English, see Dong Jiang, *Contemporary Chinese Dance* (Beijing: New Star Press, 2007); Emily Wilcox, *Revolutionary Bodies: Chinese Dance and the Socialist Legacy* (Oakland: University of California Press, 2019).

2. Wang Kefen 王克芬, *Zhongguo wudao fazhanshi* 中国舞蹈发展史 [History of the Development of Chinese Dance] (Shanghai: Shanghai People's Publishing House, 2005).

3. Kefen Wang, *The History of Chinese Dance* (Beijing: Foreign Languages Press, 1985).

4. Chinese Traditional Opera began to emerge during the Song dynasty (960–1279) and Yuan dynasty (1279–1368) and blossomed in the Ming dynasty (1368–1644) and Qing dynasty (1644–1911).

5. About 300 distinct regional forms of Chinese Traditional Opera are practiced in China today.

6. For more on these forms in relation to dance, see Bossler, Yeh, and Ma, this volume.

7. For more on the study of Western dance by Yu Rongling and Wu Xiaobang, see Nan Ma, "Dancing into Modernity: Kinesthesia, Narrative, and Revolutions in Modern China, 1900–1978" (PhD dissertation, University of Wisconsin–Madison, 2015). For more on Dai Ailian, see Wilcox, *Revolutionary Bodies,* and Wilcox, this volume.

8. For my recent collection of Chinese-language essays on this subject, see Jiang Dong 江东, *Gudianwu xinlun* 古典舞新论 [A new theory on Chinese classical dance] (Shanghai: Shanghai Music Publishing House, 2014).

9. During the 1950s, Soviet experts came to China in nearly all fields, as part of the Sino-Soviet political alliance of the time.

10. The ballet ensemble, which was established last, was attached to the Beijing Dance School until the end of 1963.

11. A fifth national ensemble, the Oriental Song and Dance Ensemble (*Dongfang gewutuan* 东方歌舞团), which specialized in music and dance of Asia, Africa, and Latin America, was established in 1962.

12. See, for example, Tang Mancheng 唐满城, *Tang Mancheng wudao wenji* 唐满城舞蹈文集 [A collection of Tang Mancheng's essays on dance] (Beijing: China Drama Publishing House, 1993); Sun Ying 孙颖, *Zhongguo gudianwu pingshuoji* 中国古典舞评说集 [Collected works on Chinese classical dance] (Beijing: China Wenlian Publishing House, 2006).

13. To see a 1963 video of Chen Ailian performing "Spring, River, and Flowers on a Moonlit Night," visit https://doi.org/10.1525/luminos.58.10

14. For a detailed history of the Chinese Classical Dance training system at the Beijing Dance Academy, see Li Zhengyi 李正一, Gao Dakun 郜大昆, and Zhu Qingyuan 朱清渊, *Zhongguo gudianwu jiaoxue tixi chuangjian fazhanshi* 中国古典舞教学体系创建发展史 [History of the creation of the Chinese classical dance educational system] (Shanghai: Shanghai Music Publishing House, 2004).

15. Jiang Dong, *Gudianwu xinlun.*

16. The Beijing Dance Academy has undergone another reorganization since 2015. According to Ms. Wang Wei 王伟 (b. 1960), vice president of Beijing Dance Academy at the time of writing, CCD is still a main Chinese dance expression at the Beijing Dance Academy and nationwide. Wang recently led a workshop for Body Rhyme, which enhanced and encouraged people's faith in the future of CCD.

17. For more on Sun's life and the founding of the Han-Tang style, see Emily E. Wil-

cox, "Han-Tang Zhongguo Gudianwu and the Problem of Chineseness in Contemporary Chinese Dance: Sixty Years of Controversy," *Asian Theater Journal* 29, no. 1 (2012): 206–32.

18. To see a 1980 video of an excerpt from *Flowers and Rain on the Silk Road*, visit https://doi.org/10.1525/luminos.58.16

19. Gao Jinrong 高金荣, *Dunhuangwu jiaocheng* 敦煌舞教程 [A textbook of Dunhuang dance style] (Shanghai: Shanghai Music Publishing House, 2002).

# CHAPTER 13

# Negotiating Chinese Identity through a Double-Minority Voice and the Female Dancing Body:

## Yang Liping's *Spirit of the Peacock* and Beyond

*Ting-Ting Chang* 張婷婷

Ten years after the end of the Cultural Revolution (1966–76), Yang Liping 楊麗萍 (b. 1958), an ethnic minority dancer from southwest China, explored and transformed traditional Dai 傣 dance elements to create her unique version of the peacock dance. Yang's dance, *Spirit of the Peacock* (*Que zhi ling* 雀之靈), won the Second China National Dance Competition in 1986 and marked a new era in the decades-long transformation of this ethnic Dai dance from an esoteric regional folk form to a globally circulating mass-mediated stage choreography.

In April 1992, Yang Liping became the first dance artist from mainland China to visit Taiwan since 1949. Yang's visit was significant because it happened just before the November 1992 Consensus, which opened the door to subsequent interaction between China and Taiwan.[1] After nearly forty years of complete separation between China and Taiwan, both governments finally started to communicate through unofficial cultural exchange programs. With the media reporting on all her activities, Yang and her peacock dance quickly became well known in all Chinese-speaking communities. As a dance major in the National Taiwan Academy of Arts, I had a fortunate opportunity to take a master class with Yang, and I was inspired by the creativity, perseverance, devoted attitude, and elegant presentation she expressed through her teaching and performance. Her passion for Chinese ethnic minority dance motivated me to begin my own research. After graduating, in 1994, I joined the Taipei Folk Dance Theatre and had an opportunity to perform a Peacock Dance choreographed by Taiwanese choreographer Yang Sue-hwa 楊淑華 on tour throughout Taiwan and South Korea. With Yang Liping's influence, Dai peacock dances became more and more popular in Taiwan, and Tsai Li-hwa

Fig 13.1. Ting-Ting Chang (the author) performing Yang Liping's *Spirit of the Peacock* in Close Up Dance at the Performing Arts Department, Washington University in St. Louis, in 2008. Photo by David Marchant courtesy of the photographer.

蔡麗華, the artistic director of Taipei Folk Dance Theatre at the time, also choreographed an evening-length production *The Peacock Princess* in 1996.

After moving to the United States in 1997, I began to work closely with various Chinese Dance groups in Southern California. With the increasing population of Chinese immigrants in the area, the practice of Chinese Dance also began to grow. Chinese Dance has a significant part in community events and holiday celebrations, such as Chinese New Year and the Mid-Autumn Festival. I have observed that many first-generation parents send their children to private dance studios in their local areas, encouraging them to learn Chinese cultural traditions, identity, and self-discipline through Chinese Dance practice. I suspect that the practice also helps connect the parents to their cultural heritage, and that this nostalgia is a mixed feeling that first-generation Chinese immigrant parents have for their homeland and childhood memories.[2] While Yang and her "Spirit of the Peacock" have been promoted nationwide through Chinese television programs, the Dai peacock dance has also become one of the most popular performances throughout Chinese-speaking communities around the world. In 2005, while touring internationally, Yang was hailed as the "Peacock Princess of China" by the *New York Times*.[3]

Tracing the changes from her 1986 solo *Spirit of the Peacock* to her large-scale 2004 production *Dynamic Yunnan* (*Yunnan yingxiang* 雲南 映象) and her 2012 dance drama *The Peacock* (*Kongque* 孔雀), I discuss how Yang incorporates the cultural aesthetics of *minzu* 民族 (ethnicity) in her productions, ultimately using her minority voice and female body to support the idea of a unified Chinese national identity. I examine how the peacock dance has been propagated in and beyond China in different times and spaces, and performed by different dancers, from its first appearances in modern stage choreography during the 1950s through Yang's latest twenty-first-century adaptations. I also examine how, through Yang's artistic entrepreneurship, the Dai peacock dance has become an integral component of China's national image and how Yang, as a person of Bai 白 ethnicity who performs dances of Dai and other ethnic groups, uses her double-minority voice and female dancing body to reflect contemporary ideas regarding race, gender, nationalism, and globalization. Finally, I argue that ethnic minority dances such as Yang's make China more visible to the world and that the peacock dance specifically serves to reinforce an imagined transnational Chinese community in an era of globalization. At the same time, as a regional cultural export that remains tied to Yunnanese identity, the dancing body in the context of Dai peacock dance also brings financial benefit back to Yunnan and its ethnic minority communities through the tourism economy.

PEACOCK DANCE:
SHIFTING EMBODIMENTS IN THE EARLY MAO ERA

Modern Chinese history is a complicated web of interaction between domestic conflicts and international forces. In the past 100 years, China has undergone major ideological shifts in terms of its concept of nation, methods of government, and the position of individuals in society. These changes were greatly influenced by outside forces. Additionally, the demographics of China, which include the majority Han 漢 and fifty-five minority groups, referred to as nationalities or *minzu*, have challenged the idea of a unified nation. Since Mao Zedong's 1942 *Talks at the Yan'an Forum on Literature and Art*, the Chinese Communist Party and the government of the People's Republic of China (PRC, est. 1949) have endorsed the use of folk-inspired cultural productions, including minority dance, to construct and promote a unified multi-ethnic vision of Chinese national identity.[4] The ethnic Dai peacock dance has undergone several transformations over time, many of which occurred in the context of this Mao-era framing of ethnic minority culture as national culture.[5]

Originally, the Dai peacock dance had a long history of being performed by male dancers and was rooted in a religious context as part of Buddhist ceremonies.[6] In the traditional version, male dancers wore masks and heavy costumes and carried wings.[7] These heavy costumes and props are known as *jiazi* 架子. In his 1953 dance, a Yunnan-based male Dai dance master named Mao Xiang 毛相 (1918–1986) carried out the first transformation of the dance by taking off the mask and *jiazi* costume to perform *The Peacock Duet* (*Shuangren kongquewu* 雙人孔雀舞). This is the first recorded staged version of a peacock duet in modern times. Photographs of Mao and his partner Bai Wenfen 白文芬, a woman of Hui 回 ethnicity from Yunnan, show elegant body lines and emotional facial expressions. Based on Mao's version, a Beijing-based male choreographer of Han ethnicity, Jin Ming 金明 (1927–2005), then choreographed a group female version, titled *Peacock Dance* (*Kongque wu* 孔雀舞).[8] This work won a gold medal representing China in the 1957 World Festival of Youth and Students in Moscow. Subsequently, Jin's version became a model for the peacock dance as a group dance primarily performed by women. Yang Liping's later versions of the peacock dance from the 1980s into the 2000s introduced yet further changes: she performed the dance solo in a Western-style white gown and used increasingly balletic movement aesthetics. In all of these forms, the Dai peacock dance represented both the Dai ethnic group and the Chinese nation.

The transformation of the peacock dance in China from the 1950s onward was part of a larger project of building national culture. Like those in many other Third World nations during the mid-twentieth century, Chinese artists and intellectuals felt the need to find or recreate the past to establish a national identity.[9] Although China was never fully colonized, the new Chinese

Figs. 13.2. Yang Liping performing a peacock dance solo in her 2012 dance drama *The Peacock*. Photo courtesy Yunnan Yang Liping Arts & Culture Co., Ltd.

Figs 13.3. Yang Liping in duet from *The Peacock*, 2012.

government was eager to build a national culture that could unite the country and speak to broader anticolonial movements. The term *minzu,* meaning ethnicity or nation, was a central concept in China's nation-building process. From the early 1950s, the Chinese socialist state promoted the idea that the territory making up China is home to various ethnicities, not only the majority Han, and that these groups together constituted a broader Chinese nation—a multiethnic *minzu* that contained many different *minzu* groups.[10] Dance became one medium through which the new PRC government created and reinforced this ideology of *minzu.*[11]

As the peacock dance shifted from Mao Xiang to Jin Ming to Yang Liping, dancing bodies reflected not only issues of ethnicity within the nation from Yunnan to Beijing and beyond, but also those of gender. The Cultural Revolution, launched in 1966, marked a turning point in Chinese performance culture. Traditional expressions of femininity that had been promoted in the 1950s and early 1960s were widely rejected; giving up traditions and adopting Western dance forms was considered a powerful and efficient way to educate people and promote the ideology of modernization. Using ballet, a European art form, to tell Chinese stories became the dominant model of dance creation, and the practice of traditional arts was suspended and even suppressed during this period. The new genre of Chinese revolutionary ballet, exemplified by productions such as the 1964 work *The Red Detachment of Women* (*Hongse niangzi jun* 紅色娘子軍), were propagated widely for mass consumption.[12] State policies called for the "equalization" of gender through a new masculine image for both men and women, and through mass distribution of these performance works ensured the larger goal of maintaining state control over the arts and ideology and advancing the Communist Party's hegemonic power. In works such as the revolutionary ballet *Red Detachment of Women*, the female dancing body conveyed an image of masculinity and power, with active energy, a strong personality, and well-defined characters and roles. Although the stories were mainly based on Han interpretation and aesthetics, the female dancing bodies in these productions delivered the Chinese communist ideology in a way that stressed women's independence, perseverance, and strength. Thus, contrary to earlier, more delicate female dancing bodies created in response to the male gaze, this new female dancing body reshaped gender ideology, offering a new model for later dance works.

In the post–Cultural Revolution period, the Chinese state expanded its international political presence through economic reforms that opened China to global markets. The Reform and Opening Up (*Gaige kaifang* 改革開放) policy, launched in 1978, brought new shifts in Chinese culture. Many

Chinese people hailed the reemergence of gender difference in dress, hairstyle, and self-presentation as one of the newfound freedoms of personal expression in this era.[13] At the same time, many people were longing for traditional arts, and a traditional sense of femininity was once again appreciated. The late 1970s and early 1980s thus became a key transitional period for the restoration of traditions and ethnic minority identities lost in the Cultural Revolution, as well as a period for rethinking the construction of gender. The Chinese female pursuit of beauty and debates about changing gender norms were also illustrated through the dancing body during this time.

YANG LIPING: A NEW PEACOCK DANCE

After Yang Liping won the Second China National Dance Competition in 1986, she performed on national television in the 1988 Chinese Spring Festival Gala (*Chunjie lianhuan wanhui* 春節聯歡晚會), the most popular television program in Chinese history.[14] Apart from being broadcast in China, the Gala has been popular in Chinese-speaking communities worldwide, distributed through media networks from satellite television, to DVDs, and, eventually, the Internet. The Gala itself helped build a virtual community of the Chinese nation-state, and to date Yang has made the most appearances in the Gala of any Chinese dance artist. In 1992, Yang performed *Timely Snow* (*Ruixue* 瑞雪); in 1993 she performed *Two Trees* (*Liang ke shu* 兩棵樹)[15]; in 1998 she performed *Plum* (*Mei* 梅 1998); in 2006 she appeared in *Three friends of Winter—Pine, Bamboo, Plum* (*Suihan sanyou—song zhu mei* 歲寒三友—松竹梅).[16] Despite being in her fifties, Yang has continued to appear in the Gala in subsequent years.

Yang's dances transformed the peacock image into an extremely feminine form with a long, extended body line, while she also incorporated some masculine characteristics. Her dancing body can be read as a hybrid that carries both female- and male-gendered elements. The audience does not see a male peacock when she performs, but rather an elegant, fragile, and curvy female beauty. However, as in earlier versions of the dance, she maintains the tail feathers that biologically symbolize the male peacock. In her choreography, Yang's dancing body bridges human and animal, delicate and compelling.

Through her promotion on television, Yang's dance career developed rapidly. Chinese people saw Yang not only as a great dancer, but as a cultural icon and a role model. Yang's private life, opinions, diet, and style all became topics of public interest, and "Spirit of the Peacock" came to stand for the nation because of the new way it depicted gender and femininity through Yang's aesthetic innovations.

Yang's dance movements combined naturalistic imitations of bird-like actions with a focus on isolated uses of the torso and limbs that especially highlighted muscular dexterity. In Yang's hand gestures, her fingers expand out with long decorative nails, mimicking a clear outline of the bird's head. The way she moves her torso corresponds to the energy that flows inside her body, and when her movements reach out, it is as if that energy is flowing out through her limbs. Yang's peacock dance is different from the traditional Dai dance, because while she keeps many traditional Dai movement elements, she no longer emphasizes the down-and-up rhythm within her body. Unlike traditional Dai music, which has a consistent rhythm, the music in the second section of Yang's version is soft and mellow, and she dances to the melody rather than to a consistent beat. This is a revelation and a departure from Dai dance, and it gives her freedom to explore new movement possibilities. At the beginning, her arm movements appear segmented with visible curves or angles, but as she picks up speed, her arm movements become so smooth that it looks as if her arms are boneless.[17]

Yang's peacock dance also incorporates clear ballet aesthetics. The ballet influence in Yang's dance can be traced back to the early period of her childhood. Growing up during the Cultural Revolution, at around the age of seven or eight, Yang saw her first ballet performance, the revolutionary ballet *White-Haired Girl* 白毛女, in Dali, Yunnan. In 1971, she started her professional dancing career by joining the Xishuangbanna Daizu Autonomous Region Cultural Work Troupe (西雙版納傣族自治區文工團), and in 1978 she danced the principle role in a new Dai dance drama, *Zhao Shutun and Nanmunuona* (*Zhao Shudun yu Nanmu Nuona* 召樹屯與婻木婼娜), also known as *The Peacock Princess* (*Kongque gongzhu* 孔雀公主).[18] Yang's performance as the peacock princess won the Outstanding Performance Award in Yunnan province and led to her joining the China National Ethnic Song and Dance Ensemble (Central Nationalities Song and Dance Ensemble, *Zhongyang minzu gewutuan* 中央民族歌舞團) in Beijing in 1980. As the largest and most prestigious minority performance ensemble in the nation, the troupe had adopted Russian ballet techniques as its fundamental training since its establishment in 1952. The Chinese dancing body had also changed over time, training the Chinese audience to appreciate a Western dance aesthetic, especially ballet. After short-term intensive ballet training with the troupe, Yang refused to take further ballet courses, but the ballet influence remained with her. Her choreography of *Spirit of the Peacock*, with or without conscious awareness, is arguably a hybrid product of Russian ballet aesthetics and Western modern dance choreographic concepts, along with her personal interpretation of traditional Dai dance movements. When Yang choreographed it in 1986, she did not expect a Western audience. However, throughout the years she has continued to develop different versions of *Spirit of the Peacock,* which some might argue reveal that she has slowly adopted some methods of self-Orientalization. By learning, adopting, and combining Chinese ethnic dance forms with Western dance elements, her peacock dance is now a complex, hybrid form—the result of a ballet aesthetic merged into ethnic minority dances.

Although Yang has danced to three different musical selections in her versions of *Spirit of the Peacock,* the basic structures of these versions are relatively constant.[19] Although Yang used a tradition-inspired Dai musical composition in her first version, Yang adopted the song "Pastorale" by European group Secret Garden in her second version of *Spirit of the Peacock* in the 1990s.[20] In this version, her dancing body drew comparisons to the classic Western ballet *The Dying Swan.* In the middle of the dance, Yang faces upstage, waving her arms with her legs in relevé, quickly traveling from stage left to stage right, resembling the internationally renowned Russian ballerina Anna Pavlova (1881–1931) bourreéing en pointe in *The Dying Swan.*[21] Yang's dancing body highlights extreme femininity through delicate movements, similar to the swan princess in the canonical ballet *Swan Lake.* Her dancing body presents how she, as a female choreographer, expresses her feelings through an exploration of the birds' movements. In contrast to the traditional Dai costume of a tight skirt with colors and patterns, Yang wears a wide white skirt with many layers, resembling the ballet tutu or even a Western wedding dress. By incorporating the Dai ethnic minority dance movements with an aesthetic of Western ballet, Yang's version of the Dai ethnic dance can reach out to international audiences, and the Chinese government understandably reaps the benefit. It connects with the state's continued promotion of its ideology of a unified nation.

Although women's independence had already been promoted by the Chinese government, as advocated in the Chinese model ballet productions of the 1960s and early 1970s, Yang's *Spirit of the Peacock* delivers a different interpretation of Chinese women's liberation and independence. In the model ballets, Chinese women's independence was based on fighting for equality between men and women. The female characters in those model ballet productions carried the responsibilities for the community, and they had to shoulder such great causes as national and even world revolution. The movement vocabularies of female dancers in revolutionary ballets were strong and firm, much like those of their male counterparts. Their body lines were regimented, and their arms and legs moved from point to point, often in large groups in unison, and the path was always direct.[22]

In contrast, "Spirit of the Peacock "expressed an individualistic aesthetic. Yang, as a Chinese woman and outspoken feminist, no longer needed to "fight" for equality, but enjoyed the freedom to express herself as an individual, in a new era in which both individualism and traditional gender aesthetics were resurgent in China.[23] Her movements and gestures were clear and firm, but she expressed a softer quality with her enhanced femininity. She constantly moved with a flowing energy, and the aesthetic of Western ballet in her hybrid dancing body projected a balance between East and West. Her body line was linear, but the path of her movements was never straight. Yang was exposed to US modern dance in Beijing during the early 1980s, and influenced by Martha Graham's technique and Western modern dance choreographic concepts. Her dancing body, in the guise of a feminine peacock, portrayed an independent woman with strong character and personality. Yang's performances, in which she withholds facial expressions and carries aggressive energy in her body movements, emulate Graham's performances.[24]

Yang's dancing body thus established the figure of a strong woman under an extremely feminine peacock image. Graham's influence can also be found in Yang's other works, such as *Moonbeam* (*Yueguang* 月光)[25] and *Daughter Kingdom* (*Nuer Guo* 女兒國). Although these presented different story themes and ethnic movement styles, Yang's dances consistently build strong female characters and images. All of these factors made her dancing body even more powerful, and the underlying meaning of her extreme femininity delivered to the public the clear image of a strong woman. Yang's personal life further contributed to the meaning of her dances, as she appeared in the media as an independent entrepreneur and strong career woman.

With a hybrid dancing body combining ballet aesthetics and modern dance choreographic concepts along with Chinese ethnic minority dance elements, Yang's performance style revived a form of femininity that had been suppressed during the Cultural Revolution. At the same time, her dancing body projected a femininity that was also distinct from Jin's female peacocks of the pre–Cultural Revolution nation-building era. Yang embodied at once the male peacock, a Western ballet aesthetic, elements of self-Orientalization, extreme femininity, and paratheatrical performance, representing a new embodiment of Chinese culture and success in a period of economic reform. As it had with Jin's *Peacock Dance*, the Chinese government saw the power of Yang's new image of an ethnic minority female dancing body, which was reflected in her tremendous popularity, especially in response to her performances in the CCTV (China Central Television, *Zhongyang Dianshitai* 中央電視台) New Year's Gala. Yang's peacock dance thus replaced the old image of the Dai peacock dance and became a new icon for both the Dai ethnic group and the Chinese nation. Although her ethnic, female dancing body has been created and presented under a unified national ideology, it now expresses the personal imagination of Yang herself as a female ethnic minority choreographer, dancer, cultural visionary, and public icon.

## LOCAL, NATIONAL, INTERNATIONAL, AND BACK TO LOCAL: *DYNAMIC YUNNAN* AND *THE PEACOCK*

In 2004, Yang created a spectacle at the Kunming Theatre, featuring the peacock dance as the grand finale of a new production, *Dynamic Yunnan.*[26] Having grown up in Xishuangbanna before becoming an internationally recognized dance artist, Yang decided to create a work focused on her home province: Yunnan. In preparation, Yang spent several years recruiting and training a troupe of more than sixty performers from Yunnan's ethnic minority regions.[27] Most of the performers were peasants and local villagers, and many had been trained in musician Tian Feng's 田丰 (1933–2001) Yunnan Institute for Preservation of Minority Cultures.[28]

Drawing on her decades of professional experience, Yang put various cultural elements together in a modern dance framework to present the cultures of different ethnic minority groups. In *Dynamic Yunnan,* Yang stages dances associated with the ethnic groups Hani 哈尼, Jingbo 景頗, Wa 瓦, Yi 彝, and Tibetan 藏. In this way, she uses her matriarchal position as a strong character and personality to speak for the entire group of ethnic minorities in Yunnan, China's most diverse province. The production ends with a group of women performing *Spirit of the Peacock* with Yang as the lead dancer. Unlike in Yang's solo, there are more than twenty dancers on the stage, making the image even more powerful. At the same time, the ensemble dancers still serve as a background to better highlight Yang, the star.

The music Yang used for this third version of *Spirit of the Peacock* was composed by Mongolian musician San Bao 三寶 (b. 1968), who used Dai musical instruments to enhance the ethnic flavor. The female silhouettes combined East and West, Dai ethnic dance and ballet, femininity, strength, and sexuality, and became a powerful weapon to deliver the feminist ideology of independence and liberation central to Yang's artistic oeuvre. Over the past thirty years, Yang's many revisions of "Spirit of the Peacock" have focused increasingly on the profile of the female figure and the movements of her torso.

After *Dynamic Yunnan* won Best Production, Best Performance, and Best Choreography in the Lotus Cup 荷花盃, one of China's largest ethnic dance competitions, Yang received sponsorship from the Yunnan government. With this continued success, *Dynamic Yunnan* has been performed more than 4,000 times, and Yang has enjoyed a successful world tour, including a tour in the United States during the 2005–06 seasons.

At the age of fifty-four, Yang was invited to perform *Peacock Love* (*Que zhi lian* 雀之戀), a new duet, in the 2012 Chinese Spring Festival Gala. *Peacock Love* was part of Yang's dance drama *The Peacock*,[29] cochoreographed with Gao Chengming 高成明 (b. 1956) and Wang Di 王迪 (b. 1978), both male dancers with strong backgrounds in modern dance. In this collaboration, Yang showed her willingness to experiment with possibilities outside of the ethnic minority dance genre. At this time, Yang defined modern dance as a "dance of feelings, a pursuit of liberation of the body and the mind, and a pursuit of individuality without traces and boundaries; it is consistent with my pursuit of the new Eastern aesthetics."[30] In this production, Yang transformed her minority dances into a form more consistent with international modern and contemporary dance, and *The Peacock* toured all over China, Hong Kong, and Taiwan during the 2012–15 seasons. Rather than focusing on issues of authority, authenticity, and representation of ethnic minority dance, Yang dedicated her efforts toward creating and developing a more contemporary reimagining of her earlier image.

During a 2007 interview, Deng Hui 鄧暉, former deputy secretary of the Yunnan Dance Artists Association, reported that the continued promotion of Yang's works attracted attention to the local cultures in Yunnan and also brought economic benefits to the region.[31] The growing tourism industry created more job opportunities for the local community, and Yang's production created even more jobs and performance opportunities for local artists. Additionally, when minority communities in Yunnan became more visible to the nation and even to the rest of the world, their political voice was boosted at the central government level. For example, artists such as Yang were selected to serve as representatives for Yunnan in the China National Congress and other major governmental decision-making groups.

The transfer of the peacock dance from local to international communities and then back to the Yunnan local community displays a Chinese gov-

ernment tactic toward the Western world of using ethnic minorities to promote its nationalist ideology. Ethnic minority dance plays a significant role in
consolidating China's national identity, and it is also consumable by a global
audience. Since 2000, several ethnic minority productions have brought a
large number of tourists to local communities. Indoor productions such as
*Dynamic Yunnan* transfer ethnic cultural elements to the proscenium stage,
whereas outdoor productions such as *Impression Lijiang* (*Yinxiang Lijing* 印
象麗江), performed over 5,000 times since its premiere in 2006, highlight the
natural environment and landscape in addition to minority culture. However,
because these productions were made for tourism, and despite the outdoor
productions' resemblance to traditional ways of dancing, their context and
purpose have changed from their original meanings. From a locally distinctive religious ritual, the peacock dance has been made into a spectacle to
be consumed by domestic and global audiences. In return, however, it has
initiated change and introduced new economic opportunities for local communities.

CONCLUSION

Yang Liping, as a female ethnic minority choreographer, has expressed her
identity both domestically and internationally, and her peacock dance is not
only a self-representation through a traditional dance form, but a representation of broader ethnic minority groups, women, and the image of the nation.
Since China's economic reforms began in 1978, the lifestyles of the Chinese
people have been constantly in flux. The Chinese nation-state and its population have undergone a dynamic modernization process to deal with rapid
social, cultural, and political changes. Along with international recognition
of its growing economic power, the Chinese nation-state has attempted to
create a national identity partially defined by Chinese ethnic dance. Yang's
female dancing body has played a role in shaping China's national identity
in different ways, positioning women artists, the female body, and ethnic
minority peoples in a unique place of agency. In this way, Yang's peacock
dance has become a new icon for China domestically and internationally.

The development of arts in China has often been dominated by the
nation's political ideologies. However, dancers such as Yang Liping have not
only retained and transformed specific choreographic elements in response
to political forces, they have responded to social, economic, and cultural
issues through their own creative interventions. From "Spirit of the Peacock"

to *Dynamic Yunnan* to *The Peacock* and her latest 2016 production *Peacock of Winter* (*Kongque zhi dong* 孔雀之冬),[32] Yang has established her unique vision of what she calls "the new Eastern aesthetic," and she continues to tour during the 2018–19 season in China. Her female dancing body continues to negotiate its multiple identities between past and present, local and regional, and national and global.

## ADDITIONAL RESOURCES

Full resolution versions of Figure 13.1 at https://doi.org/10.3998/mpub.11521701.cmp.25, Figure 13.2 at https://doi.org/10.3998/mpub.11521701.cmp.26, and Figure 13.3 at https://doi.org/10.3998/mpub.11521701.cmp.27

Link 13.1: Yang Liping performing "Spirit of the Peacock," 2007. Available at https://doi.org/10.3998/mpub.11521701.cmp.76

Link 13.2: Full video of Yang Liping's *Dynamic Yunnan* (10-year anniversary version). Available at https://doi.org/10.3998/mpub.11521701.cmp.77

Link 13.3: Promotional video and interviews about *Dynamic Yunnan*. Available at https://doi.org/10.3998/mpub.11521701.cmp.78

## *Notes*

1. "1992 Consensus" (*Jiuer gongshi* 九二共識) is a term used to describe an implicit and informal agreement between the governments of mainland China (People's Republic of China) and Taiwan (Republic of China) that both sides belong to "one China." It resulted from a meeting in Hong Kong between the mainland-based Association for Relations Across the Taiwan Strait and the Taiwan-based Straits Exchange Foundation on November, 1992.

2. Ting-Ting Chang, "Choreographing the Peacock: Gender, Ethnicity, and National Identity in Chinese Ethnic Dance" (PhD dissertation, University of California Riverside, 2008), 163–64.

3. David Barboza, "The Peacock Princess of China," *New York Times*, March 5, 2005, accessed October 16, 2018, https://www.nytimes.com/2005/03/05/arts/dance/the-peacock-princess-of-china.html

4. Mao Zedong 毛澤東, "Zai Yan'an wenyi zuotanhui shang de jianghua" 在延安文藝座談會上的講話, in Mao Tsetung, *Selected Readings from the Works of Mao Tsetung* (Beijing: Foreign Language Press, 1971).

5. For longer studies of the development of the Dai peacock dance in China in the context of Chinese dance history, see Ting-Ting Chang, "Choreographing the Peacock"; Emily Wilcox, *Revolutionary Bodies: Chinese Dance and the Socialist Legacy* (Oakland: University of California Press, 2019).

6. Yunqin Fang, "Dai Dance," in *Flying Dragon and Dancing Phoenix: An Introduction to Selected Chinese Minority Folk Dances*, ed. Weiye Chen, Lanwei Ji, and Wei Ma (Beijing: New World Press, 1987), 8–21; Haicheng Ling, "Buddhist Dance," in *Buddhism in China*, trans. Shaoqing Jin (Beijing: Chinese Intercontinental Press, 2004), 249–50.

7. *Kongquewu* 孔雀舞 [*Peacock Dance*], Dehong Television Station 德宏電視臺, Dehong, 1996 and 2000.

8. Jin Ming 金明, chor., *Kongquewu* 孔雀舞 [*Peacock Dance*] (Beijing: Central Song and Dance Ensemble of China 中央歌舞團, n.d.), VCD.

9. Frantz Fanon, "National Culture," in *The Post-Colonial Studies Reader*, ed. Bill Ashcroft, Gareth Griffiths, and Helen Tiffin (London: Routledge, 1995, 1997, 1999, 2003), 153–57.

10. Colin Mackerras, *China's Minority Cultures: Identities and Integration Since 1912* (Australia and New York: Longman Australia Pty Ltd. and St. Martin's Press, 1995). Stevan Harrell, *Ways of Being Ethnic in Southwest China* (Seattle: University of Washington Press, 2001); Thomas S. Mullaney, *Coming to Terms with the Nation: Ethnic Classification in Modern China* (Berkeley: University of California Press, 2011).

11. Emily Wilcox, "Beyond Internal Orientalism: Dance and Nationality Discourse in the Early People's Republic of China, 1949–1954," *Journal of Asian Studies* 75, no. 2 (May 2016): 363–86.

12. *Hongse niangzi jun* 紅色娘子軍 [Red Detachment of Women], 1971 film accessed via YouTube.

13. Susan Brownell and Jeffrey N. Wasserstrom, *Chinese Femininities/ Chinese Masculinities* (Berkeley: University of California Press, 2002), 331.

14. A 2007 research commissioned by China Television Research (CTR) estimated that 90 percent of Chinese families watched the Gala on television, and the audience is estimated to be around 700 million people.

15. Yang Liping 楊麗萍, *Liang ke shu* 兩棵樹 [*Two Trees*], CCTV Chinese Spring Festival Gala (Beijing: China Central Television 中央電視台, 1993).

16. Yang, Liping 楊麗萍, *Yang Liping Wudao Jingxuan* 楊麗萍舞蹈精選 [*Yang Liping's Dance Collection*], 2004, DVD.

17. For a 2007 video of Yang Liping performing *Spirit of the Peacock*, visit https://doi.org/10.1525/luminos.58.14

18. Yang Liping 楊麗萍, "Yang Liping yueliang gong ji" 楊麗萍月亮宮記 [Yang Liping's Moon Palace], *Lu Yu Youyue* 魯豫有約 [*Luyu has a day*], Southeast Television 東南衛視, March 29, 2017.

19. Yang Liping 楊麗萍, *Que zhi ling* 雀之靈 [*Spirit of the Peacock*], CCTV Chinese Spring Festival Gala (Beijing: China Central Television 中央電視台, 2004), VCD.

20. The artists of Secret Garden are Fionnula Sherry, an Irish violinist, and Rolf

Loveland, a Norwegian pianist. The music style is a combination of contemporary instrumental, new age/meditative, jazz, vocal, and classical.

21. *The Dying Swan* is a solo dance choreographed by Russian choreographer Mikhail Fokine (1880–1942) in 1905.

22. On representations of gender in the revolutionary ballets, see Xiaomei Chen, *Acting the Right Part: Political Theater and Popular Drama in Contemporary China* (Honolulu: University of Hawai'i Press, 2002); Rosemary A. Roberts, *Maoist Model Theatre: The Semiotics of Gender and Sexuality in the Chinese Cultural Revolution (1966–1976)* (Leiden: Brill, 2010).

23. On Mao-era feminism and its reversal in the 1980s and 1990s, see Wang Zheng, *Finding Women in the State: A Socialist Feminist Revolution in the People's Republic of China, 1959–1964* (Oakland: University of California Press, 2017).

24. Mark Franko, *Dancing Modernism/Performing Politics* (Bloomington: Indiana University Press, 2000), 46–47.

25. Yang Liping 楊麗萍, *Yueguang* 月光 [*Moonbeam*], *CCTV Moon Festival Gala* (Beijing: China Central Television 中央電視台), September 17, 2005.

26. *Yunnan Yingxiang* 雲南映象 [*Dynamic Yunnan*], Kunming Theatre, September 4, 2007.

27. Yamei Wang, "Yang Liping Performs Dance Drama 'Peacock' in Tianjin," ed. Yunting Liu, *Xinhua*, October 19, 2012.

28. According to a personal interview with dance master Ma Wenjing 馬文靜 (b. 1943), Ma had a chance in 1987 to conduct fieldwork in Yunnan with Tian Feng, a composer from the China Central Philharmonic 中央民族樂團, and Zhou Peiwu 周培武 (1936- ), a specialist in Chinese ethnic dance. The project was sponsored by Kunming Worker's Cultural Palace (*Kunming gongren wenhuagong* 昆明工人文化宮), and they studied various ethnic groups in the villages for two months (Ma, 2008). Ma Wenjing 馬文靜, personal interview by Ting-Ting Chang (Rowland Heights, May 7, 2008). In 1993, Tian received a donation of 100,000 RMB from a military base in Tibet and established the Yunnan Institute for Preservation of Minority Cultures (*Yunnan minzu wenhua chuanxiguan* 雲南民族文化傳習館) on the original site of the former Southwestern Forestry Institute in Anning County, thirty kilometers west of Kunming. It was China's first private institute to preserve traditional ethnic minority cultures. The teachers were local artists who taught the students their respective ethnic music and dances. Apart from tuition waivers, the students were also given free board. In 2000, seven years after the school was established, it had to be disbanded due to financial difficulties. "Tian Feng and His Institute" 田丰和傳習館, *Chinese Culture Center of San Francisco* 舊金山中華文化中心, last modified July 18, 2007, accessed October 10, 2018, https://www.cccsf.us/tian-feng-and-his-institute. Liu Xiaojin 劉曉津, dir. *Chronicle of the Minorities Institute* 傳習館春秋, 2005, film.

29. *Kongque* 孔雀 [*The Peacock*], National Theater, Taipei, July 12, 2015.

30. Li Yang, "Yang Liping wuchu 'houxiandai' kongxue" 楊麗萍舞出'後現代'孔雀 [Yang Liping Performed a 'Post-modern Peacock'], *Beijing Daily*, January 31, 2012.

31. Deng Hui 鄧輝, personal interview by Ting-Ting Chang, Kunming, September 5, 2007.

32. "Yang Liping Performs Dance Drama 'Peacock of Winter' in Kunming," *Xinhua*, November 17, 2016, accessed October 17, 2018, http://www.chinadaily.com.cn/culture/2016–11/17/content_27409990.htm

**PART 5**

Collective Technologies

# CHAPTER 14

# Cracking History's Codes in Crocodile Time

## The Sweat, Powder, and Glitter of Women Butoh Artists' Collective Choreography

*Katherine Mezur*

It's August 1988, a hot and muggy evening in Tokyo at Studio 200, Ikebukuro Seibu department store. The usher, bent over from the waist, whispers a litany of "I'm sorry, excuse me, so sorry" as he leads us into a small, stifling black-box space, already packed with 200 other bodies. The usher weaves between the tight rows to where we can kneel on tiny flat pillows on the floor. More people arrive, pressing in from all sides. The lights dim to a pale blue shimmer. A woman appears in a white *yukata* (浴衣 cotton kimono). Her white, powdered skin drips rivulets of sweat. Her hands hang limply from her wrists, floating like pale moths over her *yukata*. Her black hair hangs matted with sweat and white paste. Her toes curl and grab the floor as she drifts forward, glowing in her halo of white dust. Rolling her pupils up into her eyelids, her eyes becoming white slits, she grins. This is Ashikawa Yoko 芦川羊子.

It's August 1999. Another woman moves in the packed black box space of the Oberlin Dance Collective Theater in San Francisco, California. She crouches and rocks like a lizard in her green evening gown, which glitters with gold coins like scales in the candlelight. Her hair is pulled into curving side wings, like an Edo period *mage* (髷) wig, with a line drawn down from her part dividing her face down its center, half white, half gold. She resembles a Klimt painting. She is still, reptile-like, with her chin perched on her fists on her bent elbows. Her eyelids pressed into slits, she grins. A clock ticks. Tick-tock. This is Furukawa Anzu 古川あんず in *Crocodile Time*.

In this chapter I present the work of two outstanding Japanese women butoh performers, Ashikawa Yoko and Furukawa Anzu, whose lives and works moved across several post "wars," de- and recolonizations, and trans-national migrations. For Japanese, whose temporality is publicly measured through emperors, their creative work spanned the eras of Shōwa (昭和 1926–1989) through Heisei (平成 1989–2019) to Reiwa (令和 2019–). While

Japanese aggression throughout East Asia began in *Taishō* (大正 1912–26), *Shōwa* was the period of wars, defeat, the US occupation, and *butoh's* founding era. This brief mention of Japan's period temporalities marks the way that located "time" creates social and political relationships, which contextualize these artists and their artworks. Within these time frames, I consider these artists' contributions to the worlds of *butoh* within the confluences of Japan's gender discrimination in the arts, the US occupation and postwar conditions, and issues of single authorship in collective art making processes. Single authorship, which forms the basis for *butoh* genealogies, obstructs the recognition of collective art practices and reinforces the assigning of hierarchical racist and sexist evaluations across the arts. In *Unfinished Business*, Judith Hamera writes about the "hegemony of choreography and the presumptions of originality and range that derive from it, over techniques for executing it."[1] She warns against "choreographer credit," drawing on Sally Gardner's work concerning the separation of choreographer and dancer, where ensemble creation is erased.[2] I analyze Furukawa's and Ashikawa's dance making/performing as dancer-interactive collective processes, not "passive inscription" by a single author. Their diverse collective butoh performances offer examples of a decolonized corporeal politics embedded in located temporalities.

These two major women *butoh* artists, Ashikawa Yoko and Furukawa Anzu, both born in 1950s postwar American occupation Japan, were pivotal figures in the evolution of the Japanese avant-garde performance form *ankoku butoh* (暗黒舞踏), the Dance of Utter Darkness (hereafter, butoh). Beyond the Tokyo butoh enclave, Ashikawa and Furukawa influenced butoh performance from the 1970s to the 2000s in Japan, Europe, and the Americas. These two women's physical, visual, theatrical, and choreographic practices and training methods are integral to butoh's radical corporeal politics. Yet, butoh histories minoritized these women performers by assimilating their contributions into male butoh artists' genealogies and the legacies of butoh's founders, Ohno Kazuo 大野一雄 and Hijikata Tatsumi 土方巽.

Women did not perform in the earliest butoh works and were rarely "named" until Ashikawa Yoko, Hijikata Tatsumi's creative partner from the late 1960s until his death in 1985.[3] Women in butoh were most often described in their choruses, for example: ". . . Hijikata's female dancers, embodied ravaged Tohoku princesses, who mutated back and forward and during the performances, from addled prostitutes, to innocent collectors of herbs, to aggressively sexual doll-girl-trios."[4] Butoh scholars and critics, who left the female performers unnamed, obscured their distinctive contributions and labor by not considering the collective "princesses," girly trios, and other characters as central to butoh's corporeal politics and radicalism. For example, male dancers Murobushi Kō 室伏鴻 and Amagatsu Ushio 天児牛大 of later Sankai Juku 山海塾 are well known for the first butoh performance in Paris in 1978. Yet female dancers Yoshioka Yumiko 吉岡由美子 and Carlotta Ikeda カルロッタ池田 (or Ikeda Sanae 池田早苗), equal members of this European premiere, received little recognition. Further, Yoshioka and Ikeda created *Ariadone*, which became the first international women's butoh group and which continues today, beyond Ikeda's death in 2014.

The crisis here, in this tiny corner of butoh, reflects the skewed alignment of historiographic methods, which assign value and origin to one person, emphasizing the individual artist's power. However, this fails to recognize pivotal women artists whose dancing and choreography are foundational to the practices of collective creating with dancers. Both East Asian and Euro-American performing arts genealogies bear the markings of gender and race discrimination through the nonrecognition of many performers. The few women artists who do gain recognition become the radical exceptions, not the celebrated icons.

## THE MISSING: WOMEN IN EARLY BUTOH

Ashikawa Yoko, Furukawa Anzu, Motofuji Akiko 元藤燁子, Yoshino Hiroko 吉野弘子 (later Tamano Hiroko 玉野弘子), Kobayashi Saga 小林嵯峨, Nimura Momoko 仁村桃子, Yoshioka Yumiko 吉岡由美子, Carlotta Ikeda, Yuki Yuko 雪雄子, and Nakajima Natsu 中嶋夏 are among the notable woman butoh artists who initiated their butoh training in the early stages of its formulation in *Shōwa*, the mid to late 1960s and 1970s. Not only were they part of a postwar generation of women, they were coming of age in one of the most volatile periods of student demonstrations in Japan (and elsewhere). In Japan, these were aimed at the US-Japan Security Treaty, which made Japan the military staging ground for the US wars in Korea and Vietnam. The United States and Japan seemed to be reperforming what Vera Mackie cites as a "common imperialist project in Asia."[5] What role did women play in the political protests and broader social upheavals? How did these butoh women artists negotiate their gendered corporeal politics through their dances within these contexts?

In the following section I briefly address the major political changes that were crucial to these women artists' physical radicalization through their butoh training and performances. I follow this with more detailed examples from their dances, which illustrate the issues of gender, postwar conditions, and remilitarization within their collective choreographic practices. I chose two contrasting women artists—Ashikawa, who remained in Japan, and Furukawa, who lived in Europe and only returned to Japan to perform her works. Their differences reveal the impact of cultural and national gender and race regulations. In Ashikawa's case, her collective dance group *Hakutōbō* (白桃房) stayed largely in Japan, with the exception of a performance in New York City. However, members of her group were from several Euro-Western countries and came regularly to study and perform with her. These performers continue to create and perform and teach. SU-EN, a Swedish woman, is one of Ashikawa's exceptional performers, who extols her experience in *Hakutōbō* and how she herself extends the parameters of butoh with her own collective-based workshops and performances.[6] SU-EN founded her company in 1992 and continues today in Sweden. Ashikawa's own works are no longer performed. A Japanese male artist took over the artistic leadership of Ashikawa's group and training in the 1990s. Her direct influence has disappeared, except in the subsequent dances of her devoted international disciples (such as SU-EN), but her significant contributions to early butoh and beyond continue today.

Furukawa Anzu created many of her works in Europe with dancers from every continent. She lived in Berlin and Helsinki and served as a faculty member at Braunschweig University of Fine Arts in Germany. Furukawa died in 2001, leaving her *Dance Butter TOKIO* group archives and her dancers scattered around the globe. Bringing these two women forward into the light of performance historiography should provoke and inspire a reimagination of *butoh's* genealogy beyond any singular lineage and a recognition of the complexity of their diverse collective art labor.

## MILITARIZED AND OCCUPIED BODIES

To clarify the circumstances that propelled these butoh women, I outline moments in Japan's history of sexual politics and women's rights from the late nineteenth century to today. A key concept for the model behavior and roles for women was *ryōsai kenbo* (良妻賢母 good wife, wise mother), which was formulated in the late nineteenth century and, coupled with the constraint of Confucian relationships, continued through the wartime and postwar conditions for women. The moment of women emerging in *butoh* resonates not only with breaking through this *ryōsai kenbo*, but also with the rise of feminism in the early twentieth century and the "New Women" who formulated social policies that would enable women to fully participate as embodied citizens.[7] Then the 1930s and '40s brought oppressive state regulations of those who could best reproduce for the empire or who could best serve the empire's military.[8]

In *Feminism in Modern Japan*, Vera Mackie argues that "the history of feminist movements demonstrates that embodiment is another concept which is essential to understanding the gendered politics of citizenship." Mackie's emphasis that "we are all 'embodied' citizens," reflects the complications of equal rights and citizenship for all bodies and genders. She argues against the dichotomies of associating body with women and mind with men."[9] The 1947 revised Japanese constitution made the conflicted gendered and embodied citizenship more apparent. While the constitution prohibited sexual discrimination, it gave state control of reproductive bodies through its regulation of abortion, medicines, and artificial conception.[10]

The death of a female student protester, Kanba Michiko 樺美智子, in one of the major 1960 demonstrations radicalized some women to join in the demonstrations. However, many women found that their protest roles were largely supportive.[11] By the peak of protests in 1969 and 1970, when women were performing in butoh, Kanba had become only a symbolic martyr. Subsequently, women gave up on the "malestream left's lack of awareness of gender issues."[12] However, Mackie emphasizes that activist women turned instead to a broader view of discrimination, considering race, ethnicity, and class, pushing the women's movement to directly deal with Japanese discrimination problems concerning Okinawa, Japan-born Koreans (*Zainichi Kankoku-jin* 在日韓国人), and *Burakumin* (部落民), an outcast caste dating from the *Edo* (江戸) period (1603–1868), in Japan's 1970s soaring economic boom time.

The corporeal politics of gender roles during Japan's aggressions before and during the Pacific War, followed by its postwar US occupation and postoccupation protest era, conditioned certain attitudes toward gender roles and the physical expression of those gender roles, which dominated early butoh. Sandra Buckley's collection of interviews and articles by and about Japanese women involved in the postwar feminist movement and Karen Kelsky's later studies of the "turn to the foreign" by Japanese women emphasize how "women's continued subordination to Japanese men and 'traditional' gender roles"[13] continued into the '80s and '90s. Kelsky highlights how the US occupation was a watershed moment, when "as numerous feminist historians and scholars have been at pains to point out, ... for some women at least, Japan's defeat and occupation were experienced as a 'liberation.'"[14] She also cites how Japanese historians have distinguished the different effects that the postwar conditions of food shortages, homelessness, joblessness, exhaustion, and despair had on men compared to women. They call the extreme depressed condition of men *kyodatsu* (虚脱 collapse), but the "sense of *kaihō*" (解放 release) as a characteristically female one.[15] Early butoh women deployed this *kaihō* sensibility into their performance work.

The late 1950s and early 1960s found Japan turning its economy into a booming powerhouse. Part of this had to do with its relationship to the West and the United States military. This imprint of the US on Japanese culture had the effect of creating a tension and subsequently a resistance by many Japanese to the hegemony of US military and popular culture, especially among students, artists, critics and scholars.[16] The United States fueled this resistance with their increased military presence due to their intensification of the US war in Vietnam and their use of Japan as their military staging ground. The US secured the renewal of Anpo (Nichibei Anzen Hoshō Jōyaku 日米安全保障条約 Japan-US Treaty of Mutual Cooperation and Security) through the Japanese Diet vote. This intensified the anti-Anpo mass demonstrations in Tokyo in 1959–60 and prolonged social agitation by university students through the entire 1960s until the treaty renewal in 1970. In this public protest social space, dance, theater, and visual artists created collective works that matched the powerful waves of protest demonstrations and the tensions of enforced cultural assimilation.

## BUTOH WOMEN AND POSTWAR PERFORMANCE

The complicated status of Japanese women in the postwar period is fundamental to understanding how Ashikawa and Furukawa negotiated their roles in butoh's radical performance world. In most of East Asia, the influence of Confucian family ethics and its gender role hierarchies and practices remains woven into contemporary social structures. Japan's Confucian practices set up the entire life of a woman through her three obediences to the male members of her family: a woman obeys first her father, then her husband, and finally her son. The Japanese military exploited and strengthened this Confucian family and gender role system during the Pacific War years by demanding sacrifice to the emperor/nation and the head of the state/family and by enforcing the dedication of women to having sons to offer to the state's military agenda. Women were expected to be "breeding machines."[17] The "other" roles offered women historically from the Edo period through the Pacific War were the roles of entertainers and/or prostitutes. In the early postwar US military occupation, women suffering from extreme poverty and homelessness turned to the entertainment industry of bars that included hostessing, dancing, stripping, and prostituting. According to Matsui Yayori, an *Asahi* news-paper editor and women's rights activist, women in contemporary Japan "are divided into 'good women,' or housewives, and 'bad women,' or prostitutes. Men buying prostitutes are not socially condemned, nor is women's accep-tance of this behavior condemned."[18] This dichotomy of roles and choices for women was deeply entrenched in the early butoh era and the political demonstrations of the '60s. Even within butoh enclaves, male artists perpet-uated these subjugated roles for women performers.[19]

These prescriptions for women's roles intersected with the performance making of Ashikawa and Furukawa, creating a unique tension for each of them. As several women writers and artists have testified, a feminist consciousness arose during the protest years, but women writers and artists found that the "rhetoric of freedom and liberation did not extend to the lives of women within the movement."[20] Hijikata's butoh body revolution was not Ashikawa's or Furu-kawa's revolt.[21] But their participation in butoh's radical performances contrib-uted to this awakening to a new consciousness, what Aoki Yayoi, a scholar and eco-feminist, described as "a growing sense of doubt about what constituted civilization."[22] The dissatisfaction with butoh's gender system in Japan moti-vated Furukawa and other women butoh artists to refuse these subservient women's roles and duties and to emigrate to Europe and the US. In later dances, they choreographically provoked gender dichotomies with flamboyant gender acts. Furukawa's and Ashikawa's collaborative mode of training and devising, which empowered their dancers' personal movement choices, created new movement vocabularies with multiple gender possibilities.

## COLLECTIVE CHOREOGRAPHY

This investigation argues for the incorporation of Ashikawa's and Furuka-wa's diverse and collectively driven methods into butoh's radical emergence and complex global evolution. Two concepts serve as tools to open this sed-imented male lineage: collective choreography and the migration of gesture. These concepts work differently in different eras and cultures, which means their uses and meanings will shift in different contexts. Both require what Kai van Eikel's refers to as "looseness," which functions as an organizational qual-ity "that is part of collective self-organization," which "might help to take up, continue, further and thereby alter, the proximity between dance movement and political action."[23] Ashikawa and Furukawa's collective choreographic processes reveal this intimacy between their butoh and their corporeal politics, where different bodies open butoh's discourses to diverse collective agency.

## DECOLONIZING BODIES

Ashikawa and Furukawa negotiated the male established butoh contexts through their bodies, deftly navigating systems of hierarchy and agency deeply embedded in the larger Japanese society and entrenched in the Japanese art world. Developing a radical kinaesthetic imaginary with their bodies, Ashikawa and Furukawa performed and choreographed fantastic extensions of (often posthuman) forms, drawing on Japanese, European, and US pop and traditional cultural iconography, stereotypes, imagery, objects, media, and philosophies. Both women used specific techniques to fragment and radicalize the physical forms and socially constructed gesture patterns associated with women. They also opened *butoh* to other women and non-Japanese dancers. To survive as artists, they were also complicit, in different ways, with the male-centered butoh world of their eras.

With this context in mind, I studied Iimura Takahiko's *cinedance* (飯村 隆彦シネダンス) videos of pre-Ashikawa Hijikata and Ohno works from *Kinjiki* 禁色 (Forbidden Colors, 1959) through *Hijikata Tatsumi to Nihonjin: Nikutai no Hanran* 土方巽と日本人: 肉体の叛乱 (Hijikata Tatsumi and the Japanese: Revolt of the Flesh, 1968) and examined their gestures, patterns of movement, costuming, objects, props, and visual effects. By the late 1960s, this performance work *Nikutai no Hanran* (*Revolt of the Flesh*) had become Hijikata's iconic work of corporeal revolution.

After viewing these early works of Hijikata Tatsumi and then moving to his 1970s works with Ashikawa Yoko and other star women performers, I saw how much Hijikata performed within his training in European *ausdrucktanz* (expressionist dance), jazz, and ballet techniques. For example, Hijikata used turns, arabesques, and curving and reaching with his legs, torso, and arms to create balletic and expressionistic sculptural lines in his duet with Ohno Kazuo in *Barairo Dansu* (バラ色ダンス Rose Colored Dance, 1965). In *Hijikata Tatsumi to Nihonjin: Nikutai no Hanran* (土方巽と日本人:肉体の叛乱 Hijikata Tatsumi and the Japanese: The Revolt of the Flesh, 1968), we see the jiving striptease bar dancing style, in which Hijikata satirically burlesqued with other early butoh dancers. Hijikata also robes and disrobes in and out of satin ruffled skirts and suits, jittering and turning and prancing in a child kimono and underwear—his very own butoh? Also in 1968, Hijikata choreographed his first dance with his new disciple, Ashikawa Yoko. Then, in the early '70s, with more women disciples, he choreographed the startling *Shiki no Tame no Nijūshichiban* (四季のた めの二十七晩 Twenty-seven Nights for Four Seasons, 1972), which included the section *Hōsōtan* (疱瘡譚 Story of Smallpox, 1972). We see these transfigured bodies—not ballet, not modern dance, not cabaret, but instead bent and twisted bodies. They dance with limbs akimbo, low froggy walks (*ganimata* 蟹 股) and crumpled falls, curled, crunched spines, sucked in guts, outthrust chins, and dangling paw-like hands. The *beshimikata* 圧面形 (grimace) appeared: a pulled, wrenched, and whitened face with lips pulled over the teeth, eyes rolled up into the lids, and a slight silly grin.

The revolting body had arrived, through the bodies of women. The revolt of the body may have started in the 1960s, with the social revolution and the timely violence of political resistance and failure. But from the early 1970s something spiked the corporeal revolution into a multivalent form in earnest. If one takes the view of the female dancers, one can (even on video) experience the physical disorientation gradually usurping the everyday consciousness of propriety and technical dance form. Matching the rise of women performers in the 1970s, a popular woman-authored girl-culture phenomenon expanded in *manga* (graphic novels), *anime*, and fashion. The twisting, spiraling, and crunched bodies of these butoh women were strident outcries against the pressurized conforming roles of the late-twentieth-century female roles of office lady, elevator girl, and housewife/mother.

Crucially, it was during this time of waning political public outcry and demonstrations in the late 1960s and early '70s that young women artists entered the butoh community. This is when early butoh transforms through Ashikawa Yoko's partnership with Hijikata in his butoh movement inventions and later with Furukawa Anzu's breakaway group works and their interdisciplinary theatrical interventions. Ashikawa's entry into butoh practices initiated major shifts in butoh's trajectory of radical corporeal politics. Furukawa's butoh practices spiked another directional change and diversification of butoh in the mid-'70s. Their collective choreographic practices deployed collaborative processes of transmission through different dancer bodies' assimilation and remodeling of gestures, objects, and images. Even in their solo dances, Ashikawa and Furukawa performed collective gesture: gestures that had migrated across and through multiple bodies.

Ashikawa and Furukawa were part of the postwar and postoccupation generation of women who were working, going to university, and gaining the sense of having choices in lifestyle and life work outside the home. Tamano Hiroko, Yoshioka Yumiko, Seki Minako, and Nakajima Natsu found their initial

exposure to *butoh* liberating in its immersive and demanding physical training. I was struck by their shared exuberance when they each discovered butoh
for the first time. Yoshioka related that after trying several career paths, she
still felt unsatisfied. After seeing and participating in butoh, she felt totally
challenged: this is what she wanted to do.[24] Yet, as they trained and performed,
none of the women felt that they could stay within the confines of one company under one male artist. These women passionately embraced the radical
distorted movement, near nudity, and collective female ensemble training for
its invigorating, sensual, and flamboyant "now-ness, in the present moment-
ness."[25] While each woman had her individual entry narrative into butoh's
messy physical extremes, they also changed butoh at this crucial moment
in its growth past the initial stage of revolt. Their "present-ness" and now-
moment focus arose within their choreographic ensemble practices, where
they generated, within the chorus of other women, a collective embodiment.

In 1968, Ashikawa was among these first artists to open butoh to women,
and along with other women she continued this trajectory of diversifying
butoh. If we follow Ashikawa's process of assimilating Hijikata's visions and
concepts when they worked together, we can conjecture how she physically
interpreted his directions, images, texts, and narratives. She created these
twisted, bent, and gyrating postures and gestures and facial grimaces. Ashikawa commuted between her own creativity and compliance to Hijikata's
rigorous commands until she transmitted her butoh vocabulary to the early
female collective of dancers. Then, through these collective bodies, her transmission of butoh transformed butoh.

Similarly, Furukawa's training and performance with Maro Akaji's company Dairakudakan (麿赤兒の大駱駝館) in the 1970s changed in the 1980s,
when she initiated her collaborative works with dancers from Japan, Africa,
and Europe. Furukawa also deployed a reprocessing method through collective physicalization of images and narratives, multiplied by culturally
different bodies. Here, both Ashikawa and Furukawa processed butoh transmission with assimilation, without homogenizing the contributions of each
dancer. Their collective works revitalized butoh through diverse collectivity,
which cracked open the butoh discourse and ideology.

## GESTURE MIGRATION AND COLLECTIVITY

How does this distinct collaboration between individual gesture and collective choreography create a corporeal politics? Diana Taylor's concept of rep-

ertoire and the centrality of bodies in performance archives opens a way to differently evaluate these women and their collective works. She insists on the drive of embodied cultural memory and how much gender and ethnicity matter in shaping that embodied cultural memory and how, in performance, race, ethnicity, and gender are inseparable. This is where the repertoire has to take over the archives, and where Ashikawa's and Furukawa's choreography exhibits the process of transfer to other bodies, who maintain their differences.[26]

In their edited volume *Migrations of Gesture,* Sally Ann Ness and Carrie Noland argue how " in a rich variety of ways, . . . gestures migrate . . . and that in migrating they create unexpected combinations, new valences, and alternative cultural meanings and experiences. In a world of inescapable global circulation, gestures, too, undergo appropriations and enjoy afterlives that change their initial function."[27] In butoh, this gestural passage through bodies over time reveals its density, complexity, and adaptability to diverse processing and change through and within migration. Ness and Noland emphasize the singular significance of gesture in researching history.[28] Furukawa and Ashikawa drew directly on how this tension between the prescribed regime of gesture or techné from Hijikata and their own subjective gestures streamed through their collective of dancers. Sally Ann Ness and Deidre Sklar speak of "common sensing," which I interpret as collective sensing across dancer bodies and the many ways dancers digest, host, experiment, and unlearn gestures.[29]

In her introduction to *Collectivism in 20th-Century Japanese Art,* Tomii Reiko 富井玲子 sets out a notion of collectivism, which Ashikawa and Furukawa put into action. She explains, "The collective functions ( for the individual) as a means to mediate the relationship between the intrinsic (aesthetic/ expressive) and the extrinsic (social) forces."[30] Tomii also raises questions concerning the power of the collective: "What is the potential for artists getting together that individuals cannot achieve under the same circumstances? How did collectivism shape artists' practices of making and showing art in an environment they operate?"[31]

Tomii describes her definition of collectivism for the 1960s art practices as "strategic alliances (primarily) of artists motivated to seek and create alternatives to the existing options, be they artistic/expressive or social/operational or both."[32] She also cautions against making any generalizations or imposing any assumptions about collective methods. Instead, she emphasizes recognizing differences in process and how individuals and groups contribute to the collective work. Ashikawa and Furukawa articulate different uses of collective practices and thus offer complex ways of perceiving and evaluating their works.

Ashikawa physically processed Hijikata's visual and corporeal directions, which she taught to the male and female collective members. Watching the videos of *Hōsōtan*, the female choruses move in loose unison, with individual twists, turns, and facial grimaces. This early work of Ashikawa's female chorus reflects her fluidity of transmission and the likelihood of the female members using individual movements to formulate their sense of group expression.

## THE COLLECTIVE DANCES OF ASHIKAWA YOKO AND FURUKAWA ANZU

Ashikawa Yoko's group work in *Hōsōtan* (疱瘡譚 Story of Smallpox), *Sannin Berumeru* (3人ベルメール Three Bellmers), and *Natsu no Arashi* (夏の嵐 Summer Storm) and Furukawa Anzu's group work in *A Diamond as Big as the Ritz* stand out for their generative butoh collective creativity. Training and choreographic methods reveal how signature gestures transfigure through other bodies over time and extend the parameters of individual bodies through collective collaboration. These collective processes reflect certain Japanese performance traditions, the Japanese 1960s radical performance politics, the artists' positions as women in Japan, and their contemporary moment of corporeal politics. Exposure to European, American, African, and other Asian art, dance, theater, and performers transformed visual and choreographic designs, while their dancers' own differences of race, ethnicity, gender, sexuality, and political cultures collectively altered these forms.

## FRAMING *HŌSŌTAN* THROUGH ASHIKAWA AND THE CHORUS OF FLOATING BABY CHICKS

In the creative gestation of physical material, Ashikawa Yoko mobilized outrageous gestures and postures into a butoh vocabulary. Hijikata dictated layerings of multiple images with texts, which, according to *Hōsōtan* dancer Tamano Hiroko, Ashikawa would transform into physical shapes and qualities of movement. They all learned this movement created by Ashikawa. Tamano also reminded me that they were used to Japanese "master" learning, where no one questions and everyone represses the self. Tamano recalled how "one woman was so exhausted in rehearsal that she started crying, and Hijikata said, 'if you have the energy to cry why not laugh?'"[33] Tamano Hiroko recalled how they would learn a movement section and practice it over and over again, speeding it up each time. By increasing the momentum, she said, they would get to a point of "derangement," a one-body/mind state where their concentration would be so riveted that they vibrated together. Tamano Hiroko recalled how the women performers differed from the men because of their physical concentration: "We are different creatures . . . women are the mothers and you know, men are the children."[34]

*Hōsōtan* is only one section of five different sections of the famously extolled 1972 work, "Great Dance Mirror of Burnt Sacrifice—Performance to Commemorate the Second Unity of the School of the Dance of Utter Darkness—Twenty-Seven Nights for Four Seasons," which was held "over 27 days from October 25th to November 20th at the Shinjuku Culture Art Theater [and . . .] attracted approximately 8,500 viewers."[35] This was the turning point work with a "new dance vocabulary."[36]

Ashikawa's phrases with her female chorus sections in *Hōsōtan* are striking. The women danced: rolling onto their buttocks and kicking their feet in the air like squalling infants, flouncing in an upright tiptoe parade with arms akimbo, swaying in a hurdle of bodies with chins thrust out, eyes rolled back, and lips pulled over teeth making hollow-mouthed grimaces, jerking heads and curling, vibrating fingers—all become recognizable vocabulary throughout this work and beyond. Together the women jerk from one phrase sequence to the next, separately and together, catching up to Ashikawa. It is this slight off-balance behind-ness from the chorus that creates a chicken-like flocking effect, a flurry of bodies, slightly tipsy, rocking and squawking, resolving into and out of a fragmented collective, a single creature with many legs, heads, and mouths.

After the last male chorus member has tiptoed off, a small tribe of women enter and transfix the stage. In their hiked up, puffy winter *dotera* (褞袍) kimono, old wigs, and tall courtesan *geta* (下駄 wooden clogs), they enter like aliens, swarming and clattering women "on pointe" in their wooden geta, drumming on the ground like bent over goats. Then they rush with tiny flat-footed steps, like folded frog women. Their next pounding stampede pushes a haze of dust into the air, which settles on their black wigs. Their kimono, wrapped up around their waists for hard sweaty rice labor, make them look like chickens with thick bodies on tiny legs and giant geta feet. Movement sequences momentarily flourish, repeat, explode, and fade without cause, only their collective urgency.

In a final section, when the women slow-fall and curl down to the "butoh float" position, they are on their backs with head, legs, and arms suspended in the air, their abdominals knotted to hold the wavering limbs. In this gut-

Fig. 14.1. Women's Collective Choreography, *Hōsōtan* (1972) Women's chorus: Ashikawa Yoko, Nimura Momoko, Kobayashi Saga, Yoshino (Tamano) Hiroko, Kurosaki Midori. Photo by Onozuka Makoto.

aching position, their bodies quake and tremble. From their floating curled bodies, not unlike dying beetles, with their pinched faces shimmering with sweat and caked powder, white dust rises like a vapor cloud in the fading light. These floating bodies emerge like baby chicks from a gooey cracked egg, wet knots of skin and limbs.

### FURUKAWA ANZU'S GLITTER: ASSIMILATION PRACTICES AND EXPERIMENTS

From 1972 to 1975 Furukawa studied at the Tohogakuen College of Music. From her musical studies, she moved into performance and trained and performed in the late '70s with *Dairakudakan* (大駱駝館), founded and directed by Maro Akaji 麿赤兒 in 1972. In the 1980s Furukawa and Tamura Tetsurō 田村哲郎, a male butoh artist from Hijikata's group, founded and toured the *Dance Love Machine*. Furukawa also started her own dance school in Tokyo. From 1987 she worked mainly in Europe, and taught at Braunschweig University of Art in Germany, where many dancers studied her butoh choreographic practices.

Fig, 14.2. Women's Collective Choreography, right to left: Sano Makiko, Lilo Stahl, Torunn Robstad, and Ulrike Drescher in *Diamond as Big as the Ritz* 1991, on location rehearsal. Direction/ Co-creation by Furukawa Anzu. Photo by Okano Shoichi.

She also formed and toured the butoh group Dance Butter TOKIO from 1988 to 2001, which combined dance theater, quasi-characters, and visual surrealisms. Unlike Ashikawa, Furukawa was familiar with *ausdrucktanz*, modern dance, conceptual art, and experimental music and theater performance. Her mentor Maro Akaji originally trained in theater. His Dairakudakan scenic theatricality added to Furukawa's tools a sense of spectacle and design, which she fully developed in her own works. After her performance training in butoh of the 1970s, Furukawa struck out on her own, developing a butoh theater.

Furukawa, who moved back and forth between Europe and Japan, found it too difficult to realize her performances in Japan. While Hijikata and others advocated a corporeality of "the native (*dochyaku* 土着) or the folk (*minzoku* 民族)" Japan,[37] Furukawa *moved* into abstraction, irony, and the absurd with her international butoh theater collective. With her studies in contemporary and modern music composition, Furukawa's sensibilities tended toward the modern. In Dairakudakan, where she trained and performed, Maro Akaji enforced the separation of men and women and demanded exacting unison movement, which stifled Furukawa.[38] Subsequently Furukawa codirected and directed several butoh companies, including Dance Love Machine, Aria-done, and Dance Butter TOKIO. Furukawa's repertoire is scattered through-out other dancers' works, in modern and contemporary dance, in *tanztheater*, and in contemporary diasporic butoh. Furukawa's dancers have expressed how they felt inspired by her intensity and her way of devising images to pro-pel their movement imagination: "You wanted to watch her every move. . . . When you trained with her, you listened to everything she said, how she pic-tured something, what she thought about. You could feel the movement in it."[39] As a reviewer noted, "To think like a crocodile, instructs Berlin-based butoh artist Anzu Furukawa, 'sometime, just stop your breathing, you will get a red face, and taste crocodile time.'"[40]

### DIAMOND AS BIG AS THE RITZ (1991): COLLECTIVE GHOSTS

From the program of the *Diamond as Big as the Ritz*:

Dance Butter TOKIO Manifesto

We are dangerous passers-by cutting across the middle of the spectator's dream. We dancers, all our senses spin at hyper-light speed. Whether with the 360° maneuverability of a Zero fighter or in a 38-turn pirouette, . . . Japan, Germany, Norway, Finland, Ghana—a squad of dancing guerrillas . . . we will laugh the world off as an absurdity without meaning, knowing nothing of any-thing else . . .[41]

In the same program, Negoro Yūko 根来裕子 (ねごろ ゆうこ) places Dance Butter TOKIO's successes in the chaotic times of the crumbling of the Ber-lin Wall, "our passion being matched by the passion of great social upheaval permeating through Europe."[42] She describes the company as "The Dancing Guerrilla Command, Dance Butter TOKIO dance across all the borders of nations, races, artistic genres and what not, spinning themselves at the speed faster than light. The corps pursue love almost violently."[43] While the Berlin Wall melted and economies such as Japan's and others' plummeted, uncer-tainties in the reuniting Germany shook theaters and artists. Their two-hour spectacle danced this shocked Europe and Japan, spinning out their surreal collective dance/theater/butoh.

*Diamond as Big as the Ritz* referenced F. Scott Fitzgerald's stories and era and lifestyle, but without any story or characters. A faintly nostalgic decadence seems to haunt the movement: as if we were on the edge of a time about to implode. One section is a duet by two women, Ulrika Drescher and Toruun Robstad, who are nude with a bright glittering gold medallion over their pubic area and a square flat hat with a hanging green veil that partially covers their faces. The music is a warm rendition of George Gershwin's *Rhapsody in Blue*. They dance with these big black closed umbrellas, sometimes with the handle between their legs, curled and protruding like a wooden phallus. With the umbrella tips, they prick, stick, and tickle each other's body parts: bottoms, nipples, thighs, and tummies. It is a *butoh* tango: sweet and nasty. The women appear faceless and sometimes headless, but their bright red lips appear when they stick their tongues out to lick the edge of their sabre-like umbrellas. These objects, the curtained hat and the umbrella, come out of improvisations with objects, music, stories, and images, which the dancers and Furukawa collectively generate. This is an exchange of cultural image gestures across bodies, with the materials of harem-like veils and phallic umbrellas: collective transcultural migration.

## MONSTROUS GHOSTS: KABUKI MEETS GRIMM

A chorus of men enters, marching with thrusting martial kicks. They wear square tutu-like skirts that stick out in sharp corners from their waists. The skirts are gauze-like cloth that seems to float off the edges of the square. These square tutus also flounce and bounce when they move, and the men can lift, warp, bend, and whisk their squares and skirts about. With one leg kicked up and out, they balance, then slam it down, smacking the floor with their bare foot, and raising the next leg. They move with flouncing square tutus, kicking, crashing, and stomping towards the audience. They move back and forth upstage and downstage in these whirling bouncing skirts with these thrusting and threatening kicks. Then they back up and appear to pursue the women who have filed into a line in the darkness. The women wear only their gold medallions and bright red lipstick smeared over their lips, which they stretch into wide gaping smiles. They sing the Beatles' song *Yesterday,* with its own bittersweet memory spin, in their singsong unison.

Here the ghost stalking begins. According to Kaseki, Furukawa asked everyone to make their own monster ghost, some roving and unquiet soul from their childhood or a fairytale, from their own culture. She asked them to imagine and move the creatures that frightened them as children. They each created their own ghost body.[44] The European dancers held their arms out like giant, grizzly branches with fingers wide, reaching and shaking. They pull their mouths and eyes wide into distorted silent screams. The two Japanese women dancers, Furukawa and Sano Makiko, made the *kabuki* ghost figure, with arms drawn into the body with their hands dangling from the wrist, as if dripping blood. They curved their spines inward and thrust out their chins. They pulled their faces into grins, their pupils rolled up under their eyelids. They float forward with tiny slipping steps. The Ghanaian dancer Yaw Agyei Wiredu stamped, vibrated, and jittered, possessed by his local demon god. This staggering swarm of ghosts now begins to chant childhood rhymes in taunting punctuated voices: "London bridge is falling down falling down," and "If you go out into the woods today," while a Ghanaian chant matches a German "O Tannenbaum" round.

Then, abruptly, four of the male dancers, Ari Kalevi Tenhula, Wolfgang Graf, Gregor Weber, Harri Kuorelahti, grab the umbrellas and hold them like machine guns and proceed to pretend-shoot and fire and shake into the density of bodies. Everyone shakes. They spew sweat and spit. The men play machine gun and the women slip and fall to duck and cover. The tutu bandits turn on each other and the audience as they back into darkness. The dancers pass forms and fears from body to body. The scene flips into a ballroom dance. They pose suddenly like Swan Lake couples. The women turn into frozen statues. *Rhapsody in Blue* pulls and spins their bodies. Then the women run jumping onto the shoulders of the spinning, skirted men. Squeezing their partner's shoulders between their legs, the women twist over, swing upside down, legs thrust open into a V for victory. They smile, monstrously. The twentieth century shifts across bodies spinning Dance Butter TOKIO butoh theater.

### CONCLUSION: WHOSE SWEAT, POWDER, GLITTER?

Furukawa and Ashikawa are agents in their performances and their collective repertoire. If we look closely at enactment, as Diana Taylor emphasizes, "Humans do not simply adapt to systems. They shape them."[45] Both women performed butoh completely differently, but with a shared choreographic intent and precision: they both worked with collective creativity and tested the spectators' kinesthetic endurance. They each harnessed energy and molded their bodies into exacting and crippling architectural forms, which were then shaken from within by their controlled glacial or split-second shifts, made by and through their dancers. Their differences speak to how butoh women have invested their own butoh darkness and light. Engaging with the performances of these two women opens up and keeps open diverse butoh possibilities. Collective choreographic processes shift and open and diversify butoh, emphasizing butoh's processes of dis-identification with any originary butoh. Ashikawa and Furukawa let their dancers become the repertoire of monstrous couplings of bodies, objects, and desire, folded together and fragmented.[46]

In these works, we see the power of collective unison used in a sophisticated, diverse collective discourse, where unison explodes into antagonistic fights and power plays or when individual bodies and faces gradually add energy, shape, and timing changes to gestures and postures, and unison dissolves into tiny gestural resemblances. Like tidal waves and crosscurrents, their collective movement pulls back, hurls forward, and the "dance" momentarily dissolves. The power of the Ashikawa and Furukawa performances arises from this interplay of collectivity in tension with individuated changes.

BEFORE WE DANCE . . .

Contemporary women artists in Japan operate as a minority in their masculinist culture. Their art making is a constant process of disidentifying with the male order and building their own hybrid art. Further, while nationally Japan may appear stagnant and conservative, there is a process of change built into the arts. In traditional arts, there is a strong allegiance to head teachers, like Furukawa or Ashikawa, who are deeply venerated for their expertise and creativity. The devoted student must imitate the teacher as closely as possible, but they must eventually *yabureru* (破れる), subtly tear the self from the mentor and adapt the forms to their own bodies, minds, and energy. Their "choreography" is an unsettling process of transfer and migration through diverse bodies to other bodies. They tear, expand, and transform these differences within and through the collective action.

ADDITIONAL RESOURCES

Full resolution versions of Figure 14.1 at https://doi.org/10.3998/mpub.11521701.cmp.28 and Figure 14.2 at https://doi.org/10.3998/mpub.11521701.cmp.29

Figure 14.3: Program Furukawa Anzu Diamond as big as the Ritz. Available at https://doi.org/10.3998/mpub.11521701.cmp.79

Figure 14.4: Furukawa with Dairakudakan Women's Chorus offstage, 1975 MESU. Available at https://doi.org/10.3998/mpub.11521701.cmp.80

Video Clip 14.1: Ashikawa and Women's chorus in Hōsōtan. Accessible at https://doi.org/10.3998/mpub.11521701.cmp.81

Video Clip 14.2: Yoko Ashikawa (1986)—Wi-Fi. Accessible at https://doi.org/10.3998/mpub.11521701.cmp.82

Link 14.1: Free Visual material and introductory lectures on Hijikata Tatsumi butoh on the Keio University sponsored and supported Future Learn online course site. Available at https://doi.org/10.3998/mpub.11521701.cmp.83

Link 14.2: "Rent-a-Body Last Night at Ballhaus" Berlin 1989. Available at https://doi.org/10.3998/mpub.11521701.cmp.84

Link 14.3: Hijikata Tatsumi Archive at Keio University Art Center (in Japanese and English). Available at https://doi.org/10.3998/mpub.11521701.cmp.85

Link 14.4: Furukawa Anzu's Photographer, Okano Shoichi's website photo gallery of her works and performance programs: "Shoichi Okano Photo Office Inc." Available at https://doi.org/10.3998/mpub.11521701.cmp.86

Link 14.5: Photoblog Archive, sources and photographs of Furukawa Anzu by Gregor von Glinski. Free for public use. Available at https://doi.org/10.3998/mpub.11521701.cmp.87

Link 14.6: Short synopsis of Furukawa Anzu's works and her connections to butoh artists. Available at https://doi.org/10.3998/mpub.11521701.cmp.88

Link 14.7: Short synopsis of Ashikawa Yoko's network of butoh artists. Available at https://doi.org/10.3998/mpub.11521701.cmp.89

Link 14.8: Article on Furukawa Anzu's influence on European dance theater. Free for public use. Available at https://doi.org/10.3998/mpub.11521701.cmp.90

Link 14.9: Murobushi Ko's archive that shows the all women troupe, Ariadone, from 1973 and 1975. Furukawa Anzu was in this original all women troupe, led by Carlotta Ikeda (Ikeda Sanae), under the direction and production of Maro

Akaji's butoh troupe "Dairakudakan." Note that this is Murobushi's online archive and credits only the male butoh "choreographers." Available at https://doi.org/10.3998/mpub.11521701.cmp.91

## Notes

1. Judith Hamera, *Unfinished Business, Michael Jackson, Detroit, & the Figural Economy of American Postindustrialization* (New York: Oxford University Press, 2017), 35.

2. Ibid., 36. See Sally Gardner, "The Dancer, The Choreographer, and Modern Dance Scholarship: A Critical Reading," *Dance Research: The Journal of the Society for Dance Research* 25, no. 1 (Summer 2007): 35–53.

3. Exceptions are the female shamisen performer in *Anma* (The Masseurs), women such as Motofuji, and others in "supporting" roles such as those financing Asbestos Kan and performances.

4. Stephen Barber, *Hijikata: Revolt of the Body* (London: Creation, 2006), 84.

5. Vera Mackie, *Feminism in Modern Japan* (Cambridge: Cambridge University Press, 2003), 148.

6. SU-EN, personal interview, via Skype, 2015.

7. See *The Modern Girl Around the World: Consumption, Modernity, and Globalization*, eds. Alys Eve Weinbaum, The Modern Girl Around the World Research Group, Lynn M. Thomas, Priti Ramamurthy, Uta G. Poigner, and Madeleine Yue Dong (Durham, NC: Duke University Press, 2008). This collectively researched and edited volume offers a view of the period from the 1920s to the 1930s when the urban modern girl cultures arose and challenged the world order. Modern girls in Shanghai, Tokyo, Hong Kong, and other Asian cities initiated the first "wave" of gender role convulsions of the twentieth century.

8. Vera Mackie, *Feminism in Modern Japan* (Oxford: Oxford University Press, 2003), 6, 10.

9. Mackie, *Feminism*, 10, 11.

10. Mackie, *Feminism*, 232–33.

11. Mackie, *Feminism*, 146–47.

12. Mackie, *Feminism*, 147.

13. Karen Kelsky, *Women on the Verge: Japanese Women, Western Dreams* (Durham: Duke University Press, 2001), 3.

14. Kelsky, *Women on the Verge*, 56.

15. Kelsky, *Women on the Verge*, 56.

16. See Peter Eckersall, *Theorizing the Angura Space: Avant-garde Performance and Politics in Japan, 1960–2000* (Leiden: Brill, 2006) and *Performativity and Event in 1960s Japan* (London: Palgrave Macmillan, 2013).

17. Matsui Yayori, interview, Sandra Buckley, ed., trans., *Broken Silence, The Voices of Japanese Feminism* (Berkeley: University of California Press, 1997), 148.

18. Matsui, *Broken Silence*, 148.

19. Yoshioka Yumiko, personal interview, 2011; Tamano Hiroko, personal interview, 2015.

20. Aoki Yayoi, *Broken Silence*, 12.

21. See Bruce Baird's monograph on Hijikata's early life and creative works. *Hijikata Tatsumi and Butoh: Dancing in a Pool of Gray Grits* (New York: Palgrave Macmillan, 2012). Hijikata's butoh motivations radically differed from those of Furukawa and Ashikawa. He wrote, lectured, and experimented with movement and thought, confronting the tensions between his "native Japanese" past and simultaneously rebelling against establishment or mainstream European-centered modern dance in Japan. His danced rebellion connected with the resurgence of the 1920s nativism valorized by Yanagita Kunio (柳田 國男 1875–1962), whose influential writing and thinking promulgated the preservation of a pure "Japanese-ness," which Yanagita claimed could only be found through focusing on the Japanese common person from the undeveloped and untainted regions of Japan. His folklorist point of view flourished in the later phase of the American occupation among Japanese intellectuals. Hijikata wrote and thought deeply about this "native" butoh body and this drive to become this fictional, premodern *Tōhoku* (東北) Japanese body, with bandy legs, turned-in toes, and the bent and crumpled posture of the rice field worker. Hijikata claimed the writings of Jean Genet and Antonin Artaud as sources of inspiration, rejecting American culture and his assimilated German expressionist dance training.

22. Aoki, *Broken Silence*, 12.

23. Kai Van Eikels, "Performing Collectively," in *The Oxford Handbook of Dance and Politics*, eds. Rebekah J. Kowal, Gerald Siegmund, and Randy Martin (New York: Oxford University Press, 2017), 117–28, 125.

24. Yoshioka Yumiko, personal interview, Berlin, 2011.

25. Seki Minako, personal interview, Berlin, 2011.

26. Diana Taylor, *The Archive and the Repertoire: Performing Cultural Memory in the Americas* (Durham, NC: Duke University Press, 2003), 86.

27. Carrie Noland in *Migrations of Gesture*, eds. Sally Ann Ness and Carrie Noland (Minneapolis: University of Minnesota Press, 2008), x.

28. Noland, *Migrations*, x.

29. Sally Ann Ness, *Migrations*, 277.

30. Tomii Reiko, "Introduction: Collectivism in Twentieth-Century Japanese Art with a Focus on Operational Aspects of *Dantai*," *positions: asia critique* 21, no. 2 (Spring 2013): 225–67.

31. Tomii Reiko, "Introduction," 226.

32. Tomii Reiko, "Introduction," 232.

33. Tamano Hiroko, personal interview, 2013.

34. Tamano Hiroko, personal interview, 2013.

35. Bruce Baird, *Hijikata*, 137.

36. Baird, *Hijikata*, 137. Tamano Hiroko added that before this epic work, the shorter piece *Fin Whale*, also 1972, held the seeds of most of the actual movement vocabulary of this massive work.

37. Seiji M. Lippit, *Topographies of Japanese Modernism* (New York: Columbia University Press, 2002), 290–91.

38. Furukawa Anzu, personal interview, 1999.

39. Kaseki Yuko, personal interview, 2011, 2013, 2015.

40. Anonymous, *SF Weekly*, 1999.

41. Furukawa Anzu, *Diamond* program, 1991.

42. Negoro Yuko, *Diamond* program, 4.

43. Negoro, *Diamond program*, 4.

44. Yuko Kaseki, personal interview, Berlin, 2009, 2010.

45. Taylor, *The Archive and the Repertoire*, 7.

# CHAPTER 15

# Fans, Sashes, and Jesus

## Evangelical Activism and Anti-LGBTQ Performance in South Korea

*Soo Ryon Yoon*

Women are dancing. It is a humid and sultry June afternoon. The women's bangs, although their hair is neatly made into buns, keep sticking to their sweaty foreheads. With both hands, they each hold two large, half-circle fans adorned with artificial neon-pink feathers along the outer edges and printed with flowers painted a similar pink hue. They make quick steps in one direction in a single line, but then shift swiftly from the row to make five rings of six dancers each. In unison, each group forms a shape that is supposed to resemble a fully blossomed *mugunghwa* 무궁화 (*rose of Sharon*), the national flower of South Korea. Their arms hold the unfolded fans outward as they kneel halfway to the ground, after which they shake off their hands to flutter the fans, creating tiny petals moving in a wavelike pattern and thus becoming vibrant, blossoming flowers in motion. They quickly rise again to form another ring, this time turning their bodies inward and raising their right arms toward the center to erect a pistil-like core, still going around clockwise in circles. Most of the women appear young, but others are middle-aged. Their facial expressions vary—some violently cry in exaltation, while others smile gleefully. Some are mouthing the lyrics of the song heard in the background coming from a loud speaker: "Oh, the glory of beautiful God, we hear the roar of victory." A few, with their eyes shut, chins held up slightly toward the sky, holler "*Yesu!*" (Jesus!), while their feet move constantly to make their bodies twirl unstoppably.[1]

This was a part from the *buchaechum* 부채춤 (traditional Korean fan dance) that thirty or so of the female members affiliated with a Protestant organization All World Praise and Worship Team performed opposite the Seoul Queer Culture Festival (SQCF) (formerly Korea Queer Culture Festival until 2009), held in Seoul Plaza in front of Seoul City Hall, South Korea, in June 2016.[2] In this seventeenth annual festival, the SQCF presented its largest event ever, with over 50,000 attendees, a day-long program, multiple booths, and international support from a number of embassies in Seoul. Outside the parameters of the plaza were several church groups protesting the SQCF, either performing dance or singing songs, including the fan-dancing women described above. Rows of riot police separated these church groups from the SQCF attendees to prevent violent clashes.[3] To the SQCF attendees, the passersby, and the media, the church group's *buchaechum* displayed what the journalist Shin-Yun Donguk called a "visual shock" of an evangelical performance: church groups clad in *hanbok* 한복 (formal, traditional Korean attire) or in white dresses performing *buchaechum* along other dance movements, dancing as if to perform an exorcism of queerness that, for them, was not supposed to be part of this nation.[4]

Having followed the SQCF and its surrounding politics since 2003 as a participant, community member, and now performance studies researcher, I developed an interest in Christian Protestant anti-LGBTQ cultures.[5] This has led me to inquire into performances of hate staged by evangelical activists (the label I use to describe the church members heckling the protests and political events), their ties to nationalism, and their effects on the queer community. I argue that church groups like All World Praise and Worship Team choose a combination of dance and songs, including *buchaechum,* not simply to proselytize, but to present their nationalist political ideology with the goal of building their power in and outside of South Korea. Yet the seemingly out-of-place spectacularity of folk and traditional elements that appear in public protests against the SQCF, I also argue, is precisely what conceals the visibility of a larger community of "respectable" and reticent church groups that also push homophobic and nationalist ideologies, but often without drawing such attention. I also look at how, in counteraction to the evangelical activists, the SQCF participants build their own repertoire of "queer traditions" by restaging a 1990s Korean pop-song choreography, which also appropriates the fan dance.

In what follows, I discuss three focal points to address these central arguments. First, I briefly chronicle the performances of evangelical activists and discuss the effects of an assemblage of performances called *momchanyang* 몸찬양, or body worship, that directly relate to the performers' vision of nationalism. Second, I situate the spectacle of the evangelical activists' performances in the larger history of Christian Protestant culture in Korea and its use of performance, including folk dance elements and *buchaechum,* in tandem with the nation's promotion of nationalist ideology at times of political crisis. Lastly, I revisit the evangelical activists' performance as a nationalist response to the growing visibility of LGBTQ movement in South Korea. To close, I zoom in on some key moments from the 2017 SQCF, where I observed Korean pop-song dance during its parade. I demonstrate how the LGBTQ repertoire of queer traditions exceeds the conservative nationalist ideology undergirding South Korean Protestant culture, as festival performers and attendees repurpose the fan dance to create a space for a queer sense of belonging and community performance, while continuously citing the same forms of embodiment.[6]

What I hope to do here, by attending to the conservative hate politics of the evangelical activist performances and their stylistic features, is to cast light on the ongoing struggle of the LGBTQ polity as it responds to the emergence of Christian right-wing hate cultures in South Korea. Analyzing the specifics of the evangelical activists' choreography will help us better understand the underexamined hegemonic violence that is uniquely shaped and scripted by South Korean history, and by extension, allow us to reorient our understanding of queer politics and performance that have emerged in the same sociohistorical context. The queer parallel to the Christian fan dance, as I discuss in the latter part of this chapter, shows us how a traditional performance emblematic of "Koreanness" comes to produce new affective engagements through a "queer" choreography.

### BODY-WORSHIPPING THE NATION?

SQCF did not always have to fend off the church groups. Since its first iteration in 2000, the festival has constantly challenged pushback from nonmainstream civic groups, yet it was not until the mid-2010s that the participants saw organized large-scale counterrallies by conservative nationalist church groups, especially those that featured a series of dance performances sometimes referred to as "body worship."

The so-called "body worship" performance staged during anti-LGBTQ protests and the annual SQCF came to the general public's attention sometime in 2014. The media publicized evangelical activists' interventions in two incidents prior to the 2016 SQCF: the Seoul Metropolitan Government Declaration of Human Rights public hearing in November 2014, and the assault on the then–U.S. ambassador Mark Lippert in March 2015. While these two cases were unrelated, the evangelical activists performed the same repertoire of *buchaechum*, ballet, and drumming either in protest or support. These worship performances seemed to be in opposition to more muted bodily gestures (whether in quieter folk Christian songs performed by college students or motionless sit-ins staged by church groups) conducted by the majority of churches in South Korea that did not appear at these sites. Yet they share the common goal of preserving what they collectively deem "proper" Koreanness: a set of racially, ethnically, and culturally homogeneous qualities that signify heteronormative, family-oriented, pro-American, and anti-communist Korean bodies that adhere to nationalist and "traditional" values. Proper Koreanness would thus, in their view, serve as a foundation for a stronger nation and stability against communist and terrorist attacks, which partly explains the church groups' support for the US ambassador. Their insistence on what they deem to be proper Koreanness is related to the ongoing US intervention in South Korea. It produces a political agenda that echoes the homophobia and Islamophobia similarly prevalent among Christian right-wing groups in the US, making their "performance" both Korean and transnational.[7]

A number of evangelical activists who protested at the Seoul Metropolitan Government Declaration of Human Rights public hearing in November 2014 were directly responding to the threat that they believed the declaration's antidiscrimination clause would pose to proper Koreanness, in their words, "widely pav[ing] the way for homosexuality."[8] Conservative church groups have long existed in South Korea, but this was the first time they demonstrated in such visible ways as picketing inside the public hearing or initiating a shouting match with the declaration committee members. Protesters representing church groups and various antihomosexuality organizations were at the hearing shouting catchphrases such as "Out with Anti-Discrimination Act" and "Homosexuality, same-sex marriage OUT." Meanwhile, the "performers" waited outside the city hall in the rain, dancing to a drum rhythm in support of the anti-LGBTQ, anti–human rights declaration protesters.

A prominent image of these evangelical activists that began to circulate in news media was of dance groups, mostly women, staging a combination of *buchaechum*, ballet, and drumming, clad in white dresses with blue sashes or *hanbok*. Taken from various angles, the photographs depicted the performers with closed eyes, collectively giving concerted prayers while tapping cylindrical drums with their drum sticks or stretching both arms toward the sky holding folding fans, as if to call for God's answers. Photographs taken during the "get well" rally supporting the US ambassador Mark Lippert included the exact same performers with the same repertoire. In March 2015, Lippert was attacked by a Korean man, Kim Ki-jong, who jumped out of the audience attending Lippert's lecture to cut his cheek and wrist with a knife. Praying

Fig. 15.1. Women evangelical activists from an anti-LGBTQ church performing a Swan Lake-inspired protest dance at the 16th Seoul Queer Culture Festival on June 28, 2015. Photo ©이준헌 JoonHeon Lee courtesy of the photographer.

for Lippert's fast recovery, evangelical activists appeared in front of the Seoul Train Station and the Finance Building located not far from the US Embassy, performing, flying Korean and American national flags, and holding banners that read, "Ambassador, we Koreans are wishing you speedy recovery."[9] With these two notable cases, evangelical activists began to garner more attention by frequently appearing at various events, including the 16th SQCF in 2015.

While evangelical activists are generally known for "marshal[ling] practically every tool, every tactic employed by performance activists the world over,"[10] this eclectic combination of dance movements and music performances still raised many questions, particularly regarding their authenticity. Ballet movements unfolded in a simplified sequence of basic ballet positions accompanied by Richard Strauss's *Blue Danube*, but were always publicized as a part of *Swan Lake*. The drumming performance resembled scenes from the musical theater production *Nanta* 난타, an internationally successful Korean performance that ran at the Off-Broadway New Victory Theater in 2003. Finally, *buchaechum* included women manipulating their folding fans and performing the twirling and gather-and-spread movements, but they did not exhibit the dainty footwork originally characteristic of typical classical versions of the dance.[11] In this regard, these performances can seem like failures because they lacked formal "authenticity," as Heo Yumi has pointed out.[12] That is, these performances did not exhibit anything inherently "Korean," although that was supposedly the core identity of evangelical protests.

Yet critiques of the evangelical dance routines as an unwarranted citation of a made-up tradition are half valid and half ineffective; authenticity is, in fact, never the goal of these performances, and in any case the authenticity of Koreanness in performances is always contingent on who practices Koreanness in a specific political context. Then, the evangelical activists' singing and dancing become more about territorializing Christian hegemony and "proper" Koreanness in pursuit of stronger national security, and this process excludes queer Koreans and expresses a pro-American tendency. Ju Hui Judy Han, for example, explains that recent conservative Protestant organizations have conjoined homophobia, Islamophobia, antiterrorism, and anti-immigration to bring the politics of hate to "a new height," to protect national security that is supposedly always vulnerable to communist attacks from North Korea and terrorist attacks from Muslim countries.[13]

Therefore, it was not so much the authenticity as the familiarity of these dances and songs that helped increase the visibility of evangelical activists to the general public. These gestures are meant to both encourage "believers" to stylize their missionary work and to pique interest among "nonbelievers" less aggressively, bringing the general public's attention to the church groups even if it was negative.[14] Many of the performance components must have been already legible, if not familiar, to the general Korean public. These include *buchaechum*, which has been a Korean cultural export on the international stage since the mid-twentieth century; ballet steps appropriating one of the most famous classical ballets; and a percussive performance drawn from an internationally successful Korean show. To follow the *gidok muyong* 기독무용 (Christian dance) performer and right-wing activist Lee Ae-ra's claim, if the objective of performance has always been to "praise him with timbrel and dancing, praise him with the strings and pipe," as Psalm 150:4 states, then evangelical activists achieved this goal by taking up space and dancing movements that are already familiar to even the disinterested, non-Christian public.

This hodgepodge of different elements forms worship dance, *gidok muyong*, or body worship. Their dance, which involves choreographed expressions that articulate the messages of the Bible, forms an undeniable core of their protests and various public appearances, and it is repeatedly presented to symbolize what is presently emerging as right-wing Christian activism. More importantly, however, its relationship with more modest forms of evangelical performances complicates the seeming opposition between "frivolous worshipping" (*gidok muyong* at the protests) and "respectable worshipping" (what the majority of church groups practice).[15]

As Mirzoeff reminds us, visuality often prevents us from looking directly at the often-imperceptible essence of a problem or a power: "that authority to tell us to move on and that exclusive claim to be able to look."[16] In this case, the visual prevalence of body worshippers at the SQCF positions the worshippers against the authority of the broader, more "respectable" Protestant church communities, leading the general public/spectators of their performances to a nearsighted understanding of the larger historical context, in which performance has long played a role in advancing a conservative, Christian nationalist ideology. For example, the media have predominantly circulated photographs of evangelical women dancing *buchaechum*, ballet, and drumming with the backdrop of fluttering waves of *Taegeukgi* 태극기 (the national flag of South Korea). However, a much larger group of middle-class Christians who have distanced themselves from the more dramatic forms of protest continue to have homophobic ideas and to engage in homophobic practices while remaining largely invisible in public discourse. In other words, the public discourse so far about the evangelical performances at the SQCF or Protestant Christianity's approach to LGBTQ politics has misunderstood the uneven nature of Christian groups in South Korea, which nevertheless find commonality with one another through anti-LGBTQ politics.[17] More moderate church groups have also widely occupied the periphery of Seoul Plaza during the SQCF in 2015 and 2016; they similarly denounce LGBTQ organizations and same-sex marriage, handing out brochures and promotional tissue packs or singing folk gospel songs for the general Korean audiences who enjoy acoustic pop music. These groups differentiate themselves from the "frivolous" evangelical activists, yet still share common goals of "protecting" the nation against the increasing heterogeneity among Koreans, which is most strongly evident in the growing presence of the LGBTQ community.[18]

## FROM ANTICOLONIALISM TO OVERSEAS "K-WAVE" MISSION

The evangelical activist performance repertoire, while not authentically Korean, considerably influences the public because they find it familiar and relatable, which may suggest how the nationalist ideology of Koreanness in Christian performance emerged over time. If this is the case, it is necessary to understand the nature of relatability and the universally nationalist claim that evangelical activist performance stakes out. The effort to historicize acts of "worshipping the nation" also reveals a common goal shared by nonevangelical, "respectable" Christians whose reticent homophobia goes largely unnoticed by the media and in public discourse. In the long term, the hypervisuality of evangelical activists' *gidok muyong* prevents people from taking a careful look at and developing a deeper understanding of the historical context in which South Korean churches have long used performance to advance a more conservative, nationalist ideology. It is to an elaboration of the latter point that I now turn.

Regarding the use of performances, Christian Protestant organizations in South Korea have relied on various approaches over time. The odd combination of *buchaechum*, ballet, and drumming performance did not rise out of a vacuum; it is a product of historical changes in South Korea to which Protestant organizations have had to adapt. With the first arrival of American missionaries such as Horace Allen, Horace Underwood, Henry Appenzeller, William B. Scranton, and Scranton's mother Mary Scranton as early as September, 1884, the Korean kingdom of Joseon (1392–1897) began to see the establishment of Christian schools and "modern" medical facilities throughout its capital, Hanseong. Initially in terms of culture, American missionaries did not actively incorporate elements of local culture. As Hyaeweol Choi notes, various kinds of visual and textual accounts suggest that American missionaries were initially critical of local Joseon cultures.[19] Christian culture did not actively endorse dance, or, by extension, the public exhibition of the body; this backward "heathen" culture might have seemed to the first American missionaries to be something to be excised and repealed rather than incorporated and amalgamated.[20] For example, the missionary accounts depicted dances of Korean shamans as serving the needs of Satan, while condemning nonnoble Korean women who exposed their breasts to make breastfeeding in public more convenient. These were based on the Euro-American Victorian moral standard that emphasized the need to "protect" women's "private" bodies.[21]

Nevertheless, the relationship between the American Protestant missionaries and the local individuals who were the target of the religious conversion eventually became much more interactive as the process of Christian Protestantism's localization matured. Joseon's Protestant culture began to create an amalgamation incorporating religious messages, a musical theater style, and elements of Korean folk dance in the early twentieth century. For example, approximately 2,000 Sunday schools practiced performance in the form of *gageuk* 가극 (opera–musical theater) for children and young adults and for fundraising.[22] Because Protestant churches were centers of the independence movement against Japanese colonialism at the time, these performances reflected nationalistic themes such as the restoration and unification of the nation, the elevation of the Korean peninsula, and the preservation of national culture lost to Japanese colonialism. These musical theaters also used folk elements to denote Koreanness that was being deracinated by colonial assimilation. A case in point, Park Young-jeong describes, was the educator Kim Hyun-soon's 1920 musical theater *Yeolsejib* 열세집 (*Thirteen Houses*). The work celebrated the beauty of the Korean peninsula; young participants performed folk dances such as *dansimjulnori* 단심줄놀이 (Maypole dance) under a prop in the shape of the brightly and colorfully lit peninsula.[23] The nationalist theme took on the form of a Christian worship practice, because worship of the nation entailed and worship of God entailed similar gestures; as Park notes, the choreographic specifications in the script required the performers to "kneel halfway down" or "sit and lift two hands, while looking at the sky."[24]

Postcolonial and post–Korean War Korea (1945–) experienced an influx of conservative church leaders in the southern side, who fled the northern side for fear of persecution under the Soviet occupation. Leaders of the conservative and anticommunist Protestant churches sought to collude with then–South Korean president Rhee Syngman (1948–1960) and later Park Chung-hee (1963–1979), whose pro-US and anticommunist campaigns opened many opportunities for conservative Christian leaders.[25] During this period, Christian Protestant organizations engaged in the state campaigns of anticommunism and nationalism. The South Korean state was active in promoting folk and traditional cultures, seeking to restore a precolonial, prewar past as the fulcrum of national identity and solidarity; this was also meant to hamper dissident actions such as progressive protests and democratization movements against its authoritarian regimes.[26] *Buchaechum* was one example of the state's restoration projects: South Korea made *buchaechum* a core dance curriculum in the public education system by recognizing its *minjok muyong* 민족무용 (national dance) status in the post–Korean war period (1955–), and it also exported the dance as a cultural representative of South Korea in US Information Service–sponsored tours and performances in the 1968 Olympics in Mexico.[27] Interestingly, it was progressive church groups that adopted folk and traditional elements such as *daedongnori* 대동놀이 (seasonal village festival) to transform Western-influenced worship practices into more "indigenous" and national ones between the 1970s and 1990s, at a time of reunification, democratization, and the anti-US movement.[28]

Conservative churches did not give equal attention to the renewed importance of folk and traditional dances such as *buchaechum* until overseas missionary work became an important business enterprise for many conservative Korean Protestant churches.[29] The sudden increase in overseas missionary work was due to the lifting of a travel ban for Korean nationals in 1989; thanks to this opportunity and South Korea's continued economic and diplomatic ascendancy, South Korean evangelism gained prominence in many parts of the world. As Han observes in her ethnography of Korean missionaries in African countries, evangelicals all over the world marvel at "miraculous" economic growth and advancement in the capitalist world order, and applaud Korea's transformation from a "mission-receiving" country to the second largest "mission-sending" country in the world."[30] While it is unclear exactly when conservative churches first began actively using folk and traditional elements in their missionary performances abroad, pro-Christian news regularly shows that pastors such as Han Man-young introduced *gugak* 국악 (traditional Korean music) missionaries as members of his overseas missionary team in the mid-1990s, and Christian coalitions sent teams of *taekwondo* 태권도, *nongak* 농악 (folk Korean music that derived from communal rites, involving percussive instruments and a procession of artists and villagers), and *buchaechum* practitioners to Kazakhstan and Israel in 2000 to both proselytize and "disseminate Korean culture."[31] Some have compared this pairing of overseas missionary work with dissemination of Koreanness and Korean culture to *hallyu* 한류, or a Korean cultural wave, an international phenomenon of popularity of Korean cultures.[32]

As this long view of the history suggests, Protestant organizations in South Korea have used various performances with folk and traditional elements ranging from anticolonial folk musical theater to overseas "K-wave" missionary work. South Korean Protestant culture has consistently adopted a nationalistic tendency, strengthened by the influx of conservative right-wing leaders during the authoritarian regimes, which became an important orientation for contemporary evangelism both within and outside South Korea.

## CONTEMPORARY CHURCHES AND LGBTQ IN SOUTH KOREA: QUEER TRADITION, QUEERING TRADITION

As history reveals, Protestant groups and more recent evangelical activists and overseas missionaries have presented nationalist, "traditional" performances, depending on political needs during a given time. Because of the multivalent as well as ambivalent nature of the medium of performance, evangelical activists have adopted it as a strategy to adapt to the changing society experiencing an increasingly visible LGBTQ movement, which itself uses various styles of dance during the SQCF. South Korea has experienced growing ethnic and racial heterogeneity from the influx of migrant workers (see Yuh, this volume) and marriage-migrant women, as well as the increased visibility of dissident voices from feminist organizations and LGBTQ rights activists, especially in politics since the late 1990s. In response, leading evangelical organizations have called for concerted efforts to prevent the spread of homosexuality and what they view as the imminent demise of the nation that no longer coheres into a racially, ethnically, and culturally homogeneous whole. The Esther Prayer Movement, the Movement Center for Evangelizing the Nation, the Korean Association of Sexual Education Counselors "Holy Life," and the Chosen People Network have all appeared alongside the fan-fluttering, ballet-dancing, and drumming performers from the All World Praise and Worship Team at human rights events and progressive protests.

Indeed, the more "reserved" church groups and ministers have distanced themselves from these evangelical activists and their performances, with some pointing to these organizations as the real problem behind the crisis in Protestant churches. According to them, churches need to exhibit a more "respectable" manner that attracts even nonbelievers.[33] Nevertheless, they continue to coexist with evangelical activists, whose repeated performances have reoriented the public's attention to spectacular evangelism, preventing the public from confronting the interiority of a politics of hate within Protestant culture that seeks to "convert" queer subjects in general.[34]

While Protestant churches, regardless of their political orientation, have intensified tension between LGBTQ activists and churchgoers in general, not all churches have decided to place themselves against the LGBTQ movement. For example, Hyangrin Presbyterian Church in Myungdong, a small congregation known for its support for social justice and progressive approach to LGBTQ members, hosted a small fundraising event for the SQCF Organizing Committee in December 2015. The committee had filed an injunction against Lee Yong-hee, the leader of Esther Prayer Movement, and Song Chun-gil, the leader of the anti-LGBTQ Movement Coalition, to restrain them from disturbing the SQCF. These churches against which the committee filed its injunction had also staged sit-ins and gospel performances during the 2014 SQCF held in the Sinchon neighborhood in Seoul, and had literally barricaded the pride floats and marchers with their own bodies. The court ultimately upheld the Esther Prayer Movement members' claim that that their bodies did not actually *touch* the SQCF participants, thereby denying the charge that there was "physical" disruption of the festival. These groups have nonetheless interrupted the SQCF repeatedly over the years through threats performed through gospel or *buchaechum* performances from a distance, preventing the SQCF from fully claiming its queer "democratic public sphere."[35]

Although perhaps unintended, one of the key moments from the 2017 SQCF successfully counteracted the evangelical activists' continued appropriation of public space. Squeezing through a crowd of SQCF parade participants walking together on the main road of central Seoul in the drizzling summer rain, I followed one of the nine floats led by "Femidangdang," a group of queer, feminist women who staged a series of famous choreographies of 1990s' South Korean idol singers. In one of the performances, five women dancers in pale pink bralettes, fishnet crop tops, and black body harnesses reenacted teen idol Lee Jung-hyun's iconic fan dance routine, performed to her 1999 techno-style song, "Wa 와" blasting from the speaker. Chiding the deceitful lover, the singer demanded, "Oh, oh, oh, oh, don't you call me a heartless bitch." At the signal of this famous refrain, the twenty-something crowd around me fluttered their handheld rainbow fans and flags. Singing along with the song, the crowd mimicked Lee Jung-hyun's angular, asymmetrical limb movements, which included unfolding a giant red folding fan on the right hand, coyly covering her face at first only to violently pull the fan away from herself to snarl, "a heartless bitch."

Pleasantly surprised by the queer iteration of the fan dance, myself dancing with the performers and the participants, I took this moment to consider a different kind of energy produced by the rainbow fans, in contrast to the evangelical activists' neon pink fans fluttering at the edges of the SQCF. The collective performance momentarily transmitted the LGBT community's cultural memories carrying over from the 1990s' lesbian bar scene in Seoul into retro dance videos on YouTube, while simultaneously *queering* familiar tropes of nationalist, feminine, and "properly Korean" fan dance.[36] If traditions are indeed invented, as in the case of the anti-LGBT performances, the inventiveness may also allow minoritarian subjects to transmit their own tradition.[37] Here, the queering of fan dance does not reinsert the performing individuals into an existing norm of Koreanness, but rather gestures to a possibility to invert the public's relationship with Korean fan dance altogether.

CONCLUSION

I have discussed evangelical performance in response to the growing LGBTQ presence in South Korea. Evangelical activists use *buchaechum*, ballet, and drumming to display what they deem to be "proper" Koreanness—a racially and ethnically homogeneous quality that excludes queer as well as other minority constituencies, including Muslims and migrant workers. The performance spectacles direct the general public's attention to the evangelical activists' increasing visibility, and at the same time prevent the public from confronting more "respectable" Christians who share a similar homophobic ideology, discouraging careful understanding of the larger history of Protestant culture in South Korea. Historically, Protestant churches' uses of performance have been responses to the changing society that experienced Japanese colonialism, the Korean War, authoritarian regimes, and globalization. Yet the nationalist tendency has remained the same throughout this history.

There is no shortcut to prevent evangelical activists from performing Koreanness through their newfound repertoire of *buchaechum*, ballet, and drumming. Nevertheless, the present moment is also an opportunity to review how performance has engaged in formations of both queer subjectivity *and* conservative Protestant churches' hate culture shaped by the unique South Korean cultural history. It also redirects our attention to a different kind of tradition, one that queers a familiar nationalist repertoire such as that of fan dance and, indeed, ideological performance of Koreanness.

ADDITIONAL RESOURCES

Full resolution version of Figure 15.1 at https://doi.org/10.3998/mpub.11521701.cmp.30

Link 15.1: Seoul Queer Culture Festival Facebook page. Available at https://doi.org/10.3998/mpub.11521701.cmp.92

Link 15.2: Seoul Queer Culture Festival official website. Available at https://doi.org/10.3998/mpub.11521701.cmp.93

Link 15.3: Video of Lee Jung-hyun's musical performance in her song "Wa." Video source: MBCkpop YouTube channel. Available at https://doi.org/10.3998/mpub.11521701.cmp.94

Link 15.4: Video of rightwing evangelical activist organizations' anti-LGBTQ performance at the SQCF, 2016. Video source: Newsnjoy. Available at https://doi.org/10.3998/mpub.11521701.cmp.95

Link 15.5: Video of rightwing evangelical activists performing dance and music at the SQCF 2016. Video source: John B. Kwon. Available at https://doi.org/10.3998/mpub.11521701.cmp.96

## Notes

1. This description is based on a YouTube video of the performance held on June 11, 2016, at the Korea Queer Culture Festival (KQCF, renamed Seoul Queer Culture Festival in 2009) in Seoul Plaza in front of City Hall. Video documented by John B. Kwon, 13 Jun. 2016, 24 Jul. 2016, www.youtube.com/watch?v=p6ZAgMTCVpA

2. I use the words "perform" and "performance" expansively in this article, following performance studies perspectives that seek to understand performance as not just an aesthetic representation on stage but also cultural and identity practices in everyday social settings.

3. For instance, Kang Myeongjin, the SQCF organizing committee chair, points out that although the riot police ultimately serve to keep expanding queer space in check, the festival reluctantly relies on their service to protect its participants from physical threats posed by the anti-LGBTQ church groups. See Kim Han-ju's interview with Kang in "Olhaedo deureonaeja, uri jonjae 'kwieo': Kang Myeongjin kwieomunhwachukje jojikwiwonjang interview" 올해도 드러내자, 우리 존재 '퀴어': 강명진 퀴어문화축제 조직위원장 인터뷰 [We Will Show Our 'Queer' Selves, Yet Again This Year: Interview with Kang Myeongjin, chair of the Queer Culture Festival Organizing Committee], *Workers* 월간워커스, Jul. 7, 2017.

4. Donguk Shin-Yun 신윤동욱, "Geudeureun wae buchaechumeul chueosseulkka" 그들은 왜 부채춤을 추었을까? [Why Did the Christians Perform *Buchaechum*?], *The Hankyoreh* 한겨레, Mar. 24, 2015.

5. Analyzing the long history of queer cultural formations in South Korea and the uses of key terms in queer politics, such as "LGBTQ" or "queer," is beyond the scope of this chapter. It should nevertheless be noted that queer individuals and communities have used both Korean terms and English loan words interchangeably: *iban* (이반 different-type person), *dongseongaeja* (동성애자 homosexual/a person attracted to the same sex), *kwi-eo* (퀴어 queer), *gei* (게이 gay), and *rejeubieon* (레즈비언 lesbian) were used with similar frequency by online users in 1990s LGBTQ online forums. *Iban* in particular was introduced to the online community as an alternative to the word "homosexual," but it denoted a more expansive range of queer desires, identities, and orientations in general. See "Iban," Korean Sexual-Minority Culture and Rights Center, *Glossary of Terms for Sexual Minorities*. See also Todd Henry, ed., *Queer Korea* (Durham: Duke University Press, 2020).

6. See Diana Taylor, *The Archive and the Repertoire: Performing Cultural Memory in the Americas* (Durham: Duke University Press, 2003), 19–21.

7. Ju Hui Judy Han 한주희, "Kwieo jeongchiwa kwieo jijeonghak" 퀴어 정치와 퀴어 지정학 [Queer Politics and Queer Geopolitics], *Munhwagwahak* 문화과학 (2015): 70.

8. Seong-won Kang 강성원, "Bosudanche nanibeuro musandoen seoulsimin ing-wonhyeonjang gongcheonghoe" 보수단체 난입으로 무산된 서울시민 인권현장 공청회 [Seoul Citizen Committee's Public Hearing on Human Rights Declaration Foundered as Conservative Organizations Forced Their Way], *Media Oneul* 미디어오늘, Nov. 20, 2014.

9. "Ripeoteu mi daesa kwaeyu giwone buchaechumkkaji" 리퍼트 美 대사 쾌유 기원에 부채춤까지… [Praying and Fan-Dancing for U.S. Amb. Lippert's Recovery], *Kyunghyang shinmun* 경향신문, Mar. 8, 2015.

10. John Fletcher, *Preaching to Convert: Evangelical Outreach and Performance Activism in a Secular Age* (Ann Arbor: University of Michigan Press, 2013), 3.

11. Since a detailed analysis of *buchaechum* is beyond the scope of this article, I briefly offer descriptions of its origins and characteristics here. Fans appear in folk and traditional Korean performances such as *talchum* 탈춤 (mask dance) and *julgwangdae* 줄광대 (tightrope walking), but *buchaechum* focuses solely on the movement of the fan itself. Choe Seunghee 최승희 (see Kim, this volume) and her protégé Kim Baekbong 김백봉 have disseminated their standardized *buchaechum* choreography since the 1950s, and though the ownership of the fan dance choreography is not clear, Kim Baek-bong is known to have showcased the dance to the general South Korean public for the first time in 1954 at Shigongwan (the present National Theater of Korea) in Seoul (see Ok Jae Yoo 유옥재, "Buchaechumui munhwasajeog uiui" 부채춤의 문화사적 의의 [Cultural-Historical Meanings of Korean Fan Dance], *Daehanmuyonghakhoe* 대한무용학회 [The Korean Journal of Dance] 30 [2001]: 41–50). Accounts in the 1954 news articles note that "a number of dance works that highlight *buchaechum* were unprecedented compared to past dance works [by others] and were a great achievement in our field of dance" (see Dong-hwa Cho 조동화, "Singuinui gyoche gojeonmuyongui yesuljeog seunghwa" 신구인의 교체 고전무용의 예술적 승화 [The New Dancers Replacing the Old, Aesthetic Sublimation of Classical Dance], *Kyunghywang shinmun* 경향신문, Dec. 19, 1954). As a choreographed "repertoire," it became a popular style of *sinmuyong* 신무용 (New Dance) (see Son, this volume).

12. Yumi Heo 허유미, "Nugureul wihan buchaechumieosseulkka" 누구를 위한 부채춤이었을까 [For Whom Was Buchaechum Performed?], *The Hankyoreh* 한겨레, Mar. 16, 2015.

13. Ju Hui Judy Han, "The Politics of Homophobia in South Korea," *East Asia Forum Quarterly* 8, no. 2 (2016): 6–7.

14. Yu Oh Chun 전유오, "Muyongillyuhageul tonghae bon gidokgyo munhwaui bulgyunhyeonggwa muyongyebaeui gachi—muyongillyuhageul tonghae bon gidokgyo munhwaui muyongyebaeui gachi" 무용인류학을 통해 본 기독교 문화의 불균형과 무용예배의 가치—무용인류학을 통해 본 기독교 문화의 무용예배의 가치 I [A Study on Christian Culture and the Value of Christian Dance Service in the Perspective of Dance and Anthropology], *Yesulmunhwanonchong* 예술문화논총 3 (1994): 269–86.

15. Kwon-hyo Ku 구권효, "Pigyeog migug daesa kwaeyu bilmyeo buchaechum, bal-

let, nanta gongyeonhan gidog gyoineun?" 피격 미국 대사 쾌유 빌며 부채춤·발레·난타 공연한 기독 교인은? [Christians Who Performed Buchaechum, Ballet, and Nanta in Wishing the U.S. Amb's Recovery?], *News and Joy* 뉴스앤조이, Mar. 9, 2015.

16. Nicholas Mirzoeff, "The Right to Look," *Critical Inquiry* 37, no. 3 (2011): 474.

17. Shiwoo 시우, "Hyeomo eopsi, hyeomo apeseo, hyeomowa deobureo—hangug LGBT/kwieo sanghwangeul girokaneun noteu" 혐오 없이, 혐오 앞에서, 혐오와 더불어—한국 LGBT/퀴어 상황을 기록하는 노트 [Without Hate, Before Hate, Together With Hate—Notes Documenting the Current Situation of Korean LGBT/Queer Movement], *Munhwagwahak* 문화과학 [Cultural Science] (2015): 288–305.

18. See Yong-in Jeong 정용인, "Hangug gidokgyoneun wae dongseongae bandaee orinhana" 한국 기독교는 왜 '동성애 반대'에 올인하나 [Why Do Korean Christians Exclusively Focus on "Anti-Homosexuality?"], *Kyunghyang shinmun* 경향신문, Jun. 10, 2015; Na Young 나영, "'Ideollogijeong seongjangchi'roseoui hangugui bosu gaesingyowa jeongchijeog gibaneul tonghae bon hyeomoui peuropaganda" 이데올로기적 '성장치'로서의 한국의 보수 개신교와 정치적 기반을 통해 본 혐오의 프로파간다 [Hate Propaganda in the Case of South Korean Conservative Protestantism and Its Political Foundation as "Ideological Sexual Apparatus"], *Glocal Point* 글로컬포인트, Mar. 23, 2015.

19. Hyaeweol Choi, "(En)Gendering a New Nation in Missionary Discourse: An Analysis of W. Arthur Noble's Ewa," *Korea Journal* 46, no.1 (2006): 139–69; Hyaeweol Choi, "The Visual Embodiment of Women in the Korea Mission Field," *Korean Studies* 34 (2010): 90–126.

20. On the relationship between dance and Christianity, see Ann Wagner, *Adversaries of Dance: From the Puritans to the Present* (Urbana-Champaign: University of Illinois Press, 1997).

21. Choi, "The Visual Embodiment," 102–6.

22. Young-jeong Park 박영정, "Cheongubaekisipnyeondae cho juilhakgyo gongyeon repeotori bunseog—gojug gimhyeonsunui adonggageugeul jungsimeuro" 1920년대 초 주일학교 공연 레퍼토리 분석—고죽 김현순의 아동가극을 중심으로 [Analysis of Repertoire Played at Sunday Schools in the Early 1920s: Focusing on Juvenile Music-Dramas by Kim Hyun-soon], *Hanguk munhakgwa yesul* 한국문학과 예술 [The Korean Literature and Arts] 5 (2010): 62–101.

23. Young-jeong Park 박영정, "Gageug yeolsejibe natanan chogi gageugui han yangsang" 가극 <열세 집>에 나타난 초기 가극의 한 양상 [An Aspect of Early Korean Music-drama Presented in Kim Hyunsoon's *Yeolsejib*], *Hangukgeukyesulyeongu* 한국극예술연구 [The Journal of Korean Drama and Theatre] 28 (2008): 82–83.

24. Park, "An Aspect of Early Korean Music-drama," 96.

25. Sangkeun Kim, "Recent Rise of the Korean Missionary Movement: A Sociological Assessment," *Journal of Dharma* 32, no.4 (2007): 379–94. See also, Kai Yin Allison Haga, "Rising to the Occasion: The Role of American Missionaries and Korean Pastors in Resisting Communism throughout the Korean War," in *Religion and the Cold War: A Global Perspective*, ed. Philip Muehlenbeck (Nashville: Vanderbilt University Press,

2012); Vladimir Tikhonov, "South Korea's Christian Military Chaplaincy in the Korean War—Religion as Ideology?" *Asia-Pacific Journal* 11, no. 18 (2013): 1–16.

26. Namhee Lee, *The Making of Minjung: Democracy and the Politics of Representation in South Korea* (Ithaca: Cornell University Press, 2007).

27. Ryeo Sil Kim 김려실, "Daenseu, buchaechum, USIS yeonghwa: munhwanaeng-jeongwa 1950nyeondae USISui munhwagongbo" 댄스, 부채춤, USIS영화: 문화냉전과 1950년대 USIS의 문화공보 [Ballroom Dance, Fan Dance, and USIS Film: The Cultural Cold War and the Cultural Information Activities of USIS Korea in the 1950s], *Hyeondae munhagui yeongu* 현대문학의 연구 [Journal of Korean Modern Literature] 49 (2013): 341–75.

28. In-sik Jeong 정인식, "Urisig yebae mosaeg hwalbal" 우리식 예배 모색 활발 [Churches Active in Finding Our Way], *The Hankyoreh* 한겨레, May. 30, 1993; Sebastian C. H. Kim and Kirsteen Kim. *A History of Korean Christianity* (New York: Cambridge University Press, 2015).

29. Shin-Yun, "Why Did the Christians Perform *Buchaechum*?"

30. Ju Hui Judy Han, "'If You Don't Work, You Don't Eat': Evangelizing Development in Africa," in *New Millennium South Korea: Neoliberal Capitalism and Transnational Movements*, ed. Jesook Song (New York: Routledge, 2011), 148.

31. See Seong-hee Jeong정성희, "Saero sseuneun iryeokseo (5) daehakgyosuseo moksa byeonsin hanmanyeongssi, '[jugeum] apseo han yaksong kkog jikyeoyajyo" 새로 쓰는 이력서 (5) 대학교수서 목사 변신 한만영씨, "[죽음] 앞서 한 약속 꼭 지켜야죠" [Han Man-young, From Professor to Pastor, "I Will Keep My Promise at My Deathbed"], *Dong-a ilbo* 동아일보, Dec. 15, 1995; Mu-jeong Kim 김무정, "Icheonny-eon iseurael daeseonghoe hangug judoro" 2000년 이스라엘 대성회 . . . 한국 주도로 [Christian Gathering in Israel . . . South Korea Leads], *Kookmin ilbo* 국민일보, Sept. 21, 2000; Tae-hyeong Lee 이태형, "Dongseoyang gilmog almati bogeummulgyeol neom-chinda" 동서양 길목 알마티 복음물결 넘친다 [Good News Spreads in Every Corner of Almaty at Crossroad of East and West], *Kookmin ilbo* 국민일보, Jul. 2, 2000.

32. "Nyuyoktaimseu hallyubaegyeongen hangugui budeureoun himt" 뉴욕타임스 ' 한류배경엔 한국의 부드러운 힘' [*New York Times* Says, "Soft Power Behind Hallyu"], *The Hankyoreh*한겨레, Jan. 3, 2006.

33. Seung-hyeon Choi 최승현, "Kwieo chukje bandaehaneun gidokgyoindeul, si-cheong ap yeonhap jipoe" 퀴어 축제 반대하는 기독교인들, 시청 앞 연합 집회 [Anti-SQCF Christians Rally in Front of the City Hall], *News and Joy* 뉴스엔조이, Jun. 9, 2015.

34. Shiwoo, "Without Hate, Before Hate, Together With Hate," 303–4.

35. Han, "The Politics of Homophobia."

36. On performances of East Asian women as the subjects of nationalism, see Chang and Okada, this volume.

37. I am referring to Eric Hobsbawm's "invented tradition." See "Introduction: Inventing Traditions," in *The Invention of Tradition*, ed. Eric Hobsbawm and Terence Ranger (Cambridge: Cambridge University Press, 1983).

# CHAPTER 16

# Choreographing Digital Performance in Twenty-First-Century Taiwan

## *Huang Yi & KUKA*

*Yatin Lin* 林亞婷

On a dark stage with a light shining down from above, a man dressed in a black suit begins to move fluidly to Arvo Pärt's tranquil *tintinnabuli* music. Mechanical sounds can be heard as a bright-orange, crane-like industrial machine starts to move in close unison with Huang Yi 黃翊 (b. 1983), the choreographer, dancer, and coder of the machine KUKA. The machine is designed and produced by Keller und Knappich Augsburg (KUKA), a German company founded in 1898, now with twenty subsidiaries worldwide, including in Taiwan. Eventually, KUKA picks up a green laser torchlight to interact with Huang, using the beam of light to "guide" or "command," initiating Huang Yi's moves. Toward the end of this twenty-minute duet, which is accompanied by Johann Sebastian Bach's partita violin music, Huang dances while seated on an open folding chair, along with KUKA on the other side of the stage, moving in parallel from a stationary base. The audience's impression of this choreographic score is enhanced by a three-layered repetitional structure designed by Huang, in which he first performs the basic movement sequence and then adds lighting or other elements in each round. This section eventually ends with a duet danced in unison with his "digital double." Steve Dixon categorizes the "digital double" into four types: reflection, alter-ego, spiritual emanation, and manipulatable mannequin.[1] Huang Yi's relationship with KUKA shifts from one type to another as the piece progresses.

Huang Yi is a Taiwanese choreographer and dancer known for his innovative works incorporating dance and technology. He rose to fame around 2010, having won first prize in the first and third editions of the annual Digital Art Performance Awards in Taipei for his experimental works *Symphony Project* (*jiaoxiangyue jihua* 交響樂計畫, 2010) and *Huang Yi & KUKA* (*Huang Yi yu KUKA* 黃翊與庫卡, 2012, 2015). *Huang Yi & KUKA* is the focus of this essay. The mechanical robot is simply named after its manufacturer, KUKA, for Huang once said that he resists giving names to his objects for fear of growing personally attached to them.[2] The original twenty-minute prototype version of *Huang Yi & KUKA* consisted of a dance in three parts. In 2015, it was expanded into a seventy-minute full-length version and premiered in New York City's 3-Legged Dog (3LD) Art & Technology Center, followed by performances in China, Taiwan, the United States, Singapore, Australia, the United Arab Emirates, Switzerland, and elsewhere.

In this essay, I analyze *Huang Yi & KUKA* as a case study to discuss the production of dances involving collaboration with technology in the context of twenty-first-century Taiwan. At a macro level, I consider the arts environment in Taiwan, especially recent changes in funding policies by both the government and private sector that have enabled such works to be created. I ask how the growth and development of a younger generation of artists can be mentored and supported, so that they are funded not just during the research and development stage, but also later during promotion for subsequent touring. The local performing arts market alone is too small to support artists, and cultural exports promoting Taiwan's international visibility are often problematic due to the ambiguous nation-state status in relation to China. This could be a reason why ambitious artists do not choose topics relating to local politics, but focus on more universal themes concerning (post)humanism instead.

At the micro level, I analyze the interpretations and reception of *Huang Yi & KUKA*, especially in regard to the relationship between humans and machines. Building on the discourse on digital performance, cyborg theater, or what is also referred to as "new media dramaturgy," including writings by Donna Haraway, Katherine N. Hayles, Jane Bennett, Jennifer Parker-Starbuck, Rosi Braidotti, Peter Eckersall, Edward Scheer, and Yuji Sone, as well as theorists who have discussed the relationship of humans to nonorganic objects and/or machines, including Aneta Stojnic's concept of "digital anthropomorphism," I describe the relationship between humans and nonhuman performers, as well as the reception of audiences viewing these live performances.[3] According to Richard Allen and Shaun May, "anthropomorphism" may be used in connection with something that resembles a human, or "our natural tendency to read human characteristics in the non-human object or animal."[4] French sociologist of technology Bruno Latour insists that "anthropos and morphos together mean either that which has human shape or that which gives shape to humans."[5] In light of these ideas, I pose the following questions: How do we consider such concepts in discussing dance works involving human beings and robots? How do audiences react to such new forms of performance? Are new theories of dance needed for such readings? I offer some observations, suggesting areas for further inquiries into this new emerging field of performing arts.

## DEVELOPING DIGITAL PERFORMANCE IN TAIWAN

Huang Yi's rising career has been assisted by government and private grants he received for investigations into dance and technology. While a variety of terms exist to refer to arts that employ technology in their production—digital art, techart, new media art, and more—the awards he has received have been mainly under the "digital art" realm.[6] Internationally, digital art began with visual and installation art but has since broadened to encompass digital performance, which can be seen as an offshoot or cousin of it. According to Dixon, digital performance broadly includes "all performance works where computer technologies play a key role rather than a subsidiary one in content, techniques, aesthetics, or delivery form."[7]

In Taiwan, digital performance came about in the 1990s, around the same time as the rise of this phenomenon worldwide. In 1992, the Center for Arts and Technology was established at Taipei National University of the Arts. This led to the first Graduate School of Art and Technology in Taiwan, founded ten years later. In 2002, an important turning point arrived with the Taiwan government's release of "Challenge 2008: Important National Development Plans (2002–2007)." Under this guidance, the realm of "Cultural and Creative Industries" was promoted in Taiwan, based on past achievements of local hi-tech companies, with an optimistic outlook in terms of the unlimited possibilities of engaging creative talents in the digital arts.[8] The policy guidelines emphasized the urgency of developing digital art in Taiwan as among the ten most important investment needs.[9] By 2004, according to the White Paper published by the Ministry of Economic Affairs, "cultural and creative industries" were defined as those that "have their origins in innovation or cultural accretion, and which have the potential to create wealth or create jobs through the production and utilization of intellectual property, and which can help to enhance the living environment for society as a whole."[10]

Taiwanese digital artist, curator, and researcher Tseng Yu-chuan 曾鈺涓 pinpoints 2004 as the year digital arts took off in Taiwan.[11] It was then that the National Taiwan Museum of Fine Arts in Taichung launched the "Digital Art Project" and set up the Taiwan Digital Art and Information Center.

Drawing on the concept of Noah's Ark, it was renamed the Digiark—Digital Arts Creativity and Resource Center (Digiark) in 2007, with a focus on developing digital art in Taiwan and promoting international exchange. Also in 2004, a former meat-wholesale market building in Taipei was designated as the future site of the city's Digital Art Center (DAC). Opened to the public in 2009 with funding from the Taipei City Department of Cultural Affairs, the Digital Art Center's main tasks included organizing the annual Digital Art Festival (2006–2016) and the Digital Art Performance Awards (2010–2016).[12] In 2008, Taiwan's then–President Ma Ying-jeou's 馬英九 White Paper on cultural policy was the basis for approval of an annual budget of approximately one million US dollars to fund the Taiwan Performing Arts and Technology Flagship Project, which was launched in 2010 and executed by what is now the Ministry of Culture. This project attracted many individual artists and organizations engaged in digital performance art to apply for fairly generous funding for creation, festival curation, collaboration, and exchange.

Taiwan's successful hi-tech and computer-related private manufacturing industry has also invested in promoting the research and development of the local digital art scene. In 1999, Acer Group's founder Stan Shih 施振榮, a philanthropist and arts patron, established the Acer Digital Art Center. Meanwhile, the Quanta Arts Foundation (廣藝基金會), established in 2010 by Quanta Computer—the largest notebook-computer-manufacturing company in the world—collaborated closely with the Ministry of Culture in nurturing and promoting Taiwan's digital artists. The midsize Quanta Hall, located within its sleek headquarters in Taoyuan County, near Taiwan's international airport, was inaugurated in 2009 as part of the vision of Quanta's founder Barry Lam 林百里, an avid art collector. The Foundation hosted a few editions of the annual Digital Performing Arts Festival from 2011 to 2016, with funding from the Ministry of Culture's Flagship Project. In 2013, the Ministry further introduced the Rainbow Initiative, providing three to ten million New Taiwan dollars (approximately US$100,000 to $330,000) per proposal to fund international or interdisciplinary collaboration, research, and exchange, aimed at promoting the cultures of Taiwan internationally.[13] Inspired by Richard Wagner's concept of total arts, the Quanta Foundation introduced the QA Ring Project in 2014, co-organized with Ars Electronica from Austria, with additional collaborators including Very Mainstream Studio (Taiwan), 3LD (USA), Culture Yard (Denmark), and the Shanghai Conservatory of Music (China). Huang Yi was the only choreographer commissioned for the first year of QA Ring, while Hsieh Chieh-hua's 謝杰樺 Anarchy Dance Theatre was chosen as well in 2015. The choices of topics and aesthetics of the two choreographers are quite different, however.

## BUILDING UP A DIGITAL DANCE REPERTOIRE

It was during his graduate studies at Taipei National University of the Arts that Huang first devised various mechanical-object "partners" for his dance works. For his MFA production of *Spin* (2006–2010), he fixed on a rafter an automated revolving arm (or simply "the mechanical arm" as he anthropomorphically nicknamed it) with an attached camera to smoothly capture and project the moving images of his dancers. *Spin* took four years to develop and captured the attention of various sponsors in its development phase. The National Taiwan Museum of Fine Arts's Digiark Project hosted *Spin* in their high-ceiling museum space in 2008 to test the work's four-sided projection requirements. The Digiark Project also funded the tour of *Spin* to the Festival *bains numerique*, organized by the Centre des Arts at Enghien-les-Bains in France, an event at which Taiwanese scholars such as performance theorist Gong Jow-jiun 龔卓軍 participated in discussion panels with artists.

It would be misleading to think of Huang Yi as a choreographer who only creates dances using technology. In 2011, when the US's *Dance Magazine* listed Huang Yi as one of the top "25 to Watch," nominator Sheu Fang-yi 許芳宜—an internationally acclaimed dancer from Taiwan—emphasized, "[Huang] knows that technology is but a tool, and dancing is expressed through the body, so how to present the performance quality of each dance composition is something he continues to work on." Huang Yi constantly challenges himself and his collaborators with new possibilities for dance. Other than commissions from Cloud Gate 2 between 2008 and 2014 for their annual "Spring Riot" program, which largely features new works by emerging choreographers, Huang works on independent projects involving technology. Among his collaborators has been Yang Yu-teh 楊妤德, a freelance costume designer who has produced innovative costumes as installations or works of art, with dancers moving on stage dressed in these interactive costumes. In the 1970s and 1980s, garment export, mostly manufactured for international brands abroad, contributed to the "economic miracle" of Taiwan. With the twenty-first century emphasis on cultural and creative industries, research and development in this sector has been encouraged to emphasize the invention of innovative fabrics and the creation of local brand names to increase the value and profit of local designers and industries.

Huang and Yang collaborated on *Second Skin* (2010, 2011), a two-year project made possible by the grant from the Taiwan Performing Arts and Technology Flagship Project. Huang also invited Vietnamese-French composer Tôn-Thất An 尊室安 and XOR—a group of new media artists consisting of alumni from the Arts and Technology Graduate Program of Tapei National University of the Arts—to engage in a series of short experimental pieces showcasing different costumes for dancing bodies on stage. In one scene, a male dancer appears wearing a costume with airbags hidden in the seams. Once filled with air, the airbags balloon up to protrude from various areas of the body, appearing like tumors or exaggerated joints, thus changing the shape and function of the natural human body. I view this as a cyborg-like strategy, changing the natural operations of a material body.

A year later, in 2012, Huang Yi searched for a machine as his dancing partner. He approached a local branch of the industrial robot manufacturer KUKA, and after multiple attempts to gain approval, was finally granted permission to rent one for his performance. He learned how to program and code the robot, then observed its range of movements before eventually choreographing the twenty-minute prototype duet *Huang Yi & KUKA*. Apart from winning the top prize at the Third Annual Digital Art Performance Award, it was also nominated among the ten finalists for the 11th (2012) Taishin Arts Award (台新藝術獎) given to Taiwan's outstanding new works in the performing and visual arts. Sponsored by the Taishin Bank Foundation for Arts and Culture, this award is the most prestigious recognition given by the private sector in Taiwan.

Around this time, similar experiments were carried out in other parts of the world involving dance and robots. One such artist is Thomas Freundlich from Finland, who also has a background in dance. Like Huang Yi, Freundlich not only choreographs and performs in dance pieces involving industrial robots, he programs and codes them as well.[14] When I shared a video clip of Freundlich's dance "Human Interface" (2012) with Huang Yi in 2013, Huang responded somewhat proudly that the design of the KUKA robots he chose was based on human musculature and thus resembled human beings more closely than the Swedish ABB robots used by Freundlich.[15] Huang's comment resonates with the preference in Japan for robots resembling humans as in humanoids, or even "actroids," as used by Japanese director Hirata Oriza 平田オリザ (b. 1962) in his robot theater.[16]

## EXPERIMENTING WITH A DUET BETWEEN MAN AND MACHINE

With Huang Yi's newfound fame, the Quanta Arts Foundation purchased a KUKA robot so that his work could be further developed. In 2013, Huang Yi took up residency in New York as an Asian Cultural Council grantee and made initial contact with the 3LD Art and Technology Center there. As a commissioned artist of the QA Ring Project, Huang worked with Kevin Cunningham, the executive artistic director of 3LD. Huang Yi used the space and facilities to explore and expand his artistic vision. With stimulus from his dancers' experiences while residing in New York, he further developed the new seventy-minute full-length version, which includes two additional dancers, premiering it in February 2015 at 3LD.

Throughout this dance between a human being and an industrial robot, they seem to perform identically. The twenty-minute prototype version of *Huang Yi & KUKA* starts in darkness, with Pärt's *Für Alina* piano music introducing an introspective mood. This slow and meditative composition from 1976 is representative of Pärt's well-known *tintinnabuli* style. Pärt explained: "Tintinabuli is an area I sometimes wander into when I am searching for answers—in my life, my music, my work . . . In my dark hours, I have the certain feeling that everything outside this one thing has no meaning. What is this one thing, and how do I find my way to it? Traces of this perfect thing appear in many guises—and everything that is unimportant falls away."[17]

This search for tranquility and clarity in one's moment of darkness resonates with Huang Yi's quiet personality; he often refers to the solitude of his childhood and his dream of having a robot as a companion.[18] Thus, in this opening, Huang Yi seems to be projecting himself onto KUKA as an alter ego. However, other viewpoints are also possible. Taiwanese digital art critic Chiu Chih-yung 邱誌勇, for example, perceived the relationship between Huang Yi and KUKA here as a "split subject."[19]

Gradually, a light from above shines down on Huang Yi, who is lying on the stage right floor dressed in a dark suit and dark shirt. When he sits up, with hands over his bent knees, a beam from a flashlight shines from stage left, with the stationary crane-like robot KUKA echoing the movement of Huang Yi's head, in sync. Only after a second top light shines downstage left is the bright orange KUKA made visible to the audience. With the flashlight as if in its mouth, KUKA can be seen imitating the movement of Huang's head, while at times this Pixar-like robot seems to imitate Huang's arm movements as well.

The anthropomorphic KUKA continues to "observe" its human partner with curiosity. When Huang walks over to take the flashlight away, the robot reacts defensively, returning to its stationary base. Huang then shines the flashlight at his partner, which lowers its head as if shying away. During a moment of transition, KUKA regains the flashlight and shines it back at Huang, who raises his hands up and lowers his head in surrender. KUKA puts

Fig, 16.1. *Huang Yi & KUKA*, 2015, New York City. Original duet prototype section performed by Huang Yi and KUKA. Photo by Jacob Blickenstaff courtesy Sozo Artists.

the flashlight back into its home base in front of itself. In the following few minutes, the two slowly turn their heads in unison, checking each other out and exchanging gazes, before trust between them is established. This mutual trust is enhanced by the two circles of light merging into one, as Huang again approaches KUKA in a friendly gesture, gently laying his finger on the robot for the first time, after its initial retreat. All fears aside, Huang fully gives his weight to KUKA and relies on it for acts of balance—such as leaning over the robot and lifting his leg, followed by a turn of his body. Even when not in contact, they are one at heart, performing a breakdance-like sequence together as their heads lead them from a sideways spinal curve to a sagittal snakelike dance, with pirouettes and all. As Pärt's ten-minute music piece comes to an end, Huang lies down on the floor while KUKA shines its light over him, as if showing a sense of curiosity and concern. The robot then switches to pick up a green laser beam, as the action transitions into the second part of the duet.

The green laser beam acts as an invisible thread manipulating and conducting Huang Yi somewhat like a puppet. The preprogrammed KUKA appears to move according to its own subjectivity. With sharp and sudden changes in levels and directions, this fast-paced section picks up momentum.

With no accompanying music, the mechanical sounds of KUKA's swirls, rises, and drops can be clearly heard. About two-thirds of the way into this duet, KUKA pulls out a folded chair from underneath its base and pushes it toward Huang Yi, who opens it up and sits himself down. A three-minute excerpt from Bach's "Violin Partita No. 1 in B minor" performed by Jascha Heifetz launches an exquisite solo by Huang Yi. The dance is clear and precise; it starts by only involving his upper body, with movements mainly from his arms, fingers, and head. At times free flowing, and at times bound and mechanical, Huang Yi choreographed this part in close association with the music. Eventually, it develops into a sequence involving the whole body, ending when Huang Yi gets up from the chair, swirls it around, and sits back down.

The whole sequence is then repeated, but without music. Although only Huang Yi is in the light, KUKA can still be faintly seen in the dark, its mechanical sounds coming through the dim light, as we hear the robot moving in sync with the human dancer. The third time around, the music is brought back and the lights shine on both Huang Yi and KUKA, allowing the audience to clearly see them performing the sequence together in perfect unison. Some of the lifting, turning, twisting, and banging are familiar moves robots are programmed to perform in factory assignments. In comparison, Huang Yi's agile limbs and flexible movement highlight the freedom of the human body in movement, in contrast to the robotic mechanics of the machine. When Huang Yi returns the folded chair, KUKA carefully picks it up and sways it back before it lands. Huang then catches the chair before it hits the ground, timed perfectly as the lights go off, ending this twenty-minute duet. Similar to the proposition of director Hirata for a "total intimacy between machine and human with both becoming actor-entities that, in performance, have identical qualities," Huang Yi's goal is also to minimize the difference between the human performer and the robot machine on stage, even to the extent of ascribing subjectivity to this material object.[20]

DANCING THE DIGITAL DOUBLE

Huang Yi once said, "Dancing face to face with a KUKA robot is like looking at my face in a mirror. I make KUKA mimic my movements, and I learn from him, I make myself dance like a machine."[21] What is the nature of the relationship between the human choreographer/dancer and his nonhuman partner KUKA? How do audiences perceive such new forms of digital performance? Is kinesthetic empathy possible with nonhuman performers? In my previous description, I empathized with KUKA's anthropomorphic emotion through the projected narrative of this choreographed duet. But what new tools are needed to analyze digital performance as we enter what scholars such as Hayles term the "posthuman" age?[22] Performance studies scholar Scheer borrows from Bennet's notion of "vibrant materialism" in his study on new media dramaturgy, proposing a subject's or an object's performative potential.[23] Therefore, whether KUKA can be considered a "protosubject," "potential subjects, subjects about to be born, but not fully actualized in the world," or a "hyperobject," "a class of objects that exceed the usual parameter of objecthood," may lead to different ways of understanding this piece.[24]

In the 2015 full-length version of *Huang Yi & KUKA*, Huang Yi further complicates the robot's relationship with humans by adding two more dancers. In the first of several new scenes created for the extended version, following the previously described twenty-minute prototype, a metronome is placed on the floor between Huang Yi and KUKA. Huang Yi starts to sway side to side in relation to the movement and tempo of the metronome, with KUKA joining in as well. The ticking away of this rhythmic device is clearly decipherable as a symbol of the passing of time. This, and the inevitable passing away of human beings, is further made clear when Huang crouches and leans on KUKA for support, before gradually stumbling away like an elderly man, disappearing off stage and literally out of the picture. KUKA, as a nonorganic being, continues to sway with the metronome's beats and is not affected by death. When the metronome stops, KUKA tries to innocently restart it, but is incapable of doing so. As the lights dim, the audience should be able to relate to the somber narrative about the fates of a human and a robot, whose relationship has to end due to the former's inevitable mortality.

A second new scene includes a camera affixed to KUKA, with images, shot from the camera in real time, projected onto a screen at the back of the stage. Interpreted anthropomorphically, it seems as if KUKA has been given sight and can now "see" Huang Yi and him/herself. Ironically, a close-up shot of an illustrated sign on KUKA warning against contact with any human, for fear of danger from possible mechanical error, reveals Huang Yi's dark humor. The following series of dance phrases is another example of Huang Yi's characteristic layered choreographic strategy. First, the camera shows a rectangle of light on the stage with no dancers, as KUKA films from different angles, switching abruptly at varying speeds. Later, two dancers (Hu Chien 胡鑑 and Lin Jou-wen 林柔雯) perform fluid, graceful phrases in the lighted rectangular space while being filmed by KUKA. The peculiar angle of the shots creates the illusion that the dancers are close to the edge of a cliff, or off-balance and falling.

In contrast to the loud horns and industrial sounds by contemporary American composer David Lang that accompany the camera segment, a third new scene of another intimate duet with KUKA is danced to classical cello music by Bach. Huang holds on to KUKA for support as he swivels and turns with his new ballroom dance partner. This is reminiscent of Huang Yi's choreography for Cloud Gate 2 titled *Light* (光, 2013), a short, virtuosic work also performed by Lin, Hu, and Huang, based on quick tango moves for couples, inspired by memories of watching his parents perform and teach ballroom dancing in their home studio.

In the final scene Hu and Lin return, the latter in a white-lace dress reminiscent of Victorian times. As they sit on open folding chairs placed at each downstage corner, KUKA picks up a device that sends a red laser beam cutting across the space, as if separating the typical heterosexual couple sitting in a living room. Hearing Mozart's *Piano Concerto No. 23 in A Major (K488)*, I immediately thought of Czech choreographer Jiří Kylián's famous contemporary ballet *Petit Mort*, choreographed to the same music, which also inspired Huang Yi. However, the rigid, staccato, and somewhat robotic moves of Hu and Lin are a great juxtaposition to the graceful and fluid duets of Kylián's work. KUKA's red laser functions as an invisible string that manipulates the two mortals to move one joint at a time. They eventually come into a close embrace with each other. In an interesting twist to the opening of the work where KUKA seems to follow Huang Yi's lead, now KUKA is in charge; the puppet has become the puppeteer.

This dance raises many questions. Is Huang Yi proposing a pessimistic view of the future—a "posthuman" world in which humans and robots coexist, but in a very changed relationship? In this new world, will humans lose their embodied subjectivity? Can human consciousness be downloaded onto a computer and recreated in a robot, as imagined by science fiction writers and pondered upon by posthuman scholars such as Hayles?[25] These are questions worth investigating as we enter the age of digital performance, where live dancers may no longer need to be physically present on stage and can be represented virtually. Nevertheless, I do not think this is the direction Huang Yi is aiming toward.

Critics around the world have reacted differently as *Huang Yi & KUKA* toured across Asia, North America, Australia, and Europe since 2015. *New York Times* dance critic Gia Kourlas commends Huang Yi for his poetic *pas de deux* and hard work programming the crane-like companion, acknowledging how much time he invested, especially during the early development stages (approximately ten hours of coding labor for each minute of choreography).[26] However, in comparison to the fluid and virtuosic choreographies

Fig. 16.2. *Huang Yi & KUKA*, 2015, New York City. Expanded trio full-length version, with two additional dancers Hu Chien and Lin Jou-wen. Photo by Jacob Blickenstaff courtesy Sozo Artists.

Huang has created for live dancers (including himself) in nondigital perfor-mances, the range of movement in this piece is quite limited. After all, KUKA is permanently affixed to its base and can only move its upper crane part, which sometimes functions as a head and sometimes as an arm—somewhat frustrating for contemporary dance audiences with an appetite for quick, complex movements across space. Furthermore, Huang Yi's choreographic layering strategy—adding new elements to repeated dance phrases, which he described as analogous to Photoshop editing techniques—demands patience, stamina, and focus from his audiences.[27] Last but not least, his insistence on minimalist dark lighting throughout (using only two lights from the top as well as the flashlight and laser beam as props) does not help to brighten up the atmosphere of the performances, either.

## THINKING LIKE A MACHINE

Some of these critics may speak for audiences who felt the expanded version of *Huang Yi & KUKA* was a little difficult to appreciate—after all, the transition sections in which the stagehands (actually the dancers themselves) had to come on stage and affix the camera to KUKA took quite a while, and thus broke the momentum of the performance. Huang Yi always had a deep fascination with machines and object-figures as "partners," as in works such as *Objects* (2015, 2018, 2019). His demand for precision in his choreography and execution of movement is perhaps reason enough for his fans to admire his determination and achievement in this field.[28] Huang Yi does not treat nonhuman objects around him as lifeless; he thinks of them as having souls with feelings; he says that using light beams and a camera as extensions or props is like giving KUKA human eyes to see and hands to touch.[29] Given this, perhaps it is no surprise that his digital works with objects—be they mechanical violins, automated dance costumes, or industrial robots—come across as anthropomorphic while at the same time highlighting their materiality. *Taipei Times* dance critic Diane Baker wrote in her review of *Huang Yi & KUKA*, "Saturday night's show demonstrated how Huang has managed to blur the boundaries between magic and technology, human and non-human, as I found myself anthropomorphizing the robot in my notes, with references to its gracefulness, tenderness, playfulness, and inquisitiveness."[30]

Huang Yi likens his task as a choreographer to an operating system in a computer that coordinates the various software applications running.[31] In other words, as a producer, director, choreographer, programmer, videographer, and dancer, he needs to be adept in the various fields of knowledge of his collaborators, be they stage design, lighting design, costume design, music, and most importantly, movement. Bernadette Loacker argues, "Artist entrepreneurs must balance creation and performance of their art with increasing amount of time spent on branding, compliance, fundraising, and the logistical and commercial requirements of operating in a creative industry paradigm."[32] In short, they are expected to become "culturpreneurs." Huang Yi is a prime example of this new model for artists, demonstrating how they need to manage their careers to survive and succeed internationally.

Although Huang was fortunate to sign with Sozo Artists agency in New York in 2014 to handle his international performances, he and his team still have to manage local engagements in Taiwan and China. Huang Yi works late into the night to research, refine, solve technical details, and write his choreographic notes; he constantly shares the challenges and dilemmas he faces on his blog and at free lectures (as part of his National Theatre artist-in-residence obligations, for example). Such use of free social media was an important means of gaining exposure and fundraising at the start of his independent career. He also regularly updates his fans and supporters via his

Facebook page. He is a leader of the new breed of tech-savvy young artists who have learned to brand and promote themselves, posting excerpts of their works on the internet to gain wider visibility.

As a digital performance artist representing the dot-com generation, Huang Yi is perhaps representative of many of his generation who find themselves more at ease relating to a computer than to other human beings. He creates works based on his broad interests, drawing on his talents in fine arts, dance, photography, videography, and computer and stage technology to map out his own dance-scape. He attracts people across disciplines who are willing to engage in his performances with a new corporeal awareness as sensorially immersed audiences, setting a new model for digital performance in the twenty-first century.

### ADDITIONAL RESOURCES

Full resolution versions of Figure 16.1 at https://doi.org/10.3998/ mpub.11521701.cmp.31 and Figure16.2 at https://doi.org/10.3998/ mpub.11521701.cmp.32

Link 16.1: *Huang Yi and KUKA* Trailer, 2015. Available at https://doi. org/10.3998/mpub.11521701.cmp.97

Link 16.2: *Huang Yi and KUKA* TED Video, 2017. Available at https://doi. org/10.3998/mpub.11521701.cmp.98

### *Notes*

1. Steve Dixon, *Digital Performance: A History of New Media in Theater, Dance, Performance Art, and Installation* (Cambridge, MA: MIT Press, 2007), 241, 244.

2. Huang Yi, "*Huang Yi & KUKA*: Post-performance talk," Cloud Gate Theatre, Tamsui, New Taipei City, June 26 & 27, 2015.

3. See Donna Jeanne Haraway, "A Cyborg Manifesto: Science, Technology, and Socialist-Feminism in the Late Twentieth Century," in *Simians, Cyborgs and Women: The Reinvention of Nature* (New York: Routledge, 1991), 149–81; N. Katherine Hayles, *How We Became Posthuman: Virtual Bodies in Cybernetics, Literature, and Informatics* (Chicago: University of Chicago Press, 1999); Jane Bennett, *Vibrant Matter: A Political Ecology of Things* (Durham: Duke University Press, 2010); Jennifer Parker-Starbuck, *Cyborg Theatre: Corporeal/Technological Intersections in Multimedia Performance* (New York: Palgrave Macmillan, 2011); Rosi Braidotti, *The Posthuman* (Cambridge, UK: Polity Press: 2013); Peter Eckersall, "Towards a Dramaturgy of Robots and

Object-Figures," *TDR: The Drama Review* 59, no. 3 (T227) (Fall 2015): 123–31; Edward Scheer, "Robotics as New Media Dramaturgy," *TDR: The Drama Review* 59, no. 3 (T227) (Fall 2015): 140–49; Yuji Sone, *Japanese Robot Culture: Performance, Imagination, and Modernity* (New York: Palgrave McMillan, 2017); and Aneta Stojnic, "Digital Anthropomorphism: Performers Avatars and Chat-Bots," *Performance Research* 20, no. 2 (2015) : 70–77.

4. Richard Allen and Shaun May, "Encountering Anthropomorphism," *Performance Research* 20, no. 2 (2015): 1–3.

5. Bruno Latour, "Where Are the Missing Masses? The Sociology of a Few Mundane Artifacts," in *Shaping Technology/Building Society: Studies in Sociotechnical Change*, eds. Wiebe E. Bijiker and John Law (1992), 225–59; later revised and expanded in *Technology and Society: Building Our Sociotechnical Future*, eds. Deborah J. Johnson and Jameson M. Wetmore (Cambridge, MA: MIT Press, 2008), 151–80, 160.

6. Huang Chien-hung 黃建宏, "Preface," in *Re-TechArt: History of the Department of New Media, Taipei National University of the Arts* (Taipei, Taiwan: TNUA, 2014).

7. Dixon, *Digital Performance*, 3.

8. Executive Yuan, Taiwan, Republic of China, "Challenge 2008: Six-Year National Development Plan (2002–2007)," 2002.

9. Ibid.

10. Ministry of Economic Affairs, Taiwan, Republic of China, "White Paper on Small and Medium Enterprises (SMEs) in Taiwan, 2004" (2004), 162.

11. National Taiwan Arts Education Center 國立台灣藝術教育館, "A Timeline for the Development of Digital Art in Taiwan," http://web.arte.gov.tw/digital_teacher/art/current/p03.html, accessed July 30, 2015.

12. Founded in 2008, the Digital Art Foundation (under chief executive officer Huang Wen-hao 黃文浩) operated the Digital Art Center in Taipei since its opening in 2009 until 2017. The Foundation recently established its own DAC.TW as of August 2018. The previous municipal DAC Taipei is being run by the Association of Visual Arts in Taiwan (AVAT). See Chang Yu-yin's 張玉音 interview with Huang Wen-hao in *ARTouch*, Oct. 13, 2018. https://artouch.com/people/content-12.html

13. Ministry of Culture, Taiwan 2015, "Rainbow Initiative" website: https://english. moc.gov.tw/article/index.php?sn=825, accessed July 30, 2015.

14. Thanks to Hanna Järvinen for this reference.

15. Huang Yi, Electronic correspondence, February 4, 2013.

16. Actroids are the brainchild of Hirata's Robot Theatre collaborator Ishiguro Hiroshi, founder of the Intelligent Robotics Laboratory in Osaka, Japan. See Eckersall, "Towards a Dramaturgy of Robots and Object-Figures," 128.

17. Arvo Pärt, http://www.arvopart.org/tintinnabulation.html, accessed April 12, 2015.

18. Huang Yi, "Technology Is My Playmate, a Friend Accompanying Me Growing up," Taishin Arts Foundation webpage on Huang Yi & KUKA—http://www. taishinart.org.tw/english/2_taishinarts_award/2_2_top_detail.php?MID=

1&ID=&AID=17&AKID=46&PeID=167, 2013, accessed July 30, 2015; and *Huang Yi & KUKA: Rehearsal Notes* (Taipei, Taiwan: Huang Yi Studio+, 2015).

19. Chiu Chih-yung 邱誌勇, "*Huang Yi & KUKA*: Dancing a Beautiful Chapter of Human-Robot Co-Existence," in "FlyGlobal—Discover Digital Performing Arts in Taiwan" website, http://www.flyglobal.tw/zh/article-300, May 18, 2015, accessed July 30, 2015.

20. Eckersall, "Towards a Dramaturgy of Robots," 130.

21. Huang Yi, "Ars Electronica 2013 Total Recall" website, http:// www.aec.at/total-recall/en/2013/07/29/huang-yi-kuka/, 2013, accessed July 30, 2015.

22. Hayles, *How We Became Posthuman.*

23. Scheer, "Robotics as New Media Dramaturgy," 140.

24. Ibid., 145.

25. Hayles, *How We Became Posthuman.*

26. Gia Kourlas, "A Pas de Deux between Human and Machine," *New York Times,* February 12, 2015.

27. Huang Yi, "*Huang Yi & KUKA*: Post-performance talk," 2015.

28. Tsou Shin-ning 鄒欣寧, "*Huangyi: jingzhun zhi biyao* [The Necessity of Precision]" published online, "FlyGlobal—Discover Digital Performing Arts in Taiwan"—National Culture and Arts Foundation website: http://www.flyglobal.tw/zh/article-304, May 19, 2015, accessed July 30, 2015.

29. Hao Yong-hui 郝永慧, "《《黃翊與庫卡》:不只是人機共舞》 *Huang Yi & KUKA*: Not Just a Duet between Human and Robot" 文藝生活週刊 *Wenyi Shenghuo Zhoukan* [*Arts and Life Weekly*] http://zhoukan.cc/2015/05/11/huang-yi-and-the-library-card-not-just-people-dancing-machine/, May 11, 2015, accessed July 30, 2015.

30. Diane Baker, "The Meaning of Being Human," *Taipei Times,* July 1, 2015.

31. Huang Yi, "Artist-in-residence public talk," National Theatre, Taipei, Taiwan, November 13, 2014.

32. Bernadette Loacker, "Becoming 'Culturpreneur': How the 'Neoliberal Regime of Truth' Affects and Redefines Artistic Subject Positions," *Culture and Organization* 19, no. 2 (2012): 8.

# Coda

## To Dance East Asia

*Katherine Mezur*

In a dance class, when a slight skim of moist warmth spreads across my skin and through my muscles and joints, I begin to sense differently. The borders of my skin between my "self" and other dancers become porous and open. I meet with the other bodies and their breath, warmth, and moisture. We move together and separately, tuning slowly to each, other body. This is the beginning of the practice of practicing movement to achieve specific technical aesthetic goals in dance.

This coda is a pause, a transition, to affirm the intertwining differences of theories and practices within this collection of performance studies that connects dance studies and Asian studies. Decolonizing dance studies is a difficult process that this collection struggles with as part of our ongoing and unfinished agenda of continuing to challenge our practices, theories, and histories. Each chapter reveals the power of movement to express, control, and question. In this set of performance studies focusing on movement, we illuminate radical variations across cultures, contextualized in their temporality and geography. The coda acknowledges how much more there is to mine and deploy in an expanding context of live and virtual performance, where performers and their movement practices drive new provocations concerning their corporeal politics. In particular, it is the impact of performers' performance practices and their individual passions and perseverance that resonates across these diverse studies. This focus on practice is also an homage to the performers, teachers, and choreographers who devoted their daily lives and bodies to the labor of performance making.

Every moment we dance at the barre, in center, or across the floor, each person scans their body inside and outside to measure where there is weakness or inadequacy in line, form, and/or movement execution. We all know that the most efficient execution of the perfect prescribed form, with the aura of ease or grace, is the highest level of performance technique. We separate from each other as each person measures, adjusts, and breaks "bad" habits of body/mind synapses to slightly approximate the ideal. We practice the practice of self-surveillance and then reform and repeat the sequences over and over, again and again. We drive our bodies, separately and together, through exhaustion to incomplete desire. Practice in our collection of essays is a major force for opening up an embodied historiography of performance in East Asia.

Every chapter in this book moves across conflicting historiographies, genealogies, and technologies of dance and dancers. Many of our chapters emphasize individual dancers and dances embedded in specific circumstances, which challenged the artists to negotiate and sometimes change their artistic visions according to the political conditions of their times. Some chapters are rooted in one performance, where the details of the performance, its forms, images, and narratives, reflect and act on certain political conditions. Other chapters deal with larger theories that move across time and place, linking performers and their performances with the questions and issues that seem to continually re-emerge, still needing our attention.

Performers have traveled across geographies of place and time and many borders. They were often caught up in the process of radical changes in nation formations, social revolutions, and violent wars. What drove these artists to keep creating and performing? How did the events and economies of their times impact their artistic values? These essays examine these very moments of performance and events, when the artists' commitment empowered their creative practices. Our collection suggests that the power of movement can re-envision events, consciousness, ideologies, and beliefs with bodily actions. Our diverse corporeal politics claim stakes in decolonizing any set notions of movement, dance, and choreographic practices.

What stands out across our different approaches is *movement* and its powerful potential for deployment by artists, as agents of power, even when operating under adverse social and political systems. Our focus on movement connects to performance studies of historiography, where the shift of powers, especially in times of war and other aggressive actions, changes everyone and everything under those circumstances. Within this focus on movement, our book offers several frames with which to consider the power of movement. One of these frames is movement training, which aims to achieve certain performance goals when coupled with the discipline, focus, and technical practices of a given dance form. These goals of movement training are varied and complex, as exemplified across our chapters. The perspective of movement training has been carefully studied through somatics and other modes of body/mind theories and practices in dance and performance studies. Michel Foucault and Frantz Fanon, among others, are frequently cited for their visionary and devastating insights into the corporeal politics of human violence, colonization, segregation, incarceration, and racism.[1] However, our collection offers other perspectives on corporeal politics through embodied training and performance, which open up different views on the agency and impact of performing bodies. I suggest that these views involve deep, disciplined training that calls on an unconditional physical and mental devotion through a regimented movement training process in specialized techniques that produces specific performance forms. It is this combination of personal commitment and disciplined embodiment by performers, which threads through our chapters and demonstrates how movement practices ignite and drive aesthetic, social, and political change.

In one sense, these disciplined, exacting physical practices, which are fundamental to our collection of performance studies, are "militarized" practices. "Militarized" and "militarization" are broad concepts that may be reduced to actions by an authority to coerce a population into preparation for war or other military actions. However, to gain insight into the movement cultures of this collection, these terms and practices may clarify the ardent dedication of the performers to their art form in these studies. Brady and Mantoan demonstrate how culture-based customs deploy militarized practices, not just governments or military regimes. Their collection foregrounds the *process* of militarization within performing arts practices, which connects the performance processes here to their argument of how "Militarization is then inherently linked to performance. It is an iterative process; we are not born militarized, but through performances we repeat daily, we *become* militarized through a slow process."[2]

As essays in this volume demonstrate, performers, instructors, directors, and the performances themselves become "militarized" through disciplinary processes that repeat actions over time and which shape and tune their bodies and attitudes  to work within specific forms of physical stylization. Performance training is pivotal to understanding how the militarization of dances and dancers works. Their exacting labor conditions their bodies and attitudes to an extreme degree, which subsequently moves their spectators. Further, the designs of performance, that is, the choreographic forms that create the architecture or structure for the movement of bodies in time and space, are made up of sequences of actions to achieve a goal, such as a narrative, an abstract image or design, or sometimes the disorder of the dance makers. These forms, which may draw on established, diverse culture based modes such as unison, canon, ground base, accumulation, ritual, folk or indigenous forms, and/or avant-garde non-methods, are also invested with their politics. Drive, focus, technical skills, discipline, and structures meet in the making of meaning with movement by performers of disciplined practices. Corporeal politics foregrounds how the power of performers and their performance practices are directly involved with their cultural moment, with the caveat that the artists may or may not have been freely complicit with those in power.

Here, I apply the term "militarized" to disciplined training and performance where there is an established set of physical actions, which require specific skills to execute those actions to that set standard. I suggest that the heightened sense of focus achieved in military training practices by military personnel correlates with a performer's drive and concentration in performance and training. The purpose of this militarized performance practice is not warfare, but performers do share this personal drive to "win" through perfecting performance skills. This kind of strict, disciplined technical training is deeply ingrained in performers, and their "militarized" performance energy and focus are contagious: spectators respond viscerally to the performers' absolute driving concentration, which produces and communicates intense expressivity.

Another important aspect of this disciplined practice by individual artists is the potential for collective action because of their shared effort and devotion to these disciplined practices. All of these points, the repeated practicing of skills, the driving concentration, and the collective power of performers and production, suggest how heads of state, whether socialist, democratic, or fascist, have found that dance and other performing arts are the perfect vehicles for convincing people, even diverse populations, to comply with or join their system of thought or governance. I also argue that gaining these regimented skills opens and liberates the bodies of the performers, and allows them to access a greater variety and range of physical and expressive skills and practices. Spectators may also kinesthetically experience these expressively open and freeing aspects of disciplined practices communicated through the performers.

I would like to engage "militarized" in a complex way that might reveal the open and positive side of this kind of training and performance as well. In many of our chapters, those in power deploy this charismatic power of performers with this devotion to skill perfection to serve their causes. The artists become part of a militarized culture, even without endorsing that culture. I am not arguing that all performers or performances in this volume map onto this framework of militarized, disciplined training and performance, but I think it offers a particular point of view that reminds us to decolonize our normalized mode of thinking and performing that privileges individuality, free form creativity, and experimentation. This frame of disciplined performance skills suggests another aspect of performance practice and theory that could enrich our encounters with the complexities of corporeal politics in transcultural studies, where body stakes and meanings are often messy and convoluted due to layers of voluntary and involuntary assimilation of dominant and/or colonizing cultural practices.

These disciplined corporeal acts can also decolonize our "self"centered subjectivity, which bell hooks suggests can revolutionize our social consciousness. hooks focuses on black race and representation in film images, but she refers directly to how collectively "we must develop revolutionary attitudes" and that "militancy is an alternative to madness," to disrupt hegemonic power.[3] Emily Wilcox demonstrates, in her studies of ballet and Chinese dance practices from the early PRC dance training into the era of the Cultural Revolution, how technique, training, and prescribed stylizations of posture, gesture, and movement reveal the complexity of corporeal practices that deeply engage performer and spectator in political allegiances driven by these disciplined practices. The fervor of the performers of different styles of dance proved how much these practices were interwoven in every stage of the development of the PRC revolutionary culture.[4] Jacqueline Shea Murphy, Judith Hamera, and Broderick Chow also underline how performance training develops and produces collective fervor while practicing these physical skills.[5] Broderick Chow suggests that these body politics of practice in "communities of shared practice, rather than shared identity" connect practitioners through their repeated training in specific disciplined movements, carefully taught and corrected by teachers.[6] Chow, a committed practitioner, also acknowledges not only how powerful these practices are, but also how spectators may only see the spectacle of the movement and miss how the practice of practice may have different aims than those perceived as a result in performance. He suggests that these performer driven aims may connect with ethical practice methods, which practitioners know and feel. A spectator's "read" of a performance can ignite feelings and ideas beyond the performer's focus and execution of movement. In other words, the power of movement is deeply recognized, but very few consider how this power is coupled with ambiguity, precarity, and dynamics, which the performer must command and control from moment to moment. Performers maintain this concentration through their bodies with powerful internal focus, disciplined through and with their bodies. These body practices with such superb focus and discipline are ready-made for manipulation or redirection by any authority to use for their ends. As essays in this collection demonstrate, disciplined expressivity by one body or a collective chorus of bodies is a powerful meaning-making tool.

## Sensuous Ethnography and Corporeal Politics

Expanding the reading of our chapters through considering the training of bodies for the performances in this collection reveals the impact of movement practices. It may be facile to say that the power of the movement and its designed performance *makes* the message of the performance compelling and commanding of our total attention. The militarized drive of the performers' practices can galvanize an audience into action. Disciplined body practice is a direct sensuous act of commanding the body to do specific actions. Spectators can easily empathize with the outward display, but the complexity of performance in every case here reflects disciplined practices.

Dance movement requires focus, discipline, and a regimentation or militarization of control through physical strength, mind/body endurance, resilience, and concentration, which may be pleasurable and exciting but also directed to serve a purpose within the performance and/or the intentions of authorities. Disciplined practices and performers' conscious body/mind focus set up a network of cross-currents throughout this volume. Exacting practices and sensuous control connect the "mobile female dancer" from Beverly Bossler's tracing of women dancers in imperial China to Ji Hyon Yuh's interrogation of South Korean popular musical theater's portrayal of migrant worker characters as racialized others, to Ting-Ting Chang's reading of the contemporary use of Dai ethnic minority dances, to Yatin Lin's examining of KUKA, the robotic dance partner from twenty-first-century Taiwan. The corporeal politics of the disciplined practices of these material bodies moves across locations, temporalities, and bodies, demonstrating the significance of performers to the immediate relationship of movement, affect, and politics. Culture based disciplined practices drive the dancer and the spectator into motion, which articulates, reflects, and transforms awareness of the "self" and "other" relationship. The power of kinesthetic art practices to influence individuals and masses cannot be underestimated throughout history or the present times.

This frame of disciplined movement practices articulates corporeal politics in terms of performers and movement techniques. A focus on practice within conflicted temporalities deepens our inquiries into performative acts and interpretations of expressivity. Every author here locates the moving, gesturing, posing, and still designs of specific bodies in their specific temporal political contexts. This volume's designed encounters provide the opportunity for performance studies and East Asia studies to connect through these performances.

Within this broader frame of militarization through disciplined practices, we need to consider how specific events shape how performers and choreographers respond, transform, and survive. In particular, the nineteenth- and twentieth-century waves of British, European, and American colonizers followed by Japan's violent colonial aggression across East and Southeast Asia demonstrates how militarized practices, which demand total body/mind dedication, became the best tools for increasing fervor and commitment to the regime in power. Dance and choreography as militarized practices make powerful devices for mobilizing artists, soldiers, and the public. Japan, China, and South and North Korea frequently deploy militarized choreography and disciplined performance training to impress their citizens and the world with their power.

In his performance practice centered book, *Cultural Responses to Occupation in Japan: The Performing Body During and After the Cold War*, Adam Broinowski outlines Japan's early twentieth century aggressions, which combined Confucian and European militarized modes and "enshrined the principles of a patrilineal national family state (*kazoku kokka*) in the Imperial Rescript of Education: good wives/wise mothers (*ryōsai kenbo*); ethnic uniqueness (*minzoku*); wealth and strength (*fukoku kyōhei*); patriotic virtue (*chūkan aikoku* or *aikokuteki tokugi*); xenophobia (*sonnō jōi*)."[7] These were wrapped into a national myth of "semi-divine Emperors with a heavenly mandate to protect an exceptional national family/race."[8] While the educational system taught this message to children and recruited military cadets, in higher education, an elite class were taught this spiritual mandate of exceptionalism along with training in rational pragmatism, which embraced modern legal, political, and financial structures for competing with the European and American trade and power in the region. This combination of spiritually and racially superior characteristics fueled their system of militarizing the population with these beliefs.[9] While this process is not unique to Japan, it did guide Japan's violent domination over all its colonized, annexed, and invaded Asian states from the end of the nineteenth century to 1945. Brady and Mantoan emphasize how militarization creates a narrative where "total militarization takes place in conditions where the gun need no longer be present for hearts and minds to live in a constant state of military preparedness as well as more invisible and insidious surrender to the military machine."[10] They also suggest the profound effect on thinking, feeling, and surviving, which continues through generations with the military machine in many disguises and performances.

In the recent study, "Elegant and Militarized: Ceremonial Volunteers and the making of New Women Citizens," Ka-ming Wu noted the particularly gendered aspects of militarized embodiment, the intersection of performance and citizenship, and the connection of military and dance training in relation to megasports events such as the Olympics and Para-Olympics in contemporary China. Wu examines the process of militarizing young women volunteers, the "ceremonial hostesses," through militarized activities, which engineer bodies and their movement into machine-like precision for collective performance.[11] The collective performance of women as "ceremonial hostesses," according to Wu, brings together the combination of "Confucian discourse on etiquette, the communist party-state discourse on militarization and strong womanhood, the communist sport tradition of body training, and the latest initiatives on volunteering."[12] What stands out in this microcosm of performance training is how military training and ballet are two equal sections of the volunteer training sequence. Wu argues that these training activities have conflicting and complementary aims in the making of women citizens, which "highlight the values of discipline, physical training, compliance with authority, and collectivism."[13] Across our chapters, we can also see how dancing bodies at different places and times have supported and challenged the ideological and gendered prescriptions of militarized performance acts. For example, we might consider how Kazuko Kuniyoshi suggests that Murayama Tomoyoshi could challenge or succumb to the European dance model in 1920s in Europe, or how Ashikawa Yoko negotiated and transformed Hijikata Tatsumi's male-body-based butoh with her own interpretation of his texts and images through her disciplined practices.

While some scholars might ask if dance can move out of its own militarized practices and divest itself from the values set in its movement forms to decolonize "militarism," I suggest that dancers' disciplined practices already decolonize "militarism" through their choreographic deployment of the strategies of *militarized* practices. Jens Richard Giersdorf argues in his rich personal study, *The Body of the People: East German Dance Since 1945*, that there are "underestimated connections between aesthetic and political choices," and that corporeal resistance can be a creative agential act to make changes to those militarized aesthetic systems.[14] I wish to emphasize a crucial point that Giersdorf makes throughout his study of dance in East Germany and its relation to social and militarized physical cultures from the end of World War II to the fall of the Berlin Wall in 1989. Giersdorf was a dancer and soldier in East Germany. He emphasizes that his genealogical approach is an "historical and theoretical analysis of dance, choreography and embodiment" and "an exploration of how these organizing principles reflected social and political structures and how they created official and oppositional systems."[15] Our contributions in this volume also investigate these social and political performance systems, principles, and structures, taking to task how dance's militarized practices interweave through different temporalities of oppression and liberation.

## GENDERING CORPOREAL POLITICS

Dance's corporeal politics begins with the visual codes of race, gender, age, and ethnicity and the practices of class, sexuality, and virtuosity. While these codes may be easily recognized in many European and North American performance forms, the performances here clearly depend on these codes to create and carry the meanings of characters, gestures, and forms. Male and female gender roles are most clearly marked and divided in binary and oppositional acts, which may be performed by any body beneath. While contemporary dance in East Asia or the West appears to eschew gender role stylization, deep practices of gender acts still shape bodies inside the alternative regimes of "contemporary" art. Even in the experimental butoh forms, the major male soloists, including Hijikata Tatsumi, Ohno Kazuo, Kasai Akira, and Maro Akaji, all have had the privilege of gender play with female-like gender acts or "becoming" mother, La Argentina, or other female entities. However, until the 1990s, most women butoh artists performed in a range of female-like acts. While Butoh performers may train with embodied images and somatic theorization seemingly outside of male and female binary acts, their performances are most often strictly divided into male and female choruses with separate gender codes.

Gender equality and diversity along with women's rights in the many eras and events dealt with in this volume speak to the singular need to dismantle and decolonize the privileging of men and heterosexuality throughout dance histories and performance studies. While star-like performers here, such as Dai Ailian, Choe Seung-hui, and Furukawa Anzu, demonstrate the clear force of women's visions, training, and choreographic impact, we need to read the male dominated dance space in a more complicated way by considering how performing bodies can delink gender from gestures, postures, and costumes. The immediate outcry from many might be that the female role and male role physical stylization, from the lift of the male warrior's chin to the princess's small sliding steps, "makes" the role and underlines the tradition, the heritage, the ancestral aesthetic lineage. However, if different bodies perform the stylized vocabulary, gestures will migrate and shift across many bodies, making other multiple meanings and sensualities possible.

Walter Mignolo emphasizes that the process of decolonizing requires the commitment of both the colonizer and the colonized to break with naturalized perceptions of gender, race, ethnicity, and class.[16] Mei Lanfang, according to Catherine Yeh, extended his female role acts with the broader strokes of dance-based sequences, which narrated and amplified the role's character beyond gender binaries and set class acts. This kind of breakaway act also reveals the underlying, disciplined practices of training, where stylized forms are learned through imitation and repetition, regimenting the dancer body to perform set gender acts. Mignolo argues that artists are the "propellers" for delinking colonial systems from their own creative work, but their support and production systems are often so intertwined with the "living national treasures" or "heritage" artists and works, that delinking may require an outsider force.[17] For example, through their very exacting, disciplined, practices of gender stylization, could performers delink binary gender acts from the normalized fiction of gender matching bodies? While queering is a strategy for gender liberation in some societies, how can dancers use their militarized practices of disciplined and stylized techniques to re-envision their prescriptions for gender performance, even in the most traditional of dances? How can dance generate decolonial knowledge through practice?

"Choreography" is a Western term for "writing dance," or designing and organizing movement material for a specific purpose. How this term, choreography, moves through our chapters needs careful examination for its structuring politics and how it colonizes dance forms and performers. Not unlike gender and race, we need to think more broadly and carefully account for new and different structures, orders, and dramaturgies for dance and its corporeal politics. We need to analyze the histories and historiographies of colonization, annexation, and occupation in moments where dancers entered into the spotlight of these contexts and questioned how they should perform. In such contexts, artists had to make critical decisions, sometimes in terms of their own survival, on how to ethically and aesthetically negotiate their public acts of corporeal politics in dance.

## PROPAGANDA AND CHOREOGRAPHY

Corporeal politics are potent methods for communicating, indoctrinating, and exciting participants, live audiences, and screen viewers. Dance's power, whether in the simplest silent walk or the virtuosic leap into a backbend, impacts the body dancing and the body watching. Gesture moves us without censoring because of its direct line to our somatic system. Viewers are exposed to these visual cues, which can move them even to the point of being emotionally swept away with this kinaesthetic fuel. Dance, then, with all the above attributes, is a perfect tool for propaganda. Dance acts on our bodies.

In *Choreographies of 21st Century Wars*, Gay Morris and Jens Giersdorf emphasize that they consider "training, technique, rehearsal, performance, and reception as intrinsic parts of choreography, not only to reveal labor and agency, but also to examine discipline and resistance to it."[18] This inclusivity of the choreographic through all stages of performance production supports our use of an expanded application of choreography. Our notions of dance and choreography as well as militarization and discipline also resonate with Morris and Giersdorf's argument for choreography to move "outside any specific technique" and to function "as an operational concept in addition to a spatial and temporal one."[19] The journeys of the dancers in our essays, such as Park Yeong-in (his Korean name, also known as Kuni Masami, his Japanese name), whose dancing crisscrossed Japan, Korea, and Germany, demonstrate an expanded choreography of colonization, personal allegiances, and specific dance training. Morris and Giersdorf also warn of any "universalizing of practice and theory."[20] I extend this to dance or choreography, on one hand, and the political and social, on the other. Our volume is made up of carefully considered narratives, dances, events, theories, practices, and individual artists and their personal contexts, which our authors have dared to present as complications to Morris and Giersdorf's "choreography as a knowledge system."[21]

Dance acts and styles arise within and from a specific need from within the temporal and spatial location of an event within a specific culture. These acts become techniques, which evolve from repeated practices of organization or choreographic methodologies, which are the fundamental processes of designing bodies that perform gestures, which can communicate meanings, coupled with affect, that are needed for the dance to have both an immediate and a long lasting impact. The diverse dance worlds presented here just begin to reveal the complexity of dance and how the political, social, and aesthetic are interwoven in the range of movement from everyday to virtuosic gesture.

While every movement has consequences and multiple meanings, thinking choreographically creates a view through practices of movement organization and sequencing through time and space. Then, on top of that structural plan, each performer body distinguishes her/his/their self through unique energies and forms of the individual body itself. The rigorous demands of a dance form and its techniques shape the dancer body. The dancer becomes the grounding cornerstone to any tide of change, whether violent or celebratory because of the disciplined practices of dance. In Suzy Kim's analysis of Choe Seung-hui's extensive career across East Asia, Europe, and the Americas, but most importantly in North Korea, her legacy arises within the training processes of dancers. No matter how regime changes move and censor, the bodies of dancers form and reform multiple techniques, which resonate with layers of training. In Choe's case, her negotiations with socialist realisms, classical ballet, folk forms, and popular everyday life became a virtuosic corporeal politics.

These politics can be seen in Mariko Okada's dancing children of *Miyako Odori* and Ya-Ping Chen's examination of the slow, painful parade from the evening-length work *Jiao*. Okada discusses how the military government, overriding the managers of the *Miyako Odori*, required militarized wartime themes for the choreography of the child performers. The corporeal politics of children, with their small stature, buoyant energy, and playful gestures, strangely amplifies the beauty of national triumph over the horrors of war. The postdictatorship temporality of the Taiwanese dancers in *Jiao* reveals the interior yet corporeal manifestation of choreographic design, which reflects the earlier militarization through the suppression of energy in gesture and form. Choreography can control the dancer bodies, driving deep emotional connections through the forms of movement. In both cases, the collectivity of dancers meets and moves the collective audience, through choreographies shaped by militarized cultures.

Throughout this book, performers and performances move across controversial historiographies and genealogies of performance forms through minefields of conflict in, across, and out of East Asia. Whether it is a slow procession onto the stage in Taiwan or a human rights protest in Seoul or an imaginary pageant broadcasting the spectacle of Japanese super-nationalism and colonization in the Philippines, performance is the perfect medium to move public sentiment toward compliance, fear, joy, or passionate allegiance. The artists thrived and continue to thrive, somehow managing the impact of horrific and celebratory events. Their art labor in contexts of war, revolution, colonization, censorship, liberation, and migration reveals how their disciplined practices transform and strengthen their corporeal politics.

## DISCIPLINING DANCE

In every chapter, we recognize this power of dance to not only make meaning, but also to move, convince, and propel the performers and the audience into the role of corporeal witnessing.

It is just this power of dance movement that has made it the perfect tool for rulers, states, corporations, tribes, minorities, digital coders, and anyone or thing seeking to deeply articulate and exploit the potential of moving bodies. This volume opens a myriad of diverse paths for research in this complicated and dynamic topic of coupling public persuasion with the art of gesture and movement. Even in the absence of live bodies, the digital and filmic battles of animated or filmed warriors demonstrate our contemporary addiction to action and the meanings and purposes it serves. Each chapter presents a different method and mode of conceptualizing corporeal politics in carefully contextualized temporalities. Beverly Bossler's courtesans move and entertain within a place and time of deep gender and class restrictions, while the contemporary choreographer Huang Yi and the robot KUKA embrace stillness and exacting repetition in their structured acts of machine/human relationships. The twenty-first century and the Tang dynasty touch each other in this volume, through these interdisciplines of movement. We sense movement's power in the elegant bending and twisting of Yang Liping's torso and arms in multiple peacock dances as well as in the wild jabbing and pushing of umbrellas and breasts by Furukawa Anzu's butoh women.

Sensuality is a pivotal concern in our chapters, which problematize the reading of gesture across cultural differences and how these practices of practice become intensified through different disciplinary processes. We continue throughout this volume to examine the circumstances of the racialized and gendered milieu of each performance culture and artist. How does the dancer of Dong Jiang's chapter on contemporary classical Chinese dance

(CCD) communicate differently from the Christian South Korean dancers in Soo Ryon Yoon's chapter dealing with LGBTQI demonstrations? Even when temporalities are parallel, there are unarticulated differences in the display of bodies in their choreographic forms and in the meanings spectators derive from their kinesthetic communication. How do performers deploy their disciplined dance bodies to express, mask, and/or revolutionize their culture based sensuality?


CLOSING


Fans move across East Asian dances and beyond, like banners of different corporeal politics. In each case, fans signal a specific aesthetic and purpose within a given performance culture. Fluttering, waving, scalloping curves and crescent designs in the air, snapping shut, pointing, jabbing, and slicing like sword blades, flying high into the air and plummeting, spiral diving into waiting hands, fans move with each performer's heart and breath. Fans may also signal an "oriental" exoticism. The hand, too, with fingers wrapped into a fist, or splayed with fingers apart, or gently draped from the wrist as if water could flow from the shoulder and drip off each finger, carries the temporal and figurative meaning of the dance gesture. Not unlike brush and ink calligraphy, every gesture across our chapters resonates with a purpose and meaning, which may explode or linger resonating through the torso, arms, and hands. Dai's hands grasping or drumming in Wilcox's accounts of shifting sinophone performance, Choe's manipulation of swords in Kim's analysis of socialist dance films, and Ashikawa's paw-like curled fists in Mezur's feminist historiography are themselves different prescriptions for meaning making.

Our volume of diverse dance-centered chapters challenges the hierarchical histories that privilege the "West" in opposition to "Asia" and the theories that separate or dismiss the arts and cultural practices, especially dancing bodies, as insignificant forces during political, social, and ideological upheavals in any civilization. Dancers are cultural citizens who take responsibility and consider how their dancing bodies are a technology of politics and social change. Dancers deploy their bodies to drive action, whether it is revolution, resistance, or celebration. Their disciplined, militarized practice of practices builds their bodies to achieve nuanced gestural strategies, which ready them to drive the smallest movement toward a virtuosic level. The diverse state, institutional, or corporate strategies that carefully manipulate the arts and cultural practices to their ends, especially dancing bodies, also understand their significance in propelling political and social action. We have chosen to trouble our research, our own dancing, and our readers, by challenging common patterns of thinking and understanding of dance practices in and from East Asia. At the same time, we are well aware of the many unarticulated questions and concepts left for future studies. With the concept of "corporeal politics," we offer the reader multiple and layered provocations, each of which calls out for new research, theories, artists, and more dancing East Asia.

Together,

> Creative practitioners, activists and thinkers continue to nourish the global flow of decoloniality towards a transmodern and pluriversal world. They confront and traverse the divide of the colonial and imperial difference invented and controlled by modernity, dismantling it, and working towards "living in harmony and in plenitude" in a variety of languages and decolonial histories. The worlds emerging with decolonial and transmodern political societies have art and aesthetics as a fundamental source.

—Walter Mignolo et al. (= Working Group: Modernity/Coloniality/
Decoloniality): "Decolonial Aesthetics (I)," 2011.

## Notes

1. Jacqueline Shea Murphy's extensive research in indigenous dance studies comes closest to the movement acts of devotion in this volume. See Jacqueline Shea Murphy, *The People Have Never Stopped Dancing: Native American Modern Dance Histories* (Minneapolis: University of Minnesota Press, 2007).

2. Sara Brady and Lindsey Mantoan, ed., *Performance in a Militarized Culture* (New York: Routledge, 2018), 3.

3. hooks, bell, *Black Looks: Race and Representation* (Boston: South End Press, 1992), 7, 6.

4. Emily Wilcox, *Revolutionary Bodies: Chinese Dance and the Socialist Legacy* (Oakland: University of California Press, 2019). See chapter 4, "A Revolt from Within: Contextualizing Revolutionary Ballet," 119–55.

5. See Judith Hamera's *Dancing Communities: Performance, Difference, and Connection in the Global City* (New York: Palgrave Macmillan, 2007).

6. Broderick D. V. Chow, "Work and Shoot: Professional Wrestling and Embodied Politics," *TDR; The Drama Review* 8, no. 2 (Summer 2014) (T222): 72–86.

7. Broinowski, Adam, *Cultural Responses to Occupation in Japan: The Performing Body During and After the Cold War* (London: Bloomsbury, 2016), 16–17.

8. Broinowski, *Cultural Responses*, 17.

9. Broinowski, *Cultural Responses*, 16–17.

10. Brady and Mantoan, *Performance*, 2.

11. Ka-ming Wu, "Elegant and Militarized: Ceremonial Volunteers and the Making of New Women Citizens in China," *Journal of Asian Studies* 77, no. 1 (February 2018): 205–23, 205.

12. Ka-Ming Wu, "Elegant and Militarized," 205.

13. Ka-Ming Wu, "Elegant and Militarized," 207.

14. Giersdorf, Jens Richard. *The Body of the People: East German Dance Since 1945* (Madison: University of Wisconsin Press, 2013), 21.

15. Giersdorf. *Body of the People*, 8.

16. Walter Mignolo, quoted in program for Freie Universität Berlin workshop hand-out, "Decolonial Aesthetics in Theater and Performance," June 11–12, 2019, from Walter Mignolo et al. (=Working Group: Modernity/Colonialty/Decoloniality): "Decolonial Aesthetics (I)," (2011), 1. See also Walter Mignolo, "Geopolitics of Sensing and Knowing: On (De)coloniality, Border Thinking, and Epistemic Disobedience," in *Confero* 1, no. 1 (2013): 129–50, doi: 10.3384/confero.2001- 4562.13v1i1129

17. Mignolo, "Decolonial Aesthetics," 1.

18. Gay Morris and Jens Richard Giersdorf. "Introduction," in *Choreographies of 21st Century Wars*, ed. Gay Morris and Jens Richard Giersdorf (New York: Oxford University Press, 2016), 1–19, 7.

19. Morris and Giersdorf, *Choreographies*, 7.

20. Morris and Giersdorf, *Choreographies*, 7.

21. Morris and Giersdorf, *Choreographies*, 7.

# Contributors

**Beverly Bossler** is Chair of the Department of East Asian Studies and Professor of East Asian Studies at Brown University. She specializes in the history of gender and family in Middle Period (Tang-Song-Yuan) China. Her publications include *Courtesans, Concubines, and the Cult of Female Fidelity: Gender and Social Change in China, 1000–1400* (Cambridge: Harvard University Asia Center, Harvard University Press, 2013) and (as editor) *Gender and Chinese History, Transformative Encounters* (Seattle: University of Washington Press, 2015).

**Ting-Ting Chang** was Assistant Professor at the National Taiwan University of Arts and University of Taipei and artistic director of T.T.C. Dance, based in Taipei. She held a PhD in Critical Dance Studies from the University of California, Riverside. An active choreographer, Chang presented work in the American Dance Festival, Avignon Festival OFF (FR), Esplanade Theater (Singapore), Guangdong Dance Festival (China), Hong Kong Dance Festival, and University of Surrey (UK). She passed away in 2019.

**Ya-Ping Chen** is Associate Professor of Dance Studies at the Taipei National University of the Arts. She is the author of *Zhuti de kouwen: xiandaixing, lishi, Taiwan dangdai wudao* 主體的叩問：現代性、歷史、台灣當代舞蹈 [Enquiry into subjectivity: modernity, history, Taiwan contemporary dance]. She publishes widely in English and Chinese on dance in Taiwan and recently extended her research and publication to contemporary dance in Hong Kong. Her current research investigates dance in relation to discourses on place, senses, and crosscultural philosophy of the body.

**Dong Jiang** is Research Fellow and acting deputy director of the Dance Research Institute at the Chinese National Academy of Arts in Beijing. He is the author of *Contemporary Chinese Dance* and numerous Chinese-language books on dance, including *Gudianwu xinlun* 古典舞新论 [Rethinking classical dance], *Wu kan ba fang* 舞看八方 [Dance from all directions], and *Yindu wudao tonglun* 印度舞蹈通论 [Survey of Indian dance].

**Suzy Kim** is Associate Professor of Korean History in the Department of Asian Languages and Cultures at Rutgers University. She is the author of *Everyday Life in the North Korean Revolution, 1945–1950* and guest editor of the special issue "(De)Memorializing the Korean War" in *Cross-Currents: East Asian History & Culture Review*. She is currently working on a book about the history of North Korean women during the Cold War.

**Kazuko Kuniyoshi** is Lecturer in the Faculty of Art and Design at Tama Art University in Tokyo. Her English-language publications include *Butoh in the Late 1980s, An Overview of the Contemporary Japanese Dance Scene*, and the articles "Two Kinjiki: Diametrical Oppositions" and "On the Eve of the Birth of *Ankuko Butoh*: Postwar Japanese Modern Dance and Ohno Kazuo." Kuniyoshi is a leading Japanese dance critic who authored influential Japanese-language books on modern dance in Japan.

**Yatin Lin** is Associate Professor of Dance Studies at the Taipei National University of the Arts. Lin earned her PhD in Dance History and Theory from University of California, Riverside, and is the author of *Sino-Corporealities: Contemporary Choreographies from Taipei, Hong Kong, and New York* and book chapters in *Keywords of Taiwan Theory* [*Taiwan lilun guanjianci* 台灣理論關鍵詞] and *The Routledge Dance Studies Reader*. She serves on the Board of the Taiwan Dance Research Society, and was former director of the Society for Dance History Scholars.

**Nan Ma** is Assistant Professor of East Asian Studies at Dickinson College, where she works on modern Chinese literature, visual culture, and dance and performance studies. Ma received her PhD in the Department of Asian Languages and Cultures at the University of Wisconsin, Madison, and is the author of the article "Transmediating Kinesthesia: Wu Xiaobang and Modern Dance in China, 1929–1939." She is currently completing a book on dance, transnationalism, and modernity in twentieth-century China.

**Katherine Mezur** is Lecturer at the University of California, Berkeley. She is a dramaturg and dance/theater artist/trainer with a focus on transnational new-media performance, dance, and theater in/from the Asia-Pacific. Mezur holds a PhD in Asian Performance from the University of Hawai'i. She is author of *Beautiful Boys/Outlaw Bodies: Devising Female-likeness on the Kabuki Stage* and *Kawaii: Performing Sweet and Deviant in Japan* (forthcoming). She has taught at the Beijing Dance Academy, Georgetown, University of Washington–Seattle, McGill, and CALArts.

**Mariko Okada** is Associate Professor in the College of Arts and Sciences at J. F. Oberlin University in Tokyo. She holds a PhD from Waseda University in Tokyo and is the author of the Japanese-language book *Kyōmai Inoue-ryū no tanjō* 京舞井上流の誕生 [The birth of "Kyoto dance": *Inoue-ryu* dance in nineteenth-century Kyoto]. Her English-language essays on Japanese dance and performance appear in *Making Japanese Heritage* and *A History of Japanese Theatre*.

**Tara Rodman** is Assistant Professor of Drama at the University of California, Irvine. She holds a PhD in Theatre and Drama from Northwestern University and is the author of the articles "A Modernist Audience: The Kawakami Troupe, Matsuki Bunkio, and Boston Japonisme" and "A More Humane Mikado: Re-envisioning the Nation through Occupation-Era Productions of *The Mikado* in Japan." She is currently writing a book on Itō Michio as a figure of transnational modernism.

**Okju Son** is an independent dance researcher and dramaturg based in Seoul. She holds a PhD in Theatre and Dance Studies from the Freie Universität Berlin, for her dissertation "Zwischen Vertrautheit und Fremdheit: Modernismus im Tanz und die Entwicklung des koreanischen Sinmuyong" [Between Familiarness and Alienness: Modernism in Dance and the Development of the Korean Sinmuyong]. Recently, she participated in a research project for Korean diaspora dances supported by the Berliner Senate for Culture and Europe.

**Emily Wilcox** is Associate Professor of Modern Chinese Studies at the University of Michigan, Ann Arbor. She is the author of *Revolutionary Bodies: Chinese Dance and the Socialist Legacy* and twenty articles and book chapters about dance and performance. Wilcox co-curated the 2017 exhibition "Chinese Dance: National Movements in a Revolutionary Age, 1945–1965" and co-created the digital photograph archive *Pioneers of Chinese Dance*. Her current research concerns leftist inter-Asia dance during the Cold War.

**Catherine Yeh** is Professor of Chinese Literature and Transcultural Studies at Boston University. She is the author of *Shanghai Love: Courtesans, Intellectuals, and Entertainment Culture, 1850–1910* and *The Chinese Political Novel: Migration of a World Genre*. She is also co-editor of *Performing "Nation": Gender Politics in Literature, Theater, and the Visual Arts of China and Japan, 1880–1940*. Her current research concerns the rise of Peking opera *dan* (female role) actors and Chinese theatrical modernity in the 1910s–1930s.

**Soo Ryon Yoon**'s research concerns racial politics and performance in South Korea. Her writings on performance, Koreanness, racial politics, and sexuality are published or forthcoming in *Inter-Asia Cultural Studies, Performance Research, GPS: Global Performance Studies,* and *positions: asia critique,* among others. She received her PhD in Performance Studies from Northwestern University and was a CEAS postdoctoral associate at Yale University. She is currently Assistant Professor of Performance and Cultural Studies at Lingnan University, Hong Kong.

**Ji Hyon (Kayla) Yuh** holds a PhD in Theatre from CUNY Graduate Center. She is the author of "Korean Musical Theatre's Past: Yegrin and the Politics of 1960s Musical Theatre" in *The Palgrave Handbook of Musical Theatre Producers* and "Modern Theatre in North Korea" and "Modern Musicals in Asia (Korea)" in the *Routledge Handbook of Asian Theatre.* Her current research concerns Koreans' understanding of self and racial(ized) others through post-1960s musical theater productions in South Korea.

# Index

*Page locators to figures are indicated with italics.*